OCT 1 6 2000

P9-BZT-917

'The gigantic search for their lost heritage
which the nations of Europe have been
conducting for the last three years will
probably continue for the next fifty.'

Evelyn Tucker, US MFA&A officer, 1949

THE LOST MASTERS

World War II and the Looting
of Europe's Treasurehouses

Peter Harclerode &
Brendan Pittaway

Welcome Rain Publishers
New York

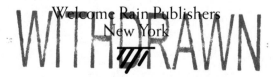

THE LOST MASTERS: WORLD WAR II AND THE LOOTING OF
EUROPE'S TREASUREHOUSES
First Welcome Rain Edition 2000.
Printed in the United States of America.

First published in Great Britain in 1999 by Victor Gollancz
An imprint of Orion Books Ltd,
Orion House, 5 Upper Saint Martin's Lane,
London WC2H 9EA, ENGLAND.

Direct any inquiries to Welcome Rain Publishers LLC,
225 West 35th Street, Suite 1100, New York, NY 10001

Library of Congress Cataloging-in-Publication Data

Harclerode, Peter, 1947–
     The lost masters : World War II and the looting of Europe's treasurehouses /
Peter Harclerode & Brendan Pittaway.—1st ed.
        p.   cm.
     Includes bibliographical references.
     ISBN 1-56649-165-7
     1. Art treasures in war—Europe—History—20th century. 2. Art
thefts—Germany—History—20th century. 3. World War, 1939–1945—
Destruction and pillage—Europe. I. Pittaway, Brendan. II. Title.

     N9160 .H373 2000
     940.53'14—dc21

                                                              00-042867

ISBN 1-56649-165-7
Manufactured in the United States of America by
BLAZE I.P.I.

First Edition: July 2000
 1   3   5   7   9   10   8   6   4   2

For Liz

ACKNOWLEDGEMENTS

Research for this book commenced in 1991 and during the seven years since then a considerable number of people have provided us with a great deal of assistance and guidance. They include the following:

Patrice Dallem of the Office Centrale pour la Repression des Vols d'Oeuvres d'Art; the late Roger Ellis, former MFA&A officer and Deputy Director of the Public Record Office in London; James Emson and Sarah Jackson of the Art Loss Register in London; Ron Tauber and Anna Kisluk of the Art Loss Register in New York; Dr Barbara Eschenburg of the Städtische Galerie im Lenbachhaus in Munich; Dr Michael Maek-Gerard of the Städelsches Kunstinstitut und Städtische Galerie in Frankfurt; Dr Anne Röver-Kann, Curator of Prints and Drawings at the Bremen Kunsthalle; Dr Josefine Leistra and Marian von Bummel of the Netherlands Institute of Cultural Heritage; Nick, Simon and Lili Goodman; Jean and Eliane de Martini; Michel d'Auberville; Henry Bondi; Lydia Braemer; Christine Koenigs; lawyer Dr Dick Schonis; Dr Gary Tinterow, Curator of Nineteenth-century European Paintings at the Metropolitan Museum of Art; Dr George Chalou, John Taylor and Larry Macdonald at the US National Archives; lawyer Clothilde Galy; Count Adam Zamoyski; journalist Philippe Sprang; Hector Feliciano, author of *The Lost Museum: The Nazi Conspiracy to Steal the World's Greatest Works of Art*; Ian Sayer, author with Douglas Botting of *Nazi Gold: The Story of the World's Greatest Robbery and its Aftermath*; author and journalist Peter Watson; journalist Michel Gardère; interpreter Barry Harrison; wartime MFA&A officer and former Deputy Director of the National Gallery, the late Ellis Gould; Professor Craig Hugh Smyth, former MFA&A officer and commander of the Munich collection point; former member of the OSS Art Looting Investigation Unit, Professor Stuart Lane Faison; John Richardson, author and friend of the late Douglas Cooper; Walter V. Robinson, art correspondent of the *Boston Globe*; Mr Bill Leckie and Mr John Lennox, both formerly of 148 (Special Duties) Squadron RAF; former OSS and CIA agent, Aline Countess of Romanones; Miss V. Schnaithmann of the German Historical Institute; Ms Jackie

McComish, researcher at the National Gallery in London; the head librarian and staff of the Wiener Library; Dr Thomas Buomberger of the Schweizer Fernsehen DRS; Saul Kagan of the Conference for Jewish Claims against Germany and Austria; Janice Lopatkin and Stephen Ward of the Holocaust Education Trust; Beth Ann Guynn and Mark Henderson of the Getty Research Institute; Ansje Burdick of Oregon University; journalist Goran Elgemyr; former Detective Sergeant Dick Ellis of the Metropolitan Police Organized Crime Group Art and Antiques Unit at New Scotland Yard; Lloyd Goldenberg of Trans-Art International; Thomas Freudenheim of the YIVO Research Institute; Dr Elizabeth Simpson of the Bard Centre for Graduate Studies; lawyer, historian and investigator of looted art Dr Willi Korte; Jeff Kleinmann of the Society to Prevent Trade in Stolen Art; Gerard Aalders, author of *The Art of Cloaking Ownership: The Secret Collaboration and Protection of the German War Industry by the Neutrals*; Marc Mazurowsky of the Holocaust Art Restitution Project; Karin Speidl of the Landeshauptmann's Office in Linz; Erika Seltzer of the Kammerhof Museum at Bad Aussee; Duncan Stuart and Valerie Collins of the SOE Adviser's Desk at the Foreign and Commonwealth Office; art historian Alexei Rastorgouev; private investigator Bill Kautz; art dealer Bernard Houthakker; journalist Antonia Kriks; lawyer Thomas Kline; Johann Linortner, author of *Die Kunstgüter im Altausser Salzberg 1943–1945*; former SOE agent and participant in Operation Ebensburg, Josef Hans Grafl; Herr Walter Tarra; Larissa Egan and Harold Holzer of the Association of Art Museum Directors; Tagarthy Patrick of Christie's, New York; Bonnie Goldblatt of the US Customs Service; Elan Steinberg, Director of the World Jewish Congress; Constance Lowenthal of the Commission for the Recovery of Art; Dr Sabine Fehlemann, Director of the von der Heydt Museum in Wuppertal; Dr Manus Brinkman, Director of the International Council of Museums; lawyer Lawrence Kaye; Louis Amigues, Director of Archives at the French Foreign Ministry; Robert Fohr and Benedicte Moreau of the French Ministry of Culture; Patrice Mounier of the Press Office at the Louvre Museum; retired diplomat Sven Fredrik Hedin; journalist Judith H. Dobrzynski of the *New York Times*; press officer Steve Coulton of the National Westminster Bank in London; Sophie Sutherland of the National Museum Directors' Conference in London; Professor Martin Kemp of Oxford University; Nicolas Vanhove of the Belgian Ministry of Economics; officials and staff of the Public Record Office at Kew, London; Michael Burke and Maggie Sutcliffe of Barraclough Carey North;

Annette Lloyd-Morgan, Assistant Librarian at the Witt Library of the Courtauld Institute of Art; Anthony Anderson; Anne Marshall; Helen Halstead; Denis and Renie Pittaway; and Lawrence Delahunty.

We are indebted to them all for their generous help and support.

In addition, the following were kind enough to permit us to draw on information previously published in books written by them: Lynn Nicholas, author of the ground-breaking book *The Rape of Europa: The Fate of Europe's Art Treasures in the Third Reich and the Second World War* (Alfred A. Knopf, 1994), who also gave us much help with contacts and photographs; Kenneth Alford, author of *The Spoils of World War II: The American Military's Role in Stealing Europe's Treasures* (Birch Lane Press, 1994), Charles de Jaeger, author of *The Linz File: Hitler's Plunder of Europe's Art* (Webb & Bower, 1981); and Konstantin Akinsha and Grigorii Kozlov, authors of *Beautiful Loot: The Soviet Plunder of Europe's Art Treasures* (Random House, 1995). We are most grateful to them for permitting us to do so.

Jane Blackstock and Sean Magee of Victor Gollancz have shown great patience and forbearance in waiting so long for everything to come to fruition, and we extend our sincere thanks to them both and to Gillian Bromley, our copy editor, who smoothed out all the wrinkles.

Above all, however, we wish to express our gratitude to Liz Knights, who commissioned this work and kept faith with us through thick and thin. We are greatly saddened that she did not live to see it published and it is with much affection that we dedicate it to her.

Peter Harclerode and Brendan Pittaway
January 1999

PREFACE

In late 1939, as his armies fanned out across Europe, Adolf Hitler dreamed of founding a new and glorious celebration of Nazi German might. His boyhood home town of Linz was to become the artistic centrepiece of the world, featuring a museum and art gallery stocked with the finest booty his forces could plunder from the Nazi-occupied countries of Europe. A massive looting operation was undertaken by special organizations formed for that purpose. Chief among these was the Einsatzstab Reichsleiter Rosenberg (ERR). Taking its name from the Nazi party's pre-eminent ideologue, Alfred Rosenberg, its role was to acquire by forced purchase, confiscation or looting the very choicest works of art. A similar organization, the Dienststelle Mühlmann, carried out looting and confiscations in the Netherlands while specially trained SS troops accompanied the Wehrmacht's divisions in Poland, Czechoslovakia, Romania, Hungary, Russia and North Africa, stripping these countries of their national treasures. Collections of priceless manuscripts, paintings, antiquities, sculptures, gold, silver, jewellery, coins, armour and a vast range of other items were removed, packed and transported back to Germany.

In Austria, France and the Netherlands, looting and confiscation were primarily concentrated on private collections belonging to Jews, who were easy prey. As they were transported en masse to concentration camps, their treasures were packed up and taken away; Nazi Germany's anti-Semitic laws allowed the seizure of Jewish property without apology or explanation. Those able to flee Europe to havens such as the United States were compelled either to abandon their collections or to have them 'Aryanized', the term coined for forced sale to a Gentile.

The entire operation, codenamed Sonderauftrag Linz, had been meticulously planned before the war began. Hitler's art advisers had established comprehensive dossiers of collections of works of art, both national and private, located in those countries to be occupied. Pre-war visits by German art experts to national museums, art institutes and galleries were in reality missions to examine and identify collections and individual works which met the criteria for entry into the Third Reich's artistic pantheon: Old Master works of

Italian and Dutch origin, as well as the Germanic pieces that were especially prized. Modern art, labelled as 'degenerate' by the high-minded Nazis, was also to be confiscated for later use in exchanges for the paintings and sculptures most sought by the Führer.

Hitler was not, however, alone in seeking to divest Europe of its art treasures. Other senior Nazis also sought to benefit from the huge quantities of valuable loot which flooded into German repositories. Foremost among them was Reichsmarschall Hermann Göring, the obese head of the Luftwaffe and heir apparent to the Führer. An avid collector whose lust for works of art knew no bounds, he had established his own network of agents throughout the German-occupied territories and in neutral countries such as Switzerland, Spain and Portugal. Their role was to identify items of interest to the Reichsmarschall and to make acquisitions on his behalf, frequently using looted paintings as payment in lieu of cash. Like Hitler, Göring had no hesitation in using threats or pressure to achieve those items he desired most.

Others benefited from the Nazis' seemingly insatiable desire for trophies of the approved genres. The art markets of Paris and Amsterdam saw frenzied activity as collaborationist dealers and collectors sought to profit from the invaders' apparent readiness to pay the highest prices. Some were happy to accept payment in the form of looted works of art, later smuggling them to Switzerland where they were sold for considerable profits.

News of the Nazi looting of Europe soon reached the Allies, who in late 1943 commenced preparations for the eventual recovery of stolen art and its restitution to the rightful owners once Germany had been defeated. From June 1944 onwards, as the Allied armies advanced through the previously German-occupied countries of Europe, officers of the Allied Monuments Fine Arts and Archives (MFA&A) organization travelled in the wake of leading formations, searching for repositories and their valuable contents. As the fighting raged in Normandy and subsequently throughout the rest of France, the French national collections were removed from Paris and transported in a caravan of trucks to a network of châteaux where it was hoped they would escape the inferno about to engulf the country. In Italy, however, little could be done to protect the country's art treasures as German forces withdrew in the face of invading Allied troops. Infuriated by their erstwhile allies' signing of an armistice with the British and Americans, the Germans not only looted large quantities of works of art but also carried out countless deliberate acts of vandalism and destruction.

Nevertheless, good intelligence helped Allied MFA&A officers to locate and secure the large number of Nazi repositories pinpointed in Germany, Austria and Italy. During the last weeks of the European war in spring 1945 a heroic operation – an account of which appears in chapter 5 of this book – was carried out successfully in Austria to prevent the deliberate last-minute destruction of Europe's most valuable art treasures.

The end of the war in Europe, however, did not see the end of looting. The Soviet Union had been planning its revenge for the wholesale looting of its national treasures by the Wehrmacht since 1943 and now proceeded to exact this with a vengeance. While the other Allies concentrated all the recovered loot at a number of collection points and commenced the lengthy process of restitution, the Red Army's trophy brigades were busy emptying Nazi repositories within the Soviet zone of occupation in eastern Germany, including those housing the collections of some of Germany's principal museums. Their contents were despatched by train to Moscow, Leningrad, Kiev and elsewhere in the Soviet Union where they were placed in museums or secret repositories, some of which came to light only as recently as 1991.

Nor were Soviet forces alone in their predations on post-war Germany. In the American zone of occupation members of the US Army and administration were also involved in blatant acts of looting. A large number of items of great value were removed from repositories and elsewhere, either being shipped to the United States or finding their way on to the black market in Germany.

In 1948 the wartime Allies effectively ended any serious attempts to track down looted works of art which were still missing and in 1954 the United States handed over the last remaining collection point to the West German authorities. In the decades since then, while some items have been recovered they are relatively few in number; the quantity of looted art still missing is huge, valued by one estimate at a staggering US$30 billion. And yet, over the last fifty years those seeking to trace and recover their treasured possessions have had to do so in the face of indifference, lack of cooperation and, in some instances, even deliberate obstruction on the part of government departments and others.

Based on over seven years' research which has revealed some startling facts, this book tells of the wholesale looting of Europe's treasurehouses during and after a war now over half a century ago. It bears witness to the determination and persistence of the survivors of the Holocaust, their families and other individuals seeking restitution of works of art which rightfully belong to them; and to the greed and naked self-interest of those trying to thwart them.

We salute all those involved in the search for missing works of art and the fight for restitution of those located. We sincerely hope that this book adds to the knowledge and appreciation of their labours and that it will in some small way assist them in completing their task one day.

THE PILLAGE OF EUROPE

The cultural pillage of Europe by the Nazis has its foundations in the Austrian city of Linz and Adolf Hitler's frustrated ambitions to become an artist and architect of renown.

It was in 1899 that the young Hitler's family moved to the village of Leonding, just outside Linz, at that time a small market town which also served as the seat of government for the province of Upper Austria. Adolf himself had been born in 1889 in Braunau am Inn, on the border between Germany and Austria. Three years later the family moved across the frontier into Bavaria but did not remain there long, returning to Austria and Leonding after two years. Hitler's education began at this point in a school at the Benedictine abbey at Lambach. Initially he proved to be an apt pupil, but failed to maintain the same degree of effort when he progressed to a secondary school in Linz in 1900, becoming lazy and regularly failing examinations. The only subject of interest to him was art, in which he showed some degree of ability. At the age of fifteen he was moved to another school at Steyr, but his academic performance did not improve and he left after twelve months.

Adolf's father, a retired customs official, died in 1903, a year after the family had moved to Linz. Lacking any paternal influence and doted on by his mother, he was able to indulge himself and do much as he pleased. He spent his days walking around Linz and along the banks of the Danube, creating in his mind a city of great architecture, or drawing and reading at a favourite spot overlooking the town; in the evening he would often go to the theatre, where he developed a passion for the music and operas of Wagner.

In May 1906 Hitler visited Vienna, and his imagination was set alight. As he wandered through the city, then the thriving capital of the Austro-Hungarian empire, he was dazzled by the beauty of its architecture and the brilliance of its society. On his return to Linz, he began redesigning the entire town in his mind; but he increasingly detested its dull provincial atmosphere, and in early September the following year, armed with a portfolio of his paintings and determined to establish himself as an artist, he returned to Vienna with the intention of entering the Academy of Fine Arts. To his amazement and dismay, his application was turned down. His reaction was explosive, an outburst into one of the towering rages which would become all too familiar to those who served him in later years. Other applicants who initially failed the examination persevered in their work and were eventually admitted; but Hitler, once baulked, made no further effort to enter the Academy and slipped back into a life of idleness and self-indulgence. He was advised to consider taking up architecture, but this proved impossible as he was entirely without educational qualifications. Shortly afterwards he returned to Linz to attend the funeral of his mother, who had died of cancer in December 1907; but, still fixated on an artistic career, returned to the capital immediately afterwards.

Vienna was at that time a centre of artistic activity and this, having attracted Hitler in the first place, now served only to aggravate his sense of grievance. Living in a series of rented apartments, he passed his days wandering the city, daydreaming, sketching and painting, visiting the Hofburg Library and attending the opera, where he fed his love of Wagner. He offered his watercolours for sale, but buyers were few and far between; inevitably and inexorably his funds dwindled until eventually, in 1910, he was forced to move into a hostel which provided accommodation for young men in penury. Morose, prone to depression and outbursts of violent temper, he was not popular among the other residents and before long he was evicted, after which his only recourse was to seek shelter in dosshouses or under archways. As his circumstances deteriorated further he developed a bitter hatred of Vienna, blaming it for cheating him of what he believed to be his just inheritance. In 1913 he left the city in order to avoid conscription for military service. During the following years, which saw him rise from ignominious poverty to supreme power as Chancellor of the Third Reich, he retained a burning desire to exact revenge for what he saw as his humiliation by the Austro-Hungarian capital.

Twenty-five years later, on the evening of 12 March 1938, Adolf Hitler returned to Linz. The streets of the town were packed with cheering crowds through which the Führer, standing in an open-topped Mercedes-Benz limousine, was driven slowly towards the town hall. Looking down from its balcony at the rapturous tumult below him, Hitler was almost overwhelmed by the adulation he was receiving. A similar welcome awaited him in Vienna two days later, although the city's worthy burghers would have trembled if they had known the fate planned for them by the man who hated their city so deeply. Hitler intended to establish Linz as the cultural centre of the

Third Reich, transforming the dull provincial town into a metropolis boasting a massive art gallery, opera house, stadium, theatres, concert hall and cinema. His plans even included his own retirement home, a large house located near the art gallery and stadium overlooking the town centre. Great museums and galleries, built to his own designs and to be known collectively as the Führermuseum,[1] were to be the new home of the greatest collection of works of art ever assembled; and Vienna was to be stripped of its treasures to fill them.

As Hitler addressed the welcoming crowds from the balcony of the Hotel Imperial, units of the Schutz Staffeln (SS) and detachments of the dreaded Geheimstaatspolizei, the secret state police better known by its acronym of Gestapo, had already moved into Vienna. Spreading swiftly through the city, they arrested known anti-Nazis and broke into the homes of Jews, forcibly removing much of their contents. Hours earlier, Austria had been annexed by Germany and now formed part of the Third Reich. The Anschluss had taken place.[2]

Almost immediately the Nazis turned their attention to the largest and most valuable Jewish-owned art collections. The fabulous treasures of Louis de Rothschild, comprising paintings, statues, books, furniture, coins and armour, were all seized and removed from his house in Vienna's Theresianumgasse, prior to the Gestapo commandeering the building as its headquarters in the city. Rothschild was subsequently forced to sign a document giving his agreement to their removal, plus the appropriation of all Rothschild assets in Austria, in return for his brother's release from the concentration camp at Dachau and safe passage for them both out of Austria.[3] Elsewhere in Vienna other collections were removed and taken to a collection point where they were examined. In all 163 confiscations, with a total value of 93 billion reichsmarks (RM), took place. From this booty 269 paintings of high value were picked out, of which 122 were later selected to be considered by Hitler for inclusion in the Linz collection.[4]

Hitler decreed that all works confiscated in Austria should remain within the country, although items purchased could be exported. This measure was introduced as a result of the acquisition by Reichsmarschall Hermann Göring of two paintings from the Lanckoronski collection.[5] Göring kept the pictures despite an order from Hitler to return them; nevertheless, the decree prevented the loss of the majority of Austria's works of art beyond its borders.

Germany itself was not spared from the Nazi cultural onslaught which commenced even before Hitler became Chancellor in 1933 and proceeded to 'cleanse' German museums and galleries of works of modern art which he deemed 'degenerate'. In 1930 Dr Wilhelm Frick, Thuringia's Minister of Interior and Education and a leading Nazi, turned his attention to the collection at the Weimar Castle Museum: frescoes by Oskar Schlemmer were obliterated with whitewash and modern paintings by artists such as Dix, Nolde, Klee, Kokoschka and Kandinsky were removed.[6] Thereafter, a similar fate was visited on other museums which suffered the removal of their collections of non-Nazi modern works of art. This process continued throughout the 1930s, with over 1,100 modern paintings removed from galleries in Berlin and 900 from the Hamburg Kunsthalle alone, culminating in 1937 with the enforced closure of the Berlin National Gallery's exhibition of modern art. The gallery lost 164 paintings as well as 326 watercolours and drawings.[7] Curators in some museums and galleries made efforts to save what they could of their collections: at the Berlin National Gallery, the curator of the modern art department removed his most important works from those selected for confiscation and substituted less valuable pieces.

This persecution extended to the artists, who found themselves shunned unless they joined a union founded by Dr Josef Goebbels, the head of the Ministry for Enlightenment and Propaganda. Some, such as the Swiss Paul Klee and the American Lyonel Kleininger, returned to their native countries. Ernst Kirchner committed suicide after having his entire life's work confiscated. Emil Nolde had two years' work removed, despite the fact that he was a member of the Nazi party and that some of his watercolours were hanging in Goebbels' sitting room. Others, such as Carl Hofer and Erich Heckel, were forced to go underground, the latter having had over 700 paintings confiscated.[8]

In 1938 the Nazis assembled an exhibition of 'degenerate' art which went on tour throughout Germany and Austria. The pictures shown were removed from their frames and hung in a haphazard fashion so as to give an impression of chaos. The intention was to show how Jewish and Bolshevik artists were responsible for a deterioration in art since the beginning of the twentieth century. The fact that some of the artists included were neither Jewish nor Bolshevik appeared to be of little or no consequence to the organizers. In early 1939 the exhibition completed its tour and the pictures were put into storage in a disused granary in Berlin while consideration was given to their disposal. It was suggested to Goebbels that any works of value could be sold abroad while the remainder were destroyed. Accordingly, an auction took place in

June 1939 at the Grand Hotel in Lucerne, Switzerland, conducted by Theodor Fischer, a leading Swiss dealer who possessed close links with the Nazis. A total of 126 paintings were auctioned, although prices paid were not as high as expected. Among the works auctioned were Gauguin's *Landscape of Tahiti with Three Female Tigers* from the Frankfurt Museum, Picasso's *The Harlequins* from the Eberfeld Museum, Franz Marc's *Three Red Horses* from the Essen Museum and a self-portrait by van Gogh from the Munich State Art Gallery.[9] Also up for sale were four more by Marc, fifteen by Lovis Corinth, nine by Oskar Kokoschka, nine by Carl Hofer, five by Ernst Barlach, a self-portrait by Paul Modersohn, three works by Max Beckmann, two by Paul Klee, seven by Emil Nolde, and three each by Erich Heckel, Ernst Kirchner, Max Pechstein and Karl Schmidt-Rottluff.[10]

Hitler's grandiose plans for transforming Linz into a world art centre were given renewed impetus by his visit to Italy in 1938 after the Anschluss. Touring the magnificent collections in Rome and Florence, he realized that if the Führermuseum was truly to outclass all other European art collections, he had to acquire the best works not only from Germany and Austria, but from throughout Europe – whether by purchase or plunder. Determined that his ideas should be realized, he set up a special commission to manage the entire project in secret. He named it Sonderauftrag Linz – 'Special Operation Linz'.[11]

Principal among those who advised Hitler on artistic matters at that time was his personal photographer, Heinrich Hoffmann, who shared his patron's taste for nineteenth-century German paintings but was otherwise largely ignorant about art. Nevertheless, such was his favoured position that his assistance was often sought in bringing to Hitler's attention paintings for the Führer's consideration. Others who advised and influenced Hitler during this period included an art dealer named Karl Haberstock, who had joined the Nazi party in 1933 and, because he too subscribed to the preference for nineteenth-century German paintings that was in accord with party dogma, soon came to the attention of Hitler and found favour. In 1936 he sold Hitler *Venus and Amor* by Paris Bordone: it was to be the first of many contributions to the Führer's collections.[12]

Haberstock used his position within Nazi circles to his own advantage. He put pressure on the directors of German museums to accept from him nineteenth-century works by artists such as Carl Schuch and Wilhelm Trübner in exchange for paintings of greater value which he would claim had no place in German museums and which he would then sell abroad at a large profit. This tactic did not always work, however: the Karlsrühe Museum refused to give up some works by Chardin and the Schloss Museum at Darmstadt resolutely held on to its *Mayer Madonna* by Holbein.

Another major supplier of paintings to Hitler, and subsequently to the Linz collection, was a dealer named Maria Almas-Dietrich, who owned the Almas Gallery in Munich's Ottostrasse. An energetic buyer, Frau Dietrich was well known among German auction houses and in particular at Lange's in Berlin, where she was notorious as a high and formidably competitive bidder. She also employed a large number of agents in other countries, notably France. She made frequent use of Hoffmann, with whom she had a close business relationship, to offer the Nazi leader pictures; she had a keen understanding of Hitler's tastes, and sold him many items, though none of them was of major importance, her emphasis apparently being on quantity rather than quality. Moreover, her limited knowledge and expertise sometimes betrayed her: she was later rebuked when a number of paintings supplied by her to Hitler were discovered to be fakes.

On his return from Italy in 1938, Hitler asked Haberstock whether it would be possible for Germany to possess museums and collections such as those which he had seen in Italy. Haberstock pointed out that the Dresden Art Gallery was already in the same category, although its director, Dr Hans Posse, had recently been dismissed by a local Nazi party official, Mutschmann, for supposedly anti-Nazi sentiments. In Haberstock's opinion, Posse was the only man capable of masterminding the Linz project. Hitler's response was to go straight to Dresden where a surprised gauleiter was strongly rebuked and an equally astonished Dr Posse reinstated. On 26 June 1939 Posse joined Sonderauftrag Linz with the title of Sonderbeauftrager (Special Envoy), bringing with him his assistant at the Dresden Art Gallery, Dr Rudolf Oertel. Posse was charged by Hitler with responsibility for the acquisition of paintings, tapestries, statuary, coins and armour. He was assisted by Dr Fritz Dworschak, an expert in coins who had previously been Curator of Coins and subsequently Director of Collections at the Kunsthistorisches Institut of Vienna. The assembly of a library for the Führermuseum at Linz was the task of Dr Friedrich Wolffhardt, a hauptsturmführer in the SS and a dedicated Nazi.[13]

Although Hitler exercised overall authority over Sonderauftrag Linz, effective power in the operation rested with the less public figure of Martin Bormann, the Führer's private secretary, over whose desk all correspondence concerning the project passed, and whose own secretary, Dr Hanssen, dealt with all its financial aspects. Since the very early days of Hitler's rise to power Bormann had exercised a formidable degree of control over the Nazi leader. It has been claimed that this influence dated back to a night in September 1931 which saw Hitler's involvement in a crime of passion, namely the murder of his 24-year-old niece who was also his mistress. In his book *The Bormann Brotherhood* William Stevenson gives an account, apparently based on information from a Nazi intelligence source, of how the girl had taunted her uncle over his sexual impotence, accused him of having Jewish blood and informed him that she was pregnant by a Jew, upon which he shot her in a fit of rage. Panic-stricken, Hitler called for Bormann – already his right-hand man – who disposed of any incriminating evidence and, with the help of Oberkriminalinspektor Heinrich Müller (later head of the Gestapo), ensured that the subsequent investigations concluded that the girl had committed suicide. Thereafter, Bormann's hold over Hitler was apparently unshakeable.[14]

Once appointed to his new role, Posse, to whom Hitler confided his dreams for the Führermuseum in Linz, was quick to seize the opportunity thus presented to him. Determined to ensure that the Linz collection would be outstanding and that its museum and galleries would become an important centre of European culture, he decided to improve the quality of Hitler's acquisitions, which had until then been heavily influenced by the ill-informed taste of Heinrich Hoffmann. Hitler insisted that the emphasis should be on nineteenth- and twentieth-century German painters such as Wald-müller, Lenbach, Makart and Spitzweg, and Posse thus commenced his search in this area. In early 1939 Gauleiter Josef Bürckel, head of the German administration in Vienna, had written to Hitler's headquarters asking for a decision on the disposal of material from the confiscated Jewish collections, which had remained in storage in the Hofburg since being seized. Now, shortly after taking up his appointment, Posse travelled to the Austrian capital to see for himself what the piles of booty contained.

Posse's inspection of the looted collections took several weeks, during which he selected those items which he deemed suitable for the Führermuseum. On 20 October 1939 he submitted a list of paintings to Martin Bormann for Hitler's approval. Of the 269 items selected from the confiscated Jewish collections as being of particular note, 122 were selected for Linz while forty-four were earmarked for the Kunsthistorisches Institut in Vienna and a further forty-three for other museums in Vienna, Graz and Innsbruck. The remaining sixty paintings would be held in reserve for Linz, pending a decision from Hitler. A further 324 paintings were also selected from the Oskar Bondy collection, which totalled some 1,500 works.[15]

Posse's recommendations, however, did not meet with unqualified approval from Hitler, who was determined that all the best works would go to the Führermuseum: annoyed at seeing that fifty-seven of the Rothschild paintings were set to remain in Vienna, he reallocated to Linz twenty of those marked down by Posse for two of the capital's museums.

During a second visit to Vienna in December 1939, Posse extended his selections for Linz to the very fabric of the buildings in which the confiscated collections had been housed. In one of his reports to Martin Bormann, he recommended that two rooms in the Palais de Rothschild be stripped of their valuable antique wainscoting, leather wallpaper, gothic and Renaissance period chimneys, portals and doors. The ever-increasing numbers of looted art treasures were sent to the headquarters of Sonderauftrag Linz in Munich; here they were stored in a special underground repository known as the Führerbau in the charge of a minor Nazi party official, Dr Hans Reger. All major items were catalogued and photographed, the prints being bound in leather volumes over which Hitler would pore for hours in his retreat at Berchtesgaden.

On a number of occasions Posse found himself competing with other German museums or collections for the same works of art, and more than once was forced to enlist Bormann's aid in acquiring items for the Linz collection. One such contested work was the famous painting *The Hay Harvest*, by Pieter Brueghel the Elder, which formed part of the Lobkowitz collection located in Radnitz Castle in Czechoslovakia. Having decided that the painting should be acquired for the Führermuseum, Posse was anxious lest it be lost to the Kaiser Friedrich Museum in Berlin. He wrote to Bormann, suggesting that the Reichsprotektor of Bohemia and Moravia, Constantin Freiherr von Neurath, be advised that all the contents of Radnitz Castle were to be inspected so that German museums and collections could subsequently make bids for them. The Führermuseum should naturally have first choice of everything. Bormann obliged and in due course Posse was successful in acquiring *The Hay Harvest*.[16]

Competition was not the only hindrance encountered by Posse in his quest for treasures for the Linz collection. He also found himself encumbered by the red tape that wound throughout the highly bureaucratic Nazi machine, and confronted on a number of occasions with opposition from senior Nazis seeking to make acquisitions of their own. Chief among these was Reichsmarschall Hermann Göring, whose activities are dealt with in detail in chapter 3. As was frequently the case among the higher levels of the Nazi party, intrigue and deceit figured largely in the machinations of those who decided to cash in on the rich haul of works of art from the occupied countries of Europe.

Where there were no grounds for confiscation or forced sale, Hitler resorted to straightforward coercion in order to acquire those items he desired most. The most prominent of the paintings commandeered in this manner was the *Portrait of an Artist in his Studio* by the Dutch master Jan Vermeer, which was in the possession of a German family living in Vienna. The head of the family, Count Czernin, had previously refused many offers for the painting from wealthy collectors throughout the world, among them reputedly one of $6 million from the American connoisseur Andrew Mellon. Hitler coveted this painting above all others and was determined to have it. All pretexts for confiscation were considered, including tax arrears; however, an investigation by the Reich finance ministry in Berlin produced only a letter of 21 September 1941 to Martin Bormann informing him that the Czernin family's tax affairs were in order and that there were no grounds for sequestration of the painting. So all pretence at subtlety was abandoned. Posse's assistant Fritz Dworschak played a major role in the negotiations in this particularly disgraceful affair: with the assistance of Baldur von Schirach, by then Gauleiter of Vienna, he personally applied pressure to the Czernin family, who were only too well aware of the fate of certain of their friends at the hands of the Gestapo. By the end of September 1941 Count Czernin had capitulated and agreed to sell the Vermeer for the paltry sum of RM1.4 million, a mere fraction of its real value. On receiving this news Posse travelled to Vienna to take delivery of the painting, which eventually arrived at the Führerbau in Munich on 12 October. There it remained until its later removal to Austria and safety in the depths of a salt mine, where it joined the rest of the Linz collection.[17]

In early 1939 Czechoslovakia suffered similar treatment to that meted out to Austria a year earlier: on 15 March the country was invaded and occupied by German troops. Such was the low esteem in which Czechs were held by the Nazis, who regarded them as subhuman Slavs, that Aryan and Jewish property alike was confiscated. The university in Prague lost its entire library; the Czech National Museum was stripped, as was the palace of Archduke

Franz Ferdinand. The Lobkowitz collection of paintings was removed, along with unique collections of armour and coins, to a repository in Munich to await their ultimate transfer to Linz.

Poland was the next country to fall victim to the Nazi juggernaut in the invasion of 3 September. Here too, the policy on works of art was quite clear: everything was to be confiscated and the Poles allowed to keep nothing. Under the overall direction of Dr Kajetan Mühlmann, an Austrian and an obersturmbannführer in the SS, a repository was established in Warsaw under Josef Mühlmann, his half-brother, and two officials of the much-feared Sicherheitsdienst, the SS security service. Another was located at Krakow under Dr Gustav Bartel and Dr Kuttlich, the directors respectively of the Breslau and Tropau Museums.[18]

The stripping of Poland had been meticulously planned. Before the war, members of the East Europe Institute, a German cultural research centre, had paid many visits to the country during which they had established friendly relationships with the directors and staffs of its museums and art collections. Now the Polish curators suffered a rude awakening with the arrival in Warsaw and Krakow of their erstwhile German friends, dressed in the black uniform of the SS and accompanied by members of the Gestapo. It transpired that the work of the institute had merely been a cover for the compiling of inventories of Polish art treasures, the listing of their locations and accumulation of information concerning measures taken by the Poles to safeguard them.[19]

Among those who followed the Wehrmacht's panzer divisions into Poland was a special unit of an organization with the cumbersome title of SS Scientific and Research Community for Heritage of the Ancestors – more usually known as the Ahnenerbe.[20] Like all German units formed on an ad hoc basis it bore the name of its commander, in this case that of Peter Paulsen, the Professor of Prehistory at the University of Berlin. Kommando Paulsen was originally tasked with carrying out archaeological work for the purpose of determining whether German tribes had once inhabited lands within Poland's frontiers. Operating under the direct command of the SS Reichsicherheithauptamt (RSHA: Reich Central Security Office), however, its remit was widened to include looting of historically significant works of art and important Polish library collections.[21]

The most valuable piece lost to Poland in this process was the Veit Stoss altarpiece from the Church of Our Lady in Krakow, carved during the period 1477–87 by the German artist Veit Stoss as a commission for the King of Poland. The centre panel depicts the Virgin Mary asleep surrounded by angels, the side panels show scenes portraying Christ and the Virgin, and the base or predella gives the genealogy of Christ himself. This altarpiece, nine paintings by Hans von Kulmbach and a number of gothic and baroque chalices all fell prey to the Kommando Paulsen.[22]

Monasteries and churches throughout Poland were systematically denuded by the Germans of all their treasures, as was the National Museum at Krakow, which lost two major works: *Venetian Palace* and *Christ Carrying the Cross* by Guardi and Rubens respectively.[23] At Warsaw's royal castle twenty-five paintings by Canaletto were taken, along with floors and wall panellings ripped out for subsequent installation in the Zwinger Palace in Dresden, considerable damage being done to them in the process by the brute force and ignorance of the removers. The Czartoryski collection, concealed in vaults at Sienewa, soon fell prey to the marauding Germans. Works by Dürer and Van Leyden were among the many items carried off, as were three paintings: Raphael's *Portrait of a Young Man*, Leonardo da Vinci's *Lady with Ermine* and Rembrandt's *Landscape with the Good Samaritan*.[24] (The fate of this collection is covered in detail in chapter 11.) Other works confiscated or stolen in Poland included *The Pretty Polish Girl* by Watteau, taken by Mühlmann and sent as a gift to Göring, and Rembrandt's *Portrait of a Young Man*, taken from the Lazienski collection by the Gestapo and presented to Poland's new ruler, Reichskommissar Hans Frank, who was only too happy to adorn his new official residences, the castles at Krakow and Kressendorf, with such treasures.

The scale of the German looting in Poland was immense. In Warsaw alone, a total of 13,512 paintings and 1,379 sculptures were confiscated. In addition to these, collections of antique furniture, books, coins, armour, tapestries and porcelain were also carried off by squads of Nazi officials and troops. Worse still were the results of wanton vandalism displayed by some of the invaders: items of valuable porcelain were used for eating from and then smashed; Gobelin tapestries were torn up and used for bedding; sculptures were used for target practice. The Oberkommando der Wehrmacht (OKW: Armed Forces High Command), unaware of Hitler's Sonderauftrag Linz and extremely unhappy about the plundering of Poland, decided to take measures to prevent such a disgraceful episode happening again. It formed a special department, named the Kunstschutz, to provide protection for all cultural material, including works of art, throughout France, the Low Countries and Italy.

In fact, though the invasion and occupation of the Low Countries and France in May and June 1940 offered Hitler access to some of the greatest treasurehouses of Europe and the opportunity to acquire yet more priceless art works, whether through purchase, forced sale, confiscation or coercion, the orgy of looting and destruction suffered by Poland was not repeated. On the contrary, orders were given by Hitler that a more subtle approach was to be used: here, the cooperation of the populations was to be won through considerate treatment by the German occupying forces, who were to ensure that normal life was maintained as far as possible. Yet despite such outward signs of apparent benevolence, Hitler never wavered in his plan for the wholesale looting of Europe. On 16 May, the day after the Netherlands surrendered, Mühlmann arrived fresh from his activities in Poland. Without delay his organization, the Dienststelle Mühlmann, was established in The Hague; here it came under the direct authority of Dr Arthur Seyss-Inquart, who had become the Nazi governor of Austria after the Anschluss before being appointed Deputy Reichskommissar of Poland and subsequently Reichskommissar of the Netherlands. Mühlmann and his staff set to work with enthusiasm to gather works of art for the Linz collection. During the next twelve months, the Dienststelle Mühlmann acquired a large number of paintings for Hitler's Führermuseum, among them works by Canaletto, Rubens, Rembrandt and several other seventeenth-century Dutch artists.

Two months after the invasion of the Netherlands Hans Posse arrived in The Hague, where he set up an office under the somewhat nebulous title of Referent für Sonderfragen (Adviser on Special Questions) and set about making acquisitions for the Führermuseum, rapidly establishing a network of informers and agents as he did in each of the Nazi-occupied countries. The majority of Hitler's art acquisitions in the Netherlands were made by purchase rather than confiscation or forced sale, and although the prices paid were in many cases far below the true value of the works in question, money was no object when it came to acquisitions for the Linz collection. Inevitably, it was not long before the Dutch art market became so overpriced that it was out of reach to all but the most affluent buyers. German works in particular fetched fantastic prices, such was the demand for them by the Nazis, who readily paid whatever was asked. A veritable army of dealers, agents and informants emerged, seeking to take advantage of the large commissions to be made from catering for the tastes of the Nazi hierarchy.

One particular collection, however, continued to elude its pursuers until after the death of its owner, a committed enemy of Hitler named Fritz Mannheimer. The priceless Mannheimer collection, comprising a large number of paintings, tapestries, crystal, silver and gold, belonged to a 50-year-old German Jew who lived in Amsterdam and was the senior controlling partner in the long-established Dutch private bank of Mendelssohn & Co. Born in Stuttgart, Mannheimer had worked as a banker in Germany, but faced with the rise to power of the Nazis and the consequent spread of anti-Semitism throughout Germany he had moved to the Netherlands and joined Mendelssohn & Co., one of the most powerful banking houses in Europe. Thereafter he had prospered greatly, and he had used a part of the huge personal fortune he amassed to assemble his fabulous art collection, which came to include paintings by Vermeer, Rembrandt, Fragonard, Watteau, Crivelli, Canaletto, Chardin and Guardi. Some of these treasures were housed in his substantial residence in Amsterdam's Hobbemastraat, the rest in France at his other home, the Château Monte Cristo at Vaucresson, not far from Paris.[25]

Mannheimer, a fervent anti-Nazi, actively used his financial expertise as a banker to frustrate the ambitions of Hitler and his henchmen. Believing that only France possessed sufficient military might to withstand Germany's increasing belligerence and expansionist ambitions, he channelled his efforts and financial acumen into supporting the neighbouring country. Some of this support took the form of donations from his own resources, amounting to several million francs. This generosity inevitably attracted a venomous response, not only from Germany but also from the Nazi party in the Netherlands. Other measures taken by Mannheimer in the attempt to support France and stem the spread of Nazism included the formation of a syndicate of Dutch and Swiss banks which handled short-term French government bond issues. With the German occupation of the Rhineland, and subsequently of Austria and Czechoslovakia, conditions became more difficult for Mendelssohn & Co. as the Nazis began to coerce banks in the occupied territories into refusing to conduct financial transactions with Mannheimer's bank. Nevertheless, Mendelssohn & Co. continued to support France in this manner and by June 1939 was heavily involved in doing so. Although the bank continued to find buyers for the French issues in Switzerland, the market in the Netherlands had fallen off dramatically under Nazi influence. Faced with a temporary shortage in liquidity the bank turned to others for short-term support in the normal way: however, no such assistance was forthcoming, as by then the Nazis had frightened most of Europe's bankers into submission.

The end came on the morning of 9 August 1939 when Mannheimer received a telephone call at his office. He left Amsterdam immediately afterwards, without disclosing the caller's identity or the substance of the call, and travelled to the Château Monte Cristo where his wife of two months was staying. On the same day, Fritz Mannheimer died. The official explanation was that he had suffered a heart attack, and this could well have been the case, as he weighed over eighteen stone and suffered from a weak heart. However, there were strong suspicions – never investigated – of suicide.

The immediate consequence of Mannheimer's death was that Mendelssohn & Co. was forced to cease trading. It was subsequently declared insolvent with a deficit of over Fl 5 million. Mannheimer's assets in the Netherlands were frozen and the bank's creditors seized the Dutch part of his collection. In February 1941, eighteen months after Mannheimer's death, they came under considerable pressure to sell. Responsibility for negotiations with the new owners on behalf of Hitler was given to Seyss-Inquart and Mühlmann. Faced with competition from other German organizations which also wished to acquire parts of the collection, Mühlmann appealed for support from Hitler; this soon arrived in the form of a letter from Martin Bormann to Generalkommissar Schmidt in The Hague, instructing him to block any bids other than those made on the Führer's behalf. Mühlmann's offer of Fl 5.5 million for the Dutch part of the collection, which included Rembrandt's *Jewish Doctor*, was initially turned down as it was considerably less than the collection's true value, estimated to be at least Fl 7.5 million.[26] Threats of confiscation followed, and eventually Mendelssohn & Co.'s creditors, in the absence – unsurprisingly – of interest from other quarters, resigned themselves to the inevitable and accepted Mühlmann's offer. Shortly afterwards the collection was transported to the Führerbau in Munich, where it was catalogued and where it remained until 1944 when, because of the increasing threat from Allied air raids, it was moved to safety in an Austrian salt mine. The rest of the collection, meanwhile, had been moved by Mannheimer's widow from the Château Monte Cristo to a temporary refuge in the unoccupied zone of Vichy just before the German invasion of France in June 1940. Here it stayed undisturbed for three years until Hitler once again turned his attention to acquiring it.

Belgium also fell prey to Hitler's insatiable lust for art treasures, losing its most precious artwork of all: the fabulous twelve-panel altarpiece called *The Adoration of the Mystic Lamb* in the cathedral of Ghent, painted in 1432 by the van Eyck brothers, Jan and Hubert. In 1939, after the outbreak of war, the altarpiece was moved for safe keeping by the French to a repository in the town of Pau, in the Pyrenees. This was not the first time that the altarpiece had been removed from its home city. During the sixteenth century, which was a period of Protestant rule in Ghent, it had been hidden for safe keeping until such time as Catholicism should be restored. Subsequently, after the invasion of Belgium by France under Napoleon Bonaparte, the four central panels were taken to Paris and placed in the Louvre. After Napoleon's defeat by the British at Waterloo in 1815 and his subsequent exile, the French king Louis XVIII, restored to his throne, returned them to Ghent. Six of the twelve panels were later sold by the Vicar General of Ghent, in the bishop's absence; these were eventually purchased by King Frederick William III of Prussia, who presented them to the Kaiser Friedrich Museum in Berlin where they were kept until 1920. The remaining panels were left in the cathedral at Ghent until the outbreak of the First World War, when they were removed and hidden in a house in the city. The invading Germans, demanding to know the whereabouts of the altarpiece, were told that it had been evacuated to Britain. In the aftermath of the war the altarpiece was reassembled, with the return by Germany of the six panels from the Kaiser Friedrich Museum and of the remainder from their hiding place in Ghent. In 1930, however, one of the panels was stolen; and despite the success of the Belgian police in tracing the thief, who died in custody from a heart attack while being questioned, it was never recovered and was replaced by a copy.

Two years after the next invasion of Belgium, and of France, Hitler set about attempting to obtain the altarpiece. Pau lay within the territory under the control of the Vichy regime, but the Germans were well aware where the paintings were being kept. The French obtained written agreement that they could not be moved without the express agreement of the Mayor of Ghent, the French authorities and the Kunstschutz, and initially the Vichy regime of Marshal Philippe Pétain resisted pressure to relinquish them. The collaborationist Prime Minister Pierre Laval, however, proved more amenable to the German demands and on 3 August 1942, under conditions of great secrecy, the altarpiece was taken from the repository at Pau and transported under armed escort to Germany.[27]

Nor did the Germans waste much time in laying their hands on France's own art treasures. On 30 June 1940 Generalfeldmarschall

Wilhelm Keitel, Chief of Staff of the OKW, ordered that all publicly and privately owned collections and works of art were to be 'safeguarded against possible loss'. On 17 September he issued a directive that any disposals of French-owned property which had taken place since 1 September 1939 were null and void and that the German military authorities in France were empowered to confiscate Jewish-owned works of art for transportation to Germany. Three months later Hitler proclaimed his right of disposition over all confiscated works of art, decreeing that German commanders throughout occupied France were to keep Hans Posse fully informed of their efforts to acquire such booty.[28]

In addition to appropriating entire collections, Hitler's representatives were active in the French art market. In March 1941 Posse was allocated an account at the Reichskreditbank in Paris containing RM500,000 with which to purchase works of art for the Führermuseum at Linz. As will be described in further detail in chapter 3, some French dealers joined those from Germany and elsewhere flocking to Paris to take advantage of the Nazis' willingness to spend large sums of money in the effort to satisfy the Führer's dreams. As in the Netherlands, prices rocketed and dealers unencumbered by conscience made large profits. Where neither confiscation nor straightforward purchase would serve, because the owners were non-Jewish and refused to sell, Hitler and his representatives resorted to forced sale. A notable example of this method of acquisition was the case of the Schloss collection of 333 paintings, including a number of Dutch masters signed and dated by the artists. A detailed account of the forced sale of this collection and its ultimate fate is given in chapter 12.

In 1943 Hitler renewed his efforts to secure the French part of the Mannheimer collection, which was still in the possession of Mannheimer's widow. The paintings included Chardin's *Soap Bubbles* and *Mary Magdalene* by Crivelli, as well as works by Guardi, Watteau, van Ruisdael, Molenaer, Ingres and Canaletto.[29] Once again, Kajetan Mühlmann was tasked with handling the negotiations. Instead of making a direct approach to Mme Mannheimer, who was by this time in Argentina, he employed the services of Ferdinand Niedermeyer, who had been appointed Administrator of Property Seized by the Reich in France. In May 1944 negotiations were successfully concluded and the paintings sold for a price of FFr 15 million, paid to Mannheimer's creditors. Shortly afterwards they were shipped from Paris to Austria, where they joined the rest of the collection.

Hitler's plundering of collections in France was confined for the most part to those owned by Jews and private individuals and did not extend – openly, at least – to those belonging to museums. The only exceptions to this rule related to certain works of art of German origin, which he ruled were to be returned to Germany forthwith – notably 2,000 items acquired by the French during the Napoleonic, Franco-Prussian and First World Wars which were removed from the Musée de l'Armée and sent to Germany. The reasoning behind this relative restraint lay not in any affection on Hitler's part for the French but in his ultimate plan that all France's most valuable treasures would form part of the compensation to be paid to Germany as one of the conditions to be laid down in any peace negotiations. Until then, he knew he could rest assured that such treasures, whether remaining in the museums or hidden away, would be well looked after by their French custodians.

Such was Hitler's determination that the Linz collection should possess the finest of the world's art treasures that the tentacles of Sonderauftrag Linz even found their way into the territory of Italy, Germany's principal ally. Hans Posse was represented in Rome by Prince Philipp von Hessen, a descendant of Britain's Queen Victoria and Emperor Frederick III of Prussia. An architect by profession, von Hessen had settled in Italy and married Princess Malfada, one of the daughters of King Victor Emmanuel. Having joined the Fascists, he maintained strong links with the Nazi party in Germany, and his extensive network of contacts among Italian dealers and collectors made him extremely useful to Posse. The latter paid his first visit to Italy in March 1941 and stayed for two weeks, during which he travelled to Rome, Florence, Naples, Genoa and Turin, acquiring a total of twenty-five paintings for the Linz collection and paying for them from a special fund of RM500,000 which had been established for him at the German embassy. Only a few days after returning to Germany in late March, Posse was back in Italy at the request of von Hessen, who had located some works of art which he knew would be of great interest to Hitler. Having exhausted his special fund at the embassy on his first visit, Posse had to request additional finance; this was arranged by Reichsminister Dr Hans Lammers, the Head of the Reichskanzlei (State Chancellery), who supplied a further RM500,000. June of the same year saw Posse returning for a third visit. Once again he exhausted his initial allocation and had to call for supplementary funds; once again these were forthcoming, when at the end of June Bormann sanctioned the despatch of a further RM1.65 million to the German embassy in Rome. All of Posse's purchases in Italy were legitimate, effected on the open art market. On instructions from Hitler, he and his representatives were careful to avoid any contact with those acting on behalf of Göring, who was also busy making a large number of acquisitions in Italy (described in detail in chapter 3).

A point of dispute between the Germans and their Italian allies was the status of the South Tyrol, which the former claimed as belonging to Germany, the latter to Italy. An agreement had been drawn up and signed in October 1939 in which the Italians had consented to the return to Germany of monuments, archives and works of art of German origin in the disputed region. During the following year a special commission was established by the Ahnenerbe of the SS to protect German interests in the South Tyrol, and Posse was appointed as its art adviser.

Posse's tireless quest for additions to the Linz collections came to an end in mid-December 1942, when he died of cancer of the mouth. His health had been poor for some time but he had refused to lighten his workload. He had been the driving force behind Sonderauftrag Linz and his death left a gap that would be hard to fill. Indeed, such was the esteem in which he was held by Hitler that the Führer ordered a state funeral for him, which was attended by every museum director in Germany; the eulogy was read by Goebbels. The rivalry among those who sought to replace Posse was fierce, and the selection of his successor took some weeks. On 22 March it was announced that Dr Hermann Voss, the Director of the Dresden Gallery, had been chosen for the post. This appointment sent shock waves through the German museum and art establishment: Voss was not a member of the Nazi party and indeed was well known for his antipathy towards senior Nazis.

Changes were made in the management structure of Sonderauftrag Linz. Voss was placed in sole charge of the Führermuseum, but with reduced responsibilities and powers, confined principally to paintings. The collections of armour and coins became the responsibilities of two experts in the respective fields, Drs Leopold Ruprecht and Fritz Dworschak, while overall day-to-day control of the project was vested in Dr Helmut von Hummel, who had been appointed personal secretary to Martin Bormann in October 1942 and reported to the Reichsleiter on all matters concerning the Linz project.

After the Allied invasion of Sicily on 10 July 1943, and of the Italian mainland two months later, the Germans abandoned any pretence at consideration for the feelings and property of their erstwhile allies. As Generalfeldmarschall Albert Kesselring, the commander of German forces in Italy, was forced to withdraw his forces northwards under relentless pressure from the advancing Allies, SS units indulged in a wanton orgy of destruction and looting of works of art – despite the presence of Kunstchutz personnel who had been tasked with protection of monuments and art works. In at least one instance they were reported to have killed Italian guards attempting to prevent the terrible and senseless devastation. The Royal Society Library in Naples was set ablaze, as was the Villa Montezone at Livardi which housed the Naples State Archives, earlier evacuated there for safety. Archives of immense historical value were lost, including those of several of Europe's monarchies. Among scores of works of art destroyed were seventy paintings including Luini's *Madonna and Child*.[30] The Ahnenerbe played its own part in the looting, albeit acquisitive rather than merely destructive, and established large repositories in the South Tyrol, at the Castle of San Leonardo and at Campo Tures. The latter was used to store paintings taken from the Uffizi, the Pitti Palace and other museums and galleries in Florence.

The Italian authorities were not entirely unprepared for this onslaught, having taken some measures to protect the country's art treasures when it was realized that the collapse of the Fascist regime meant an increased threat of looting and destruction from German forces, principally those of the SS. A former official of the Uffizi Palace Gallery, Rodolfo Siviero, had formed an underground organization, its members recruited from among art experts, artists and museum officials, which had contacts within the Italian army's intelligence arm, the SIM (Servizio Informazioni Militari), elements of which had been incorporated into the SS Sicherheitsdienst in Italy. SIM officers provided Siviero's group with information about German plans and warned of impending confiscations of collections or major works of art.[31] On one occasion, a former SIM officer provided the leader of the underground group in Florence with copies of German documents which contained details of a meeting to be held between the German consul and two members of the Sicherheitsdienst to discuss plans for the removal of the city's art treasures. Siviero himself discovered that the Sicherheitsdienst was equipped with lists of the works of art stored in repositories at Montegufoni and Montagnana.

The underground activists succeeded in removing a large number of individual works of art before the Germans could lay their hands on them; on many occasions this work was carried out at great risk to the lives of those involved. One such item under threat of confiscation was Fra Angelico's *Annunciation* which, until spirited away by two monks working for Siviero's organization, was in a monastery near Giovanni Valdarno. Göring coveted the painting and the Kunstchutz had been instructed to obtain it for him. On demanding to know the reasons for its removal, Kunstschutz officials were told that it had been carried out on the orders of the Vatican.[32]

When it came to looting or confiscation on a large scale, however, there was little the Italians could do to stop the Germans. In June 1944 orders were issued by Standartenführer Dr Alexander Langsdorff of the Kunstschutz for the contents of the Montagnana repository to be evacuated by troops of the 362nd Infantry Division, commanded by Generalmajor Greiner. The operation began in the following month and convoys of trucks transported the art treasures northwards to the repositories in the South Tyrol, from where they would eventually be sent to Germany. Complete collections, including those of Finaly Landau and the Duke of Parma, were seized and despatched to the South Tyrol under orders from the Kunstschutz.

The movement of these convoys and their precious cargoes, by both road and rail, was closely monitored by Siviero's organization and its allies in the Italian partisan movement, difficult as this was at times because of tight security maintained by the Germans. Through their contacts within the SIM, the underground activists were able to pinpoint the location of works of art belonging to Florence which, as noted above, had been taken to the repositories at San Leonardo and Campo Tures; among them were Botticelli's *Judith with the Head of Holofernes*, Cranach's *Adam and Eve*, Rubens' *Return of the Peasants*, Donatello's *St George* and Michelangelo's *Bacchus*, as well as works by Brueghel, Tintoretto and other great masters.[33]

The tentacles of Hitler's mass looting stretched ever further eastwards as the war unfolded. Before the German invasion of Russia in June 1941, responsibility for stripping Russia of its art treasures was given to a special organization formed for the task, the Einsatzstab Reichsleiter Rosenberg (ERR), which will be discussed in detail in chapter 2. However, the task proved beyond the capability of the ERR and three months later was taken over by the foreign minister, Joachim von Ribbentrop, who formed a special unit to carry out looting in countries invaded by Germany. Commanded by Sturmbannführer Eberhard Freiherr von Künsberg, the Sonderkommando Künsberg comprised four companies, each of which was assigned to a different area of operations. The unit first saw service in 1939 when elements took part in the invasion of Poland, during which they captured and looted embassies and other buildings belonging to enemy or neutral nations. Thereafter detachments were deployed in Norway, the Netherlands, Belgium, France, Greece and the Balkans.[34] The role of the unit was to seize items on behalf of other German organizations, including the OKW, the Sicherheitsdienst and the foreign ministry. On occasions, Ribbentrop issued orders to the unit on his own account: in France it seized works of art on his personal instructions.

During Operation Barbarossa, the invasion of the Soviet Union, Ribbentrop ordered von Künsberg to deploy his unit to Russia to undertake the confiscation of works of art there. This move was opposed by the High Command of the Army and several other bodies, including elements in Ribbentrop's own foreign ministry, which attempted to limit the unit's role to confiscations of records and documents from embassies and diplomatic missions. Despite such disapproval and von Künsberg's own reluctance, the 2nd, 3rd and 4th Companies were subsequently despatched, each being attached to one of the three Army Groups operating in the Soviet Union; logistical support was provided by units of the Waffen-SS. The 1st Company was meanwhile sent to North Africa, where it joined Generalfeldmarschall Erwin Rommel's Afrika Korps.[35]

Assisted by Waffen-SS troops, the 2nd Company laid waste to the palaces and museums of Leningrad, emptying Pavlosk, Peterhof and Tsarskoe Selo of paintings, tapestries, sculptures, porcelain, antique furniture and other treasures, as well as complete libraries of priceless books and manuscripts.[36] Meanwhile the 4th Company accorded similar treatment to the city of Kiev, ransacking the Museum of Ukrainian, Russian and Western Art and the Schevtchenko Museum. The Medical and Research Institute and the Ukrainian Academy of Science also fell victim to the marauders, losing valuable equipment, books and documents. So vast were the quantities of looted items that large freight trains were employed to transport them back to Germany and Hitler's repositories.[37] Nor did the Germans restrict themselves to looting alone: they also waged a campaign of deliberate destruction which resulted in 427 museums in Stalingrad, Leningrad, Smolensk, Poltava and Novgorod being razed to the ground.

One of the most priceless of Russian treasures to fall into German hands was the panelling of the Amber Room in the palace of Catherine the Great at Tsarskoe Selo. The room was so called because its panelling was formed from sheets of amber, and it was furnished with tables, chairs, chests and ornaments also fashioned from solid amber. Whereas the Russians had been able to evacuate the furniture before the arrival of the Germans, the panelling had had to be left behind. The 2nd Company had been given the Amber Room as one of its primary objectives on reaching the palace and had thus come fully equipped for the task of dismantling and packing it for shipment. Within a relatively short space of time, the panelling had been removed and packed into twenty-nine crates which were then despatched to the museum at Königsberg, where the amber was subsequently installed.[38]

In March 1942 the Sonderkommando Künsberg held an exhibition in Berlin, displaying a selection of the items confiscated – museum exhibits, archives, books and valuables – during the campaigns in which it had been deployed. By the end of 1942 the unit had confiscated 304,694 works of art which had been distributed to other organizations, principally the Reich Ministry for the Occupied Eastern Regions, which also received four library collections totalling 97,500 books looted from the Soviet Union. At the beginning of August, the unit was absorbed into the Waffen-SS and given the designation of 'Waffen-SS Special Disposal Battalion'. By then, however, von Künsberg had fallen from grace: von Ribbentrop considered that he had taken too many decisions on his own authority, and shortly afterwards removed him from his post as commanding officer. In 1943 the Waffen-SS Special Disposal Battalion was itself disbanded and its personnel dispersed among other SS units.[39]

Meanwhile, such was the volume of art – looted, confiscated or purchased, forcibly or otherwise – which continued to pour into the Führerbau in Munich that it was not long before other secure locations had to be found for storage. Three main ones were established, at the Schloss Neuschwanstein near Füssen in Bavaria, the Schloss Thürntal near Kremsmünster and a monastery at Hohenfurth in Czechoslovakia, close to the border with Austria. The first of these to be used as a repository was the Schloss Thürntal. Between August 1941 and November 1943 a total of 1,732 paintings and other works of art were transferred there in convoys under military escort. They included most of the collection of Baron Cassel, taken from the south of France; valued at at least RM1.5 million, its most important element was a group of late nineteenth-century French paintings. When the Thürntal repository was full, subsequent consignments were transported to the monastery at Hohenfurth. Among the treasures stored there were a large number of items from the Rothschild collection, over 1,000 pieces of silver from that of the David Weill family, and furniture and *objets d'art* from the

Mannheimer collection. The largest of the three repositories, however, was that at the Schloss Neuschwanstein, which ultimately was filled almost to overflowing with art treasures. By 1944 its contents numbered 21,903 works of art (including some 6,000 paintings) from 203 collections – almost all of them Jewish.[40]

Lesser repositories containing works destined for the Linz collection included the Schloss Kogl at St Georgen in Attergau, the Schloss Steiersberg near Wiener-Neustadt, which housed the Lanckoronski collection from Poland, and the Schloss Weesenstein near Dresden, which contained not only art treasures but also the card index listing the items intended for Linz; other works of art were concealed in an old monastery at Buxheim which housed among other things 200 paintings looted from Russia.

As the threat from Allied bombers increased in the spring of 1944, Hitler gave orders that all art treasures were to be evacuated to places of greater safety. Collections in German museums were moved underground, to the salt mines: those from Karlsruhe and Mannheim and part of the collection at Stuttgart to Heilbronn, the remainder of Stuttgart's along with those of Cologne and Heidelberg to Kochendorf, and Vienna's collection, including 1,408 paintings by Brueghel, Rembrandt, Dürer and Titian, near Bad Ischl.[41]

By far the largest repository was in a huge salt mine north of the Austrian spa town of Bad Aussee, in the mountains fifty-six kilometres east of Salzburg, just outside the summer resort of Alt Aussee. Here, from early 1944, large convoys of trucks arrived bearing the contents of the Führerbau in Munich in an evacuation overseen by Hans Reger, the officer in charge of the Führerbau since the beginnings of Sonderauftrag Linz. During the months of May to October, most of the contents of the Führerbau, numbering some 1,788 paintings and other works of art, were transferred to Alt Aussee.[42] At the same time, works of art were still arriving in large quantities at the Führerbau from other smaller repositories which were being closed. Inevitably this resulted in a huge workload for those responsible for recording and cataloguing, and eventually, at both the Führerbau and Alt Aussee, the system broke down.

2

LICENSED TO LOOT

Europe's greatest storehouses of major works of art lay in France and the Netherlands, and these great prizes had long been at the forefront of Hitler's aspirations for his Führermuseum in Linz. For them he harboured particular plans, and during the invasion of the Low Countries and France in 1940, the Wehrmacht's panzer divisions were closely followed by units of a special organization called the Einsatzstab Reichsleiter Rosenberg (ERR).

Formed under Hauptabteilung III: Sonderaufgaben (Division 3: Special Projects) of the Aussenpolitischesamt (Foreign Political Office), headed by Reichsleiter Alfred Rosenberg, the ERR had originally been tasked with collecting political material in German-occupied territories.[1] Rosenberg, who was responsible for all matters concerning political indoctrination within the Nazi party, was also Reichsminister responsible for the Occupied Territories of the East. The ERR was entirely self-contained and independent in its operations, possessing its own intelligence agents for tracking down and locating collections or individual works of art that had been targeted, as well as expert appraisers to identify and authenticate them. Squads of ERR troops carried out raids, securing target areas and sealing them off. A force of ERR packers, carpenters and transport personnel carried out the physical removal of works of art, while the ERR registry department was responsible for recording details of all confiscated items. These activities were supported by the ERR's own administrative and quartermaster branches.

The ERR carried out operations in both eastern and western Europe. It took part in the seizures of collections in Czechoslovakia; among the items of great value taken from that country was the 'Hohenfurth altarpiece', which had been painted in the fourteenth century for the monastery at Hohenfurth in Bohemia. In western Europe, the ERR was organized under three headquarters located in France, Belgium and the Netherlands, each with responsibility for a number of sectors. The French sectors were centred on Paris, St Germain, Angers and Dijon; Belgium was divided into two based in Brussels and Lille; the Netherlands into three based in Amsterdam, The Hague and Rotterdam. The entire western area was the responsibility of Amt Westen, which was established in Paris in July 1940.[2]

On 17 September that year Generalfeldmarschall Wilhelm Keitel, Chief of Staff of the OKW, gave orders that German forces in France were to provide assistance to the ERR. On 5 November, Göring issued an edict which extended the role of the ERR to locating and confiscating collections owned by Jews, a task hitherto the responsibility of the Wehrmacht, which had undertaken it with reluctance and distaste, and the German embassy in Paris. On 18 November Hitler gave orders that all confiscated works of art were to be sent to Germany, where they would come under the authority of Hans Posse. During the following year, collections seized in Paris included those belonging to the Schloss, David Weill, Wassermann, Hamburger, Solomon Flavian, Rosenstein, Sauerbach, Kronig, Rosenfeld, Thierry, Federer, Hamperzounian and Rothschild families. Thereafter, this work of confiscation – mainly, but not exclusively, of Jewish collections – became the primary role of the ERR, in which it was assisted by other organizations as described later in this chapter.

Initially, Amt Westen was headed by Stabsführer Dr Ebert, whose deputy was a senior German Red Cross official, Oberführer Baron Kurt von Behr. Early in 1941, however, Ebert was forced to retire as a result of injuries received in a car accident; he was succeeded by Stabsführer Gerhard Utikal, who was subsequently promoted, with the lengthy and somewhat cumbersome title of Hauptstellenleiter des Aussenpolitisches Amt und Leiter der ERR, and given responsibility for the activities of the ERR throughout all German-occupied territories. Thereafter, von Behr, as Deputy Director of Amt Westen and Director of the Paris Kunststab, was responsible for ERR operations throughout the French capital and surrounding areas.[3]

Based initially in Paris at the Hotel Commodore, and then subsequently at 54 avenue d'Iena, Amt Westen included a small group of professional art historians, called the Arbeitsgruppe Louvre, backed up by a number of photographers and research assistants. They were responsible for the preparation of all confiscated works of art for transportation to Germany. Among those who comprised the group initially were Drs Günther Schiedlausky, Hans Ulrich Wirth, Esser, Jerchel and Friedrich Franz Kuntze.[4] As was frequently the case with Nazi organizations, there was a degree of duplication of authority which inevitably caused a certain amount of administrative confusion. The Berlin-based Amt Bildende Kunst (Office for Pictorial Arts) was a department of the Hauptamt Kunstpflege (Central Office for Art Administration), which was headed by Hauptamtsleiter Dr

Walter Stang. This in turn formed part of the Amt für Weltanschauliche Schulung und Erziehung (Office for World-Political Indoctrination and Education), which was an independent element of Alfred Rosenberg's organization, separate from and possessing equal authority to the Aussenpolitisches Amt.[5] The Director of the Amt Bildende Kunst was Bereichsleiter Dr Robert Scholz, who was not only Rosenberg's personal adviser on all matters concerning art but was also responsible for the professional guidance provided the art historians of the Arbeitsgruppe Louvre which, as part of Amt Westen, was under the command of von Behr. Scholz frequently attempted to exercise his authority over the members of the Arbeitsgruppe Louvre but was always frustrated by von Behr.

Another organization which had a direct role to play in matters concerning works of art was the Kunstschutz which, as mentioned in chapter 1, had been formed in 1940 by the OKW to prevent a repetition of the wanton destruction and looting that had taken place in Poland. Kunstschutz personnel were subsequently deployed wherever German military administrations were established – France, Belgium, the Netherlands, Greece, Italy and Yugoslavia – and were tasked with the protection of all monuments and works of art in those countries. The re-formation of the Kunstschutz, which had existed in the First World War, had been the brainchild of Professor Count Wolff Metternich, chief curator of the museums in the Rhineland and Westphalia, whose representative in Paris, on the staff of the Military Governor, was Dr Herman Bunjes.[6]

Planning for Kunstschutz operations in France was carried out in Germany at the Art Historical Institute of the University of Marburg, renowned for its library of photographs of French and German art assembled over a period of thirty years. Here a group of the Institute's art experts drew up the plans for the photographic survey of French works of art and monuments which had been commissioned by the OKW and the Reich Education Ministry, and put together the considerable quantity of photographic and other equipment required for the Kunstschutz units. Kunstschutz personnel, including a number of art scholars, arrived in France towards the end of September 1940, having travelled by road from Marburg to Paris where they were initially employed on tasks at Versailles. A laboratory was established, comprising several darkrooms in which two photographers developed plates and produced proofs. Secretarial support and the cataloguing of photographs was carried out by two female assistants from Marburg. Meanwhile, other members of staff were busy inspecting the library of 200,000 plates at the Central

Depot of the French Monuments Historiques: one specialist was tasked with producing four prints from each plate which were subsequently sent to the respective research institutes of the universities at Marburg, Berlin, Bonn and Strasbourg.[7]

On 26 September a delegation of French dealers attended a meeting with Count Metternich and asked for permission for auctions to be resumed at the famous Hôtel Drouot in Paris in order to revitalize the art trade, which had been paralysed by the outbreak of war and the occupation of France. Permission was granted with the proviso that records be kept of works of art worth over FFr100,000, with details of the price paid and the new owner. Jews were not permitted to take part in the auctions.[8]

In early October, three groups of photographers were despatched from Paris to individual areas assigned to them: Normandy, Amiens-Laon and Rheims-Troyes and their surrounding districts. Each was commanded by a civilian member of the Kunstschutz, who had been accorded officer status, and was equipped with a vehicle and trailer. These groups worked in their respective areas until the beginning of December, when they returned to Paris to continue their work in the city's museums and libraries.

The main functions of the Kunstschutz staff in the Paris area were to administer the museums in and around the city and the photographic survey. In addition, they were tasked with preparing publications on the protection of monuments in German-occupied areas and on French art history, as well as making preparations for the establishment of a German art research institute in Paris. More ominously, however, they were also given responsibility for the 'transfer of certain large French art collections in a state of dissolution into German State and museum possession' and 'execution of personal jobs for the Reichsmarschall and Führer'. It was in these two latter roles that it was to cooperate with the ERR.[9]

The operations of the ERR were divided in the first instance into three separate elements: confiscation, sorting and disposal. Once items had been removed from their original locations, they were collected together at ERR depots where they were sorted. Selected items were then despatched to the central ERR clearing house at the Musée de Jeu de Paume in Paris, where they were once again sorted by ERR art experts before being sent to Germany. In the early stages, the ERR's efficiency in handling the confiscation of large quantities of works of art left much to be desired. By the time Ebert and his staff established themselves at the Hôtel Commodore, there was already a plethora of material appropriated earlier by the Wehrmacht under the aegis of the German embassy in Paris; while ERR staff worked on inventories of items already received, yet more confiscated items would arrive at the Musée de Jeu de Paume by the truckload. Subsequent attempts to produce inventories for them proved difficult, even impossible, as little or no information was given at the time of delivery about the owners from whom they had been confiscated.

This lack of organization and proper procedure elicited a strong protest from the members of the Arbeitsgruppe Louvre, who refused to permit the despatch of collections to Germany until inventories had been properly prepared. Von Behr, who cared little for the opinions of his staff, responded by giving orders to two other members of his ERR personnel, Wolff Braumüller and Fritz Busse, that such uncatalogued items were to be packed and sent to the principal repository at the Schloss Neuschwanstein at Füssen in Germany, the crates being marked 'Unknown'. Both these men frequently led confiscation missions, accompanied by French police, which were mounted after receipt of information from the SS Sicherheitsdienst.[10]

Despite the fact that all ERR operations in France were in theory under the overall authority of Rosenberg, in practice they were controlled by Göring. From the very start Hitler's edict of 18 November 1940, decreeing that all confiscated works of art were to be sent to Germany, was ignored by the Reichsmarschall who exploited Amt Westen's operations to his own advantage. Rosenberg, although vested with authority by Hitler and despite the latter's resentment at Göring's influence over the ERR, ranked well below the Reichsmarschall and possessed insufficient political authority to oppose his superior; he was also a somewhat weak character, lacking the courage to stand up to the likes of Göring or other senior Nazis such as Goebbels, von Ribbentrop, Himmler and Bormann, and prone to be influenced by the stronger characters within the ERR, such as von Behr. Rosenberg personally disapproved strongly of the ERR's role as confiscator of works of art and never attempted to use his position as head of the organization to profit from it. Indeed, he only visited Amt Westen twice, and often forbade his staff even to mention the ERR to him.

In early December 1940 Scholz was sent to Paris by Rosenberg to discover the extent of Göring's influence over Amt Westen. On questioning Ebert and von Behr, he was told that Göring had received permission from Hitler to examine confiscated collections and to determine their fate. Scholz gained the clear impression, and reported to Rosenberg on his return to Berlin, that the two men were working in Göring's interests and that the Reichsmarschall had already begun to remove items for his own collection at his palace at Karinhall in Germany. Rosenberg immediately attempted to block any transfer of works of art to Karinhall – but with little success. In March 1941 Dr Hermann Bunjes travelled to Berlin with a large portfolio containing photographs of works of art for Göring's inspection. Before showing them to the Reichsmarschall, however, he attended a meeting with Rosenberg and Utikal to discuss the selected items. No sooner had Bunjes departed than Rosenberg despatched Scholz to Paris to pre-empt the transfer to Karinhall; but the emissary was informed by von Behr that the works of art in question had already been loaded aboard a train and that nothing could be done to stop the shipment.[11]

Early in 1941, with von Behr's approval, Göring appointed one of the group of art historians on the staff of Amt Westen, Dr Bruno Lohse, as his personal representative. Although Lohse continued to work with the Arbeitsgruppe Louvre, he thereafter enjoyed independent status through his appointment to Sonderauftrag Göring (Special Operation Göring). He was issued with letters of authority, signed by the Reichsmarshall himself, instructing all German military and civil units and departments to accord him all assistance in carrying out his mission.[12] Together with another member of the Arbeitsgruppe Louvre, Dr Günther Schiedlausky, Lohse was given the responsibility of organizing exhibitions of confiscated works of art which he thought would be of interest to Göring, as well as making periodic surveys of the Paris art market.

Göring had a large number of agents in the occupied territories who kept him supplied with information. Among those in France was a German officer working in the military administration in Paris, who obtained the cooperation of a French police officer in the Sûreté Nationale called Dufour and a Frenchwoman named Lucie Botton who had previously been employed by the wealthy French Jewish art dealer André Seligmann in his gallery in Paris.

These two collaborators provided the German officer with details of Jewish art collections which had been hidden in an attempt to avoid confiscation by the ERR. Eventually, however, these activities came to the attention of General Karl Heinrich von Stülpnagel, the Commander-in-Chief of German forces in France, who put a stop to them by having the officer posted to Berlin.

In mid-1940, Göring had established a procedure for 'legitimizing' his acquisition of confiscated works of art through the ERR. He appointed a French artist, Professor Jacques Beltrand, as 'official appraiser' for the French government with the role of placing valuations on those which the Reichsmarshall wished to acquire from collections confiscated by the ERR.[13] The works valued by Beltrand were ultimately sent to Göring for payment. Needless to say, payment was never forthcoming and indeed no method of payment was ever established.

Göring would give little notice of his visits to Paris. Accompanied by his art adviser, Walter Andreas Hofer, he would go in person to the Musée de Jeu de Paume, where ERR staff would have set up an exhibition. The Reichsmarschall would inspect the exhibits, placing them in four categories: those selected for consideration by Hitler; those for his own collection at his palace at Karinhall; those for universities and places of higher learning; and those for other German collections. The works of art earmarked for Karinhall would then be packed and taken immediately to Göring's special train, accompanying him back to Germany. Between February 1941 and November 1942 a total of eight such consignments were transported to Karinhall. By these means Göring ensured that he always received first choice from any newly arrived confiscations; he acquired approximately 700 items from France for his collection, which is covered in detail in chapter 3. Among them were Chardin's *Joyeuse de Volant*, Teniers' *Adam and Eve in Paradise*, Fragonard's *Young Girl with Chinese Figure*, Boucher's *Venus* and works by Cranach the Elder and Younger. Those items set aside for Hitler's own personal collection were in fact chosen by Göring during a visit to Paris on 5 February 1941. Initially, Hitler had made his choice from an album of photographs sent to him, but it was Göring who made the final selection with Hitler's agreement. A total of fifty-three works of art, which with one or two exceptions came from the Rothschild and Seligmann collections, were selected and transported on Göring's train to Munich where they were placed in the Führerbau.[14] Surprisingly, Hitler personally made no further selections from ERR confiscated material, despite the large number of leather-bound albums, containing photographs of selected works of art, which were sent to him.

Göring sought to cloak the ERR's operations with respectability by using the pretext that they were being conducted within the rules of international law. In early 1942, in response to French official protests against the confiscations, he instructed Dr Hermann Bunjes to produce a document which laid out in detail the background to the ERR's operations. Entitled *French Protests against the Safeguard-ing of Ownerless Jewish Art Properties in Occupied France*, it rejected French protests as ingratitude and sought to justify the confiscations on the grounds that they were carried out for purely altruistic reasons, namely to secure valuable works of art to protect them from damage or destruction.[15]

Bunjes also claimed a legal justification for the confiscations. Article 46 of the Hague Convention of 1907, which was signed by Germany and France and observed in the terms of the Armistice of May 1940, called for the inviolability of private property. Bunjes argued that the Armistice of 1940 was between Germany and the French state and people. The latter, in German eyes, excluded Jews, and so Germany was not bound to respect their property. He continued by accusing the Jews, in alliance with communists, of carrying out attacks on Wehrmacht personnel and German civilians, which constituted grounds for measures to be taken against them. Bunjes maintained that the real reason for the French protests against the seizure of Jewish property was a desire to deceive Germany and promote subversive activity, including anti-German cultural propaganda. He also claimed that such protests were designed to create opposition to German claims for the return of German cultural material destroyed or stolen by French forces during and after the First World War, and ultimately to denigrate the altruistic motives behind the German measures taken to protect French works of art. He strongly recommended that French officials not be allowed access to ERR repositories throughout France, on the grounds that this would permit espionage, and concluded by advising against giving any response to the French until Hitler had decided on the disposal of all the confiscated items.

Towards the end of March 1942 von Behr was appointed Leiter der Dienststelle Westen der Ostministeriums (Director of the Western Branch of the Ministry for the Occupied Countries of the East). Three months earlier, Alfred Rosenberg had suggested to Hitler that the furnishings of 'ownerless' Jewish houses in the western German-occupied countries should be seized for use by those officials of the Nazi party whose houses in the eastern territories had been bombed.[16] During the following month, having obtained Hitler's agreement to this idea, Rosenberg suggested that responsibility for this new task, called the 'M-Action', should be allocated directly to his own department, the Ministry for the Occupied Territories of the East, on the grounds that using existing ERR channels would create difficulties. Once again, Rosenberg obtained Hitler's assent and orders were issued for the establishment of the Dienststelle Westen with its headquarters in Paris and offices throughout France, Belgium and the Netherlands. Von Behr was placed in charge of the new organization which, while working alongside the ERR, would have a separate role. Although he remained titular head of the ERR art staff in Paris, he was to relinquish operational responsibility. It was strongly suspected that the establishment of Dienststelle Westen was in fact the brainchild of von Behr himself, who considered that it would give him greater freedom to lay his hands on large quantities of valuable items such as furniture which would not be subject to such close scrutiny and rigorous accounting procedures as the fine art collections seized by the ERR.

Von Behr's transfer to his new appointment was cause for considerable satisfaction among the members of the Arbeitsgruppe Louvre and senior staff of the ERR, including Robert Scholz, with whom he had come into conflict on more than one occasion and whom he had antagonized with his arrogant and patronizing manner. A member of an aristocratic German family from Macklenburg, von Behr was totally ignorant about art yet had consistently scorned the advice and opinions of his own art specialists. He had also shown himself to be utterly unscrupulous in his methods, using his position to make substantial personal profit, which he used to finance an extravagant lifestyle. Counting Göring among his customers, he sold confiscated paintings and pocketed the proceeds. Although a civilian, von Behr, who was renowned within the ERR for his great vanity, always wore the uniform of the German Red Cross or that of a civilian employee of the Wehrmacht. During the First World War he had served as a non-commissioned officer and had been captured by the British, spending the rest of the war as a prisoner. During the early 1930s he had become an ardent Nazi and before the outbreak of war had joined the Red Cross. Although only the equivalent of an oberleutnant (lieutenant) in 1940, he eventually acquired the rank equivalent to oberstleutnant (lieutenant colonel) by playing the Red Cross off against the headquarters of the local Wehrmacht military administration, claiming to each that the other was offering him promotion. Well known for his sycophancy, he courted the favour of senior officers and influential figures, plying them with lavish gifts. For example, on Göring's birthday in 1942 von Behr arrived in Berlin bringing a gift in the form of the original copy of the Treaty of Versailles bearing all the signatures and an original letter to Napoleon III from Richard Wagner. Both these items had been part of collections confiscated by the ERR.[17]

Von Behr worked closely with Darquier de Pellepoix, the notoriously anti-Semitic French Commissioner for Jewish Affairs. In 1941 he forced members of the ERR to work closely with the Sicherheitsdienst in searching for wanted Jews, and personally attended conferences held by the Judenreferat of the Sicherheitsdienst at which he gave and received information which led to the arrest of Jews and the confiscation of their property: he was later stated to have been responsible for initiating action for the confiscation of the Schloss collection. In his new post as head of Dienststelle Westen, he used Jews as forced labour in repairing and packing furnishings for transportation to Germany, housing them in a small prison camp in Paris.[18]

Robert Scholz took over responsibility for the work of the ERR art staff, while von Behr's administrative duties within the ERR were assumed by Dr Karl Brethauer. Shortly afterwards, Amt Westen moved to a new location at 12 rue Dumont d'Urville, leaving the Dienststelle Westen in occupation at 54 avenue d'Iena. Assisted by Abschnittsleiter Oberleutnant Hermann von Ingram, who had taken charge of administrative and business affairs under Brethauer, Scholz produced a report for Rosenberg which was highly critical of the activities of the ERR art staff in Paris and recommended that in future it should be restricted to cataloguing and conservation of works of art and to meticulous control of all material confiscated by the Dienststelle Westen, with the power to withdraw any art objects from consignments prior to shipment to Germany. So strong was Göring's influence, however, that Rosenberg was in no position to act on these proposals.

In theory, von Behr's connection with the ERR's art staff ceased with his appointment as Director of the Dienststelle Westen. In practice, however, he managed to prolong his activities by enlisting the support of Göring who, on his visits to Paris, gave temporary authority for von Behr to continue in his dealings with confiscated works of art. In June 1942 Rosenberg wrote to Göring, informing him that it would no longer be possible for the ERR to present works of art for inspection and selection, although the services of the Arbeitsgruppe Louvre would still be available for consultation and advice. Despite this, however, Göring continued to obtain works of art from the ERR via von Behr until the latter was removed as deputy head of the Amt Westen in January 1943. In April that year, Martin Bormann wrote to von Behr, informing him that Dr Hermann Voss, Dr Friedrich Wolffhardt and Dr Helmut von Hummel had been appointed as the official experts for Hitler's collections and would accordingly make the decisions concerning disposal of works of art confiscated by the ERR.

Within the ranks of the ERR, jealousy and back-biting were rife. The special position of Bruno Lohse, Göring's personal adviser, aroused particular resentment and jealousy among his colleagues, who objected to the privileges it brought him. Indeed, Göring's influence undermined morale throughout the organization, preventing it from carrying out its role as originally dictated by Hitler; but Rosenberg was politically too weak to counter it. Lohse himself was involved in disputes with his colleagues on more than one occasion, exacerbating existing frictions. Shortly after he took over the administration of the Arbeitsgruppe Louvre, Oberleutnant von Ingram dismissed two of the female research assistants who were on very bad terms with his wife, an art historian on the staff of Amt Westen. Lohse intervened and persuaded von Ingram to reinstate the women, one of whom, Dr Helga Eggemann, then stated that she would be unable to work on a full-time basis for the ERR as she had by then obtained a part-time post with the German embassy. Lohse gave her an ultimatum: work full-time or resign. Dr Eggemann remained in post, but her resentment towards Lohse endured and she eventually caused a rift between him and Dr Walter Borchers, with whom he shared responsibility for the Arbeitsgruppe Louvre.

The ERR's operations in Paris were perpetually hampered by the lack of sufficient properly qualified personnel and of adequate facilities. The members of the Arbeitsgruppe Louvre had no art reference library, yet all relevant confiscated books were the responsibility of another section of the ERR which was under orders to 'freeze' all such written works pending instructions from the Amt für Weltanschauliche Schulung und Erziehung. Consequently, the art historians possessed almost no reference material to aid them in their work. As for personnel, some of the ERR's staff were available to it only on a part-time basis or for limited periods of time on loan from the Kunstschutz. These included members of the Arbeitsgruppe Louvre. Dr Hans Ulrich Wirth had been conscripted into the army, posted to the Kunstschutz unit in Paris and then subsequently detached on temporary duty to the ERR. Similarly, Dr Jerchel, a very learned scholar who was later deemed to have been the most knowledgeable of all the art historians who worked for the ERR in Paris, had seen active service with the Wehrmacht and had been awarded the Iron Cross 2nd Class before being posted to the Kunstschutz and subsequently detached to the ERR.

The military ranks of members of the Kunstschutz serving on

attachment to the Arbeitsgruppe Louvre bore little relation to their degree of expertise and standing in the world of art. Dr Günther Schiedlausky was a mere corporal in the army while Dr Walter Borchers, an eminent art historian who was eventually placed in charge of the group, held the lowly rank of obergefreiter in the Luftwaffe. Several individuals in the ERR had seen active service before joining the Kunstschutz or the ERR: among these was Oberleutnant Hermann von Ingram, who, as an infantryman during the campaign in Belgium in 1940, was one of the first German soldiers to be awarded the Ritterkreuz (Knight's Cross of the Iron Cross) in the war. Commissioned in the field, he had been retired to the reserve before being posted to the ERR.

In a report dated 22 August 1942, prepared at the request of Oberleutnant von Ingram, Dr Günther Schiedlausky stated that the shortage of trained personnel was preventing the construction of proper inventories of confiscated works of art. Three members of the Kunstschutz on loan to the ERR, photographers by training, now found themselves cataloguing works of art. Furthermore, Schiedlausky complained, because Bruno Lohse had been appointed as a special representative of Göring, he could no longer be relied upon to carry out research under Schiedlausky's direction. This left only Dr Friedrich Franz Kuntze and himself to work on recording and compiling inventories on a full-time basis. He went on to express his strong disapproval of the exhibitions demanded by Göring, complaining that they were time-consuming and diverted already the overstretched ERR staff from their proper employment where they were sorely needed.

Much of the problem facing the ERR in Paris was caused by the huge quantities of confiscated art which flooded into the Musée du Jeu de Paume in the months following the German invasion of France. Between the end of 1940 and the beginning of 1941, the flow of works from large collections, such as those of Rothschild, Kann, Weil-Picard and Wildenstein, was such that the overstretched members of the Arbeitsgruppe Louvre were unable to cope with the amount of work heaped upon them. After the departure of von Behr, the ERR in France became more discriminating in selecting works of art for confiscation, with one of its art historians evaluating items beforehand.

Relations between the ERR and other German military and civil departments in the occupied territories were poor. Many officials disapproved strongly of its activities, which were regarded as little better than larceny, and the ERR frequently encountered obstruction in the course of its operations. Rosenberg and von Behr were well aware of the low esteem in which the organization was held by the Wehrmacht, and von Behr, who lived in Paris in great luxury, was encouraged by Rosenberg to entertain lavishly in order to improve relations with the military.

One Nazi body which took more than a passing interest in the ERR was the SS, and in particular its leader, Reichsführer Heinrich Himmler. His attention was attracted by Hitler's repeating in March 1942 that the ERR had sole responsibility for the confiscation of works of art, archives, libraries and other cultural material from the enemies of the Third Reich. In response, Himmler wrote to Hitler to determine the rights of the Sicherheitsdienst (SD) and the Sicherheitspolizei (SIPO) with regard to any documentary material relating to such enemies which might be confiscated. Consequently, Alfred Rosenberg was instructed to have the ERR send all documents having relevance to security matters to the SD and SIPO. Notwithstanding this concession, however, neither Himmler nor Reichsminister Dr Hans Lammers, the head of the Reichskanzlei, had much time for the ERR, and firmly opposed its confiscatory remit. Their considerable influence with the OKW and in army circles was such that only minimum cooperation was ever extended to the ERR.

After von Behr's departure from Amt Westen, the activity of the ERR in France assumed a more passive nature. Work proceeded on the compilation of catalogues and inventories of the several thousand works of art in its possession, notably on the production of an extensive inventory of the Jewish-owned collections, work on which continued until the withdrawal of German forces from Paris.

The ERR's arch-enemy in Paris was Count Wolff Metternich, the head of the Kunstschutz and its representative at the OKW, who frequently and publicly condemned the activities of the ERR and von Behr. Soon after his arrival in Paris in the wake of the German occupying forces, Metternich had discovered that a representative of the German foreign ministry, Sturmbannführer Freiherr von Künsberg, who commanded Ribbentrop's specially formed looting unit, had been sent to the French capital with the secret task of producing an inventory of the contents of all the French national collections and to select the choicest items for despatch to Germany as a 'gift' from the people of France.[19] He was assisted by an unnamed German art expert who had lived in France for some years and was well acquainted with the French national collections and with the French art market in general. Metternich succeeded in countering this plan by obtaining an edict from Generalfeldmarschall Walter von Brauchitsch, the Commander in Chief of the army, which forbade unauthorized entry to the five hundred or so châteaux and historic buildings to which all the French national collections had been evacuated in 1939 on the outbreak of war, and placed all these repositories out of bounds to German troops. This incurred the displeasure of the Nazi hierarchy, but Metternich suffered no repercussions: he later stated that he believed this was because the Nazis did not wish their secret plans for the French national collections to become public knowledge.

One collection, however, had not been evacuated from Paris. This was the Musée de l'Armée, located in the Hôtel des Invalides. Consequently, the Germans selected some two thousand items which they claimed to be of German origin from the Napoleonic and Franco-Prussian Wars and the First World War. These were removed and despatched to the Zeughaus military museum in Berlin by its director, Admiral Lorey.[20]

As the ERR strengthened its grip in France and confiscated an increasing number of French Jewish-owned collections, Metternich's position became increasingly precarious. Opposed by von Behr, who was supported by Göring, he found himself virtually powerless. However, although unable to stop the confiscations, he was determined to impede the activities of the ERR where and whenever he could: on at least one occasion he warned an owner that his collection was to be confiscated, enabling it to be handed over to a French museum for safe keeping beyond the reach of the ERR. According to Charles de Jaeger, who interviewed him at length during his research for his book *The Linz File*, Metternich also held secret meetings with the French authorities during which he handed over lists of works of art despatched to Germany by the ERR. This information was to prove invaluable after the end of the war in the efforts to return the items to their rightful owners. Metternich would later receive the Légion d'Honneur from General de Gaulle himself as a mark of French gratitude.[21]

Göring became increasingly irritated by the obstructive attitude and activities of the Kunstschutz in France, and eventually Metternich was reported to Hitler. The OKW was ordered to recall him and he returned to Germany, where he resumed his previous post as chief curator of the museums in the Rhineland. His fears that he might subsequently suffer at the hands of the Nazis proved groundless. This was undoubtedly due not only to his high-level contacts in the OKW but also to his extensive knowledge of the involvement of Göring and the ERR in wholesale looting throughout Europe and of Sonderauf-trag Linz.

Metternich was not the only individual who took active measures to oppose the activities of the ERR. Working in the recording centre at the Musée du Jeu de Paume was a Frenchwoman named Rose Valland who had worked for the Louvre as an art historian before the war. In 1940, on hearing that the ERR was establishing a collecting point at the Jeu de Paume, she volunteered her services and, because of her qualifications and previous experience in the world of art, was employed as a clerk in the recording section of Amt Westen. Her work involved compiling inventories and filing details of all works of art confiscated by the ERR in France, brought to the Musée du Jeu de Paume and ultimately despatched to Germany, as well as recording the details of the original owners and the recipients.[22] Despite the supervision of ERR officials, and at great risk to herself, Rose Valland duplicated all the records which she made and filed during her work for the ERR. She then passed this information to Jacques Jaujard, the French Director of National Museums, who was a member of the Resistance. Jaujard in turn sent the information to the Free French government-in-exile in London. Like the information handed to the French authorities by Count Metternich, this material would also eventually prove of immense value in helping to return looted works of art to their rightful owners.

It was in 1944 that Rose Valland made her greatest contribution to saving France's art treasures. With the Allies advancing on Paris, the Germans were making urgent preparations to withdraw from the city. The ERR had been ordered by the Wehrmacht military administration to put its staff on forty-eight hours' notice to be available for the defence of the city; all its able-bodied younger male members had already been called away for service with front-line army units. The remaining contents of the repository at the Musée du Jeu de Paume had been packed into a total of 148 cases and loaded aboard a train already heavily laden with a large quantity of furniture and other items looted by von Behr's Dienststelle Westen. Von Behr himself was also due to depart from Paris on the same train.[23] Through Jacques Jaujard, Rose Valland succeeded in making contact with a railway official who was also a member of the Resistance, and enlisted his aid. This official arranged for the crates containing the works of art to be marked and at the same time made discreet enquiries concerning the train's initial destination. He learned that it was Abbeville, which lies to the north of Paris on the

River Somme near the French coast. This information was given to Rose Valland who turned once again to the Resistance, contacting another group and asking it to ensure that the train did not leave the Paris area. When the train, carrying von Behr and his consignment of loot from the Louvre, reached Le Bourget, it was discovered that a stretch of railway line had been removed. The train was forced to return to Paris and remain there for forty-eight hours before it could recommence its journey. On the second attempt the engine's brakes failed and the train was forced to return to Paris again. Further attempts to leave the city met with similar mishaps or obstructions. Eventually von Behr, becoming increasingly desperate with the advancing Allied forces having reached Rambouillet on the south-west approaches to the city, commandeered a brand new engine and placed it under heavy guard. This was coupled to the wagons and, after a thorough inspection, the train departed once more. By this time, however, the leading elements of General Jacques Leclerc's 2nd French Armoured Division had advanced into Paris and secured the marshalling yards through which the train had to travel. By sheer coincidence, the officer commanding the leading troops who inter-cepted the train was Capitaine Alexandre Rosenberg, the son of the Jewish dealer and collector Paul Rosenberg whose collections in Paris and Libourne, near Bordeaux, had been confiscated by the ERR. When the cases containing the ERR loot were eventually opened, Rosenberg found himself looking at a large number of his father's paintings.[24]

Von Behr, who was accompanied by his wife, had meanwhile succeeded in escaping and eventually made his way to Germany. There he was re-employed in his role as head of the Dienststelle Westen's M-Action, this time moving large quantities of looted furniture, books and other items from the Netherlands to Germany. Eventually, however, with the Allies advancing into Germany, he and his wife, who was an Englishwoman, committed suicide by drinking poisoned champagne in their home at the Schloss Banz near Lichtenfels.[25]

In addition to confiscating art collections, the ERR also acted as intermediary in a number of exchanges of confiscated works of art between a small group of dealers and certain senior Nazis who sought to use the organization to profit personally from its activities. Eighteen of these exchanges were undertaken on behalf of Göring; seven for Hitler and the Reichskanzlei; one for Bormann; and one, or possibly two, for von Ribbentrop.[26] The exchanges took place between February 1941 and November 1943 and involved mainly late nineteenth- and twentieth-century French paintings confiscated principally from the Rosenberg-Bernstein collection. They took place largely as a result of the edict by Hitler which forbade the transportation to Germany of French Impressionist or twentieth-century works of art, which he had declared to be 'degenerate'. Part of the processing of confiscated collections by the ERR consisted of the separation of such works from the remainder. It was not long before it was realized that the increasing number of 'degenerate' works in the hands of the ERR possessed great potential for commercial exploitation, and the suggestion of exchanging them for Old Masters and German nineteenth-century paintings was put to Göring who, renowned for his reluctance to part with money, responded enthusiastically. Responsibility for the idea was later laid on the shoulders of von Behr and the art historian Bruno Lohse, although the latter claimed that it had originated from von Behr. Indeed, Lohse and Scholz subsequently stated that von Behr had proposed to Göring's chief of staff that confiscated 'degenerate' works could be smuggled into Portugal where they could be bartered for uncut diamonds.[27]

Fifteen of the exchanges effected for Göring, and three of those for the Reichskanzlei, were organized by a German dealer named Gustav Rochlitz who had entered the art world in 1921 as a result of meeting a well-known museum director, Wilhelm Bode. Encouraged by Bode, Rochlitz had become a dealer, travelling throughout Europe, mainly in the Netherlands and Italy, and from 1925 onwards spending the majority of his time outside Germany. He established a loose partnership with a Swiss dealer named Stoeri in Zurich and associations with the Galerie Weder in Lausanne and Galerie van Diemen in Berlin. In 1924, he opened his own gallery in Berlin and ran it until 1930. In 1928, however, business took a downturn for Rochlitz as his association with the Galerie Weder was terminated; and three years later, in 1931, the business of his Swiss partner, Stoeri, went into liquidation owing Rochlitz 200,000 Swiss francs. Nothing daunted, however, Rochlitz opened another gallery in Zurich in the same year, running it for a banker named Guhl and holding an exhibition of Old Masters at the Muralto Gallery which proved very popular and received favourable acclaim. In the same year, however, the Swiss authorities barred him from operating a business in Switzerland because of his German citizenship. (Rochlitz later suspected that this was due to pressure from Theodor Fischer, the dealer in Lucerne who conducted the auction of 'degenerate art' in June 1939.[28]) The following year, 1933, Rochlitz moved to Paris and went into business under his own name and that of his book-keeper, Paul Weill, initially at premises in the Cité Bergère in Montmartre and later at 222 rue de Rivoli. Shortly after the beginning of the war Rochlitz, as a German national, was interned by the French; but he was freed two weeks later because his daughter, Sylvia, who had been born in Paris in 1934, held French citizenship. In early 1940, as German forces were advancing on Paris, he was interned again amid fears of fifth column activity; once more, after the fall of the city, he was released. He was permitted to re-establish his German nationality, but only on a month-by-month basis as he and his wife had previously applied for French citizenship, the granting of which had been delayed by the onset of war.[29]

Immediately after the German occupation of Paris, Rochlitz had learned from friends that a large number of German dealers and museum officials were in the city for the purpose of purchasing works of art in quantity. He lost no time in taking advantage of the situation and soon re-established his business. His first customer was the Director of the Düsseldorf Museum, Dr Hupp, to whom he sold five paintings in a deal arranged by another German, Adolf Wüster, who was an art adviser to the German embassy in Paris and whom Rochlitz had known previously in Germany.[30] Thereafter, Rochlitz conducted a considerable amount of business with German clients and with the ERR in the person of Bruno Lohse, who approached him while looking for works of art on behalf of Göring. In February 1941 Rochlitz put forward two paintings, *Portrait of a Man* by Titian and *Still Life* by Jan Weenix, which were taken away for a private exhibition being arranged for Göring at the Musée de Jeu de Paume. Lohse subsequently returned and informed Rochlitz that both paintings had been turned down because of their high prices but that he wished to acquire them by exchange.[31] Initially Rochlitz was reluctant to agree to this proposal, as was his co-owner, a French dealer named Birtschansky who had a two-thirds share in both paintings. However, the latter's interest was bought out for the sum of just under US$20,000 by another German dealer, Hans Wendland, and Rochlitz gave in to pressure from Göring to agree to an exchange rather than a cash sale. The deal was subsequently concluded and Wendland received six paintings which had been confiscated by the ERR from the Alphonse Kann and Rosenberg-Bernstein collections: *Mother and Child* by Corot, *Madame Camus at the Piano* by Degas, *Still Life* by Braque, and *Woman at a Table*, *Still Life* and *Sleeping Woman* by Matisse.[32]

Thereafter, Rochlitz participated in a further seventeen exchanges with the ERR, receiving confiscated paintings which he kept or sold to other dealers. Among the works which passed through his hands were the following: *Women at the Races* and *Mother and Child* by Picasso; *Still Life: Roses* by Manet; *Tuileries Gardens* and *View of Paris* by Pissarro; *Oriental Women* and *Woman in a Red Coat* by Matisse; *Bathers* and *Flower Piece* by Cézanne; *Rearing Horses* by de Chirico; *Two Girls of Tahiti* and *Crucifixion* by Gauguin; *Portrait of a Woman* by Modigliani; *Girl Reading in Front of a Bunch of Flowers* and *Two Nudes* by Renoir; *Forest Scene* by Courbet; *Village Street (Une Rue de Conquet)* and *Rue Froideveaux* by Utrillo; *Wooded Landscape* by Corot; *Abstraction* and *Still Life* by Braque; *Still Life* by Bonnard; *Café Scene* by Toulouse-Lautrec; *Spring Landscape* and *River Scene* by Sisley; *Children on a Staircase with Sunflowers* and *Street Scene with Banner* by Monet; *Mont St Michel* by Signac; and *The Beach at Trouville* and *Seascape* by Boudin.[33]

Adolf Wüster, the German embassy's art adviser who had initiated Rochlitz's first sale, was directly involved in two ERR exchanges on behalf of Göring and von Ribbentrop. In the first, the ERR handed over *Lion with a Snake* by Delacroix and *Forest Scene* by Courbet, and received a Gobelins tapestry entitled *Maximilian Hunting Scene* and a painting, *The Hen Yard*, in the manner of Albert Cuyp. The second exchange saw the ERR receiving *Chapel of the Rocks* by Jodocus de Momper in exchange for *Suburban Street Scene* by Utrillo.[34] Two exchanges were transacted with a confidence trickster named Arthur Pfannstiel who worked for von Behr. In these, the ERR gave *Winter Landscape* by Sisley, *Girl with a Guitar* by Laurencin and *Portrait of a Woman* by Degas in exchange for *Farmers Gambling* by Cornelis Bega and a French fifteenth-century portrait. The ERR also conducted two exchanges with another dealer in Paris, Max Stöcklin, who represented the Reichskanzlei in the first and Hitler in the second. It gave *View through a Window* and *Female Nude in a Yellow Chair* by Matisse and *Still Life, Coffee Table* by Bonnard in exchange for *Woodland Landscape with Figures* by Winants and *The Temple of Faustina* by Rudolf Alt.[35]

A number of exchanges were carried out with dealers in Germany and the Netherlands. The Galerie Almas-Dietrich in Munich, owned by Maria Almas-Dietrich, represented the Reichskanzlei in a transaction in which the ERR gave *The Harbour of Honfleur in the Rain* by Pissarro and received two early sixteenth-century Franco-Portuguese paintings: *Scourging of Christ* and *Betrayal of Christ*.[36] A dealer in Frankfurt named Bödecker represented either Hitler or Bormann in an exchange in which the ERR gave *Boy with a Butterfly Net* by

Renoir, receiving *Painter Seated on Bough of Tree, Surrounded by Children* by Ludwig Knaus.[37] A Dutch dealer in Amsterdam named Jan Dik Jr represented Göring in an exchange in which the latter received from the ERR *Pause before a Country Inn* from the school of Isaak van Ostade and gave in return three paintings: *River Landscape* by Brueghel, *Farm Village* by van Stalbent and *Procession in a Grotto* by Jodocus de Momper.[38] Finally, a German dealer with Hungarian citizenship, Dr Alexander von Frey, acted on behalf of Göring in an exchange in which the latter received *Portrait of a Girl* by Renoir, *Apple* by Picasso and *Country Road* by Pissarro and gave the ERR *Mill in Saxony* by Karl von Blechen and *Study of Figures* by Makart.[39]

An exchange involving a painting previously confiscated by the ERR was effected in late November 1942 by Walter Andreas Hofer, the art dealer who was Göring's principal buyer, and Bruno Lohse on behalf of the ERR. A French Jewish dealer and director of the firm Kleinberger, Allen Loebl, had offered the entire Kleinberger library to Göring in gratitude for the latter's having secured him, through Hofer, certain exemptions from the anti-Jewish laws being enforced by the Germans in occupied France. Göring refused to accept the library as a gift and proposed an exchange. This was agreed and he gave in return a painting by Utrillo which had been confiscated from the Bernheim-Jeune collection.[40]

According to an official report produced by Alfred Rosenberg in 1944 the ERR had between October 1940 and July 1944 confiscated 22,000 works of art which had been subsequently despatched to Germany. More detail is provided by one of three lengthy and detailed documents produced after the end of the war by the Art Looting Investigation Unit (ALIU) of the Office of Strategic Services (OSS), the forerunner of the US Central Intelligence Agency, of which more will be said in chapter 4. Consolidated Interrogation Report No. 1, *The ERR in France*, gives a detailed breakdown of the confiscations made by the ERR in France: 10,890 paintings, watercolours, drawings, pastels, engravings, miniatures, etc.; 583 sculptures; 2,477 pieces of seventeenth- and eighteenth-century furniture; 583 tapestries, carpets, embroideries, etc.; 5,825 *objets d'art* (porcelain, glass, jewellery, coins, rare gems, etc.; 1,286 works of Asiatic art (sculptures, porcelain, paintings, screens, etc); and 259 items of classical antiquity (Greek, Roman, Egyptian, Assyrian; sculptures, vases, jewellery etc.).[41] The estimated value, at that time, of the acquisitions from France alone was US$1 billion. OSS ALIU examination of the ERR files revealed a detailed inventory which gave figures relating to the numbers of confiscated works of art belonging to some of the major Jewish collections: 2,687 from the David Weill collection; 1,202 from Alphonse Kann; 989 from Levy de Benzion; and 302 from Georges Wildenstein. Other figures, 558 from Seligmann and 123 from Weil-Picard, represent only fractions of the total numbers of items confiscated from these two collections.[42]

The majority of the works of art confiscated by the ERR were despatched to Germany as stipulated in Hitler's edict of 18 November 1940. A report by Robert Scholz, dated July 1944, stated that a total of twenty-nine shipments to Germany took place between April 1941 and July 1944. These consisted of 138 railway wagonloads which contained 4,174 cases and crates. Problems arose over a lack of rolling stock and thirty suitably constructed wagons, fitted with heating systems, had to be commandeered from all over Germany.[43] The first major shipment, consisting of items from the Rothschild, David Weill, Weil-Picard, Seligmann and Wildenstein collections, left Paris in April 1941 for the repository at the Schloss Neuschwanstein at Füssen under a heavy escort of Luftwaffe troops and accompanied by Günther Schiedlausky and Friedrich Franz Kuntze. Travelling via Belfort, Stuttgart and Augsburg, the train took three days to reach Füssen. The second major consignment was despatched in October 1941 and was also delivered to the Schloss Neuschwanstein.[44] In 1942 the Bacri and Cramer collections were sent to the Schloss Kogl at St Georgen in the district of Vocklabruck, and other items were sent to two further repositories at the Schloss Nickolsburg and the Cloister Buxheim, the latter located in the Memmingen area. Two other repositories, at the Schloss Chiemsee at Herreninsel, in the district of Traunstein, and at the Schloss Seisenegg at Amstetten, also came into use.[45]

By the beginning of 1944, however, the threat from Allied bombing raids on Munich was such that on 6 February Hitler gave orders to Alfred Rosenberg, via Martin Bormann, that the Führerbau's most important contents, together with those of the other repositories, were to be moved to safety as soon as possible. A few days later Robert Scholz was summoned to Berlin, where he attended a conference with Dr Helmut von Hümmel, Bormann's personal accountant. There he learned that the contents of the Führerbau and the repositories were to be moved to the salt mine at Alt Aussee. The removal posed considerable logistical problems. Any movement of such valuable works of art required special packing materials; but these had been returned to Paris after each shipment for further use.

They now had to be retrieved and the art treasures repacked before being despatched by road to Alt Aussee. It took a total of thirteen large convoys to transfer the contents of the six ERR repositories to the subterranean vaults of the mine, a process which commenced in February 1944 and was not completed until March 1945.

Thus the ERR carried out its assigned task of stripping Europe of its great art treasures and moving them to Germany. Although nominally under the control of Reichsleiter Alfred Rosenberg, it was in fact largely dominated by one man whose insatiable lust for works of art, combined with his great power and influence, made him the most formidable of all the thieves in the Third Reich: Hermann Göring.

3

THE THIEF OF KARINHALL

On several occasions Reichsmarschall Hermann Göring publicly declared that he would never permit any confiscated or looted works of art to adorn the walls of his palace at Karinhall, and that it was unthinkable for him even to consider coercing anyone into selling a work of art which he desired. Furthermore, when visiting the ERR collection point at the Musée du Jeu de Paume in Paris, he always loudly avowed his intention of paying for those items which he selected. The truth about the obese Reichsmarschall was, however, somewhat different. The fact was that Göring was an unscrupulous hypocrite and a fanatical, avaricious collector who would go to virtually any lengths to acquire items he wanted; and he would subsequently avoid paying for them if at all possible, being notoriously reluctant to part with money.

Göring had started collecting works of art in the 1920s. After the rise of the Nazis to power in the early 1930s, he and Hitler had formed a plan that he would assemble a large collection which would eventually be presented to the German nation and be located either in Berlin or at his palace at Karinhall, although no decision on this was ever reached. As the two men began to collect seriously, they made a gentleman's agreement that either would keep whatever he found. Göring's collecting covered a wide field, from Roman artefacts to nineteenth-century German paintings as well as jewellery, *objets d'art*, carpets and tapestries. His personal taste dominated the collection, which as a result included a large number of female nudes, portraits and triptychs. He possessed no knowledge of art himself, and as a consequence relied heavily on his specialist advisers for guidance. The first of these, a Berlin art historian and dealer named Binder, was replaced in 1937 by an individual who would play a major role in the history of the Göring collection: Walter Andreas Hofer. Göring, who tended to be somewhat extrovert and bombastic in public, would frequently override the advice of Binder, and subsequently Hofer, in front of others but change his mind later in private, when he would meekly give way to his adviser's superior knowledge.

Göring employed a large number of people to administer his

collection and to act as his agents in acquiring additions to it. Such was his fanaticism towards his art collection that he devoted inordinately large amounts of time and resources to augmenting it. If news reached him of a particularly choice work of art becoming available, he would divert not only himself but also members of his staff from other duties to the business of obtaining it. Pressing matters of high priority were often ignored as the Reichsmarschall pursued his latest quarry. His personal trains were frequently pressed into service, not only transporting him and his staff to visit dealers or collectors with items for sale but also carrying large quantities of works of art back to Karinhall.

The administration of the collection was carried out by his Stabsamt (personal staff) of civil servants and Luftwaffe officers, which was based at Karinhall and at his headquarters in Berlin. The Stabsamt was headed by Göring's Chief of Staff, Dr Erich Gritzbach, who played an active role in the assembling of the collection. A particular responsibility of his was the selection of birthday presents for Göring, who was fond of receiving works of art as gifts but wanted to ensure that he was not given items which would not fit into his collection. During visits throughout the German-occupied countries, therefore, he would visit dealers and earmark works of art which were then reserved for him. When senior Nazis subsequently wished to present him with a gift they would consult Gritzbach, who would put them in touch with the appropriate dealer.

Despite his public declarations against coercion, Göring was not averse to applying pressure on owners of works of art which he wished to acquire. An illustration of his methods is provided by the purchase of the Renders collection in Belgium, an acquisition in which Gritzbach played a part. This collection, comprising the most important assemblage of Flemish primitives in private hands at that time, was owned by a Belgian named Emile Renders living in Brussels. In September 1940 information that it was for sale reached the ears of Walter Paech, a German dealer resident in the Nether-lands who was a friend and business partner of Hofer. Paech contacted Hofer, who visited the collection twice that month, accompanied on the second occasion by Gritzbach to discuss the matter of payment.[1] The accounts of the negotiation process given later by Hofer and Gritzbach differ from that of Renders, who maintained that he never wanted to sell the collection and that he was coerced into doing so. Both men maintained that the Belgian wished to sell because he feared that the collection would be broken up as a result of litigation between his heirs after his death. However, after the war Allied investigators unearthed documentary evidence which proved that Göring had brought pressure to bear on Renders to force him to sell.[2]

Renders had apparently succeeded in prolonging the negotiations over the sale by constantly changing his mind over the type of currency in which he wished to be paid. Eventually, however, Hofer and Gritzbach became exasperated at the endless delays and enlisted the help of another of Göring's agents: a German banker, resident in the Netherlands, named Alois Miedl, of whom more will be said later. On 25 September 1940 the collection was 'frozen' by the German authorities. This was in fact a ploy, later admitted by Hofer, to force Renders into finally coming to a decision. When Miedl met the Belgian shortly afterwards, he showed him a copy of a letter from Göring which rescinded the freezing order. On 17 March of the following year Göring took the unusual step of writing directly to Renders, rather than communicating through Hofer or Miedl, and advising him to make up his mind once and for all or he, Göring, would not be able to answer for the consequences. This threat had the desired effect and Miedl was able to complete negotiations for the sale of the collection at an agreed price of Fl 800,000, to be paid in Belgian securities chosen by Renders' banker. The six paintings thus acquired by Göring from Renders were: *Madonna and Child* by Roger van der Weyden, *Madonna and Child* and *The Annunciation* (two wings of an altarpiece) by Hans Memling, *Christ the Saviour with the Madonna and Child and St Catherine* by Master Wilhelm of Cologne, *Madonna and Child* by Quentin Massis and *Annunciation* by the Master of the Baroncelli Portraits. Subsequent investigations also revealed, however, that Renders had used the situation to inflate the price, playing for time in order to drive a hard bargain rather than genuinely to resist a sale. He voiced few complaints after the transaction had been concluded and even attempted to sell his sculpture collection to Göring under similar conditions. As an Allied report later stated, 'Like many collaborationists converted by the Allied victory, he is probably trying to have his cake and eat it too.'[3]

Göring's staff was divided into three Abteilungen (sections). Abteilung I was headed by Ministerialdirigent Fritz Görnnert. Formerly a senior member of the Nazi Brownshirt organization, the Sturmabteilung (SA), Görnnert acted as a liaison officer between Göring and Martin Bormann, Hitler's private secretary, as well as with the Nazi party. As far as the collection was concerned, his main responsibility was that of transportation: he was responsible for Göring's four special trains. Abteilung II was headed by Göring's personal secretary, Gisela Limberger, who was in charge of the collection. Abteilung III comprised Göring's military staff which consisted of Luftwaffe officers commanded by Oberstleutnant Brauchitsch. Göring frequently used his military aides to carry out errands connected with his collection, including visiting dealers on his behalf.[4]

In addition to his Stabsamt, Göring also maintained a liaison department at the Berlin-based headquarters of the Luftwaffe, of which it was part. It was commanded by Generalleutnant Karl Bodenschatz, deputy chief of the Luftwaffe general staff, who acted as liaison officer between Hitler and Göring, and between the latter and the OKW. Bodenschatz was in charge of Göring's art fund and all requests for payments had to be sanctioned by him. Attached to Göring's staff in Berlin and at Karinhall was the Staatliche Bauleitung für Sonderaufgaben (State Architectural Bureau for Special Projects) which was a section of the finance ministry assigned specially to work for Göring. This was headed by Oberaurat Professor F. Hetzelt, the architect at Karinhall. His responsibility, and that of his staff, was architectural repairs, installation of sculpture and monumental items, and the unpacking and storage of works of an architectural nature.

Another department of the finance ministry which worked closely with Göring's Stabsamt was the Devisenschutzkommando (DSK: Foreign Currency Authority), headquartered in Berlin. In addition to Germans, some of whom were members of the SS, the DSK also included collaborators in its ranks. Referred to as Vertrauensmänner or V-men, these proved invaluable in providing information on their fellow countrymen; they received their 'thirty pieces of silver' in the form of a commission of 10 per cent of the value of any loot acquired by the DSK as a result of their efforts. In France the V-men numbered eighty in total and performed their highly lucrative duties assiduously.[5] The DSK was divided into two branches, one covering France and Belgium and the other the Netherlands, and had offices in Paris, Brussels, Amsterdam and The Hague.[6] The France and Belgium branch, which was subordinated to the financial section of the Wehrmacht military administration headed by Göring's friend General Ministerialrat Michel, was the more active. The chief of the branch, Regierungsrat Staffeldt, was ordered by Michel to place his services at the Reichsmarschall's disposal. Consequently, when the DSK uncovered an art collection concealed in the vaults of one of the banks which came under its authority, it would freeze it and advise the Stabsamt. One of Göring's agents would then be despatched to inspect the collection and indicate those items which he considered suitable for the Reichsmarschall's collection. These would then be sent to the ERR repository at the Musée du Jeu de Paume to await Göring's next visit.

In some cases the DSK sent collections to the ERR without examination beforehand, reporting to the Wehrmacht military administration that the entire collection had been confiscated and handed over to the ERR on the authority of the Reichsmarschall. Among those confiscated in France in this manner were the Wassermann, Hirsch, Erlanger-Rosenfeld, Meyer, Heilbronn, Hamburger, Flavian, Rosenstein, Kronig, Erlanger, Thierry, Wildenstein, Seligmann, Rosenberg, Stern, Weiss, Weinberger, Federer, Hamperzounian, Rothschild, Dreyfus and Jacobson collections.[7] In Belgium, the collection belonging to Baron Cassel was discovered in a bank in Brussels and, after a visit from Göring himself, selected paintings, items of furniture and rugs were taken from it. For some reason, however, these never reached Karinhall.

In the Netherlands the DSK was not as active on behalf of Göring, although it had taken over the Lippman Rosenthal Bank in Amsterdam as a repository for confiscated Jewish property. In this country the chief confiscation organization was the Feind Veremoegen Stelle (Enemy Property Control) under the directorship of Dr von Boeck, which formed part of the economic division of Seyss-Inquart's Reichskommissariat headed by Dr Fishboeck.[8] Relatively few items were acquired by Göring from confiscated Dutch Jewish sources, and most of these came from the Offenheim and Jaffe collections.

Acquisitions for Göring's collection were made with the assistance of a large number of agents throughout the German-occupied countries of Europe. These were for the most part dealers who, while having no official connection with the Reichsmarschall or his staff, frequently carried letters of authorization which stated that they were acting on behalf of Göring. His principal agent, and from 1937 his official art adviser, was Walter Andreas Hofer, who had started his career as a dealer in the early 1920s while working for his brother-in-law, Kurt Bachstitz, in Munich and The Hague. He had also worked for a German collector and dealer named Gottlieb Reber, based in Switzerland, who later acted for Göring in Italy. Hofer first met Göring in his capacity as a dealer; a friendship developed between the two men and eventually, in 1937, Hofer succeeded in replacing Binder as the Reichsmarschall's art adviser. The arrangement which Hofer negotiated with Göring, and which continued after he was appointed director of the collection at Karinhall, was that he would act as Göring's buyer while remaining an independent dealer and retaining the right to any works of art which the Reichsmarschall did not wish to acquire.

For Hofer, this arrangement offered limitless opportunities. He had acquired the patronage of the second most powerful man in the Third Reich which in turn offered him access to all collections throughout the German-occupied territories. He was also free to travel at will, a privilege denied to many Germans at that time, and to obtain foreign currency whenever he needed it. As director of the Göring collection, Hofer's main responsibility was supposed to be the conservation of its contents, including cataloguing and storage. In practice, however, his purchasing activities occupied most of his time, and he spent long periods travelling on behalf of Göring, who accorded him authority to make final decisions on all acquisitions, as well as to carry out negotiations over payment. This was not a popular arrangement with other dealers, who complained of encountering endless problems in attempting to sell to the Reichsmarschall whenever Hofer was called in to give his opinion. Moreover, like Göring, Hofer never spent more than he had to and always bargained sellers down to rock-bottom prices.

Hofer maintained contact with all the major dealers throughout Europe and ensured that any approaches to Göring were made via him. He attended auctions, occasionally purchasing items but with the primary purpose of keeping himself up to date with trends in prices and markets in general. His travels were always planned with Göring and sometimes took place in conjunction with him. On those occasions, Hofer would travel ahead and look over the local art market, subsequently making arrangements for particular works to be brought to Göring or for him to visit the owners. If a decision was taken to buy, he would pay another visit to arrange payment and transportation to Karinhall.

When travelling alone, Hofer kept in contact with his employer by letter and telephone. Copies of some of this correspondence show how he regularly submitted detailed reports to Göring. In a letter dated 26 September 1941, he describes how he had selected items of 'degenerate' art to be used as 'currency' in exchange for items destined for the Göring collection:

Dear Reichsmarschall,
    Lange Auction: The results were in part really sensational. You will meanwhile have received the catalogue with prices through Miss Limberger. I could only purchase for you the Grimmer (appraised value

RM4,000); the Nic. Maes went unusually high for RM31,000 (appraised value RM8,000) and as for the Is. van Ostade (appraised value RM20,000), I stopped bidding at RM25,000 since the co-bidder was a commissioner whom I knew to have a higher order. The very beautiful, unfortunately very Jewish looking portrait of a boy by Aert de Gelder (appraised value RM8,000) climbed to RM25,000 and also the Goyen (appraised value RM30,000) was adjudicated only at RM38,000. The picture was not a very pleasing one, though, too blackish in tone. The Grimmer is, however, a very beautiful, colourful picture which is likely to gain by cleaning. But the sensation was the French pictures of the 19th Century which brought prices hitherto unobtained. And this, in spite of the fact that they were not even of absolutely first quality. I am very glad to be able to tell you that the French 19th Century pictures, which I recently selected for you in Paris, are of much higher quality.

Collection of the Jew Paul Rosenberg, Paris: I have chosen for you and reserved with Mr von Behr: 2 Ingres drawings, 7 pictures and 1 drawing by Corot, 1 watercolour by Daumier, 3 pictures by Courbet, 1 by Pissarro, 4 pastels and 1 picture by Degas, 1 picture by Manet, 5 by Sisley, 3 watercolours by Cézanne, 4 pictures by Monet, 3 drawings and 5 pictures by Renoir, 1 picture by van Gogh, 1 picture and 2 drawings by Seurat and 1 picture by Toulouse Lautrec. All are of outstanding quality, and measured by the results of the Lange auction, exceedingly cheap and particularly suitable for exchange. I shall bring you, in addition to Haberstock, very willing purchasers for it! Since Professor Beltrand, who acts in Paris as our expert (and always appraises the French 19th Century very high) gave the pictures a total appraisal value of 9,030,000 French francs, I naturally accepted the value set by the expert of the former proprietor, representing a total of 3,795,000 French francs. I told Mr von Behr that this sum will be put at his disposal through General Hanesse for payment from the account known to him. The remaining pictures from the property of the Jew Paul Rosenberg I left to the Einsatzstab Rosenberg. They are mainly degenerate art and 19th Century pictures, not appropriate, in my opinion, for exchange.

Collection of the Jew Seligmann, Paris: I had these pictures also transferred to Mr von Behr, a number of them reserved for you, appraised and put aside until your next visit to Paris. These pictures of the 16th–19th Century are particularly rather interesting and suitable for your collection, partly to be used for exchanges.

Braque Collection, Paris: Braque is an Aryan and lives in Paris as a painter. His collection in Bordeaux, put into security by the Devisen-schutzkommando, must therefore be unblocked. I negotiated with him personally about his Cranach *Portrait of a Girl*, and held out to him the prospect of an early release of his collection if he were ready to sell his Cranach! He is reserving his picture for me, which he intended never to sell, and will notify me of his decision on my next visit to Paris. His other pictures are of no interest to us.

Joseph Rottier Collection: The residence of the proprietor is reported to be in Holland. The Devisenschutzkommando has safeguarded in a Parisian bank very important pictures of his, which I inspected. Among them is a Rubens, *Portrait of the Scholar Jean Woverius* from the collection of the Duke of Arenberg, a beautiful *Parc Scene* by Pater and two further pictures by Rubens and van Dyck. I am now ascertaining whether the proprietor is a Jew; till then the pictures will remain in safekeeping with the bank.

Collection of The Rothschild Family, Paris: I inspected the pictures of the Baroness Alexandrine Rothschild, which you have not yet seen, and which the Devisenschutzkommando has safeguarded. This certainly was a sensation! They are twenty-five pictures of utmost quality and highest importance, among them an enchanting *Portrait of the Infanta Margherita* by Velázquez which by all means you must acquire for your collection. You will never again get a Velázquez of such exquisite quality combined with absolutely faultless condition. The picture constitutes a wonderful addition to your collection, in which Velázquez, probably the greatest painter, is not yet represented. In addition, there are among others a wonderful picture by Pieter de Hoogh, a *Head of a Child* by van Dyck, very beautiful pictures of the French 18th Century, and first rate pictures by van Gogh and Cézanne, highly welcome as exchange pictures. The Devisenschutzkommando will safeguard these pictures until you come to Paris. This collection, which also comprises the voluminous collection of modern family jewels, naturally remains blocked pending your decision.[9]

This particular report is also interesting in that the account of Hofer's visit to the painter Georges Braque illustrates his and Göring's willingness to put pressure on an owner reluctant to sell a work of art.

Hofer possessed a number of contacts outside Germany who kept him abreast of movements in the art markets. Chief among these was Hans Wendland, who represented his interests in France and Switzerland. Wendland was a German dealer who had begun his career in the art world as a historian in the Islamic Department of the Kaiser Friedrich Museum in Berlin. He had left the museum after a disagreement with his superior over the results of an excavation which he had conducted for the museum in Persia, having been accused of stealing some of the items found and selling them in Budapest. After service as an officer in the First World War, Wendland had established himself as an independent dealer in Berlin working almost exclusively on commission. He soon gained a good reputation and in the early 1920s moved to Switzerland. He prospered and bought two large estates near Basle and Lugano, but in 1929 his affairs suffered a reverse and he was forced into bankruptcy. In the early 1930s he moved to Paris where he restored his fortune as a dealer before returning to Switzerland in 1939.

Wendland was the most important agent for the Göring collection in France. Based in Paris, where he lived in the Hôtel Ritz, he was described by Hofer as the 'unofficial king of the art world'. He travelled extensively throughout the country, including the unoccupied Vichy zone, and frequently visited the area of the Midi where the majority of French Jewish dealers had taken refuge. He conducted business with a large number of others in the art trade and established an informal syndicate, which was used on occasions by other dealers to camouflage sales to the Germans, with three dealers: Achille Boitel, Allen Loebl and Yves Perdoux.[10]

These three men had widely differing backgrounds. Boitel was a wealthy Frenchman who owned an aircraft engine factory and other interests, including a factory which produced wooden packing cases for von Behr's Dienststelle Westen. He was a notorious collaborator and was later reported as having been killed by the Resistance, who apparently booby-trapped his car with an explosive device.[11] Allen Loebl, a French Jew, was a director of a firm of dealers called Kleinberger and carried out a great deal of work for Hofer and Bruno Lohse, Göring's agent inside the ERR's Arbeitsgruppe Louvre. He enjoyed the protection of Göring on the recommendation of both Hofer and Lohse, who obtained special privileges for him from Standartenführer Knocken of the Sicherheitsdienst at its Paris headquarters. It was in gratitude for such protection that, as mentioned in chapter 2, Loebl had offered the valuable library of books owned by Kleinberger as a gift to Göring.[12] Yves Perdoux was a Paris art dealer who worked for the firm of Guynot and had one of the worst reputations in Paris for involvement in very shady deals. His value to Wendland, however, was based on his extensive range of contacts in the provinces throughout France. Another Paris-based dealer, Charles Michel, was apparently also involved with the syndicate and was later suspected of having provided the finance for it.[13]

Wendland also made use of a small number of middlemen in Paris.

Among these were Mme Chesnier Duchesne, who specialized in tapestries and acted as an intermediary on a number of occasions; Professor Dr Simon Meller, a former director of the Budapest Museum and an expert on drawings, who combined writing on art history with dealing; and an Italian dealer and middleman named D'Atri, who had been resident in France for many years.[14]

Wendland's own permanent residence was in Switzerland, near Geneva. When not living there, he was in the habit of staying at the Palace Hotel in St Moritz, the National Victoria Hotel in Basle, the Monopol Metropol in Lucerne – or the Habis Royal in Zurich, where he had rooms permanently reserved for him. He paid frequent visits to Germany, either alone or accompanied by dealers, as well as to France. His standing with Hofer is illustrated by the exceptional ease with which he was able to travel throughout the German-occupied countries, a privilege granted only to those who enjoyed powerful patronage within the Third Reich. Indeed, it was eventually suspected that Wendland had connections with either the Abwehr, the Wehrmacht's military intelligence service, or the Sicherheitsdienst, and he was eventually questioned at length by the Swiss Fremde Polizei (Foreign Police).[15]

After Hofer, the next most important of Göring's agents was Sepp Angerer, a dealer specializing in tapestries, textiles, rugs, sculpture and stained glass. As the owner of the Berlin-based company of Quantmeyer & Eike, Angerer had travelled throughout the world and had extensive contacts in France, Switzerland, Italy, Spain, South America and Persia. Like Hofer, he carried a letter of authority from Göring and was able to obtain foreign currency from the Stabsamt.[16] Acquisitions for Göring's collections were paid for either by the Stabsamt or through his own company, which was used on occasion to camouflage disposals of items at auction by Göring.

In 1940 and 1941 Angerer preceded Hofer to France, where he established contact with the military administration of the Wehrmacht and the DSK. He was apparently responsible for the first shipments of confiscated works of art from France to Karinhall, and also for introducing Hofer to many of the dealers in France and Italy. Like Hofer, Angerer had his agents in place in all the occupied countries. Among them was an American named Tudor Wilkinson who lived in Paris throughout the war and apparently acted as a scout, notifying Angerer of any particularly worthwhile items. When his English wife was sent to a concentration camp Wilkinson turned for help to Angerer who, with the further help of Göring, contrived to obtain her release.[17]

Angerer was later reported to have worked variously for Hitler, the Reichskanzlei, the Sicherheitsdienst and the Abwehr, although this was never confirmed. However, on at least two occasions in 1937 he used the threat of the Gestapo to put pressure on an unwilling owner to sell. In both cases, the individual concerned was a dealer in Munich named Walter Bornheim who later worked for Göring. Angerer wanted to purchase, firstly, the Cumberland Tapestry (Beauvais, c. 1700) and secondly the Maximilian Court Tapestry (Brussels, sixteenth century). In the face of these threats Bornheim acquiesced, and the two tapestries went to Hitler and Göring respectively.[18]

Having first met the Reichsmarschall when the latter visited his shop, Bornheim was subsequently summoned to Berlin and thereafter appointed buyer of sculpture for the Göring collection. He had fought in the First World War and had been captured by the French; as a result of their treatment of him during his years of captivity he had never returned to France, and was unwilling to do so when Göring asked him to make the journey in early 1941 to acquire some pieces. Nevertheless, he acquiesced and thereafter made regular lengthy visits to the country to buy not only on behalf of Göring – on one occasion venturing into Vichy – but also on his own account. Like all the Reichsmarschall's major agents, he was invariably armed with letters of accreditation from the Stabsamt.[19]

The most notorious of all Göring's agents was the Austrian Dr Kajetan Mühlmann who, after the invasion of Poland in 1939, had been appointed by the Reichsmarschall as Sonderbeauftragter für die Sicherung der Kunstschätze in den besetzten Gebieten (Special Commissioner for the Protection of Works of Art in the Occupied Territories). The two men had first met Göring in Vienna after the Anschluss in 1938, when Mühlmann sold Göring a number of works of art confiscated from Jewish collections. In October 1939, after taking up his post in Poland, Mühlmann had sent Göring three paintings from the Czartoryski collection in Sienewa Castle: Raphael's *Portrait of a Young Man*, Leonardo da Vinci's *Lady with the Ermine* and Rembrandt's *Landscape with the Good Samaritan*.[20] (The full story of the looting of the Czartoryski collection and its subsequent fate is covered fully in chapter 11.) Later on, in early 1941, Mühlmann also sent Göring *The Pretty Polish Girl* by Watteau, part of the Lazienski collection, which had been removed by his half-brother, Josef Mühlmann, and then taken to Berlin for restoration before being presented to Göring.[21] Of these four works, Göring kept only the Watteau; he refused the others and sent them to the Kaiser Friedrich Museum in Berlin. Shortly afterwards, Hans Posse requested that they be reserved for the Linz collection; but he never received them. Mühlmann later insisted that the Watteau, like the three paintings from the Czartoryski collection, had not been confiscated but simply removed for safe keeping, and that it was on loan. Göring, however, was definitely under the impression that it was a permanent addition to his collection, as was Hofer who included it in the catalogue.

Mühlmann also sent Göring thirty drawings by Dürer: two from the Czartoryski collection and twenty-eight from the Lubomirski collection in Lvov. Göring in turn gave them to Hitler, who kept them at his headquarters for his own personal pleasure, rather than handing them over to the Linz collection.[22]

In 1940, Mühlmann was summoned to The Hague by Arthur Seyss-Inquart, the newly appointed Reichskommissar of the Netherlands, and, as described in chapter 1, directed to establish his own organization, the Dienststelle Mühlmann, with the task of acquiring works of art for Hitler. He was given a small staff which included, as well as an administrator, a secretary and a chauffeur, Dr Eduard Plietzsch, a German art historian specializing in Dutch paintings and author of a book on Vermeer, who acted as Mühlmann's art expert and chief purchaser; Dr Franz Kieslinger, an Austrian art historian who was a specialist in sculpture and *objets d'art*; Dr Josef Mühlmann, his half-brother; and Dr Bernard Degenhart, another Austrian art historian.[23] Of these, Plietzsch and Kieslinger played the most important roles in that Mühlmann relied on them entirely for selection of works of art. His own expertise lay in organizing large-scale confiscation and looting operations, and in managing the commercial transactions that followed. Despite the fact that the Dienststelle Mühlmann had been established primarily to obtain works of art for Hitler, Göring made the best possible use of it, exploiting Mühlmann's debt to him for having secured him his previous position in Poland. As a result, Mühlmann made constant efforts to keep Göring happy.

Most of the work of the Dienststelle Mühlmann was done in cooperation with the Feind Veremoegen Stelle (Enemy Property Control). When the confiscation of a Jewish collection had taken place, Mühlmann's organization made its selection at the same time as the representatives of Sonderauftrag Linz, who were also based in The Hague. Mühlmann also purchased works of art on the open market, paying for his acquisitions from a special fund established for his organization by Seyss-Inquart. On occasions, the fund was augmented by sales of acquisitions. Items acquired for Göring were paid for by the Stabsamt. On one occasion, Mühlmann attempted to obtain foreign currency through Göring but was unsuccessful. Unlike other agents such as Hofer and Angerer, Mühlmann did not enjoy good personal relations with the Reichsmarschall, who disliked him.

Whenever possible, Göring maintained a hold over his agents. A good illustration of this was his relationship with Alois Miedl, a banker and entrepreneur from Munich who had lived in the Netherlands since 1932 and whom Göring had known for a number of years. Married to a Jewess, Miedl was beholden to the Reichsmarschall for his wife's protection and thus was only too willing to serve him when it came to matters concerning business or art. Göring was well aware of this and never missed an opportunity to take advantage of Miedl's debt to him. Whenever the two men were involved in a transaction, Miedl always paid heavily.

The last of the agents employed by Göring in a major capacity was Dr Hermann Bunjes, who had been the Kunstschutz representative in Paris until dismissed by Count Wolff Metternich. On his dismissal, Bunjes had almost immediately been transferred to the Luftwaffe by Göring and appointed Director of the Deutsche Kunsthistorische Forschungsstätte (German Fine Arts Institute) in the French capital.[24] Bunjes' main role as an agent of Göring was that of liaison officer between the Reichsmarshall and the French government's Ministry of Public Education, headed by Abel Bonnard, and its Fine Arts Secretariat. The more mundane of his responsibilities, such as the transportation of sculptures and other works of art to Karinhall, were handled by his assistant, Dr Frantz. Göring used Bunjes to procure for his collection some bronze copies of famous French monuments. Among these were the *Dianas* of Fontainebleau and Anet as well as a number of Rodins, including the *Gates of Hell*.[25] Bunjes had also been given the task of supplying Göring's library with books on art, but in this he was not always successful: on one occasion Göring sent back a large shipment of books which he had found to be uninteresting.

In late November 1942, after the German occupation of the previously unoccupied Vichy zone, Bunjes was tasked by Göring with organizing an exchange of works of art between the Louvre and the Reichsmarschall.[26] Göring wished to acquire works of German origin from the French national collections and was sufficiently shrewd to realize that any attempt at confiscation or further presentations of 'gifts' to him would only serve to alienate the French and result in adverse publicity both in France and abroad. An exchange, on the other hand, could more plausibly be seen as scrupulously fair.

Among the objects of Göring's desire was a nude statue in wood of St Mary Magdalen by Gregor Erhart, called *La Belle Allemande*. This the Reichsmarschall had long coveted; indeed, he had previously told Hofer that the French had promised to present it to him as a gift.[27] He proposed to give two items in exchange for this prize: a statue of the Madonna and Child of the Nuremberg school, attributed to Leinberger, and a fifteenth-century Austrian statue of St George and the Dragon which had formerly been part of the Krebs collection, until acquired by Hofer in 1941.[28] In the ensuing negotiations, held in Paris and Berlin and lasting from late 1943 to March 1944, the French government was represented by Abel Bonnard, the Minister of Public Education, and Jacques Jaujard, the Director of National Museums and of the Louvre. The counsellor at the German embassy, named Gerlach, was also present throughout as an observer.

A further exchange was also proposed by Bunjes at the same time. Göring would give three paintings – *Open Air Theatre* by Charles Coypel, previously part of the Rothschild collection confiscated by the ERR and acquired by Göring in November 1942; *The Betrothal of St Catherine* from the school of Hans von Kumbach, acquired by Hofer from the Dutch dealer Hoogendijk in 1941; and *Biblical Scene* from the seventeenth-century school of the Danube – in return for a triptych, the *Presentation of Christ in the Temple* by the Master of the Holy Family.[29]

Bunjes had also been holding discussions with Bonnard over yet another exchange in which Göring would give a number of well-known works of art in Germany, such as the *Enseigne de Guersaint* and *Madonna and the Saints* by Benozzi Gozzoli, which had been acquired for the Reichsmarschall by Bornheim from the Wallraf Richartz Museum in Cologne, in exchange for the *Basle Antependium*, which was in the collection belonging to the Cluny Museum, now in safe keeping at Chambord. Of solid gold, this was part of an eleventh-century altarpiece and showed the Holy Roman Emperor Henry II and his wife praying before St Benedict.[30]

Jaujard and the other directors of the French museums were implacably opposed to Bunjes' proposals and resorted to every possible method to thwart Göring; so the Reichsmarschall later turned to Marshal Pétain and Prime Minister Laval, who succumbed to pressure and gave orders that the *Basle Antependium* was to be taken from Chambord, where it had been inspected by Hofer and Dr Hermann Voss, and despatched to Paris.

In December 1943, tired of the procrastinations of the French, Göring arrived in Paris to take part in the negotiations personally. Accompanied by Bunjes, Hofer and Gerlach, he met Bonnard, who astonished the Germans by announcing without any warning that the exchange could not take place. Infuriated by the apparent intransigence of the French, Göring insisted that it had to do so and demanded that *La Belle Allemande* and the triptych be despatched immediately to Germany. Bonnard, apparently somewhat cowed by the Reichsmarschall's wrath, eventually agreed to seek permission from the Vichy leader, Marshal Pétain, for the *Antependium* to be given to Göring as a gift, but the Reichsmarschall refused, demanding an exchange as he left the meeting in a towering rage.

In the event, *La Belle Allemande* and the triptych were eventually sent to Germany and delivered to Karinhall. The items from German national collections for which they were to be exchanged never arrived; in their place came items from Göring's collection which the Reichsmarschall no longer wished to retain. To add insult to injury, some of these were items confiscated from French Jewish-owned collections, including that of Jacques Seligmann, and were recognized as such. Thanks to the stiff resistance put up by officials of the French museums, however, the *Basle Antependium* remained in France.[31]

The majority of purchases for the Göring collection were made in France, the Paris art market being the most active in occupied Europe. German buyers flocked to the city and this resulted in vastly inflated prices, particularly in the last years of the war. Armed with large quantities of the wartime German paper currency, the Reichs-kassenscheine (invasion Reichsmark), which cost Germany nothing, they had a massive advantage over domestic bidders. Furthermore, they were well aware that no matter what prices they paid for works of art in Paris, they would make a hundred per cent profit on their return to Germany. Even works of art classed as 'degenerate' fetched very high prices. For the most part, the French dealers had no qualms about dealing with the Germans; they were joined by a large army of middlemen and hangers-on who were keen to join in on the bonanza. The Galerie Garin in Paris became the popular meeting place of the collaborationist art world. Such was the frenzy of the market that at its peak works of art were frequently sold and then rapidly resold at different auctions at ever-increasing prices.[32]

Some of the dealers acted independently, while others formed syndicates which specialized in particular areas of the market, of which the most prominent and important was that established by Hans Wendland with Boitel, Loebl and Perdoux. Another important group was formed by two major French dealers, Martin Fabiani and Roger Dequoy, and a number of more minor ones such as Georges Destrem and Hugo Engel. Although it was in contact with some of Göring's agents, this syndicate dealt mainly with the buyers representing the Sonderauftrag Linz, such as Karl Haberstock, one of Hitler's art advisers.[33] A third syndicate was formed by two dealers named Birtschansky and Mandl, together with a hanger-on named Makowsky. While maintaining contact with Göring through Bruno Lohse of the ERR's Arbeitsgruppe Louvre, these three individuals conducted most of their business with German museums.[34]

Of all the dealers who collaborated with the Germans, the most prominent was Roger Dequoy, a former employee of Wildenstein et Cie at 57 rue de Boetie in Paris. Until shortly after the end of the war, the activities of the company during the German occupation of France remained a mystery. In 1945, however, a report was produced by the British War Office which sheds a considerable amount of light on its fate during this period.[35]

In October 1940, after France had fallen to Germany, Karl Haberstock travelled to Paris to visit his contacts among the French dealers and discuss with them the possibilities of acquisitions for the Linz collection. One of his visits was to the Galerie Wildenstein, with which he had conducted a considerable amount of business before the war. There Haberstock found Roger Dequoy, whom he knew well, in charge of the gallery, its owner, Georges Wildenstein, having taken refuge from the Germans at Aix-en-Provence in Vichy while awaiting passage by ship to the United States. Dequoy told Haberstock that the company's stock had already been confiscated by the ERR but that another collection of eighty-seven pictures owned by Wildenstein was being stored by the Louvre in a repository at the Château de Sourches, in a village about two hours' journey from Paris, where it was in danger of confiscation.[36] Dequoy further mentioned to his visitor that he was anxious to travel to Vichy to discuss matters with Wildenstein before the latter left the country. Haberstock decided to make the necessary arrangements for himself and Dequoy to visit Wildenstein. Accordingly, during the following month of November, the two men travelled to Aix. Here they spent four or five days with Wildenstein, who was later reported to have been enthusiastic about doing business and apparently proposed that he give a large Tiepolo and other pictures from his stock in exchange for Impressionist works from Germany which would be sent to him in the United States. He also raised the subject of extracting his collection from the Château de Sourches, in order that Dequoy could continue to run the Paris gallery, and agreed that Haberstock should be given first option on it. Wildenstein gave Dequoy full authority to administer his collection, to sell anything to the Germans and to Haberstock in particular, and to make every effort to trace important collections or individual works of art in France which the Germans might be interested in acquiring.[37]

On their return to Paris, Haberstock and Dequoy decided that the first step in the removal of the collection from the Château de Sourches would be to have it 'Aryanized' – a process by which Jewish companies' names and assets were sold to Gentiles. Using his semi-official position with the Reichskanzlei as Hitler's art adviser, Haberstock supported Dequoy as the latter conducted lengthy negotiations with the German authorities in Paris and in particular with the Commissioner for Jewish Affairs, Dr Stenger. Haberstock also called upon Hans Posse, the Sonderbeauftrager of Sonderauftrag Linz, to lend his support to Dequoy. Eventually, Haberstock and Dequoy were successful in their efforts. On 24 April 1941 a letter was written by an accountant named Gras, who had been appointed temporary administrator of the collection by Stenger, instructing the Jewish dealer Hugo Engels, who was a friend of Haberstock and Dequoy, to take possession of the collection and to arrange for its return to the Galerie Wildenstein. Another friend of Haberstock's, a Luftwaffe officer named Major Baron von Pöllnitz, provided the transport.[38]

The 'Aryanization' process was completed just in time: the ERR, which knew of the collection's whereabouts, was planning to remove it to the Musée du Jeu de Paume on 15 May. However, before it could act, the ERR was informed by Dr Pfitzner, the assistant to Dr Kütgens, the Kunstschutz representative on the staff of General von Stülpnagel, the Commander in Chief of the Wehrmacht in France, that the collection was to be returned to the Galerie Wildenstein on 13 May. A member of the ERR, Wolff Braumüller, immediately telephoned Göring in Berlin in the hope that he would intervene and prevent the collection from slipping through the clutches of the ERR. However, Göring's view was that if the collection was Jewish-owned then it should be handed over to the ERR; on the other hand, if it had been 'Aryanized' then it was the property of the new owner.[39] Braumüller, assisted by Günther Schiedlausky, proceeded to make enquiries at the Louvre, where they were informed that 'Aryaniza-tion' had taken place. They also asked Haberstock about the identity of the new owner of the collection, but to no avail. On 14 May, all eighty-seven paintings were removed from the Château de Sourches and taken to the Galerie Wildenstein. Two days later, Göring and the ERR were informed by Haberstock that 'by arrangement with Dr Posse the collection was reserved, that it was not to be offered or sold to anyone else, but that of course everything which was not wanted by the Führer would be offered to the Reichsmarschall'.[40]

Dequoy proceeded to re-establish Wildenstein's business, operating it under the new name of Roger Dequoy et Cie. In 1942 problems arose when the German authorities attempted to requisition the gallery's premises, and both Posse and Haberstock had to intervene on Dequoy's behalf. Dequoy, however, was soon doing well and in April 1942 was commissioned to sell two important Rembrandts, *Landscape with Castle* and *Portrait of Titus*, from the collection of Etienne Nicolas, to whom they had been sold by Wildenstein in 1933. Dequoy succeeded in selling them via Haberstock to the Führermuseum for the sum of FFr60 million – a transaction for which he received a commission of FFr1.8 million from Haber-stock.[41]

Dequoy sold large numbers of paintings to all the big German dealers and museums, although the full extent of his business during the period 1940–4 has still not been discovered. Among those who acted as commission agents for him were Adolf Wüster, art adviser to the German embassy in Paris; the Jewish dealer Hugo Engels, who also worked for Haberstock; Allen Loebl, the director of Kleinberger; and Georges Destrem, a dealer associate of Haberstock's. According to Haberstock, when questioned by Allied investigators after the war, the profits from all these transactions were paid into a special account which was later allegedly handed over to Georges Wildenstein on his return to France from the United States after the end of the war.[42]

Göring acquired a number of paintings from the confiscated Wildenstein collection via the ERR between November 1940 and November 1942. These included *Romantic Park Landscape* by Hubert Robert, two *Venuses* by Boucher, *Fête in St Cloud* by Fragonard, *Madonna and Child with Donor* by Joos van Cleve, *Portrait of Frederick the Wise* by Lucas Cranach the Elder, *Summer Landscape* by van Goyen, and *Woman's Head* and *Portrait of a Woman* by Boldini.[43]

As far as so-called 'legitimate purchases' were concerned, the most important market in respect of Göring's acquisitions was the Netherlands. There were fewer opportunities for confiscation there than in France because of the smaller number of Jewish collections; moreover, any confiscations that did take place were carried out by the Feind Vermoegen Stelle, supported by the DSK, while the ERR concentrated on its political indoctrination and general property seizure remits. The first choice of works of art from confiscated collections was given to the Dienststelle Mühlmann which then sold items to Hitler, Göring and German museums.

In 1938 and 1939 the threat of war had caused a severe slump in the Dutch art market. After 1940, the German occupation revived it dramatically, bringing large numbers of German buyers with apparently limitless funds at their disposal. Dealers and collectors alike participated in the ensuing boom; their willingness to do so is well illustrated by the case of Smit van Gelder. A wealthy paper-mill owner who was resident in Belgium but whose family lived at Haarlem in the Netherlands, van Gelder approached the Dienststelle Mühlmann of his own volition in 1940, offering to sell paintings from his own collection while requesting an exit visa for Belgium (necessitated by the travel restrictions in force across all Nazi-occupied territories). Kajetan Mühlmann and Eduard Plietzsch selected a total of fifteen pictures and van Gelder obtained his visa. Thereafter he was a regular visitor to Mühlmann's office and was always keen that he should be mentioned to both Hitler and Göring as a source of works of art.

Most of the major Dutch dealers were happy to deal direct with their country's new masters, although a few employed middlemen to camouflage their transactions. Surprisingly, the figure at the centre of the collaborationist art market in the Netherlands was a German Jewish refugee: Max Friedländer, a well-known art historian and specialist in early Flemish paintings who had previously been a director of the Kaiser Friedrich Museum in Berlin. At the time of the German occupation of the Netherlands he had been imprisoned along with other German Jews who had fled Germany at the start of their persecution there. He had been released after Göring had intervened at Hofer's request, and thereafter was employed by Hofer and others, providing valuations and information concerning the locations of paintings of interest to German buyers.[44]

Hofer, who represented Göring in the Netherlands, had an extensive network of contacts there from his days in The Hague as an employee of his brother-in-law in the 1920s. When absent, Hofer in turn was represented by his friend and business partner Walter

Paech. Göring was also unofficially represented by four other individuals: a dealer named Jan Dik Jr, the banker Alois Miedl, a Dutchman named Wiedt and Kajetan Mühlmann, the director of the Dienststelle Mühlmann.

During 1940 and 1941 Göring made a number of trips to the Netherlands with Hofer to conduct negotiations in person. It was during the former year that he made two major acquisitions in the form of the Koenigs and Goudstikker collections. A detailed account of the acquisition of the Koenigs collection and its eventual fate appears in chapter 12. Negotiations began in June 1940 for the purchase by Göring of the Goudstikker collection. This had been the property of Jacques Goudstikker, a dealer in Amsterdam who had died the previous month as the result of an accident, falling into the hold of a ship at Dover while en route with his wife and child to South America. It was not long before the two trustees appointed after Goudstikker's death were approached by a number of prospective purchasers, including Alois Miedl.

Gritzbach, Göring's Chief of Staff, had initially proposed that the entire business, including the premises at Heerengracht 458 in Amsterdam, should be purchased, but Hofer advised against this. The matter was referred to Göring himself and it was eventually decided that he would buy the collection while Miedl purchased the business and the real estate, which comprised the gallery in Amsterdam and several properties in the area of the city: Castle Nyenrode, the Villa Oostermeer and another house situated by the River Amstel.

Through this deal Göring acquired approximately 600 paintings, including a number of important works. Four of these – *Two Philosophers* by Rembrandt, *Portrait of a Young Man* by Franz Hals, *River Landscape* by Salomon van Ruysdael, and *Duke Cosimo dei Medici* by Ter Borch – were valued together at Fl 992,600. After an inventory had been compiled by Hofer and Fräulein Limberger in Amsterdam, Göring's new acquisitions were despatched to Berlin. The remaining pictures in the collection were subsequently bought back by Miedl for the sum of RM1.75 million.[45]

A large number of purchases for the Göring collection were made in Italy. Here too, buying was carried out by the Reichsmarschall himself or his agents. In their absence, matters were handled by Generalmajor Ritter von Pohl, who commanded the Luftwaffe administrative headquarters in Rome, and Oberst von Veltheim, the Luftwaffe attaché at the German embassy, which handled all documentation and stored works of art before they were despatched to Germany on one of Göring's special trains. As in France and Holland, the art market in Italy reached unparalleled levels of activity during the war. Once the Italians learned of what was happening in the rest of Europe, prices spiralled until they exceeded even those being asked in Paris and Amsterdam. Large numbers of dealers and middlemen joined in the rush to profit from the boom as Göring's agents sought to buy large quantities of paintings and furniture. Eventually, however, the numbers of works of art being exported to Germany reached such a level that the Italian government was driven to step in. On 9 May 1942 the Ministry of National Education announced a new law banning the export of works of art. Thereafter it was difficult for Göring to take his purchases out of Italy, and he was forced to seek the diplomatic services of the German ambassador, Hans Georg von Mackensen, to obtain special permission from the Italians to move his acquisitions.

Although Hofer was nominated as Göring's chief agent in Italy his contacts there were not extensive, and initially the Reichsmarschall's principal intermediary was Gottlieb Reber. Reber was a German collector and dealer who lived in Lausanne; during one of Hofer's visits to Switzerland, Reber mentioned that he could introduce him to his contacts in Italy and advise him of opportunities for acquisitions. Hofer was quick to appreciate the offer and in 1941, armed with the requisite travel documents, procured by Hofer, and a letter signed by Fritz Görnnert, the head of Abteilung I of the Stabsamt, which confirmed that he was proceeding on business for Göring, Reber travelled to Italy.

Reber's most important contact in Italy was Count Alessandro Contini Bonacossi, a senator who had formerly been one of Mussolini's financial advisers and had been made a count by the Duce in exchange for his art collection which was presented to the nation. Bonacossi himself was very wealthy, with extensive commercial interests as well as vineyards and farms. Although not a dealer, he was the principal figure in the wartime Italian art market to whom dealers frequently gave first refusal on works they were offering for sale. He sold a total of thirty-one paintings and sculptures to Göring through Hofer, including works by Tintoretto, Titian and Botticelli, as well as several pieces of fifteenth- and sixteenth-century furniture.[46] This was a departure from normal practice for Göring, who had hitherto made all his furniture acquisitions through the ERR. Another source of furniture for the Reichsmarschall was Luigi Bellini, a musician, sculptor and painter who owned a shop in Florence. Reber introduced him to Hofer who subsequently visited him on a number of occasions, sometimes bringing Göring with him. Bellini sold the Reichsmarschall some pieces of sixteenth-century Florentine furniture and a small number of paintings.[47] Reber also introduced Hofer to Count Paolo Labia, a member of a well-known Milan family and owner of a collection which included some important paintings by Tiepolo. Hofer established a good working relationship with Labia, who maintained almost daily contact during his visits to Rome, either bringing him works of art for consideration or introducing him to dealers or collectors with items for sale.[48]

However, about six months after Reber's initial journey into Italy, at the time when the Italian government began to be concerned at the level of exports of works of art to Germany, it came to Göring's attention that his agent was making excessive use of his letter of authority and it was withdrawn. Reber was later questioned by the Gestapo about his activities but Hofer vouched for him and confirmed that he had been working for Göring.

Other agents of Göring were also very active in Italy. Sepp Angerer had his own network of dealers and collectors and occasionally used Reber as an intermediary. Kajetan Mühlmann also travelled to Italy on a number of occasions from 1942 onwards, buying pictures and subsequently selling some of them to Göring. One of these was *St Florian* by Michael Pacher, which was purchased from Lodovico Pollak, a dealer in Rome. Another dealer with whom Mühlmann conducted business was Francesco Pospisil of Florence, a specialist in nineteenth-century paintings. He attempted to sell Göring two large pictures of battle scenes, later suspected as being *The Story of Horatius* by Tiepolo. However, the price proved too high even for the avaricious Reichsmarschall and the offer was declined.[49]

Among Göring's acquisitions from Italy was the Sterzing Altarpiece, a German work which comprised four panels depicting eight scenes from the life of Christ, painted by the Master of the Sterzing Altar, and a number of statues. The altarpiece had been dismantled and its various elements distributed among ecclesiastical buildings in the town of Vipiteno in northern Italy, just south of the border with Austria. Göring had coveted it since 1941 when he had mentioned it to Hofer, saying that he wished to reassemble it at Karinhall. On the Reichsmarschall's instructions, Hofer travelled to Vipiteno in June 1941 and subsequently reported on the condition of the altarpiece and the locations of its various parts. Göring had told Hofer that he intended to approach Mussolini with a proposal for an exchange: the Sterzing Altarpiece for some well-known Italian works of art in Germany. A few months after Hofer had submitted his report, however, Göring informed him that he was to receive the altarpiece as a birthday gift from Mussolini. On 12 January 1942, Ambassador von Mackensen presented Göring with the four panels; the statues were to follow in due course.

Göring also received another gift from Italy – but this time he was not at all enthusiastic about accepting it. As mentioned in chapter 1, a large number of works of art were looted by German troops after the fall of Mussolini and the Allied invasion of Italy in September 1943. Among them were a number of paintings by Titian, Raphael, Tiepolo, Palma Vecchio and Lorrain which, together with the rest of the contents of Naples' National Museum, had been evacuated to the monastery at Monte Cassino. In January 1944 the collection was evacuated again to Rome, where it was placed in the Vatican. On its arrival, however, it was found that nineteen paintings, including a Titian and a Claude Lorrain, and a number of bronzes were missing. Subsequent investigations revealed that they had been stolen by troops of the Hermann Göring Division, who had been escorting the collection, and sent to Germany by their officers as a gift for Göring himself. The Reichsmarschall, unwilling to be associated with such an outrageously blatant act of looting, sent the paintings and bronzes to the Führerbau at Munich.[50]

The only neutral country to contribute significantly to the Göring collection was Switzerland, which prior to the war had never been of interest to either Hitler or the Reichsmarschall because the market there comprised mainly Impressionist and modern works. During the war, however, the situation changed: large numbers of German paintings appeared in Switzerland and Göring purchased several Cranachs there. As there were very few, if any, collectors of early German art in the country at that time, Allied investigators later suspected that these pictures were owned by Germans who were aware that Göring was purchasing in Switzerland and took advantage of the fact. The additional attractions of selling through Switzerland would have been the very low Swiss import tax for works of art, and payment in Swiss francs which could be kept out of Germany. A considerable amount of firm evidence led Allied investigators to believe that a number of Swiss bank accounts were established for the purpose of handling the financial aspects of these transactions.

Göring was represented in Switzerland principally by Hofer and, to a lesser degree, by Angerer. Hofer, having previously lived in the country, had a large number of contacts among dealers and collectors, a number of whom conducted business with Göring and his representatives during the war. Principal among these were Theodor Fischer and Hans Wendland. Some of Wendland's efforts on Göring's behalf have been described earlier in this chapter; Fischer, as mentioned in chapter 1, had conducted the auction of 'degenerate' art at the Grand Hotel National in Lucerne in June 1939. Their activities, and those of others in Switzerland, are covered in greater detail in chapter 6.

The prominence of exchange as opposed to purchase as a means of acquiring works for the Göring collection is attributable not only to the Reichsmarschall's notorious reluctance to part with money but also to the scarcity of foreign currency available to him. Whereas he was outwardly opposed to receiving confiscated works, he was perfectly content to use them as payment in kind for acquisitions, particularly as they had cost him nothing in the first place. Furthermore, the works of art used instead of currency belonged to the categories declared 'degenerate' and thus were considered of little value. Göring was involved in a total of fourteen exchanges, through his various agents and intermediaries, in France, the Netherlands, Italy, Switzerland and even Germany. These were in addition to those carried out by the ERR and comprised one in France, which has already been covered earlier in this chapter; three in Switzerland, covered in detail in chapter 6; four in the Netherlands; one in Italy; and five in Germany.

In the first of the exchanges in the Netherlands, conducted with the trustees of the Kroller-Muller Museums, Göring was represented initially by Hofer and then by Mühlmann. He acquired three paintings: *Venus and Cupid* by Hans Baldung Grien, *Portrait of a Lady* by Barthel Bruyn and *Venus and Cupid* by Lucas Cranach the Elder. In exchange, he gave fifteen paintings purchased with a fund of Fl 600,000 provided by Reichskommissar Seyss-Inquart. Among these were works by Fragonard, Boucher, Delacroix, Degas, Corot, Toulouse-Lautrec and van Gogh.[51] The next exchange, effected with Nathan Katz, a businessman and dealer in The Hague, was negotiated in March 1941 and concluded in Switzerland the following year. Katz gave eight Dutch works which included *Peasants* by Jan Steen, *Adam and Eve* by Peter Cook van Aalst, *Peasants Drinking* by Isaak van Ostade and *Autumn* by Cornelis van Haarlem; Göring gave *Forest Landscape* by Hobbema.[52] The third exchange was effected in 1942 by Hofer on behalf of Göring, who gave *Tobias and Sarah* by Jan Steen in exchange for *Peasant Scene* by the same artist.[53]

Negotiations for the fourth and final exchange in the Netherlands commenced in September 1943 and lasted until February 1944. Göring was represented once again by Hofer, while Alois Miedl represented the vendors, the Amsterdam dealers D. A. Hoogendijk and Pieter de Boer. Shortly beforehand, during a visit to Berlin, Miedl had shown Hofer a painting by Vermeer, *Christ and the Woman Taken in Adultery*, which had been brought to him by a Dutch artist on behalf of an anonymous owner who wished to sell it for the very large sum of Fl 2 million. Miedl had also shown the picture to Heinrich Hoffmann, Hitler's personal photographer and self-styled art expert, who had immediately wished to acquire it for the Führer; but Hofer, reminding Miedl of his earlier promise to give Göring first refusal on everything, prevailed on him to take the painting to Karinhall.

Much as he desired the Vermeer for his collection, however, Göring turned the painting down, on the grounds of cost and because he was concerned that it might have been stolen. Nevertheless, he kept it at Karinhall and refused to return it to Miedl, despite the fact that the latter had received an offer from a group of Dutch collectors. Eventually Göring agreed to take it, together with seven paintings from the Renders collection which he had acquired but not paid for, for the equivalent of Fl 1.65 million. In return, he gave a total of 150 paintings, 54 of them from the Goudstikker collection and all of them later classified as of secondary value and importance.[54]

There was a twist to this tale, however. In August 1945 the painting was discovered in the possession of Göring's wife. Subsequent examination of the work and of another Vermeer, *Christ in the House of Mary and Martha*, which had been purchased from a dealer by the Dutch Rijksmuseum for Fl 1.34 million, revealed that both works were fakes. Investigations by the Dutch revealed that they had been produced, together with a number of other 'Vermeers', by an artist named Hans van Meegeren.

Göring's single exchange in Italy between December 1942 and March 1943 was transacted with Eugenio Ventura, a dealer in Florence whom Hofer considered to be second only to Count Alessandro Contini Bonacossi in the quality of the items he offered for sale. Hofer had previously purchased a *Madonna and Child* by Giovanni di Paolo from him on behalf of Göring. In exchange for seven Italian paintings, two statues, a female bust and a garland of flowers in terracotta by Giovanni della Robbia, valued together at RM540,000, Göring gave nine paintings: *Mont Sainte Victoire* by Cézanne, *Seated Nude* by Degas, *View of Saint Remy* by van Gogh,

Landscape with Poplars, *Winter Landscape* and *Walk in the Parc Monceau* by Monet, *Seated Nude at the Dressing Table* by Renoir, and *The River Seine at Argenteuil* and *The Thames at Hampton Court* by Sisley. All of these Impressionist works, classed as 'degenerate' by the Nazis, had been confiscated from the Kann, Rosenberg, Weinberger and Lindenbaum collections by the ERR and deposited in the Musée du Jeu de Paume in Paris.[55]

It is worth noting the discrepancy between the total values given to these nine paintings by the ERR and DSK, and by Hofer. The former had valued them at a total of RM37,750, based on an assessment by Professor Jacques Beltrand, the ERR's official appraiser appointed by Göring to represent the French government. Hofer's valuation was over fourteen times this. In September 1941, Beltrand had appraised the Rosenberg collection in Hofer's presence; however, the values recorded at the time by the DSK were considerably lower. Thus it is clear that the values of items were manipulated to suit Göring and his representatives, being kept low when confiscated and vastly increased when sold or used in exchanges.

One of Göring's exchanges in Germany, negotiated in June 1941, was with Baron Kurt von Behr, the head of the ERR's Amt Westen: von Behr gave a painting, *Diana at the Bath* by Luca Giordano, in exchange for *Seascape* by van der Velde. The second exchange, in November 1941, was between Göring and Hofer: the latter gave *Venus and Cupid in a Landscape* by Francesco Albani and *Venus and Sachus* by Bartholamus Spranger, and received in return a sixteenth-century South German painting entitled St Andrew.[56] Two other exchanges in Germany were transacted with Karl Haberstock, Hitler's art adviser, in 1941 and 1943. In the first, Göring gave *Bacchanale* by Hans Makart and received *Still Life with Game* by Frans Snyders.[57] In the second, he gave *War and Peace* by Hendrik van Balen in exchange for *Shepherdess* by Moreelse and *Portrait of a Lady* by Franz Pourbus. The fifth exchange, carried out in December 1942, was with Dr von Mangoldt-Reiboldt, a banker, to whom Göring gave *Landscape with Figures* by Salomon van Ruysdael, a painting from the Goudstikker collection, and from whom he received a gilded bronze table centrepiece attributed to Thomire.[58]

Despite being a fanatical collector with massive funds available to him, Göring was not averse to selling some of his acquisitions at a profit, particularly when they were confiscated works of art for which he had not paid. One such sale was made to Alois Miedl, who approached Göring with a request for his help in transferring money to Switzerland, where he wanted to send his Jewish wife and family to escape the anti-Jewish laws being enforced in the Netherlands by the Nazis. Instead, Göring offered to sell Miedl six Impressionist works, confiscated from the Rosenberg, Rothschild and Goudstikker collections, agreeing as a condition of the sale that they would be delivered to Miedl in Switzerland. Hofer negotiated the transaction, which was concluded for a price of RM750,000. The six paintings involved in this exchange were *Self Portrait with a Bandaged Ear* by van Gogh; *The Mill, Young Man with a Red Waistcoat, Harlequin* and *Still Life* by Cézanne; and *The Marriage at Cana* by Jan Steen. They were sent in the diplomatic bag to the German legation in Berne, from where they were collected by Hofer who delivered them to Miedl's lawyer.

Göring also sold confiscated works of art to his employees, including his military aides. A landscape by Gilles Rombouts, from the Hamburger collection, was sold together with one by Hendrik de Hont, *Landscape with Horsemen*, to Oberst von Brauchitsch, while Major Teske purchased *Chapel in the Rocks* by Joos de Momper, and Major Wolhlermann bought *Seashore Landscape* by Richard Bonington from the Cramer collection.[59] Other items sold on by Göring included some which he had purchased on the open market. The most significant of these disposals were sales to some of his friends of a number of paintings which had formed part of the Goudstikker collection, and others purchased from a number of Dutch dealers. These numbered thirty-four in all and included *The Pedlar* by Jan Steen, *Scene in the Temple Prison* by Leonard de France, *Forest Landscape with Figures* by Jan Brueghel, four views of Venice by Canaletto, *The Annunciation to the Shepherds* by Jacopo Bassano, *The Resurrection* by Alvise Vivarini and *Bacchanale* by Francesco Mazzuela.[60]

All money received from these sales was paid into Göring's art fund, which was controlled by Generalleutnant Bodenschatz until 1945 when Göring took it over himself, and whose records were kept by Gisela Limberger, his personal secretary. The fund, whose average balance was between one and two million Reichsmarks, was kept at the Preussischer Staatsbank until early 1945, when it was moved to the Thyssen Bank. Payments from the fund were used for new purchases, restoration, framing, transportation when the special trains were not used, insurance and photography of all items in the collection. Göring was an extremely wealthy man, who possessed a personal fortune and enjoyed an income from his estates as well as from his salaries as Reichsmarschall and Minister of State of Prussia. He was also extremely secretive in all his financial dealings which, though frequently dubious, were always cloaked with apparent rectitude. He insisted on scrutinizing all expenditure, no matter how small the amounts, and only Fräulein Limberger was permitted to handle correspondence dealing with his financial matters. He took a very hard-headed approach to all transactions concerning works of art, always bargaining and ultimately buying at only the lowest prices, while demanding extremely high prices when selling, even for those works of art for which he had not paid.

By February 1945, the increasing threat from the advancing Allies was such that Göring decided to move his collection to southern Germany for greater safety. He and Hofer compiled lists of those top priority items which had to be moved immediately and those which would follow in due course. Hofer later claimed that Göring wanted to leave behind all the works of art acquired from the ERR but that he had persuaded the Reichsmarschall against doing so and thus saved them. The collection was transported by Göring's special trains. The original plan had been for part of the first load, despatched in the first week of February 1945, to go to a castle at Veldenstein and the rest to Obersalzberg at Berchtesgaden.[61] However, Göring learned that the air raid shelters in which the works of art were to be stored had not been completed and so the entire first consignment had to be despatched to the Schloss Veldenstein. This meant that only the smaller items could be sent, because the corridors and rooms of the castle were too narrow and small to accommodate the larger pieces. The second consignment was despatched from Berlin on 13 March 1945 for the Schloss Veldenstein where it was stored. The third, due to leave for Veldenstein at the beginning of April, contained most of the remaining items at Karinhall and everything from Kurfürst, near Potsdam, where all the best items in the Göring collection had been stored from 1942 onwards under the supervision of one of his officials, Oberinspektor Krawczak, in a large air raid shelter guarded by Luftwaffe troops commanded by Oberst Shomburg. However, the consignment was delayed at the last minute and Hofer received instructions to travel to Veldenstein alone.

On 15 April Fritz Görnnert, the head of Abteilung I of the Stabsamt, arrived at Veldenstein with instructions from Göring for everything in the castle to be loaded on to one of the special trains and moved as quickly as possible.[62] The train travelled to Piding, near Reichenhall, where it met the third consignment from Berlin before heading on 16 April for Berchtesgaden, where it arrived ten days later. There it was parked inside the station tunnel with Hofer living in one of the carriages. Two days later, the train was divided in two, with eight of the carriages being moved to Unterstein and the remaining three, containing Göring's library, furniture and Stabsamt records, being left in the tunnel.[63]

A few days later, Göring and Görnnert arrived at Berchtesgaden to decide on the locations for the storage of the collection. By then, however, the Third Reich was in its death throes and Hitler a seemingly spent figure. Anxious to negotiate peace with the Allies, the OKW suggested to Göring that he, as Hitler's successor (nominated as such in a decree of 29 June 1941), should take over the leadership of the Third Reich. Himmler too, also under the misapprehension that Hitler would shortly die, was likewise making preparations to assume the latter's mantle of authority. Both were premature in their assumptions.

Encouraged by the OKW, Göring despatched a telegram to Hitler, asking for his authority to assume the leadership. However, Martin Bormann, his long-time enemy, successfully seized the opportunity to present it as evidence of the Reichsmarschall's treachery. Hitler was enraged and demanded the latter's resignation from all his positions of office. On 30 April, acting on Bormann's orders, the Sicherheitsdienst arrested Göring and Görnnert, although the latter was released the following day and returned to Berchtesgaden to supervise the unloading of the collection and its storage in the air raid shelter. The eight carriages were brought back from Unterstein and unloaded; but such was the quantity of material that the shelter was soon filled to capacity, and some of the paintings had to be stored on the premises of a local Nazi official. The rest were reloaded on to the train and sent back to Unterstein. The three carriages containing the library, furniture and records were left in the tunnel at Berchtesgaden, where they were found by American troops of the 101st US Airborne Division on 4 May.[64]

During the six years from 1939 to 1945, the Göring collection grew from around 200 works of art to over 2,000: approximately 1,375 paintings, 250 sculptures, 108 tapestries, 200 pieces of period furniture, sixty Persian and French rugs, seventy-five stained glass windows and 175 objets d'art. As has been stressed above, while Göring refused to be directly associated with any form of confiscation or looting, he was perfectly content to receive forcibly removed items from the organizations responsible for their appropriation. Although the Einsatzstab Reichsleiter Rosenberg was the most notorious of the German bodies involved in the confiscation of Jewish-owned collections, it was Göring who encouraged its efforts and ultimately benefited most from its activities. Göring used his position as the second most powerful man in the Third Reich ruthlessly to his advantage, applying pressure and forcing down prices whenever he wished to make acquisitions. He had no scruples about breaking the laws of Germany, of Germany's allies and of neutral countries, particularly when the latter attempted to make it difficult for him to acquire his intended targets, or about using such measures as the diplomatic bag to circumvent regulations and restrictions which otherwise would have limited his activities and those of his representatives.

It is ironic that, at the end, it was the Nazis' own security apparatus, the Sicherheitsdienst, that removed him from power. A grasping, cruel and hypocritical bully, he was subsequently found guilty of war crimes at Nuremberg and condemned to death; but he avoided retribution by taking poison hours before he was due to be executed by hanging. The world was well rid of him.

4

THE TREASURE HUNTERS

The Nazi pillaging of Europe received a considerable amount of publicity from the very start. Reports of the looting of museums, galleries and Jewish-owned art collections were reaching Britain and the United States even before the beginning of the war. On 7 August 1939 the *Pariser Tageszeitung* newspaper carried a report of the auction in Lucerne that June of confiscated Jewish-owned works of art, presided over by the Swiss gallery owner Theodor Fischer. During 1940 further reports were published including, in October, that of the seizure of a consignment of 635 paintings en route from Lisbon to New York on board the steamer SS *Excalibur*.[1] This comprised a collection which had formerly belonged to a well-known French dealer, Ambroise Vollard, and included a large number of works by Renoir as well as others by Gauguin and Cézanne. After Vollard's death in 1939, his brother had sold the collection to another French dealer, Martin Fabiani, who, in partnership with fellow dealers who included in their number Roger Dequoy, Georges Destrem and Hugo Engels, had formed a syndicate to deal with German buyers representing the Sonderauftrag Linz. The British Ministry of Economic Warfare, which was monitoring the movement of assets of potential value to Germany, was well aware of the shipment and of Fabiani's dealings with the Germans. Accordingly, the *Excalibur* was searched on arrival at Bermuda, en route for New York, and the paintings removed and impounded.

Subsequent press reports carried further details of German looting. In February 1941 a report in the *Daily Telegraph* referred to attempts by the Germans to sell looted works of art on the American market, these being frustrated by dealers and collectors refusing to touch a number of Old Masters on offer.[2] July 1942 saw a report in *The Times* announcing the enforced sale of the Goudstikker collection a year earlier to Alois Miedl, the German banker and entrepreneur who represented Göring.[3] In January 1943 the *Daily Telegraph* and the *New York Herald Tribune* published accounts of the operations of the battalions of the Sonderkommando Künsberg in North Africa, Italy, the Balkans and Russia, based in large part on the confession of Haupsturmführer Norman Förster, an SS officer commanding one of the units, who had been captured and interrogated by the Russians.[4]

In Britain during the early years of the war, however, relatively little attention was paid to such reports as the government was primarily concerned with the Nazi occupation of Czechoslovakia, Poland, the Low Countries and France, and ultimately with the threat of invasion to Britain itself. Relentless bombing by the Germans preoccupied most people and it was not until after the Royal Air Force had driven Göring's Luftwaffe from the skies over Britain during the summer of 1942 that less pressing matters could be addressed.

Problems concerning the protection of items of major cultural value first reared their heads for British and Commonwealth forces during the campaign being fought in North Africa, where they found themselves occupying areas in which there were large numbers of sites of great archaeological value. Among these was Libya, which had until then formed part of Mussolini's so-called 'New Roman Empire'. The British occupied the area of Cyrenaica, on the Libyan coast, in early 1941, but it was recaptured by the Italians a few months later. The latter, as part of a black propaganda campaign against their enemy, accused the British of vandalism and published a booklet illustrated with photographs which purported to show examples of damage and destruction carried out by the troops of General Bernard Montgomery's Eighth Army.[5] While such accusations were totally false, the photographs subsequently proving to have been faked, the propaganda found its mark and questions were asked at high levels. Orders were subsequently issued to the effect that all monuments and sites of archaeological importance in areas occupied by British forces were to be treated with care and damage avoided wherever possible.

Responsibility for the protection of works of art and other valuable cultural material in areas liberated from enemy occupation by British forces was vested in the War Office. There was, however, no department nor any specialist personnel tasked with carrying out such duties, and the only suitably qualified individual serving in the War Office at that time was Major Leonard Woolley (later Lieutenant Colonel Sir Leonard Woolley), an eminent archaeologist who was employed on staff duties but also acted as an unofficial adviser on matters relating to the protection of sites of archaeological importance. As the war in North Africa and elsewhere turned in the Allies' favour, with a consequent increase in areas under British control, the protection of works of art and monuments became a matter of increasing importance. In October 1943 the War Office decided to establish a specialist department headed by an officer who would be responsible to the Director of Civil Affairs. Accordingly, during the same month, an Archaeological Adviser's Branch was formed with Woolley appointed to head it, albeit comprising in the early stages merely himself, his wife and a clerk.[6] The advantage of this arrangement was that Woolley held military rank and his department was an integral part of the War Office establishment. This would subsequently prove to be an advantage when requesting facilities and support in the field.

One of Woolley's functions was to liaise with organizations such as the British Academy, the Courtauld Institute and the Institute of Archaeology at the University of London. Others subsequently consulted by him would include the Royal Institute of British Architects and, after his branch's responsibilities had been extended to include the protection of archives, the Public Record Office. Much advice and assistance was obtained from these august bodies, particularly with regard to nomination of suitably qualified personnel to serve in the Archaeological Adviser's Branch (subsequently renamed the Monuments Fine Arts & Archives Sub-Commission). Assistance was also sought and given in obtaining lists of contents of museums, galleries, private collections, churches, archaeological sites and archives in the German-occupied territories. Also subsequently accumulated over a period of time was a wealth of data on art dealers in Germany, France, the Low Countries and neutral states such as Switzerland, Portugal and Spain.

One of the major problems facing Woolley was the recruitment of suitable personnel for service as Monuments Fine Arts & Archives (MFA&A) officers who would ultimately be attached to Allied formations in the field. Such individuals had to possess not only extensive knowledge and experience in their own specialist field, as well as full fluency in the language of the country to which they would be deployed, but also the necessary military expertise and qualifications to enable them to hold their own among the formations and units whose support would be essential for the protection of monuments, works of art and archives in areas liberated from enemy occupation. This was particularly important if MFA&A officers were to avoid being regarded with resentment by the officers and troops of fighting units who might otherwise see them as being more concerned with the protection of cultural property than with defeating the enemy. Wherever possible, therefore, prospective candidates were sought from among suitably qualified officers who had already seen active service.

Despite the fact that it was also stipulated that such personnel had to be of an age which would enable them to be excused active service with fighting units, Woolley found great difficulty in recruiting sufficient numbers. Those officers with suitable qualifications as well as the requisite military and intellectual abilities were few and far between, and most of them were already employed on specialist duties. Nevertheless, Woolley persevered and eventually succeeded in assembling a team of officers who would subsequently perform sterling work in the various theatres of operations where British and Allied forces were deployed. Among the more senior of the MFA&A personnel recruited by him were Lieutenant Colonel (later Brigadier) Mortimer Wheeler, formerly Director of the London Museum, who was despatched to North Africa as Director of the MFA&A Branch at GHQ Middle East. He was assisted by Major J. B. Ward Perkins, who had previously worked under Wheeler at the London Museum. Two other MFA&A officers who would see service in North Africa were Major Geddes Hyslop of the Royal Engineers, who had formerly been at the British School of Rome, and Major D. E. L. Haynes, who had previously been on the staff of the Greek and Roman Department of the British Museum.[7]

One of the senior members of the MFA&A Sub-Commission was Lieutenant Colonel Geoffrey Webb, well known in the pre-war art world as Slade Professor of Fine Arts at Cambridge, who had previously been employed on intelligence duties at the Admiralty. Others included Lieutenant Colonel Stanley Casson, formerly the Assistant Director of the British School in Athens, who was appointed Director of the MFA&A Branch at the headquarters of the British forces in Greece. He had served in the Intelligence Corps during the First World War and had returned to it during the early days of the Second, subsequently serving throughout the Greek campaign of 1941. After his tragic death in May 1944 in an air crash while en route from Athens to Cairo, he was replaced by Lieutenant Colonel Dunbabin, a former assistant director of the British School in Athens. The latter was assisted by Captain (later Major) J. M. Cook and Lieutenant (later Captain) T. W. French, both of whom had been students of the School.[8]

Other officers who were transferred to MFA&A duties included: Major P. K. Baillie-Reynolds, formerly Inspector of Ancient Monuments for England at the Ministry of Works; Major The Lord Methuen of the Scots Guards; Captain (later Major) Robert Balfour of the 60th Rifles (King's Royal Rifle Corps), formerly Fellow and Tutor at King's College, Cambridge; Captain Roger Ellis of the Royal Northumberland Fusiliers, formerly an archivist at the Public Record Office; Captain Croft Murray, formerly of the British Museum; Captain F. H. J. Maxse; Captain Ellis Waterhouse; Squadron Leader Jack Goodison; Squadron Leader Dixon-Spain; Flight Lieutenant Christopher Norris; and Flight Lieutenant Cecil Gould.[9]

One officer who would play a particularly significant role in MFA&A Sub-Commission operations was Flight Lieutenant (later Wing Commander) Douglas Cooper, who joined as Intelligence Officer. Cooper, a well-known art historian and collector of Impressionist works, was the ideal choice for such a role. Educated at Repton, followed by Cambridge, Marburg in Hessen and the Sorbonne, he had devoted himself, after a brief period as a dealer, to the study and chronicling of modern art. Indeed, as his obituary recorded forty-one years later, he was the first to devote the same depth and extent of study to Cubism as was customarily applied to Old Masters. Concentrating on the four most important Cubist artists, Picasso, Braque, Léger and Gris, he assembled in less than ten years a collection which was considered unique in both content and quality. Cooper's prize possession was Picasso's *Trois Mosques*. He also became a personal friend of several artists, including Picasso and Matisse.[10]

A brilliant linguist, Cooper had chosen to remain in Paris when war broke out and had subsequently joined a French army ambulance unit, being awarded the Médaille Militaire during the German invasion of France. After the French surrender he had succeeded in making his way to Britain where, immediately after disembarkation, he was arrested for reasons which are obscure but which he later put down to the fact that he was wearing French uniform. However, he was not without contacts in the right places and, thanks to a former Minister of Air, was soon released and subsequently commissioned in the Royal Air Force.[11] Due to his considerable linguistic abilities Cooper was employed on intelligence duties and, on being posted to North Africa, proved particularly adept at interrogating enemy prisoners of war, including shot-down Luftwaffe aircrew. Thereafter he had been posted to Malta before being transferred to the MFA&A Sub-Commission in 1943.

Cooper was tasked with accumulating all available intelligence on the forcible confiscation of collections by the Germans, the large number of transactions being effected in the art markets within the occupied territories, and the organizations and individuals, including art dealers, involved in trafficking in looted works of art. He took to his new duties with relish, also compiling information on the ERR, individual officials of German museums and galleries, and the Kunstschutz organization of the Wehrmacht. Cooper's efforts resulted in the assembly of a formidable database comprising a number of card indices containing an extensive amount of information which would later play its part in the identification and tracing of the principals involved in the looting of Europe's treasures.

In May 1944 a special committee was formed on the orders of the Prime Minister, Winston Churchill. Called the British Committee on the Preservation and Restitution of Works of Art, Archives and Other Material in Enemy Hands, it was better known as the Macmillan Committee after its chairman Lord Macmillan. As its formal title suggests, its primary concern was with post-war restitution of, or compensation in lieu for, looted works of art. Close liaison was established between the committee and the MFA&A Sub-Commission, which was tasked with supplying it with reports which would eventually include those of MFA&A officers attached to Allied formations in the field. The committee also had close links with the Ministry of Economic Warfare, Foreign Office, Air Ministry and Ministry of Information.

The previous month, on 10 April 1944, another committee had been established by the Conference of the Allied Ministers of Education under the auspices of the British Minister of Education, R. A. Butler. An unofficial body which had not been given any terms of reference by the Allied governments, it was named the Commission for the Protection and Restitution of Cultural Material but was usually known as the Vaucher Commission after its chairman Professor Paul Vaucher, the Cultural Counsellor at the French embassy in London. The committee was formed in recognition of the increasing need for a body to pool information on works of art which had been confiscated or forcibly purchased by the Germans, and on the subsequent trafficking in them. The work of the Vaucher Commission was divided into three main categories – places, personnel and objects – in each of which an index was to be compiled. The first was intended to cover monuments which might be damaged or destroyed, and accordingly represented the most urgent task. The second, which eventually comprised some 2,000 dossiers, was designed to assist the tracking down of those individuals involved in the looting, confiscation or enforced sale of works of art. At the request of Sir Leonard Woolley, the Commission also compiled lists of art dealers in Germany, Austria, France, the Netherlands, Belgium, Denmark, Italy, Hungary, Sweden and Switzerland who were known to have been involved in trafficking in looted art.[12]

Compilation of the third index posed a problem to the Vaucher Commission in that it required more staff and resources than were available. Efforts to raise the necessary funds were unsuccessful and eventually it was suggested that the work should be carried out by the London-based headquarters of the MFA&A Sub-Commission. This, it was suggested, would become the central point to which all information relating to looted works of art should be sent for collation and subsequent despatch to Allied formations and their respective MFA&A personnel in the field. In the event, however, this proposal was dropped, and it was later decided that the national restitution commissions (established by each of the occupied countries) would submit lists of missing works of art to the authorities controlling the Allied zones of occupation in Germany and Austria.

Meanwhile, the United States had not been idle. Many art experts from countries occupied by the Germans had fled to America to avoid Nazi persecution, bringing with them harrowing accounts of wholesale confiscation and looting of national and private collections. After the Japanese attack on Pearl Harbor in December 1941, however, the American museum and art establishments, like their British counterparts in the dark days of 1939–42, were primarily concerned with the threat to their own collections in the event of German or Japanese attacks on the United States. Indeed, preparations to withstand such incursions had already begun in March 1941 with the formation of the Committee on Conservation of Cultural Resources, which was given the task of laying plans for the protection and conservation of all the United States' collections of art treasures and items of major cultural value.[13] However, once it became apparent that fears of invasion by the Japanese were groundless, the leading organizations and individuals of the American museum and art world turned their attention to the question of works of art and cultural material of major importance and value in German-occupied territories and to the measures which could be taken to alleviate losses once the war spread to those areas.

Initial suggestions that a body should be formed to study the problems of protection and conservation of works of art in theatres of war were put forward by two individuals: George C. Stout, Head of the Department of Conservation at the Fogg Museum of Art at Harvard University; and W. G. Constable, the Chief Curator of the

Museum of Fine Arts in Boston. Their proposals were submitted to the Committee on Conservation of Cultural Resources in September 1942 but met with little response beyond polite acknowledgement. They were not, however, alone in their concern: others were also contemplating the threat to Europe's art treasures, among them Francis Taylor, the Director of the Metropolitan Museum in New York, who discussed his ideas with George Stout before approaching officials and members of the board of the National Gallery, which included the US Secretary of State and the Secretary of the Treasury, in November 1942.[14] Taylor's ideas fell on more fertile ground and in due course became the subject of a meeting of the board of directors of the National Gallery. Support was also forthcoming from other influential individuals. Taylor proposed the formation of a national committee of experts who would not only study the problem of protection and conservation of works in war areas but also gather information on looted works of art with a view to their eventual restitution. This plan was included in a document submitted in early December 1942 to President Franklin D. Roosevelt by the Chief Justice, Harlan Stone, who was also on the board of the National Gallery. Roosevelt's response was positive, but no action resulted.

In March of the following year, however, the US Army made contact with American Defense Harvard, one of a number of organizations established by universities in 1940, after the fall of France, to act as conduits through which academic expertise could be directed in support of any future American involvement in the war. The army requested the assistance of George Stout in providing information for use by its Civil Affairs Division, which would be responsible for administration of areas liberated from German occupation by US forces; and it asked for lists of works of art, monuments, libraries, archives and buildings of major cultural value in each country under Nazi domination. Francis Taylor, meanwhile, had persevered in his efforts and in the same month he and Archibald McLeish, the Librarian of Congress, approached the Secretary of War, Henry Stimson, who lost little time in putting their proposals forward with his support to the War Department's Operations Division. This resulted in the decision to form a small pool of officers with the requisite expertise and experience in conservation of works of art and items of cultural value. It was also decided to produce appropriate technical information, in the form of manuals, for use by the army when occupying liberated areas.

In January 1943 an ad hoc committee had been formed under the auspices of the American Council of Learned Societies to press the cause of the protection of works of art. This was followed by the formation on about 23 June of the American Commission for the Protection and Salvage of Artistic and Historic Monuments in War Areas, subsequently known as the Roberts Commission after its chairman, Supreme Court Justice Owen J. Roberts.[15] The role of the Commission, of which Taylor was a member, was 'to cooperate with the appropriate branches of the Army and Department of State as well as with appropriate civilian agencies' and 'to advise and work with the School of Military Government at Charlottesville, Virginia, and subsequent organisations of civilian character which may take over control of occupied territory'. In addition, the Commission was also to be prepared to 'furnish museum officials and art historians to the General Staff of the Army so that, so far as is consistent with military necessity, works of cultural value may be protected in countries occupied by the armies of the United Nations' as well as to 'act as a channel of communications between the Army and the various universities, museums and other scholarly organisations, institutions and individuals from whom information and services are required'. Finally, the Commission was to 'function under the auspices of the United States Government and in conjunction with similar groups in other countries for the protection and conservation of works of art and of artistic and historic records in Europe, and to aid in salvaging and restoring to the lawful owners such objects as have been appropriated by the Axis powers or individuals acting under their authority or consent'.[16]

Three weeks earlier, the first American MFA&A officer had been appointed. He was Captain (later Lieutenant Colonel) Mason Hammond, a United States Army Air Force officer employed on intelligence duties but formerly Professor of Classics at Harvard University.[17] Other suitably qualified officers appointed or transferred to MFA&A duties during the coming months would include Major Theodore Sizer, formerly Director of the Museum of Fine Arts at Yale University, who was attached to the School of Military Government, Charlottesville, as an MFA&A instructor; Major Paul Gardener; Major Norman T. Newton; Major Ernest T. de Wald; Major Deane Keller; Captain Marvin Ross; Captain Walker Hancock; Captain Bancel Lafarge; Captain Robert Posey; Captain Hammett; Captain Walter Huchthausen; Lieutenant Perry Cott; Lieutenant Walter Horn; Lieutenant Daniel Kern: Lieutenant Kenneth Lippmann; Lieutenant Young; 2nd Lieutenant Calvin Hathaway and 2nd Lieutenant James Rorimer. Also among them was George Stout, who had earlier left his post at the Fogg Museum of

Art at Harvard on being commissioned into the United States Navy Reserve and had been employed initially on naval duties.

Like their British counterparts, on completion of their training these officers were attached to the headquarters of Allied formations deployed overseas. The first to be deployed was Captain Mason Hammond who, three or four days after his transfer from USAAF intelligence duties, was sent on 3 June 1943 to Algeria where he joined the headquarters of the Allied military government waiting to take control of Sicily on successful completion of Operation Husky, the Allied invasion of that country which would take place on 10 July.[18] Two months later, the Allies landed on the Italian mainland. Additional MFA&A officers were deployed as Allied forces advanced northwards and Allied military governments established control over areas liberated from the enemy. Among the British MFA&A officers were Major P. K. Baillie-Reynolds, who was appointed Acting Director of the MFA&A Sub-Commission in the country until the arrival of an American officer, Major Ernest de Wald, who took over the post; Major F. H. J. Maxse, who joined Captain Mason Hammond as the latter's British counterpart; and Major J. B. Ward Perkins, who was appointed Deputy Director, having served previously in Tripolitania and Cyrenaica. Their American counterparts included Major Paul Gardener, who was assigned to Naples, and Major Norman Newton, who was sent to the headquarters governing the Calabria and Lucania regions.[19]

During November and December 1943, Lieutenant Colonel Sir Leonard Woolley visited the areas of Italy under Allied control; such was the concern expressed in his subsequent report of the situation there, reinforced by public anxiety in both Britain and the United States, that a court of inquiry was convened. Its findings resulted in the Supreme Allied Commander in Europe, General Dwight Eisenhower, issuing orders to all theatre commanders that a much higher priority was to be accorded to the protection of Italian works of art, cultural material, monuments and sites of archaeological value. The MFA&A officers were few in number and thinly spread over the ever-increasing area being liberated by Allied forces. Nevertheless, on encountering serious damage to cathedrals, churches, monuments and buildings of great historic value, they set about organizing repairs and securing their contents.

Most of the damage to monuments and archaeological sites was caused by Allied bombing. The RAF was aware of the problem and asked for a report, which was produced by Flight Lieutenant Christopher Norris, one of the MFA&A Sub-Commission's RAF officers. As a result, photographic reconnaissance flights were flown over a total of seventy-nine cities and large towns in Italy and their respective monuments and areas of cultural and archaeological value. The resulting air photographs were incorporated in handbooks which were issued to all Allied air formations operating over Italy and were subsequently used in the briefing of bomber crews.

Meanwhile the date of the Allied invasion of Normandy was drawing near. During January 1944 a British officer, Lieutenant Colonel Geoffrey Webb, was appointed Director of the newly formed MFA&A Branch of Supreme Headquarters Allied Expeditionary Force (SHAEF) with an American assistant, Captain Marvin Ross. The branch comprised a mixture of British and American MFA&A officers, some forming French, German and Belgian Country Units, others attached to formations of the Allied armies.[20] The first MFA&A officer to land in Normandy in June was Captain Bancel Lafarge, attached to the headquarters of Lieutenant General Sir Miles Dempsey's Second British Army; three weeks later, Squadron Leader Dixon-Spain and Lieutenant George Stout arrived to join First US Army and Captain Robert Posey made his way to Headquarters Third US Army. In 21st Army Group, Major Robert Balfour was attached to First Canadian Army while Major The Lord Methuen assumed responsibility for the area covered by the British line of communications.[21]

In the early stages of their work, MFA&A officers found that transport and other facilities were scarce and were forced to use their initiative to overcome such problems, which inevitably hampered their activities. While George Stout succeeded in commandeering a captured German staff car shortly after his arrival, Bancel Lafarge was less fortunate, being forced to hitchhike for ten days before obtaining his own personal vehicle and driver. As the Allied armies advanced through France, the MFA&A officers found themselves heavily committed in organizing protection for monuments and buildings at risk, or repairs to those which had been damaged earlier during the fighting. While the Allied forces provided the necessary transport and materials for the latter, the local French authorities were approached to provide labour, which they did readily.

With the capture of Paris, a major responsibility of the SHAEF MFA&A Branch was the collection of documents relating to German looting of works of art and in particular those concerned with the work of the ERR and the activities of Reichsmarschall Göring and his agents. A wealth of evidence was discovered at the Musée du Jeu de

Paume, the ERR's collection point, including documentation belonging to Schenkers, the German freight forwarding company which was responsible for moving consignments of confiscated works of art from Paris to Germany.[22] All such documentation, together with reports from MFA&A officers in the liberated countries, interrogation reports of prisoners of war and information obtained from refugees, was despatched to Douglas Cooper's German Country Unit in London, where it was responsible for collecting and collating all material relating to looted works of art and the locations of Nazi repositories in Germany. Cooper and his assistants made good use of their extensive personnel card index containing details of all those individuals reported as being involved in dealings in looted art: art dealers, officials of German museums and galleries, members of the ERR, officials of the Nazi party and others.

At this time the major part of the intelligence-gathering effort, which also covered the Low Countries and Italy, was with American agreement conducted by the British, who processed a vast amount of material, including captured enemy documents, MFA&A field reports, transcripts of interrogations of enemy prisoners and reports from refugees. From November 1944 onwards, Cooper and his German Country Unit were assisted in their task of accumulating intelligence by a newly formed unit of the US Office of Strategic Services (OSS). Headed by General 'Wild Bill' Donovan, an eminent peacetime lawyer, the OSS was the American wartime forerunner of today's Central Intelligence Agency. In London, it was headed by David Bruce who had formerly been president of the National Gallery. The OSS became involved with MFA&A operations as a result of an approach by Francis Taylor of the Roberts Commission, after it had become apparent that the US Army was reluctant to provide the commission with intelligence. Bruce had earlier approached the commission with a view to having an OSS officer attend its meetings, and had conceived the idea of inserting some of his agents into Europe in the guise of MFA&A personnel. That idea had been rejected by the army and by General Eisenhower himself, but contact had been maintained between the Roberts Commission and the OSS; and in August 1944 Taylor had raised with Bruce the idea of OSS involvement in investigations of German looting of works of art.[23]

Together with its British counterpart, which came under the auspices of the Ministry of Economic Warfare, the OSS was already involved in the Safehaven Programme: the Allied operation to track down Nazi assets hidden in neutral countries such as Switzerland,

Spain and Portugal, which will be discussed in more detail in later chapters. The result of Taylor's discussions with Bruce was the formation of the OSS Art Looting Investigation Unit (ALIU), which was staffed by American art historians proposed by the Roberts Commission. Its role would be totally independent from that of the Allied MFA&A organization and its officers would report directly to the commission.

The creation of the ALIU was a coup for Taylor and the Roberts Commission, which until then had experienced great difficulty in obtaining information concerning MFA&A activities in Britain where SHAEF was located. Furthermore, there had been increasing resentment within the commission at the apparent assumption by the British of control of the entire Allied MFA&A organization. Such was its concern that the commission had proposed that an officer of brigadier general rank take over the role of MFA&A adviser at SHAEF from Lieutenant Colonel Geoffrey Webb. The individual concerned was Brigadier Henry Newton, an engineer officer in the US Army Reserve who had been an architect in civilian life.[24] On 6 May 1944 Newton flew to Britain, having been appointed by both the US War Department and the Roberts Commission as their representative. Far from being greeted with open arms, however, he discovered to his dismay that he was most unwelcome. He quickly found that his anti-British sentiments fell on stony ground among the American MFA&A officers working in close cooperation with their British counterparts, and the fact that he represented the US War Department as well as the Roberts Commission cut little ice with them. Indeed, one of them forcefully pointed out that all SHAEF policies were laid down by General Eisenhower and not the War Department.[25]

Newton had a similar lack of success in his dealings with the staff at SHAEF, succeeding only in causing a considerable amount of resentment by his overbearing and aggressive behaviour. This eventually resulted in the Deputy Chief of Staff at SHAEF sending a complaint to the US Army's Civil Affairs Division, which informed the Roberts Commission that Newton could no longer act as the commission's representative and that it would have to appoint a civilian to do so. This was a setback to the commission, which was by then under the impression that Newton was performing an important role as a member of Eisenhower's staff. In fact, the reverse was the case, with Newton regarded at SHAEF as an outsider who represented the War Department and was thus excluded from SHAEF councils. Nevertheless, the commission continued in its efforts to wrest control of Allied MFA&A operations from the British, and from Lieutenant Colonel Sir Leonard Woolley in particular. This was despite the fact that Woolley corresponded regularly with the commission: indeed, his letters were one of the few sources of information for it.

Frustrated and disillusioned at his lack of progress, and having been left in London after SHAEF moved to France in the wake of the invasion, Newton travelled to Italy where he busied himself by visiting MFA&A personnel. His copious reports addressed to the Roberts Commission were, however, blocked at some point along the channels through which they passed and thus were never received. The extent to which the Roberts Commission was kept in the dark is illustrated by the fact that a month after D-Day it had still not received any copies of SHAEF MFA&A reports from the field. Eventually, such was its exasperation that it despatched Francis Taylor to France, where he arrived shortly after the liberation of Paris. There he made contact with the French authorities, including Jacques Jaujard, the Director of National Museums and of the Louvre, from whom he obtained much useful information. It was not long, however, before his presence in Paris was discovered by a senior American officer, who gave vent to his displeasure at seeing a civilian in an operational theatre at a time when civilians were barred from it. This resulted in a letter of censure and yet further deterioration in relations between SHAEF and the commission, the latter having become even more unpopular. Thus it was that the formation of the OSS ALIU in November 1944 came at a very welcome time for the Roberts Commission.

As the Allies advanced through France during the summer of 1944, the fighting brought an increasing risk to the repositories containing the French national collections located in châteaux, monasteries, convents and similar establishments throughout the country. There was also a threat from German troops engaged on counter-guerrilla operations against the Resistance. One repository, located in a château at Valençay and containing works of art belonging to the Louvre, was attacked by troops of the 2nd Das Reich SS Panzer Division who subjected the building to heavy machine-gun fire, setting it alight. When the Louvre staff, who had been forced to prostrate themselves on the ground outside, attempted to extinguish the fire, they were fired upon and one of their number was killed.[26]

A few months earlier, prior to the Allied invasion, SS troops had also been involved in the disappearance of works of art belonging to a French Jewish family named Bernheim-Jeune, who had owned a gallery in Paris until it had been sequestered in late 1941: paintings found in the gallery were confiscated by the ERR and the buildings seized by the Commissioner General for Jewish Affairs, who put them up for sale. The two heads of the family had, however, already fled Paris: Gaston Bernheim-Jeune with his paintings to Monte Carlo, where he spent the rest of the war suffering no further disturbance, and his brother Josse to Lyon, where he was subsequently joined by his two sons, Jean and Henri. Shortly afterwards, however, Josse died and his sons fled to Switzerland, contriving to smuggle in some of their paintings with the aid of a Japanese diplomat who was an old friend from their schooldays.[27] Meanwhile Gaston's son Claude was suffering from the unwelcome attentions of the Nazis and their Vichy allies. His collection was located in a private hotel, owned until his death by Josse Bernheim-Jeune, in the rue Desbordes-Valmore in Paris. In early 1941, this was occupied by the Germans. Once again, the ERR was foremost in the pillaging which ensued. Among the items which fell prey to the looters was a painting by Bonnard, *The Venus of Cyrène*. A gift from the artist to Josse Bernheim-Jeune, it portrayed a vase of flowers on a table with some books, one of which bore the title of a novel written by the recipient. The painting was taken from the hotel and subsequently disappeared. It would be some years before it would be seen again.[28]

In 1942, it was decided to move a further collection of paintings, belonging to Josse Bernheim-Jeune's wife, to a safe hiding place in a château at Rastignac, in the Dordogne, to avoid confiscation. Built in 1811 as a replica of the White House in Washington, the château was owned by an Anglo-American family, the Lauwicks, who were close friends of Jean Bernheim-Jeune's parents-in-law. The collection comprised thirty works by a number of artists and included Cézanne's *Le Jas de Bouffan*, *Bathers*, *Portrait of the Master with Long Hair* and *Auvers under Snow*; Renoir's *L'Algérienne Accoudée* and *Portrait of Coco*; Toulouse-Lautrec's *La Goulue et son Cavalier*, *En Meublé* and *Le Bal du Moulin Rouge*; van Gogh's *Flowers on a Yellow Background*; and others by Bonnard, Manet, Matisse, Morisot, and Vuillard.[29] Before their despatch from Paris, all thirty paintings were removed from their frames, carefully rolled up and packed in special brown paper wrappings. On arrival at the château they were hidden in the attics, concealed in a trunk with a false bottom. Shortly afterwards, they were joined by a small but highly valuable Renoir, *Les Roses Mousseuses*, which belonged to Jean Bernheim-Jeune.[30]

The collection remained safely hidden until early 1944, when, in the small hours of 30 March, a detachment of SS troops under the command of Obersturmführer Thalman arrived at the château. Mrs Lauwick, her son Jacques, her daughter Mrs Fairweather, and other members of the family and staff were ordered outside into the courtyard where they remained under armed guard while the SS systematically tore apart the interior of the building. As they listened to the sounds of doors being smashed and furniture being reduced to matchwood, the Lauwicks heard shots coming from a nearby village as the mayor of the town of Azerat, together with two of his officials, were executed by an SS firing squad. At midday Thalman left the château and, taking Jacques Lauwick and his sister with him under escort, drove to the town hall in Azerat. There Jacques Lauwick was submitted to lengthy interrogation which led him to believe that the Germans had not found the paintings. His interrogators seemed preoccupied by matters relating to the construction of the château, which suggested to him that they were looking for secret caches of arms and money possibly hidden there by local Resistance groups. Meanwhile, his mother and the rest of the family, together with the château's staff, had been told to leave the area. As they did so, the SS loaded furniture, linen, tapestries, rugs and other looted items on to vehicles on which they were subsequently driven away. Not long afterwards, another detachment of SS arrived and proceeded to set the château ablaze. The resulting fire totally engulfed the building and its contents.[31]

The fate of the thirty-one paintings remains a mystery to this day, and many questions are still unanswered. There is no explanation as to why the Germans suddenly descended upon the château and tore it apart. Were they looking for caches of Resistance arms and money? Did they know of the existence of the hidden paintings and, if so, who betrayed them? Did they find the paintings and take them away? There are indications that the paintings may well have survived the conflagration at Rastignac. Witnesses who observed the Germans loading the contents of the villa on to their vehicles, and indeed some individuals who were forced to assist them, later reported having seen the canvases, rolled and packed in their special brown paper wrappings, being loaded aboard the trucks. Despite lengthy enquiries and investigations on the part of the Bernheim-Jeune family, however, none of the paintings hidden in the Château de Rastignac has ever been seen again.

As the Allied armies advanced further through France and the Low Countries, heading towards Germany, one subject which was at the forefront of the minds of MFA&A personnel at SHAEF and in the field was the whereabouts of the German repositories which were known to have been established by the Nazis for the storage of the huge quantities of looted works of art. Individual MFA&A officers had already learned of some of these as the Allies progressively liberated Europe from German control: Rose Valland at the Musée du Jeu de Paume had provided details of several repositories to which the ERR in Paris had despatched trainloads of works of art.

Initial reports concerning the largest repository came about partly through information given to Captain Robert Posey, the American MFA&A officer attached to the Third US Army. Along with other MFA&A personnel, he was investigating the whereabouts of the Ghent altarpiece, the *Adoration of the Mystic Lamb* by the van Eyck brothers, which was rumoured to be in a number of different locations ranging from Hitler's Berghof headquarters at Berchtesgaden to Göring's palace at Karinhall. Some reports, received from museums in Luxembourg, stated that the altarpiece was concealed in a salt mine; others indicated that it was in the vaults of the Reichsbank in Berlin. It was by sheer coincidence that Posey obtained reliable information about the work's whereabouts. While undergoing treatment for toothache in the town of Trier, on the border of Germany and Luxembourg, Posey learned from the dentist that the latter's son-in-law had previously been a member of the Kunstschutz. Accompanied by his assistant, Private Lincoln Kirstein, Posey subsequently visited the dentist's daughter and son-in-law, discovering that the latter was none other than Dr Hermann Bunjes, the representative of the Kunstschutz in Paris until dismissed by Count Wolff Metternich.[32] Under questioning from Posey, Bunjes revealed the existence of the huge repository at Alt Aussee in the Austrian Alps near the spa town of Bad Aussee. He told Posey that he was certain that the Ghent altarpiece was hidden there. The saga of the eventual discovery of the repository at Alt Aussee, and the events surrounding it, is related in the following chapter.

In March 1945, as the Allied armies crossed into Germany, the primary role of MFA&A officers in the field switched from that of securing and protecting buildings and monuments to that of locating and securing works of art. MFA&A personnel soon uncovered a considerable number of repositories, some of them containing large quantities of stolen material. The majority of the repositories which had been officially established by the Nazis possessed detailed inventories and their contents had been carefully preserved. Other, smaller repositories, comprising for the most part the ill-gotten gains of unscrupulous Nazi officials, contained no records of the origins of their contents. Among the most important of the former kind was the Schloss Neuschwanstein, which contained not only collections belonging to French Jews, including treasures from the Rothschild and David Weill gold and silver collections, but also the records of the ERR which provided invaluable information on works of art looted by that organization.[33] Another repository, located in the Schloss Tambach a few miles from Coburg, included among its contents paintings from the royal palace at Warsaw which had been removed by the Reichskommissar of Poland, Hans Frank, including nine great eighteenth-century Venetian works by Bellotto.[34]

More works of art continued to be discovered as further repositories and hiding places were uncovered. The number of repositories discovered in Germany eventually reached over 1,000. Unfortunately, many of these were totally unsuited to the storage of delicate works of art which normally required careful maintenance. It was inevitable, therefore, that many items suffered irreparable damage or even destruction.

The multiplicity and variety of the locations and contents of the repositories, as well as the size of the task facing the overstretched Allied MFA&A officers as they sought to secure and protect the vast amounts of art treasures coming to light, are illustrated in the following extracts from two MFA&A reports written in May 1945:

> The ducal palace at Karlsruhe, now the provincial museum, is in ruins; the cellars still contain some collections which are being salvaged and sorted. There is an important repository of works of art in the Chateau of Baden Baden, some of which belong to the Cathedral of Strasbourg. The local jail of Pfullendorf contains a vast collection of art from the Karlsruhe museum and a certain number of pieces from Alsatian museums. As a general rule all historical monuments and depositories of works of art have been entrusted to the care of the persons previously appointed to the post by the German authorities, under the responsibility of the Burgermeister.[35]

> The most important repository of works of art known to exist in western Germany was uncovered in the tunnels of a mine under Siegen. It contains paintings and sculpture of major importance from museums of Aachen, Köln and Münster, as well as the treasuries of Aachen Cathedral and many other churches of the Rheinprovinz. The entire contents of the repository are intact. Another accumulation of important works of art from Köln was found in the undamaged castle of Langenauin in the charge of members of the Wallraf-Richartz Museum. German officials

have supplied names of more than seventy-five repositories of art and archives in western Germany. This information is being disseminated to corps and divisions. Paintings and sculpture from a number of the finest collections in western Germany were found in two air raid shelters in Bad Wildungen.[36]

It was extremely difficult to secure and guard this large number of repositories, dispersed over such a wide area, as the Allied fighting formations could ill afford to spare manpower to carry out such tasks. Their contents were under threat not only from deterioration through unsuitable accommodation and lack of proper care but also from damage or looting at the hands of some of the large numbers of displaced people, mainly slave labourers, who were wandering through Germany in the wake of the liberating Allied forces. A number of repositories suffered from such unwelcome attention. To avoid further depredations the MFA&A Branch at SHAEF decided to establish a number of collection points to which works of art would be taken for rehousing in secure accommodation in which they could be inspected and remedial restoration work carried out before the task began of tracing their rightful owners with a view to eventual restitution. The American collection points were established by the 12th US Army Group at Munich, Frankfurt, Marburg and Wiesbaden; the British located theirs at Celle.

The task of moving the vast numbers of works of art stored in the repositories to the collection points was a huge undertaking. This is well illustrated by the extensive operation required to empty the repository found in a large salt mine at Bernterode, which had also been used as a munitions manufacturing plant and depot and in which some 40,000 tons of ammunition were also found. The mine was being inspected by American troops of the 350th Ordnance Depot Company when it was noticed that a wall of masonry had recently been built into the side of the main corridor of the mine. On breaking through the wall, the Americans discovered a large repository, comprising several chambers hung with Nazi regalia and Wehrmacht regimental banners and containing numerous paintings, books, tapestries, porcelain and priceless treasures belonging to the Hohenzollern Museum.[37] On the following day, 28 April, an American MFA&A officer, Captain Greenspan, arrived and began a detailed inspection of the repository. In one of the chambers he found three coffins in which lay the remains of the eighteenth-century Prussian warrior king, Frederick the Great, alongside those of another famous soldier, Generalfeldmarschall von Hindenburg, and his wife. Among the paintings, which numbered 271 in total, were works by Lucas Cranach the Elder including the portrait of Adam and Eve from the Uffizi Palace in Florence, nine panels from the *Passion of Christ*, a *Crucifixion* and a number of portraits. Among others were *Venus and Adonis* by Boucher, Watteau's *Departure for Cythera* and two works by Chardin: *Femme Cachetant une Lettre* and *La Cuisinière*.[38]

Orders were given to evacuate the mine of its contents, and two days later Captain Greenspan was joined by Lieutenant George Stout. Further reinforcements arrived in the form of men from the 3052nd Engineer Combat Battalion which established a power supply and lighting in the mine. During the next ten days, working in two shifts from 8 a.m. until 10 p.m., the Americans steadily emptied the repository. This had to be done with extreme care as none of the paintings, tapestries or other works of art were in frames or cases and all had to be carefully packed before being hoisted 553 metres up the mine's elevator shaft to ground level. After all the items had been carefully recorded, they were taken to the collection point at Marburg by trucks of the 413th Transport Company.[39]

Earlier in the month, another vast repository had been discovered almost by accident in an isolated mine some 200 miles south-west of Berlin. Thirty miles from the nearest town of Merkers, the Kaiseroda mine and its contents might well have escaped notice for some time had not two military policemen (MPs) of the Third US Army met two Frenchwomen, both of them displaced persons, as they were driving along a remote country road in their jeep. Movement of civilians was being restricted at that time, so the MPs loaded the two women aboard their vehicle and proceeded to take them back to Merkers. As they passed the entrance to the mine, the women pointed it out and mentioned that it contained a large amount of gold bullion.[40] Three days later, on 7 April, American military personnel entered the mine. Descending by the elevator 2,100 feet, they found in the depths below 500 sacks containing RM1 billion and, after blowing open a steel door with explosives, 8,527 gold ingots, a large amount of gold coinage, further quantities of paper currency and crates of gold and silver plate. It was subsequently discovered that this hoard of gold and currency formed the major part of the Reichsbank reserves. Also discovered were a large number of cases containing precious stones and gold dental fillings, the latter taken from the bodies of concentration camp inmates.

As the Americans probed further into the depths of Kaiseroda, they also found large numbers of works of art and considerable quantities of valuable books belonging to German museums. Among the paintings they found were Lorenzo Lotto's *Saint Sebastian*, Cecchino Salviati's *Two Musicians* and Botticelli's *Virgin with a Choir of Angels*. Together with the gold, silver, precious stones and vast amounts of paper currency, these were brought to the surface and loaded on to convoys of trucks for transportation to Frankfurt, where they were subsequently secured in the vaults of a bank.

Those Allied MFA&A personnel tasked with establishing the collection points had to start with little or nothing in the way of resources. The first priority was to acquire buildings of suitable types and sizes and to render their accommodation for the preservation and storage of works of art. One of the primary American collection points was in Munich, and the responsibility for setting this up had been given to Lieutenant Craig Hugh Smyth, previously a member of staff at the National Gallery of Art in Washington. He succeeded in commandeering the Führerbau, the building which had served as Hitler's headquarters as leader of the Nazi party and which had been used as a store for looted works of art, and the Verwaltungsbau, which had been the party's central administrative headquarters. Both were found to contain a wealth of valuable documentation in the form of files and records which were handed over to intelligence personnel from Third US Army. These and similar buildings in Wiesbaden had to be cleaned, thoroughly renovated, fitted with storage facilities and secured by armed guards before they could be put to good use in their new role.[41]

A major problem facing the officers tasked with organizing the collection points was the acute shortage of qualified labour capable of carrying out construction and maintenance. For these they were forced to turn to the local German population and particularly individuals who were already familiar with the large buildings. Many of these were inevitably Nazis and thus precautions had to be taken against theft and sabotage, with troops positioned as guards inside and outside the buildings. Despite this vigilance, several paintings were stolen from the Führerbau, and a bomb was placed in one of the tunnels connecting the Führerbau and Verwaltungsbau; although little damage was caused by the explosion, it reinforced the need for a high level of security.

Germans were also employed on the staffs of the collecting points. Among those recruited were a number of individuals who had been curators of museums and galleries in Germany and who thus had knowledge and expertise which could be put to good use in the process of restitution. Secretarial and administrative personnel were also needed to establish and maintain filing systems, compile inventories and process the enormous amount of information which started to flow into the collection points. Experienced conservators were also required to carry out sometimes urgent remedial work on items suffering from the effects of having been stored in unsuitable conditions, as were photographers to help in identifying and compiling inventories of the recovered works.[42]

One of the major problems faced by MFA&A personnel was the lack of information about the vast number of works of art recovered from repositories. The highly comprehensive records covering those works destined for the Linz collection would have done much to facilitate the task of restitution; these records, however, had been placed in the repository at the Schloss Weesenstein near the city of Dresden, now in the area occupied by the Soviet Red Army destined to become post-war East Germany. As recounted in chapter 9, the Soviets discovered the Sonderauftrag Linz records and subsequently moved them to Moscow together with the contents of the repository. Nevertheless, some valuable information was uncovered by the Western Allies, notably the records of the ERR discovered at the Schloss Neuschwanstein. These and other documentary materials discovered in Germany and Austria by British MFA&A and American OSS ALIU personnel were sent to a documentation centre which was established alongside the collection point at Munich.

Despite such difficulties, restitution was high on the list of priorities of the Allied MFA&A organization. The Macmillan Committee and the Vaucher Commission had been formed with this as their primary concern, and the Roberts Commission had from the outset adopted the policy that all works of art looted or forcibly purchased by the Germans should be returned to their rightful owners as soon as the cessation of hostilities permitted. The idea of a post-war inter-Allied commission for restitution had also been mooted, but agreement on its composition and terms of reference could not be reached and thus it was never formed. Eventually, in July 1945, the Americans decided to proceed with restitution of their own accord.

The task of restitution was vast, involving a lengthy and painstaking process of research and investigation into the countless works of art purloined from areas of Europe which had been occupied by the Germans for almost five years. The majority of the Nazi repositories had been found in western and central Germany and north-west Austria, areas occupied by the 6th and 12th US Army Groups. Inevitably, therefore, the American MFA&A personnel attached to those formations found themselves under great pressure. The problems facing their British counterparts were somewhat different. The majority of the repositories in their areas of responsibility were located in castles and large houses in rural regions, and one of the principal threats to them was from looting by displaced persons living nearby or moving through the area. While these repositories held little in the way of looted works of art, a number of them were found to contain large numbers of items from German-occupied territories purchased by German museums in north Germany. One such repository discovered in a large house in Westphalia was found to contain a hoard of works of art, silver and antique weapons belonging to Heinrich Himmler, the much-feared head of the SS.

Fortunately, the already overstretched Allied MFA&A personnel were reinforced at this stage by suitably qualified officers who had been released from active service on the cessation of hostilities in Germany. Each of the Allied powers sent representatives who would assist in identifying items suspected as having originated in their respective countries: France, the Netherlands, Belgium, Poland, Czechoslovakia and Russia. Some major works of art were so easily identifiable and their origins so well known that their return to their rightful owners was merely a matter of time. The first restitution shipment took place on 21 August 1945, when the van Eyck altarpiece was despatched in an aircraft to Belgium and its home in the Cathedral of Ghent. It was followed shortly afterwards by Michelangelo's *Madonna and Child*, which was returned to its home city of Bruges. As recounted in the following chapter, both of these items had been discovered in the huge repository at Alt Aussee. The latter part of the following month saw the despatch of further shipments, including the first to France. In early October, the first shipment to the Netherlands took place, followed eleven days later by a second.[43]

As increasingly large numbers of works of art were being unearthed from Nazi repositories throughout Germany, the search continued for others documented as still missing. The OSS ALIU had already established an interrogation centre known as 'House 71', located at Bad Aussee, to which several of those individuals who had played prominent roles in the looting of Europe's treasurehouses were brought for interrogation. Nearby were Alt Aussee and the salt mine which held the ill-gotten fruits of their labours.

5

OPERATION EBENSBURG

At 2345 hours on the night of Sunday 8 April 1945, Halifax bomber 'T – Tommy' of 148 (Special Duties) Squadron, Royal Air Force took off from its base at Brindisi, a former fortress town of the Holy Roman Empire on the north coast of the 'heel' of southern Italy.[1] The night was clear with a full moon. Heading north-west, the aircraft flew parallel to the northern coastline of Italy before turning north off the port of Ancona and heading between Venice to the west and Trieste to the east. The pilot and captain was Pilot Officer Bill Leckie.[2] In addition to the rest of the crew – navigator, bomb aimer, flight engineer, wireless operator, rear gunner and despatcher – the aircraft carried a four-man team of the Special Operations Executive (SOE), the British organization charged with the conduct of clandestine warfare in enemy-occupied countries. All were Austrians and would shortly carry out one of the most significant missions undertaken by SOE, one that would ultimately prove to be of the utmost importance in saving some of Europe's most priceless art treasures from destruction.

Until now few details of the operation have been available; over half a century later, the account of it reads like a classic tale of high adventure. The authors of this book have managed to gather together previously classified documents from Britain and Austria and have interviewed survivors of the mission to tell the story. In so doing, their research into one of the most heroic single episodes of the entire war has brought to light an unresolved mystery involving a lady with an enigmatic smile.

In the spring of 1945, as the Allied armies advanced further into Austria and Germany, there were two primary concerns uppermost in the minds of the members of the MFA&A staff at SHAEF. First, they were only too well aware that the Russians were also advancing into Germany from the east and that any art treasures which fell into their hands would be lost. Secondly, they were in possession of reliable information that Hitler had ordered the destruction of the repositories and their contents in order to prevent them falling into Allied hands. On 2 November 1944, Lieutenant Colonel Sir Leonard

99

Woolley had written to Lord Macmillan, the chairman of the Macmillan Committee:

Dear Lord Macmillan,

The following statement, which has recently been obtained from a reliable source, is of such consequence for the artistic and cultural heritage of Europe, that I feel impelled to bring it immediately to the notice of your Committee.

Our informant reports that he was in Munich in October 1943 and there learnt from a Bavarian state functionary to whom it had been officially circulated, that Hitler had issued a secret order to all responsible authorities to the effect that in the last resort all historic buildings and works of art in Germany, whether of German or of foreign origin, whether legally or illegally acquired, should be destroyed rather than allowed to fall into the hands of Germany's enemies. This information was confided to our informant by his great friend Dr Max Göring, a reputable German art historian and one of the members of the Bavarian Commission for the Preservation of Art and Monuments. (He is no relation of the Reichsmarschall and has since been killed in an air raid on Munich.)

Other considerations apart, there is already enough evidence to show that this may indeed be Nazi policy. I would remind you on the one hand of the burning of the deposit of Neapolitan pictures and archives at Nola, on the other of the burning of the Lauwick collection of French Impressionist paintings at the Chateau de Rastignac. Again it is reliably reported that recently the German commander in The Hague summoned the leading members of the city's administration and read a proclamation stating that The Hague would not fall into the hands of the Allies in the same state as did Brussels and Paris, and that nothing would be left of it but ruins.

Literal obedience to Hitler's orders will result not only in the destruction of the artistic treasures of Germany itself, but of a great deal of the artistic heritage of many of our Allies. In view of this threat, therefore, it seems essential that His Majesty's Government be now recommended to take some anticipatory action . . .[3]

Such fears were wholly justified, particularly in the case of the largest and most important of all the German repositories: the salt mine at Alt Aussee.

In early April 1945 Gauleiter August Eigruber, the Nazi official ruling Ober-Donau, the region of Upper Austria in which Alt Aussee was situated, received a letter from Hitler's private secretary Martin Bormann. This instructed him to take all measures necessary to prevent the repository from being captured by the Allies. As far as Eigruber was concerned, this meant destroying the mine and its contents with explosives. A fanatical Nazi, he intended to see that this was carried out at all costs.[4] However, by the time Eigruber received the death sentence for the treasures stored in the network of caverns deep inside the mine, the Allies had learned of the existence of the repository and had taken measures to discover more about the situation there. News of the vast store of art treasures in the salt mine had reached the British in late 1944 after the Allied invasion of southern France, confirming information obtained earlier by American MFA&A officer Captain Robert Posey from the former Kunstschutz official Hermann Bunjes (as described in chapter 4).[5]

In April of that year a member of the Luftwaffe had defected to the French Resistance. An Austrian named Albrecht Gaiswinkler, he had been born in Bad Aussee in 1905. On leaving school he had worked in various jobs in the timber industry, railways and farming before joining the civil service in 1929, thereafter being employed in the social security office in Graz, the capital of the south-eastern Austrian province of Styria.[6] A Social Democrat and active in the trades union movement, Gaiswinkler was staunchly anti-Nazi in his sympathies and joined the Styrian Resistance shortly after the Anschluss in 1938. Eventually, however, his activities had attracted the attention of the authorities, including the Gestapo, and he thus enlisted in the Luftwaffe on 20 March 1943 to avoid retribution. After completing his training, Gaiswinkler was posted to Flieger Ausbildungs Regiment 90,[7] with which he served in Belgium and then France. During this time, members of his family wrote to him regularly and on a number of occasions made mention in their letters of convoys transporting large consignments of crated works of art at night to the salt mine at Alt Aussee.

While serving in Paris, Gaiswinkler made contact with a Resistance group. He later claimed that, with the assistance of the mayor of the town of St Jouan, he had delivered four trucks of munitions and a large sum of money, belonging to the imprest account of his unit, to the Resistance fighters. In April 1944 he deserted from his unit and joined the Resistance himself, remaining with it until September when he surrendered himself to the Americans at Dinan.[8] During his initial interrogation, Gaiswinkler not only made clear his anti-Nazi sentiments but also mentioned his knowledge of the storage of works of art at Alt Aussee. This information was swiftly passed back to London and shortly afterwards he was flown to Britain, where he was interrogated further about his political leanings as well as his knowledge of the salt mine and its contents. Gaiswinkler also had other information to offer: the letters from his family had mentioned mysterious explosions in the area of the Töplitzsee, a large lake situated near Bad Aussee.[9] Satisfied that his information was reliable, and recognizing that his detailed knowledge of the area of Alt Aussee would be invaluable, the British offered Gaiswinkler the opportunity of being trained as an agent and saboteur for operations in Austria.

The SOE archives are today controlled by an administrator based in an uninspiring grey room inside the Foreign and Commonwealth Office in central London, a short distance down Pall Mall from Buckingham Palace. In 1946, prior to their move from SOE's Baker Street headquarters, a mysterious fire destroyed a large number of the organization's files; just 7,000 or so of a total of around 20,000 survived. Most of them have been declassified in recent years, but Albrecht Gaiswinkler's file has not been made available to researchers before and previous accounts of events at Alt Aussee in April and early May 1945 have been based on other, mainly American, accounts. During their research, the authors of this book uncovered some startling, previously unknown facts.

After accepting the British offer, Gaiswinkler was sent to SOE's Special Training School (STS) No. 2 at Dorking in Surrey where he joined a group of anti-Nazi Austrians, nicknamed the 'Bonzos', who had either been captured by, or deserted to, the Allies. Two other members of this group were Karl Standhartinger, who used the aliases Josef Ludwig Roth and Karl Schmidt, and Karl Litzer, whose aliases were Franz Karl Wallner and Karl Fischer. During their time at STS No. 2 the group underwent initial selection procedures to determine their suitability for employment as agents. Having successfully passed these, Gaiswinkler, Standhartinger and Litzer were sent in early October 1944 to STS No. 5 at Wanborough Manor, near Guildford, where they were trained in military skills such as marksmanship, tactics, demolitions, camouflage and concealment, fieldcraft and map reading.[10] Then the men were sent to STS No. 51 in Cheshire for parachute training, which was carried out at nearby Ringway, just outside Manchester. Gaiswinkler unfortunately suffered a sprained ankle on his second descent and this prevented him from completing the course; nevertheless, he was considered capable of carrying out an operational jump and duly accompanied his companions to STS No. 44 at Market Harborough, in Leicestershire, for training in clandestine skills. At this juncture he was enlisted in the Pioneer Corps and given the alias of 13122230 Sergeant Karl Hans Schumacher. The use of false identities by members of SOE was normal practice when operating in enemy-occupied countries, agents being required to learn in minutest detail every facet of their aliases in order to be able to pass scrutiny if stopped and questioned by police or enemy troops.[11]

By the end of January 1945 the three men had completed their training. On 28 February they were flown to 'Maryland', the SOE forward operations base near Bari in southern Italy, Gaiswinkler travelling under the further alias of Major Thomas. There they met a fellow Austrian named Josef Grafl who used the aliases Johann Bönisch or John Green. He was to be the fourth member of their team and its radio operator.[12]

Grafl had a similar background to Gaiswinkler. Coming from a family bitterly opposed to the Nazis, he had been imprisoned prior to the Anschluss for voicing dangerously left-wing sentiments. One of his brothers-in-law was also jailed in late 1940 for being a communist. After his release, however, Grafl enlisted in the army and in November 1940 was posted to a specialist radio communications unit, the 1st Funkkompanie, having previously learned how to use a radio while a member of the Socialist Youth movement near his childhood home in Schattendorf. In the late summer of 1941 he was posted with his unit to take part in the invasion of Russia, but after only a few months succeeded in deserting.[13] Using his family's contacts with the Austrian resistance movement, Grafl made his way via the Romanian port of Constanta through Bulgaria to Greece, where he joined a partisan unit in the port of Piraeus, a short distance from Athens, in autumn 1942; and it was here that he met SOE agents operating in support of the partisans and organizing supplies of weapons and equipment. (This was not, apparently, the first time that Grafl had encountered members of Britain's clandestine services: in 1939 he had been in contact with two agents, named Miller and Hopson, who had been sent into Austria to gather intelligence on military dispositions within the country.) After several months of involvement in guerrilla operations, Grafl decided to throw in his lot completely with the Allies and was despatched by submarine to Alexandria in northern Egypt. Volunteering for the Royal Air Force, he was subsequently sent to Haifa, in Palestine, where he underwent training as a pilot. In early 1945, however, he was transferred to SOE and underwent further training as a wireless operator and parachutist.[14]

At Bari, the team carried out a further period of training and eventually was briefed on its forthcoming mission, codenamed Operation Ebensburg.[15] Its primary task was to make its way to Alt

Aussee and there to investigate and report on the situation at the mine repository. Thereafter it was to organize local Resistance groups in the area and gather intelligence on the locations and deployments of Wehrmacht formations and units. This latter task included investigation of the area of the nearby lake of Töplitzsee. All reports were to be transmitted by radio to the SOE base at Bari. Gaiswinkler, who led the team, and his men were warned that none of their tasks would be easy as the entire area was heavily populated with troops of the German Sixth Army which had been withdrawn from the Balkans to defend the Alpenfestung, the alpine redoubt in which Hitler's forces would apparently make their last stand.

In mid-March, having completed their training and final preparations for the operation, the team took off from Brindisi for Austria, where a reception committee from the local Resistance group had been alerted of their imminent arrival. However, the drop had to be aborted because of bad weather, and the aircraft returned with its passengers to Italy. It was three weeks before the operation could be mounted again. On the evening of 8 April, Gaiswinkler and his companions were once again transported from Bari to Brindisi in a closed truck. On arrival at the airfield, the vehicle drove straight to the waiting bomber and reversed up to it so that the four men could transfer to the aircraft completely unobserved.

At 0250 hours, thirty minutes before the designated 'P-Hour', the Halifax's despatcher, Flight Sergeant John Lennox, indicated to the four Austrians that they should commence preparing for the drop. It was a relief for them to do so; it was chilly in the unheated fuselage and they were cold and stiff. Under their parachutist's helmets and jumpsuits they wore civilian clothes and boots suitable for the mountainous terrain over which they would have to make their way. Each was armed with a Beretta 7.65mm calibre pistol and fighting knife, carried in the pockets of their jumpsuits. Their other weapons and equipment, including Josef Grafl's high-frequency transmitter/receiver, were in four containers carried in the aircraft's bomb bay.

When all four had checked their personal equipment and pronounced themselves ready, Flight Sergeant Lennox led them towards the tail of the aircraft where he positioned them sitting in pairs by the trapdoor covering the large circular aperture in the floor through which they would make their exit. Lennox clipped the end of the static line of each man's parachute to a D-ring set in the port side of the fuselage.[16] Shortly afterwards the Halifax banked gently and began the first of two flights over the dropping zone at an altitude of 800 feet. The bomb aimer, Flight Sergeant Brian Douglas, opened the doors of the bomb bay containing the team's four equipment containers; minutes later, he released the containers and the aircraft flew on in a wide circle. From his turret in the tail the rear gunner, Flight Sergeant Charlie Leslie, watched the four container parachutes floating earthwards. At this point Flight Sergeant Lennox opened the trapdoor covering the aperture, and a loud blast of cold air and noise filled the aircraft interior.

As the aircraft began to line itself up for the second approach, the four men readied themselves for the jump. When the command to drop came through Lennox's headset and the green jump light came on, he shouted 'Go!', tapping Gaiswinkler and Grafl on the shoulder. As the two men dropped down through the aperture, Lennox gave a thumbs-up signal to Standhartinger and Litzer, who followed immediately.[17] As each man fell away from the aircraft, his parachute was extracted from its pack by its static line and all four were soon descending towards the dark mountainside below.

A strong wind caused the parachutes to drift rapidly away from the centre of the drop zone; nevertheless, Gaiswinkler and his companions all landed safely and, having buried their parachutes in the deep snow, regrouped. There was, however, no sign of the expected Resistance reception committee, nor of the four equipment containers. Shaking his head almost in disbelief, Josef Grafl, now in his late seventies, recalls the drop. 'It was terrifying. It was dark and there was snow, plenty of snow. I landed in a drift which came up to my shoulders. I lost my emergency kit. On top of this, it was my first time in the mountains. But I realized that there might be situations like this. When I was asked by a British officer to parachute, I said all right because I thought I would jump and then go home.'[18]

One container, containing Grafl's precious transmitter/receiver, was eventually located, but the team's relief at finding it soon turned to dismay on discovering that the set had been irreparably damaged on landing. They had lost their means of communicating with the SOE base at Bari. Shortly afterwards, the situation looked even worse when it became apparent that the team had been dropped in the wrong place and were a considerable distance from where they should have been. As he and his companions continued their search for the other three containers, Gaiswinkler succeeded in regaining his bearings and realized that instead of being on the Zielgebiet am Zinken Plateau, they were several kilometres away from it on the slopes of the Höllingebirge – which, translated literally, means 'Hell Mountains' – above the town of Feuerkogel and overlooking one of the area's most notorious prison camps.

The discrepancy between where the team expected to be landed and where they were actually dropped has remained a mystery. When interviewed fifty-three years later by the authors of this book the pilot of the aircraft, Bill Leckie, recalled the operation quite clearly. 'It was the only occasion on which we dropped four "Joes", as we called our passengers; we normally only carried one or two plus their containers. The weather was fine, otherwise the drop would not have taken place, and I remember clearly seeing the lights of villages in the valleys below.' He also dismisses any suggestion that the team was dropped far from its intended DZ. 'There is no way that could have happened. We were a very experienced crew of a special duties squadron which had carried out a large number of operations of this type previously. On each run-in my tail gunner, Charlie Leslie, watched the chutes going down and it was his job to let me know that all had gone okay.'[19]

The explanation may lie in the files of SOE's Austrian Section. According to those covering the early part of 1945, there were suspicions of double agents among both the section's Austrian personnel and the Austrian Resistance movement. Furthermore, two agents of the Abwehr, the Wehrmacht's military intelligence service, had previously been intercepted in Italy and, under interrogation, had revealed that their missions were to make their way to Bari and reconnoitre the SOE base there.[20] It is thus possible that, for additional security, SOE had briefed the RAF to drop the team at a point different from that notified beforehand to the team and the Resistance group meeting them.

When told that the team had found no Resistance reception committee waiting for them, Bill Leckie commented: 'We would have been briefed beforehand on whether or not there would be a reception committee. If there was to be one, we would have been told the pre-arranged pattern in which the flares would be laid out on the DZ and the code letter which would be flashed at us by a torch from the ground. If the flare pattern or code letter was not correct, or if we could not see any, I would have aborted the drop. On the other hand, if we had been told the team was jumping blind, with no one down below to meet them, we would have dropped them accordingly. In this instance, where there was no one on the ground, we must have been told that they were jumping blind otherwise we would not have dropped them.'[21]

The search for the remaining containers proved fruitless. As the four men debated their next move, they suddenly realized they were not alone on the mountains that night. In the distance they could hear the sounds of troops approaching up the mountainside. As they had been warned during their briefing in Bari, the area was heavily garrisoned: having heard the aircraft, and suspecting that parachutists had been dropped, the Germans had reacted swiftly and despatched patrols to scour the area.

The bare, snow-covered terrain offered little chance of concealment and so Gaiswinkler and his companions had no option but to flee, carrying only their personal weapons and what little else they had been unable to unpack from the single recovered container, which was left buried in the deep snow. It was not long, however, before they realized that the main paths from the mountain slopes to the valleys below were blocked, and they were thus forced to adopt a more precarious route, struggling through snow which came up almost to their armpits to make their slippery descent down the steep, icy mountainside in pitch darkness. Finally they reached the valley below and headed for the nearby town of Steinkogl bei Ebensee.

'In the end,' remembers Josef Grafl, 'we came down the mountain without difficulty because the Germans checked only the roads. We went directly to the town's railway station and went by train to Bad Aussee. We heard rumours about the Englishmen who had landed.'[22] Their journey to Bad Aussee was a hazardous one; in constant danger of arrest, they jumped from the train before it arrived at their destination. They had good reason to be wary. Not only did they have the troops of General Fabianku's Sixth Army to contend with; also in evidence were the SS and Gestapo, who were conducting courts martial and summary executions of anyone suspected of anti-Nazi activities or sympathies, and large numbers of other Nazis seeking to escape the advancing Allied armies – among them the German Foreign Office, which had arrived in Bad Aussee in its entirety, along with the pro-Nazi governments of Croatia, Serbia, Hungary and Bulgaria, which had brought with them their gold and currency reserves.[23]

On reaching Bad Aussee, Gaiswinkler immediately made contact with his brother, Max, who agreed to shelter the team temporarily despite the great risk to himself and his family. Over the course of the next three weeks, Gaiswinkler and his men carried out the tasks allotted to them. First they made contact with the local Resistance group, which was led by the communist Valentin Tarra. Until Gaiswinkler's arrival, the Resistance movement in the area had been diffuse, operating in small independent cells without any form of coordination and thus with little effect.[24] He set about reorganizing it, assisted by the arrival of men of the local mountain rescue service and local gendarmerie, the latter bringing with them vital weapons and equipment. The team also established contact with a number of miners and the two Germans in charge of the repository in the salt mine at Alt Aussee: Hofrat Professor Hermann Michel and Karl Sieber, the latter a restorer in charge of the work being carried out on the repository's contents. Unbeknown to his Nazi compatriots, Michel was a communist and a member of the Resistance; a geologist by profession, it was he who had originally approved the use of the mine as a repository.[25]

Meanwhile, Josef Grafl succeeded in obtaining a transmitter/receiver to replace his own damaged set. This was achieved with the help of the Resistance, which had an agent working on the staff of Oberstgruppenführer Ernst Kaltenbrunner, the chief of the Reichsicherheithauptamt (Reich Central Security Office) and second-in-command of the SS under Reichsführer Heinrich Himmler. Like other senior Nazis, Kaltenbrunner had fled before the Allied advance into Germany and retreated to Austria, where he had recently established his personal headquarters in the Villa Castiglione, a large house near Bad Aussee which had previously been used as a summer residence by Josef Goebbels, the Nazi propaganda chief, and which contained the major part of Hitler's Linz library collection. The Resistance agent, a Sicherheitsdienst wireless operator, acquired a spare set and passed it to Grafl, enabling him to re-establish contact with the SOE base at Bari.[26]

All this time, lines of trucks were continuing to arrive at the mine at Alt Aussee, bringing in further large quantities of art treasures. On 10 April, two days after his team's arrival, Gaiswinkler was informed that a convoy had arrived at the mine with a heavy escort of SS troops, carrying six large crates ostensibly containing slabs of marble and marked 'Marmor Nicht Stürzen' (Marble Do Not Drop). Accompanying the convoy was an individual named Glinz, who was the gauinspektor for the region of Ober-Donau, together with another local senior Nazi official for the area.[27] The crates contained six 500lb aircraft bombs which, on the instructions of Gauleiter Eigruber, were to be placed at certain locations within the mine, carefully sited so that when detonated they would destroy the tunnels, damage the chambers containing the art treasures and destroy the pumps which were in constant use extracting any water in the mine workings.[28]

Loaded on to trolleys which ran along the narrow-gauge rails within the tunnels, the crates were pushed into the mine and placed in their designated locations. The detonators were not fitted but stored separately. Meanwhile a detachment of SS troops took up positions guarding the entrance to the mine. Much of this activity took place under observation from the SOE team, which had swiftly established itself in some woods nearby on receiving news from the Resistance of the convoy's arrival. That night, on orders from Gaiswinkler who was anxious to discover the contents of the crates, two miners succeeded in infiltrating themselves into the mine and opening one of the crates. When news of its contents reached Gaiswinkler and his colleagues, including the two repository officials, they realized that the Nazis planned to destroy the repository and its priceless contents.

Twenty-four hours later, while a close watch was kept by miners who were also members of the Resistance, Professor Michel, two miners and his female assistant secretly moved the most valuable works of art from the caverns in which they had hitherto been kept to the mine's underground chapel, where it was felt there was the least chance of damage from blast and falling rock. The first item to be transferred was the Ghent altarpiece. All this was achieved without the knowledge of the SS guards outside the mine entrance.[29]

On 13 April the repository received a visit from Martin Bormann's personal secretary, Dr Helmut von Hummel, accompanied by Gauinspektor Glinz and a number of officials who had been charged with ensuring that the mine was sealed and its contents preserved. Eigruber refused to accept this interpretation of the orders which he had already received, despite a telephone call from von Hummel to Berlin to obtain confirmation that the contents of the mine were not to be destroyed. He was determined to press on with preparations for the destruction of the repository.[30] Meanwhile, Gaiswinkler made contact with Dr Wilhelm Hoettl, an obersturmbannführer in the SS and a member of the Sicherheitsdienst. A native of Bad Aussee, he had returned in March from Budapest, where he had worked in the SS headquarters. The numerous reports which crossed his desk soon made it clear to him that Germany had lost the war, and his response to this realization was swiftly to establish contact with the American OSS in Switzerland, headed by Allen Dulles and based in Berne.

Gaiswinkler knew that Hoettl had returned to Bad Aussee and somehow also of his secret contact with the Americans. He was concerned that the latter, like the British, had been convinced by Nazi propaganda that the entire area of the Austrian Alps comprised the Alpenfestung and thus might subject it to bombing prior to advancing into it. Summoning Hoettl to his headquarters deep in the

woods near Alt Aussee, Gaiswinkler asked him to despatch a
message to the Americans, stating that the area should not be
bombed.[31] The reason behind Gaiswinkler's approach to Hoettl has
yet to be explained, bearing in mind that he should have made any
such request via Grafl's transmitter to his own operational headquarters at Maryland, the SOE base at Bari. Whether or not Hoettl
obliged is also unknown; in any event, fortunately, the Americans
did not bomb the area.

By now the German forces in the region were withdrawing in some
disorder in the face of advancing American troops of General George
Patton's Third US Army, the leading elements of which had reached
Salzburg. Gaiswinkler was, however, under no illusions as to the
capability of his lightly armed band to withstand any attack on the
mine by a well-armed and determined force. He and his team thus
decided to take the war to the enemy. Dressing themselves in
captured SS officers' uniforms, they proceeded to spread mayhem
among the retreating forces passing through the area. On more than
one occasion, large numbers of bewildered and demoralized troops
suddenly found themselves covered by armed Resistance men who
proceeded to strip them of their weapons. In one instance, Gaiswinkler succeeded in capturing two armoured personnel carriers which
were soon put to good use.[32]

Nor did Gaiswinkler and his three fellow SOE agents confine
themselves merely to capturing weapons and equipment. They also
carried out an operation to kidnap three leading Nazis, two of them
members of the Gestapo: Schöningh, the commander of the local
unit; and one of his officers, Ortsgruppenleiter Cain. The third, an SS
obersturmführer named Blaha, was Gauleiter Eigruber's deputy and
had been charged by him with overseeing the destruction of the salt
mine and its contents. All three were immediately subjected to a
mock trial conducted by Gaiswinkler and the Resistance group,
found guilty and condemned to death. They were informed that the
sentence would be suspended if they agreed to cooperate with the
Resistance. The three men, all of whom were Austrian, agreed with
alacrity and were released. Despite Gaiswinkler's doubts about them,
they kept their word and proceeded to pass information and
documents to him, also supplying him with official Gestapo stamps
and stationery to assist with his work of deception and misinforma-
tion.

As German troops continued to pour into the area over the
Pötschen Pass, Gaiswinkler and his team, who were hiding in the
hills, used bluff in an attempt to discourage any attack on the mine.

Rumours were spread of the approach of Yugoslav partisans over the mountains and fires were lit on mountainsides to reinforce these claims. The two captured armoured vehicles were pressed into service in the defence of the mine and the surrounding area. The Resistance also captured the region's principal radio station, located a dozen miles away at the Teichschloss, and used it to good effect, broadcasting misleading reports to cause confusion within the enemy formations and units. All these measures proved highly effective and were later credited with having forestalled an attack by an SS battalion. 'It was an alarmingly easy operation,' recalled Josef Grafl. 'We put an Austrian on the air who said repeatedly, "This is Austria, red, white and red [the colours of the national flag]." There was no resistance to it at all. We didn't have many resources with which to defend the transmitter. If the Germans had still wanted to, they could have taken it back quite easily but they did nothing. We were able to take weapons and vehicles from SS officers without any trouble at all.'[33]

Despite the success of these tactics, Gaiswinkler was becoming increasingly anxious about the mine and its contents. Von Hummel had failed to make Eigruber change his mind about the import of his instructions, and no appeal to Bormann was possible as the Reichsleiter had disappeared while escaping from Russian forces advancing into Berlin. Furthermore, all lines of communication with the German capital had been cut. So Gaiswinkler turned to the senior Nazi official in Austria, SS chief Ernst Kaltenbrunner, making direct contact with him at his headquarters and demanding that he countermand Gauleiter Eigruber's orders to destroy the repository. Kaltenbrunner initially refused to do so, but was eventually persuaded to change his mind by one of his staff who was an Austrian and a member of the Resistance. However, Eigruber soon learned of this and gave orders for a detachment of SS engineers at Innsbruck, equipped with explosives and flamethrowers, to travel with all haste to Alt Aussee and destroy the repository.[34] Gaiswinkler's informers in Kaltenbrunner's headquarters were quick to pass this information on to him.

By this time rumours of the imminent arrival of American forces were spreading throughout the region. The SS guards entrusted with protecting the mine deserted their posts and fled to the mountains, where they joined other bands of SS troops roaming aimlessly around the area. Gaiswinkler realized that the mine had to be secured and defended until the Americans arrived. On 3 May, the combined force of his team, the miners and members of the Resistance established a defensive perimeter and secured the area of the mine.[35] The miners, whose principal motive was preservation of the mine itself and their livelihood, suggested to Gaiswinkler and Michel that the six bombs and their detonators should be removed and the main tunnel of the mine demolished with explosives, sealing it off. Both agreed and the miners set to work removing the bombs. Two days later, on 5 May, the main tunnel was blown up, leaving the repository and its priceless contents sealed safely inside.[36]

However, one threat still remained. The activities of Gaiswinkler's group had by now reached the point where General Fabianku, the commander of the Sixth Army, was provoked into retaliation. Hearing that the Resistance had taken the mine, he gave orders for an immediate attack to be mounted against Gaiswinkler's base. This took place on 6 May but failed in the face of determined opposition on the part of the Resistance. Not content with having fought off Fabianku's troops, Gaiswinkler retaliated by mounting a raid on the general's headquarters and capturing him in person. Taken to Gaiswinkler's headquarters and threatened with being shot out of hand, Fabianku was forced to give orders for the release of a Resistance courier who had been captured earlier and despatched to Bad Mittendorf for execution.[37]

While Gaiswinkler was thus engaged, other members of the SOE team were carrying out another of their tasks, that of reconnoitring the area of the Töplitzsee, from where a series of explosions could be heard. They found that the lake had been used by the Kriegsmarine for development of torpedoes and mines. On this occasion the explosions were those of demolition charges destroying the lake's research station and installations.[38]

By now time was running out, and Gaiswinkler realized that he would have to make contact as soon as possible with the American forces, whose leading elements had reached the town of Vocklabruck, some thirty-five miles by road north of Alt Aussee. On 6 May, while the defenders of the mine were staving off Fabianku's attack, two members of the Resistance, Leopold Köberl and Julius Stockl, were despatched in a vehicle to establish contact with the Americans and plead for reinforcements. They succeeded in making their way to Vocklabruck, where they met the vanguard of the Third US Army and reported the situation at Alt Aussee. While returning, however, the two men were stopped at an SS roadblock and arrested. Only a subsequent rescue operation by the Resistance saved them from certain execution.[39]

The Americans pushed forward to the Pötschen Pass, where on 7

May they met Gaiswinkler and some of his men in their two captured armoured personnel carriers. To the SOE agent's concern, the new arrivals seemed in no hurry as the area appeared already to have been liberated by the Resistance. There were, however, still large numbers of armed German troops, including units of SS, in the area and Gaiswinkler was concerned at the risk they posed. It was with a profound sense of relief, therefore, that on the following day he witnessed the arrival in Alt Aussee of troops of the 80th US Infantry Division who immediately took over the area and secured the mine itself.[40]

Shortly afterwards Captain Robert Posey, the MFA&A officer attached to the Third US Army, arrived with his assistant, Private Lincoln Kirstein, to investigate the contents of the mine and to supervise their eventual evacuation to safety. Equipped with lamps, the two men entered the mine and moved gingerly along the main tunnel until they found themselves blocked by the debris from the explosions set off by the miners. By the following day, the obstruction had been cleared by engineers and they were able to enter the mine's chambers.

Having visited the mine, it is easy for the authors to imagine how Posey and Kirstein felt as they made their way along the narrow passages leading miles underground. Today the mine is open to tourists; but there is nothing outside to suggest its crucial place in the twentieth-century world of art, not even a plaque to boast of its previous illustrious contents. A guide leads visitors down cool, moist walkways lined with smooth red rock, illuminated by aged electrical lighting which picks out the glistening salt crystals, shuffling slowly forward while taking care to avoid the low ceilings. Steep slides and staircases take one even further into the heart of the mine, which is now the scene of summer theatre performances and *son et lumière* shows, but which fifty-three years ago housed an estimated $500 million worth of works of art. The art treasures are of course long gone; but evidence of their presence in the mine is still visible. In several chambers the racking on which they were stacked is still in place, now bearing only some of the crates which contained Gauleiter Eigruber's bombs.

As they worked their way into the mine, Posey and Kirstein discovered a number of huge caverns and galleries interconnected by a honeycomb of tunnels. One of these caverns was known as the Springerwerke. Measuring about 50 feet in length and 30 feet in width, it contained some 2,000 paintings stored in two tiers of racking around the three sides of the cavern and down the centre.

Among the items in this cavern examined by Posey and Kirstein were around forty Italian paintings of the famous Lanz collection from Amsterdam, along with paintings by Brueghel, Titian, Rembrandt, Tintoretto, van Dyck, Rubens, Reynolds, Nattier, Lancret and Hals.[41]

The largest of the caverns was the Kammergraf, which lay three-quarters of a mile from the entrance of the mine. This comprised several galleries which were on different levels and were so high that those on the first level could accommodate three tiers of paintings on racks. Among the numerous paintings secreted here were works by Titian, Tintoretto, van Dyck, Rubens, Rembrandt and Veronese. Many of them had been appropriated from private owners in Austria, the Netherlands, Belgium and France, including the Rothschild, Gutmann and Mannheimer collections. Others were from the Dutch Goudstikker and French Sammlung Berta collections.[42] Also found in the Kammergraf, which was devoted to works for the Linz collections, was the fourteenth-century Hohenfurth altarpiece; drawings and prints of the sixteenth to eighteenth centuries; tapestries from Krakow Castle in Poland; cases of porcelain; decorations from the Reichskanzlei in Berlin; and furniture from the castle at Posen. The most important discovery in the Kammergraf, however, was Vermeer's *Portrait of the Artist in His Studio*. Other major works stacked nearby in the Kammergraf were some of the fifteen paintings and sculptures removed from the famous monastery at Monte Cassino in Italy. These included Raphael's *Madonna of the Divine Love*, Titian's *Danae*, an *Annunciation* by Filippino Lippi, *Crucifixion* by van Dyck, *Sacra Conversazione* by Palma Vecchio, Sebastiano del Piombo's *Portrait of Pope Clement VI*, Pieter Brueghel's *The Blind Leading the Blind* and a landscape by Claude Lorrain.[43]

However, it was on entering the mine's chapel – a cavern called the Kapelle and complete with an altar carved in salt – that Posey made his most important discovery. There, to his great joy, was the Ghent altarpiece, van Eyck's *Adoration of the Mystic Lamb*: the principal item he had been seeking which, as mentioned previously, Hermann Bunjes had assured him was at Alt Aussee. Shortly afterwards it was moved to a more secure location in another cavern, the Mineral Kabinett, where it was placed under lock and key. The altarpiece was one of the two most important single items in the mine, the other being Michelangelo's statue *The Madonna of Bruges*, which Posey and Kirstein subsequently found in the Kaiser Josef cavern. The Kapelle cavern also contained Archduke Franz Ferdinand's collection

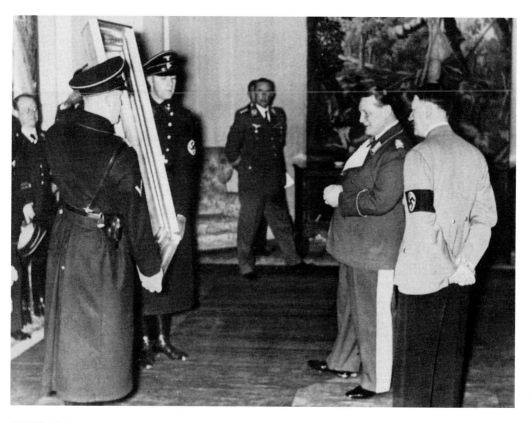

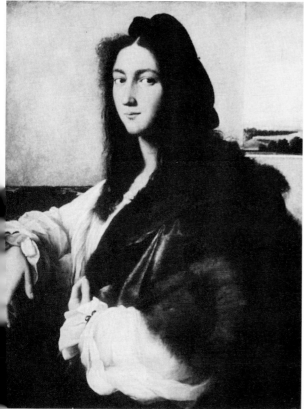

ABOVE: Adolf Hitler and Hermann Göring admiring a painting given to the latter on his 45th birthday by the Führer. (Hulton Getty Picture Library)

LEFT: *Portrait of a Young Man* by Raphael, which is still missing. Belonging to the Czartoryski collection, it was last seen in the possession of Reichskommissar Hans Frank in January 1945 but disappeared there-after. (Czartoryski Museum)

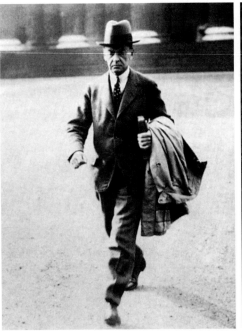

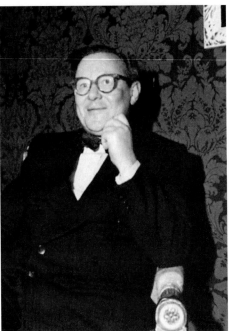

Sir Leonard Woolley, Archaeological Adviser to the British War Office and head of its MFA & A Sub-Commission. (British Museum)

Douglas Cooper, British MFA & A intelligence officer and subsequently Deputy Director MFA & A at SHAEF, who conducted investigations into trafficking in looted works of art in Switzerland. (Hulton Getty Picture Library)

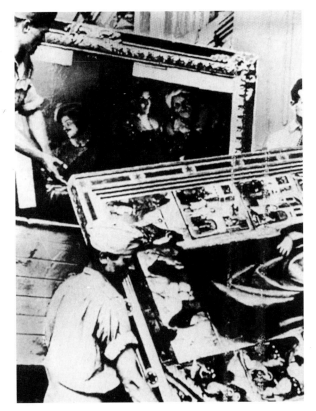

German troops removing works of art from Florence during their withdrawal from the city in July 1944. (Hulton Getty Picture Library)

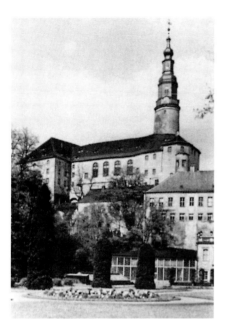

LEFT: The Schloss Weesenstein, near Dresden. A major Nazi repository, it also contained the records of the Linz collection. The castle was captured by the Red Army in 1945 and its contents transported to Moscow. (Ullstein Bilderdienst, Berlin)

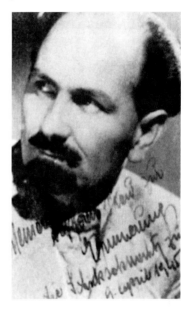

RIGHT: Albrecht Gaiswinkler, Austrian leader of the SOE team which saved the repository at Alt Aussee from destruction by the Nazis. (Bad Kammerhof Museum)

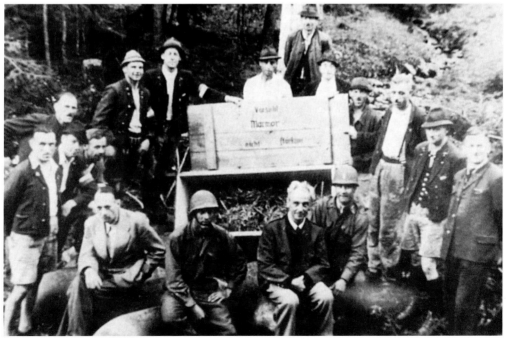

Professor Hermann Michel and some of the miners at the salt mine at Alt Aussee with three of the defused bombs earlier placed in the mine by SS troops to destroy the huge repository of works of art. (Bad Kammerhof Museum)

Dl/!

    Gendarmeriemajor Valentin T a r r a hat sich als Österr. Freiheitskämpfer mit der Waffe in der Hand bei der Widerstandsbewegung im Ausserland ganz hervorragend bewährt.

    Durch sein initiatives Handeln hat er im wesentlichen dazu beigetragen, dass die Kampfhandlungen im Ausserland abgekürzt wurden und dabei rund 6000 Mann deutscher Truppen entwaffnet werden konnten.

    Seiner besonders tatkräftigen Mitwirkung an leitender und verantwortungsvoller Stelle ist es auch zu verdanken, dass enorme Kultur- und Kunstschätze, die von den Deutschen verschleppt und verborgen gehalten wurden, wie die österr. Kaiserkrone, die Mona Lisa aus Paris Tizian und 80 Waggons Kunst- und Kulturgüter von ganz Europa im Werte von 21 Milliarden Dollar gerettet werden konnten.

    Die Bitte um Wiedergutmachung der finanziellen Schädigung des GendMajors Valentin Tarra und seiner Gattin wird wegen der einmalig herrvorragenden Leistung dieses aussergewöhnlich pflichttreuen und vom österreichischen Geiste durchdrungenen GendOffiziers besonders befürwortet.

    Seine Ernennung zum GendMajor mmm vom Gend RevInspektor erfolgte durch die Besatzungsmacht bezw, mit deren Zustimmung und dürfte aller Voraussicht nach auch seine Ernennung zum GendMajor von der österr. Staatskanzlei im Zuge der Rehabilitierung demnächst erfolgen.

        Wien, am 12. Dezember 1945.

                    I. V.

An Austrian Ministry of Interior report mentioning the discovery of the *Mona Lisa* at Alt Aussee in May 1945. Investigations by the authors revealed that the painting was a copy of Leonardo da Vinci's masterpiece. (Paul Mealey)

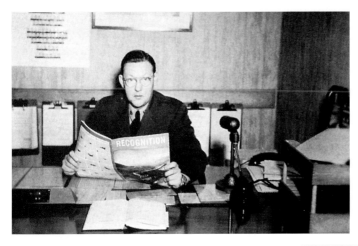

LEFT: Professor S. Lane Faison who, as a member of the OSS Art Looting Investigation Unit, interrogated individuals principally involved in the Nazi trafficking in looted works of art. (Professor S. Lane Faison)

RIGHT: OSS agent Aline Griffith who sought to track down looted works of art smuggled into Spain. While working for the CIA in the 1960s, she uncovered the identity of the head of the Nazi smuggling ring. (Kit Talbot)

BELOW: The Führerbau in Munich, initially the principal destination for works of art looted by the ERR which were later evacuated to repositories in Austria. It was subsequently used by US forces as the location for one of their two major collection points. (Craig Hugh Smyth)

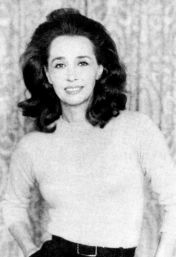

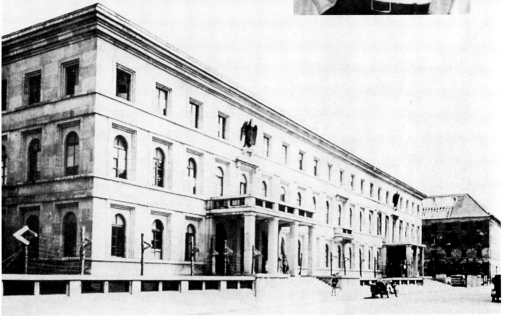

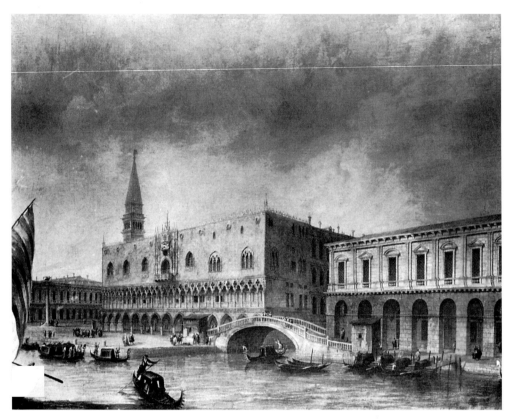

View of the Doge's Place in Venice by Canaletto. Looted by American troops in 1945 from a Städel Museum repository, it was later acquired by a London collector and appeared at auction in London in 1962. It subsequently disappeared again and is still missing. (Bildarchiv Foto Marburg)

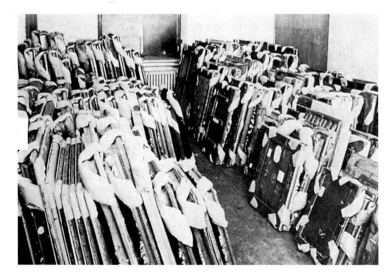

An interior view of the American collection point at Munich, showing stacked works of art recovered from Nazi repositories. (Craig Hugh Smyth)

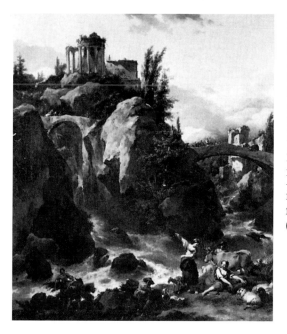

Motiv aus Tivoli by Nicolaes Berchem. Looted in April 1945 by a US Army officer from the Städel Museum repository in the Schloss Büdingen, it appeared at auction in London in 1962 and was later located in the possession of the Custodia Foundation at the Dutch Institute in Paris. However, it is still listed as missing from the Städel collection. (Bildarchiv Foto Marburg)

Mariners Loading Freight in a Southern Harbour by Johannes Lingelbach. Looted by American troops in 1945 from the Städel Museum repository in the Schloss Amorbach, this painting reappeared in 1963 when it was offered for sale by a New York art dealer acting on behalf of a collector. It disappeared again and is still missing. (Bildarchiv Foto Marburg)

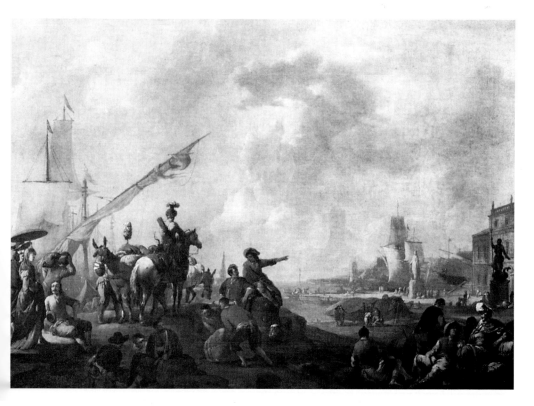

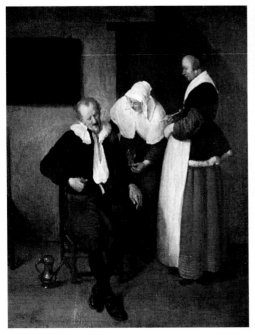

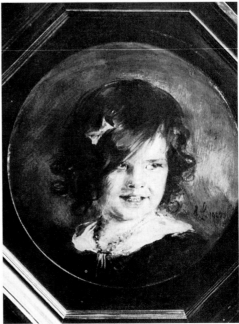

The Fainting Fit by Quiringh
Gerritsz van Brekelencam. Looted
by American troops in 1945 from
a Städel Museum repository, it
appeared at auction in London in
1962. Located in Germany by the
museum in 1980, negotiations for
the painting's recovery failed and it
is still missing. (Bildarchiv Foto
Marburg)

Gabriele Lenbach by Franz von
Lenbach. Looted in September
1945 from the Lenbachhaus
repository in the Schloss
Hohenaschau in Bavaria, it is
still missing. (Städtische Galerie
im Lenbachhaus)

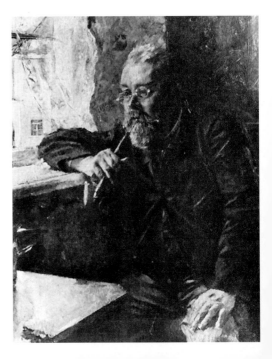

In a Small Town by
Wilhelm Leibl. Looted in
September 1945 from
the Lenbachhaus reposi-
tory in the Schloss
Hohenaschau
in Bavaria, it is still
missing. (Städtische
Galerie im Lenbachhaus)

of Spanish arms and armour, which belonged to Czechoslovakia, and the Linz coin collections.

As they probed their way further into the mine, Posey and Kirstein discovered a large number of paintings in another cavern called the Mondberg; among these were several sixteenth-century Venetian works, including Paris Bordone's *Portrait of a Young Woman*. Subsequent reports stated that the mine contained in total some 6,755 paintings, principally Old Masters, which had been intended for the Führermuseum at Linz. Other items included a large number of nineteenth-century German paintings, over 2,000 drawings and watercolours, in excess of 900 prints, some 130 pieces of sculpture, collections of books and manuscripts (including those of the Biblioteca Herziana in Rome), archives, tapestries, collections of coins and armour, and the Millionen Zimmer and Chinesisches Kabinett from the Imperial summer palace at Schönbrunn.[44] One particularly interesting item found by Captain Posey was a letter from Martin Bormann, directing that at all costs the repository should not be permitted to be captured by Allied forces; but that its contents must not be harmed.[45]

Posey and Kirstein were subsequently joined at Alt Aussee by other American MFA&A personnel to assist in the mammoth task of evacuating all the art treasures from the mine. Among these were Lieutenant George Stout; Lieutenant Thomas C. Howe, previously Director of the California Palace of the Legion of Honor; Lieutenant Lamont Moore, previously Director of educational programmes at the National Gallery in Washington; Lieutenant Steve Kovalyak and Lieutenant Frederick Shrady. Evacuation of the mine began on 16 June, with the first consignment departing for the collection point at Munich on the same day. The most important works were brought to the surface first, some having to be wrapped in protective materials before being placed on small flat-cars or *hünde*, pulled by a small engine, and taken out on the mine's narrow-gauge railway. Thereafter they were loaded aboard convoys of trucks which transported them to Munich, escorted by troops of the 11th US Armored Division. The contents of each truck were listed in duplicate, one copy accompanying the consignment to the collection point, the other remaining with the records established at the mine office.

There remains, however, one as yet unresolved mystery concerning the contents of the repository at Alt Aussee. In 1997 the SOE Adviser, the official in charge of the SOE archive at the Foreign and Commonwealth Office, telephoned the authors of this book in a state of some excitement. Responding to their request for the service record of Albrecht Gaiswinkler, he had stumbled upon a potentially explosive discovery. Several documents, compiled by British intelligence officers, referred in detail to the events at Alt Aussee and the discoveries at the salt mine. One, by 'GSI [General Staff Intelligence], British Troops, Austria', entitled 'Resistance in Bad Aussee',[46] is based on information sources in Austria and begins by stating, 'There is no reason to suppose that the picture they present is over-drawn'. It goes on to describe how Gaiswinkler and his team 'saved such priceless objects as the Louvre's *Mona Lisa*'. Yet that painting, arguably the most famous in the world, does not feature on any of the lists of the contents of the salt mine at Alt Aussee. A second British report, detailing the history of SOE in Austria at the end of the war,[47] again details how Gaiswinkler's team secured 'the preservation of the *Mona Lisa*'.

The authors' research led them to the Louvre, the home of the *Mona Lisa* since the completion of the museum's Grand Gallery in 1804 – apart from a brief period in 1911 when it was stolen by an Italian, Vicenzo Peruggia, who planned on taking the painting 'home' to Italy. A spokeswoman for the museum, however, informed them that it was 'inappropriate' to offer comment on a particular piece in the Louvre's sizeable collections. Further enquiries took the authors back to Austria and Alt Aussee. A local museum produced another official document, dated 12 December 1945, which once more stated that 'the *Mona Lisa* from Paris' had been among '80 wagons of art and cultural objects from across Europe' which had been packed into the salt mine.[48] An official Austrian government publication from 1946, telling the story of the country during the occupation by German forces, only added to the mystery by again listing the *Mona Lisa* as one of the works of art housed in the Third Reich's largest repository – works of art which, if Gauleiter August Eigruber had had his way, would have been obliterated with the explosion of six 500lb bombs.[49]

Even Lieutenant Colonel Ralph Pearson, the first senior American officer to arrive at the mine entrance, is drawn into the discussion over whether the *Mona Lisa* was present in the mine. He subsequently wrote an account of his days at Alt Aussee which was published in the *Kansas City Times* in 1958. In it he quotes from his diaries at the time he was stationed in northern Austria. While not mentioning the painting by name, he intriguingly lists the mine as having housed 'the master works of Goya, Raphael, Rembrandt, da Vinci, Michelangelo and other equally famous masters'.[50] Nowhere other than in the documents seen by the authors is there any suggestion that a work by Leonardo da Vinci was stored at the salt mine. Of course, references made to the painting in wartime documents do not amount to concrete proof and are certainly not taken as such by the authors of this book. However, they do raise the question of the *Mona Lisa*'s whereabouts throughout the war.

After repeated demands for comment, the Musée du Louvre broke with official protocol and took the unusual step of releasing certain limited details which confirmed the little which was already known of the painting's movements after its evacuation from Paris. Already published accounts outlined how the operation to remove French state collections from the country's capital began on 6 September 1938.[51] The *Mona Lisa* left in a specially marked and constructed case on 28 August 1939.[52] Together with the other essential parts of the national collections, she made her way through France via a series of temporary repositories. The Louvre collections moved first to Chambord in the Loire; then, on 5 June 1940, they moved on to Chauvigny and the Abbaye de Loc-Dieu in the Aveyron, 'part of the mountainous heart of the country'. In September that year they moved again to the Ingres Museum at Montauban in the south of France, where they remained for two years until their apparent final wartime switch to Montal near to the town of Saint-Cere, according to an official Louvre chronology supplied to the authors.[53]

But this first release of information did little to put the matter of da Vinci's lady to rest. The documents contained no information about any further dramas until her safe arrival back at the Louvre on 16 June 1945 – leaving a crucial gap of two and a half years in the picture's history at the same point that official paperwork from other European nations placed her in the Alt Aussee salt mine. Nor is the confusion cleared up by interviews and additional post-war accounts from former MFA&A officers who worked at Alt Aussee. They make no mention of the *Mona Lisa*. Lynn Nicholas does, however, refer in her book *The Rape of Europa* to an agreement in June 1945 that a number of easily recognizable and well-known works of art, such as the Ghent altarpiece and the Bruges Madonna, should be returned to their respective owner-nations on an interim basis.[54] Among such items designated for immediate return to France were fifty paintings, mainly from the Rothschild and Mannheimer collections. Whether the *Mona Lisa* was among those treasures returned swiftly to their permanent homes, thus avoiding the indignity of passing through one of the Allied collection points, is again uncertain.

Is it possible that the *Mona Lisa* was seized by the Germans as they withdrew northwards through southern France to counter the Allied invasion of Normandy? As mentioned in chapter 4, troops of the 2nd Das Reich SS Panzer Division chanced upon the Louvre's temporary repository in the château at Valençay in the summer of 1944, attacking it, setting it alight and killing a member of the museum's staff. Did they take the painting? Have the French authorities, through embarrassment or for other reasons best known to themselves, concealed the fact that elements of France's state collections, including their most treasured work of art, were confiscated by the Germans? Is it even conceivably possible that the Louvre was forced into some form of transaction with the Germans? As mentioned earlier, it is known that Hitler had secret plans for the French national collections. Moreover, Allied reports document how the museum's directors exchanged certain works with Hermann Göring for other pieces and it is known that Henri Verne, the former Director of French national museums, worked with two of the principal Nazi agents in occupied France, Hans Wendland and Bruno Lohse.

The mystery is not easily solved, particularly when most of those who took part in the rescue and evacuation of the mine's contents are no longer alive. Even those who are appear to be able to shed no further light on the matter. Craig Hugh Smyth, who established the American collection point at Munich to which the contents of the mine were taken, remarked during a telephone conversation with one of the authors, 'I never heard anything about the *Mona Lisa* and I'm quite sure I would have done. It would have been truly remarkable if it had been there.'[55] Josef Grafl, whose home is no more than a few miles from the mine he helped to rescue, has no clearer idea. 'I can't help you,' he apologizes. 'I never went inside the salt mine. The artworks were taken out by the Americans. To be honest, nobody was really interested in paintings, food was more important at that time. I certainly didn't hear anything about the *Mona Lisa*.' At the time of writing, the only authority which may perhaps know the truth, the Louvre, is refusing to comment fully on the mystery. Thus the question remains – for now at least.

Early in 1999 officials at the Louvre, responding to yet more detailed questions from the authors, attempted once again to dismiss the 'absurd' notion that their priceless da Vinci had been only hours away from obliteration.[56] However, they succeeded only in increasing the number of question marks hanging over the painting's authenticity. Finally, they admitted that the *Mona Lisa* was in the Alt Aussee salt mine. But with the help of letters and bills of lading which dated from December 1947,[57] they argued that it had been a sixteenth- or seventeenth-century exact copy: a rendition of the masterpiece that had been returned to Paris from Salzburg as part of a four-wagon shipment of French possessions seized by the Nazis.

The defence reignited the age-old debate about which version of the noblewoman known to the French as 'La Joconde' was the one painted by da Vinci himself. Professor Martin Kemp, a Leonardo expert at Oxford University, gave his explanation. 'There are quite a few copies of the Mona Lisa,' he said, 'some of which were painted almost as soon as da Vinci died. Ordinarily a portrait would not necessarily have excited such fervour but this was quickly seen as a very special picture.'[58]

'I have inspected the *Mona Lisa* and been allowed to remove it from its frame for analysis. Under infra-red inspection you can see how the painting developed and changes were made. That's not something you tend to get with a copy. Copyists like the effect without the effort. As a result, I'm 99 per cent certain that the one on display to the public is the same one which Leonardo painted and that his right-hand man, Giangiacomo Caprotti, gave to the French.'

The Alt Aussee *Mona Lisa* was, according to the Louvre, entered on to the list of the Musées Nationaux de la Récupération – an inventory of several thousand works whose owners could not be traced after the war. It was given the number MNR 265.[59] According to officials, 'this fine copy' was presented to the Louvre in 1950 and now hangs in a corridor outside the office of the museum's director, Pierre Rosenberg.[60] The questions persist, however. If it was not the genuine article, was the presence of the fake *Mona Lisa* in the Nazis' Austrian art cache the result of a clever piece of hoodwinking by the French looking to protect their state collections, or was it a result of one of the wartime trades between Parisian art officials and their counterparts in the Third Reich? Or even the outcome of a forced confiscation by Germans believing they had finally laid hands on the most famous painting in the world? And why did this picture alone return to Paris via Salzburg rather than Munich? Was there a particular need in this case to sidestep the usual procedures? The Louvre, the apparent authority on the matter, is not willing to say. After being prompted to respond to demands for information about the whereabouts of the *Mona Lisa*, they are refusing to explain how it – or a copy of it – ended up in a cold salt mine in the Alps.

What is not in doubt is the heroism of the four Austrians who rescued the mine and its priceless contents. And yet, considering their feats of bravery and the staggering value of the works of art which they saved, their reward was pitiful to the point of being insulting. All four received a suit of clothes; but SOE recommendations for a lump sum of cash for each man were lost in haggling with officials in other British government departments. The only member of the team known to have received any money was Josef Grafl, and he was paid the paltry sum of £45 instead of the recommended amount of £100. Standhartinger and Litzer both had their £100 payments deferred pending deliberation in London.[61] Albrecht Gaiswinkler received a glowing report for his performance as team leader. An appraisal of his service with SOE was entered on his hitherto secret records, stating: 'In view of success achieved, rousing and organising Austrian resisters and qualities shown in leading his party and organising Austrian civil life after the surrender, recommend on discharge: £250 (two hundred and fifty), 1 suit of clothes.'[62] Yet even his award was queried and it is not known how much he eventually received.

Recognition of his services was, however, forthcoming from elsewhere. Appointed bezirkshauptmann (district captain) after the war, he progressed through the civil service and eventually became a member of parliament for the Social Democratic party. He wrote a book about his experiences, *Sprung in die Freiheit* ('Jump into Freedom'), which was published but did not become a best-seller. He died in 1979, having received no significant reward from the British for his outstanding achievements during Operation Ebensburg and his success in rescuing many of Europe's principal art treasures from destruction. He was nominated for the award of the King's Medal,[63] a personal gift from the British sovereign, but that honour was apparently refused him.[64]

Standing in the garden of his neat cottage home in Bad Aussee, Josef Grafl bids the authors goodbye. As he shakes hands, he chuckles to himself. 'We didn't receive any pension after the war was over. Not from the British or the Austrians. You know, I could have got a bit more money but instead of getting paid at the end of our mission, I took my money weekly. I spent it as soon as I got it. I was young and I figured there would be no use for it if I died.

'The British offered me an army job later but I turned it down. Austria is free, I told them. I'm happy. All four of us remained in Austria. I saw Gaiswinkler from time to time but we hardly had anything to say to one another. I met up with the other two now and then; they had gone to live in Vienna. They're both dead as well now. A few years ago, I tried to get in touch with some of the others I had worked with through the British military during the war. There was no reaction.'

There was significantly more reaction in Herr Grafl's home village. Instead of being regarded as a hero, he found himself treated as an outcast for daring to assist the Allies. 'Many people would not even talk to me after the war because I was "an Englishman" to them. I couldn't make friends in Aussee because of what I had done. Whenever I walked into a bar, they would stop talking and say "here is the Englander".'

Even though the feats of Grafl, Gaiswinkler and their two compatriots were recognized by the Austrian government, the latter's response matched that of the British. 'After the war I just went back to work like before. I didn't get anything from the state. No thank you, no medal, no money.'

With that, Josef Grafl turns and gestures to the mountains which encircle the land around his house. 'It seems like we all stopped mattering when that job in the mine was done.'[65]

6

THE SWISS CONNECTION

While the mine at Alt Aussee was being emptied of its contents, in London Wing Commander Douglas Cooper, the head of the SHAEF MFA&A Branch's German Country Unit, was concentrating his attention elsewhere, directing his quest beyond the countries recently liberated from German occupation towards those neutral states where it was known that German assets had been concealed. One country in particular was of interest to him: Switzerland.

Since early 1943 the British and Americans had been receiving intelligence that the Germans had been covertly exporting vasts quantities of assets, in the form of gold, looted works of art, money and securities, to the neutral countries of Switzerland, Sweden, Spain and Portugal, and further afield to certain South American states such as Argentina. They had responded by setting up the Safehaven Programme: an operation to track down and monitor the movement in neutral countries of German assets which in many cases had been secreted in the vaults of banks. Principal among these havens for Nazi assets was Switzerland, whose geographical position, secretive banks, large German population and rail links with Germany made it the first choice of destination for Nazis seeking to extricate and conceal their ill-gotten gains. Furthermore, many German industrial concerns had Swiss subsidiaries which were used to export items such as aircraft and electrical components, chemicals and ammunition which were essential to the German war effort. Despite their officially neutral status, and despite Allied protests, the Swiss permitted the Germans to use their rail links to move troops and equipment to and from Italy. In return, the Germans supplied coal and steel which were in constant demand for Switzerland's industries.

During the latter part of the war, the British legation in Berne had kept a watchful eye out for confiscated works of art arriving in Switzerland and despatched regular reports to the Ministry of Economic Warfare and to the MFA&A Sub-Commission in London. At the beginning of 1945, Allied concern about looted works concealed in Switzerland was such that it was decided to send an MFA&A officer to carry out investigations there. Accordingly, after consultation between the Ministry of Economic Warfare and the War Office in London, SHAEF issued orders for Wing Commander Cooper to travel to Switzerland to carry out the task of tracking down looted works of art and to report on the extent to which the Swiss art trade was involved in dealing in them.

Cooper arrived in Berne on 17 February 1945 from Paris, where he had been carrying out investigations into the activities of the ERR in France. Making his way to the British legation, he made contact with the Commercial Counsellor, W. J. Sullivan, and his deputy, Jackson Smith, explaining that his mission was to carry out an investigation into looted works of art and their whereabouts in Switzerland.[1] In order to give him some official standing with the Swiss government, Cooper was appointed as a technical adviser to the British trade delegation which was at that time taking part in discussions with the Swiss on the delicate subject of Swiss–German economic relations. This appointment proved useful, later enabling him to keep himself informed about the proposals and measures agreed by the Swiss with regard to German assets in Switzerland. Moreover, his diplomatic status could only facilitate his task of tracking down stolen works of art.

The British, American and French delegations had been jointly conducting negotiations with the Swiss government over the question of German assets, including works of art, in Switzerland. As a result of these, it had been decided that all such assets would be 'frozen' by a Swiss decree which would make it impossible for them to be realized while still deposited in Switzerland. This measure would not, however, bring into the open any assets that were hidden; these would remain undetected unless the Allies could provide information as to their whereabouts. The Allies therefore also obtained the agreement of the Swiss government to order a census of all German assets in Switzerland to be carried out. It would be compulsory for all assets to be declared, and failure by any party to do so would be an offence under Swiss law. Moreover, the Swiss declared that they were willing to act immediately in cases where the Allies could inform them of any hidden deposits of works of art which had been smuggled into the country in contravention of Swiss law. The Allies were satisfied that these measures would prevent the export of looted works of art; but neither the freezing decree nor the census was ever implemented.

Having – as it then seemed – dealt with that particular problem, Cooper began the task of unearthing the missing paintings on his list known or suspected to be in Switzerland. He was armed with a considerable amount of information which had been gathered during the past year or so by the commercial section of the British legation, which had passed it to his intelligence section in the MFA&A Sub-Commission and to the Ministry of Economic Warfare. Cooper visited Basle, Berne, Lausanne, Lucerne and Zurich; for some unexplained reason, he was advised against going to Geneva. Among those whom he visited were a number of Swiss dealers suspected of having been involved in trading in looted works of art, including the proprietors of the Galeries Tanner, Neupert, Schmidlin, Gasser, Aktuaryus and Epoques in Zurich, the Galeries Fischer and Rosengart in Lucerne and the Galeries Bollag and Vallotten in Lausanne. As he was also representing the MFA&A Branch of the US Group of the Control Commission for Germany, and the French Restitution Commission, he made contact with the American legation and the French embassy and with the US and French trade delegations.[2]

One of the first to be questioned by Cooper on his involvement with looted pictures was Arthur Wiederkehr, a lawyer who lived in Zurich. He was found to be in possession of paintings left in his care by one of Göring's agents, Alois Miedl, who had been responsible for the purchase of the Goudstikker collection in the Netherlands. Under questioning, Wiederkehr stated that he had been in the Netherlands on several occasions during 1941 and 1942, and in the summer of the latter year had been introduced to Miedl by a close friend, Dr Lanz, who was the Swiss consul in Amsterdam.[3] As a result of that meeting, Wiederkehr had taken over the handling of Miedl's affairs in Switzerland, which had until then been handled by a Dr Wilhelm Frick, who also lived in Zurich. Frick was holding a number of pictures for Miedl and was instructed by the latter to send them to the Schweizer Bank Gesellschaft in Zurich, which in turn received instructions to hand them over to Wiederkehr. On the arrival of the pictures, Wiederkehr found the containers secured with the seals of the German legation in Berne.

The paintings, which had a total value of SwFr800,000, included *Marriage at Cana* by Jan Steen, from the Goudstikker collection; Cézanne's *Le Moulin*, which belonged to the Rothschild collection; *L'Homme à l'Oreille Coupée* by van Gogh, from the Paul Rosenberg collection; and *Nature Morte*, *Harlequin* and *Jeune Homme au Gilet Rouge*, all by Cézanne, also confiscated from the Paul Rosenberg collection.[4] Between 1942 and 1944 these pictures, which were stored in the vaults of the Volksbank in Zurich, were inspected only once, by Hans Wendland on the request of Alois Miedl. In late 1944 Miedl had telephoned Wiederkehr and asked him if he could make arrangements for the paintings to be sent to Spain; however, Wiederkehr had ignored this request and the pictures remained in Switzerland.[5] On being interviewed and questioned by Cooper, Wiederkehr admitted he was aware that the paintings had been smuggled into Switzerland via the German diplomatic bag. However, he maintained that he had not known they were looted works of art until he heard of the Bretton Woods conference announcement in July 1944, when his suspicions were aroused.

On 7 March Cooper continued his investigations by visiting the Lucerne gallery of Theodor Fischer, who had been identified by the British legation in Berne as one of a number of dealers engaged in transactions involving looted works of art. Cooper confronted Fischer and was shown a list of forty-two works including paintings and drawings by Corot, Monet, Rousseau, Renoir, Degas, Manet, Sisley and van Gogh. Cooper identified the majority as belonging to the Rosenberg collection, with others belonging to the Levy-Benzion, Alphonse Kann and Bernheim-Jeune collections. A small number of paintings belonging to individuals, including Miriam de Rothschild and two British nationals, Alfred Linden and Peter Watson, who had both lived in France, were also among them.[6]

Fischer denied knowing that the items were looted and that he or his gallery had been involved in the auction or sale of any such items. He also maintained that he was an expert in antiques and tapestries, rather than paintings and drawings, and thus was unaware of either the value or the origin of the items in question until they were examined by an expert. Cooper knew that he was lying; he was well aware that as early as 1939 Fischer had been disposing of 'degenerate' works of art on behalf of the Nazis. On inspecting Fischer's records, Cooper saw that a few of the looted pictures had already been sold, but that a total of thirty-one were still in the gallery's possession. He instructed Fischer not to dispose of any more.[7]

From Switzerland Cooper moved on to Italy, where he continued his investigative work before returning to England at the end of March. During the following months, prior to his next visit to Switzerland, he amassed further evidence relating to Swiss dealings in looted works of art, including documentary proof of visits by Theodor Fischer and Hans Wendland to the headquarters of the Stabsamt Göring in Berlin to select paintings for payment in kind from the Reichsmarschall. This evidence included a number of invoices covering transactions between Fischer and Göring.[8] In September, on his way back to Switzerland, Cooper travelled to

Austria where he visited the special interrogation centre established by the OSS ALIU at Bad Aussee. Among those detained here were several of the individuals who had played principal roles in the looting of Europe's art collections, including Robert Scholz, chief art adviser to Alfred Rosenberg; Bruno Lohse, the ERR art historian and member of the Arbeitsgruppe Louvre, and one of Göring's agents; Günther Schiedlausky, another leading member of the ERR who had been responsible for a number of its repositories; Walter Andreas Hofer, Göring's principal agent (somewhat cumbersomely entitled Direktor der Kunstsammlungen des Reichsmarschalls); Gustav Rochlitz, the German art dealer responsible for many of the transactions involving the export of looted art to Switzerland; Karl Kress, one of the ERR's photographers; Gisela Limberger, Göring's personal secretary; Walter Bornheim, one of the buyers for the Göring collection; and Hermann Voss, the Sonderbeauftrager of Sonderauftrag Linz.[9]

Cooper's interrogation of Hofer proved to be a lengthy process, with the German trying to give the impression that his role was merely one of advising Göring on purchases for his collection and denying that he had played any part in selecting works of art from confiscated collections. Eventually, however, when confronted by evidence in the form of his own letters to Göring, Hofer admitted that he had done so. In one letter he described how he had offered the painter Georges Braque the possibility of a speedy release of his confiscated collection in return for selling Göring his Cranach, which Hofer knew Braque would never willingly relinquish. In another letter Hofer had advised Göring to take certain paintings from the Rothschild collections and had drawn his attention to their large collections of jewellery.[10]

Hofer also tried to deny any knowledge of the exchanges conducted between Göring and the ERR; but documents produced by the OSS interrogators, concerning the exchange between the Reichsmarschall and the French Jewish dealer Allen Loebl of a painting by Utrillo from the Bernheim-Jeune collection for the art library of the Kleinberger gallery in Paris, bore Hofer's signature.[11] Furthermore, the OSS possessed firm evidence of the fact that it was Hofer who had selected the paintings from the Rosenberg collection for the exchange with Wendland described below, and that it was to him that ERR staff at the Schloss Neuschwanstein repository had handed confiscated Impressionist paintings for the exchange with Theodor Fischer.[12]

During the last days of his interrogation, Hofer admitted that he had enjoyed a close business relationship with Wendland, who had been his principal agent in Switzerland. Further evidence of this was found in his account book, which provided Cooper and the OSS interrogators with much useful information about the transactions in which he had engaged. Wendland had apparently supplied Hofer with Swiss francs from Göring without the latter being aware of it. When Wendland had a painting for sale which he had acquired in Paris, Hofer would inform Göring that it had come from Switzerland for acquisition and that it had to be paid for in Swiss francs. (No one outside German-occupied territory would deal in the Reichskassenscheine or invasion mark.) Five paintings were sold to Göring in this manner: *The Betrothal* by Lucas van Leyden; *Adoration of the Magi* by Lucas Cranach the Elder; *The Madonna Painted by St Luke* by a follower of Roger van der Weyden; and *Portrait of Suzanne Fourment* by the school of Rubens.[13] Hofer also admitted that he had conducted business in Switzerland with Theodor Fischer, most of it being connected in some way with Wendland who acted as the Swiss dealer's agent in the selection of Impressionist paintings offered for exchange by Göring. Hofer stated that Fischer had paid him commissions, sometimes through marking up the prices of paintings sold to the Reichsmarschall, such as *Madonna and Child* by Montagna, *The Last Supper* by Lucas Cranach the Elder and *St Magdalen* by the Master of the Female Half-Lengths.[14] By assembling such information, extracted from Hofer during his interrogation, Cooper managed to put together an accurate picture of the various transactions which had culminated in the secret and illegal export of looted works of art to Switzerland.

As mentioned in chapter 3, Göring appointed a French artist, Professor Jacques Beltrand, as an 'official appraiser' to represent the French government in valuing any works which he wished to acquire, the idea being that any payments for such items would be placed in a special fund to be held by the French government. Once the Reichsmarschall had made his choice from the 'exhibitions' of confiscated collections at the Musée du Jeu de Paume organized for him by the ERR, a list of the selected items was drawn up by either Hofer or von Behr, and Beltrand would then appraise the items concerned. The list would then be sent to Göring's headquarters in Berlin for filing against future payment. In practice, however, this system was ignored. Hofer, on behalf of Göring, would always disagree with Beltrand over his appraisals and would persuade him to reduce his valuations by at least 50 per cent; the works of art would be packed in the Musée du Jeu de Paume and removed at once to one of the Reichsmarschall's special trains without any payment being made. Göring's excuse was that he always preferred to have his acquisitions accompany him back to Germany. In two and a half years, during which he paid twenty visits to the Musée du Jeu de Paume, Göring had acquired some 700 works of art for his collection in this fashion. No payment had ever been made for any of them.

Hofer went on to tell Cooper that (as mentioned in chapter 2) the ERR had carried out a total of twenty-eight exchanges of looted works of art between February 1941 and the end of 1943. A number of these had involved Hofer himself, Hans Wendland, Gustav Rochlitz and Theodor Fischer. In February 1941 Hofer had chosen a number of works of art in the Galerie Fischer in Lucerne, and these had been despatched to the Reichsmarschall's palace at Karinhall. Initially Göring had agreed to pay in Swiss francs, but subsequently had decided that payment would be effected by exchange. Fischer had agreed to this arrangement, stating that he would accept French Impressionist pictures. In mid-July Fischer had visited Göring's Stabsamt headquarters in Berlin, where he was shown a selection of paintings and had agreed to the deal. The export of paintings, however, required an export permit from the Reichskammer der Bildenden Kunste (Reich Office for Pictorial Arts). Fischer had agreed to obtain such a permit and to arrange transport to Switzerland, his application supported by an official document from the Stabsamt Göring which had stated that the export was being carried out on behalf of the Reichsmarschall.

In this exchange, Fischer had supplied six pictures: four by Cranach the Elder – *Madonna and Child in a Landscape, Crucifixion with a Knight as Donor, St Anne and The Virgin, Portrait of a Bearded Kurfurst* – along with a triptych by a Frankfurt master and a sculpture of a female saint of the Nuremberg School. In return, Fischer had received twenty-five Impressionist paintings, including four Corots, four Degas, three Sisleys, and two van Goghs. The other works were by Cottet, Courbet, Daubigny, Daumier, Lucas, Manet, Monnier, Renoir, Rousseau, Rodin and an anonymous artist. These paintings had previously formed parts of the Levy-Benzion and Alphonse Kann collections, with the exception of one, *Flowers in a Vase* by van Gogh, which was from the Lindon collection.[15]

The second direct exchange had been carried out between Göring and Wendland, with Hofer once again playing the role of negotiator during a visit to Switzerland in November 1941. Wendland had supplied Göring with a painting by Rembrandt, *Portrait of an Old Man with a Beard*, which he had purchased from a Frenchman in

Marseilles in 1941, and two sixteenth-century Brussels tapestries after cartoons by Lucas van Leyden. These latter items had been presented by Napoleon in 1808 to the Princess de Franceville of the Château de Bezanos, near Pau, where Wendland had purchased them. In this instance Göring had agreed to pay SwFr250,000 in cash into one of Wendland's accounts in Switzerland, this representing half the sum owed, with the balance being payable in the form of twenty-five Impressionist paintings; these included four Corots, four Degas, two Ingres, four Renoirs, three Seurats and two Sisleys, the remaining individual works being by Courbet, Daumier, Manet, van Gogh, Monet and Pissarro. All were from the Paul Rosenberg collection with the exception of one painting, a small landscape by van Gogh, which belonged to the Miriam Rothschild collection.[16] They had been acquired by Göring from the ERR in September and December 1941 during two of his frequent visits to the Musée du Jeu de Paume.

On this occasion, the pictures had not been officially imported into Switzerland. In early 1942 Wendland travelled to Berlin, where he made his selection at the headquarters of Göring's Stabsamt. In April, at his suggestion and with Göring's agreement, the paintings were sent to Switzerland via the German diplomatic bag and accompanied by a courier. Hofer also travelled with the consignment and, on its arrival at the German legation in Berne, took delivery of it from the head of the legation's courier section, an individual named Riekmann. Hofer then took the paintings to Lucerne, where he delivered them to Wendland.

Indirect exchanges had also been effected: this involved the ERR in Paris supplying pictures, on instructions from Göring's headquarters in Berlin, in order to acquire other works of art for the Reichsmarschall. According to Hofer, the first of these transactions had involved Hans Wendland and Gustav Rochlitz, in liaison with the ERR in Paris. Hofer told Cooper that Wendland and Rochlitz had supplied two pictures, *Portrait of a Bearded Man* by a north Italian artist (possibly Titian) and *Hunting Still Life* by Jan Weenix, which were jointly owned by the two men and Birtschansky, the Parisian art dealer. In exchange the ERR, on behalf of Göring, had supplied eleven pictures selected by Hofer in the Musée du Jeu de Paume, his choice being approved by Göring, which included three Matisses and two Picassos. The other six were paintings by Braque, Cézanne, Corot, Degas, Renoir and Sisley. All were from the Paul Rosenberg collection except for the Braque, *Still Life with Grapes and Peaches*, and the Degas, *Madame Camus au Piano*, which belonged to the

Alphonse Kann collection. Wendland had subsequently bought out Birtschansky's interest and had received the Braque, Corot, Degas and the three Matisses as his share of the proceeds. All these paintings also eventually found their way to Switzerland and the Galerie Fischer.[17]

The revelations which resulted from the interrogation of Hofer raised several questions in Douglas Cooper's mind with regard to the role played by Fischer, who had eventually acquired all the Impressionist paintings received as payment by Wendland and Rochlitz as well as those which he received directly from Göring. Cooper suspected Fischer not only of holding money and further works of art belonging to Wendland, but also of holding funds for a large number of Germans resident in Switzerland and elsewhere. He had also obtained evidence that Fischer had sold to Göring, in addition to the transactions already mentioned, works of art of a total value of SwFr1.142 million. Many of the pictures sold to Göring by Fischer were procured for the latter by his agent, Carl Bümming, an art dealer in Darmstadt in Germany.[18]

Cooper also learned from Hofer that Fischer had maintained very close connections with two other Swiss galleries known to have dealt with looted works of art: the Galerie Schmidlin and the Galerie Neupert, both located in Zurich. Other Swiss dealers who also sold paintings to Göring and Hofer included the Galerie Giese in Zurich and the Galerie Schulthess in Basle.

The interrogation of Hofer and of some of the other individuals detained at Bad Aussee confirmed Cooper's suspicions that a large number of dealers and other individuals had been involved in the export of looted works of art to Switzerland. Principal among these was Hans Wendland, who was living at that time at Bois d'Avault, Bellevue, near Geneva. Before the war, Wendland had played a key role in arranging many exchanges of pictures between German art dealers and their counterparts and museums in London, Paris, Switzerland and New York. With a large number of contacts among dealers in several countries throughout Europe, he had an extensive knowledge of the contents of major private collections. Between 1940 and 1943, while living in Switzerland, he made a number of expeditions to France, Germany and Italy to acquire works of art.

During the war Wendland's main business was acquiring looted works of art and importing them into Switzerland. In November 1942 he took delivery of a large consignment which arrived from Paris in a railway wagon which it had filled completely. This had been cleared for import through a Lausanne-based firm of freight forwarding agents called Lavanchy.[19] When he moved from Lucerne to Geneva in 1944, Wendland took two van-loads from Lucerne and one from Basle, all of which were reported as having contained works of art which had arrived from Italy in early November of the previous year.

Cooper discovered that Wendland had acted as principal purchasing and commission agent for Theodor Fischer in negotiating deals over looted pictures with Hofer. Wendland had known Fischer since 1931, when the latter had rescued him from major financial difficulties by advancing him a large credit. Both men had financial interests in the majority of each other's transactions; in the case of the deals with Hofer, the bartered works of art belonged jointly to both of them.

Wendland was directly involved on his own account in at least one major direct exchange of pictures with Göring, this being the transaction negotiated by Hofer in November 1941, mentioned above, in which *Portrait of an old Man with a Beard* by Rembrandt and two tapestries were exchanged for twenty-five Impressionist paintings from the Paul Rosenberg and Miriam Rothschild collections. This consignment was included in the same shipment as another smaller one which comprised pictures featuring in a direct exchange between Göring and the Galerie Fischer. In this instance, Theodor Fischer had supplied three sixteenth-century Brussels tapestries depicting *Scenes from the Life of Scipio*. In return, he received *Girl in Red Bodice* by Corot, a seascape by Monet and *Landscape with Orchard* by Sisley. All three paintings were from the Paul Rosenberg collection and had been selected by Wendland at the headquarters of the Stabsamt Göring.[20]

As noted above, Cooper learned that a number of indirect exchanges had also taken place in which Göring or Hitler was represented by the ERR. In one particular instance, Wendland had been in partnership with another individual heavily involved in the illegal export of looted works of art from France to Switzerland: Gustav Rochlitz. A notoriously dishonest art dealer based in Paris and Baden-Baden, Rochlitz worked closely with the ERR – so closely, indeed, that his participation in looting activities had been officially authorized: like several of Göring's agents, he had been issued with documents which confirmed that 'Herr Rochlitz is employed by arrangement with the Office for the Protection of Works of Art of the Headquarters of the Supreme Military Commander in France, for the purchase of important works of art for German museums, as well as for high officials of the State and

Party. All authorities are requested to offer him the maximum of assistance in the carrying out of his mission.'[21] In mid-July 1944 Rochlitz had despatched 200 cases of paintings from Paris to Switzerland by train.[22] Despite the efforts of Cooper and other Allied investigators, these were never found.

A number of other indirect exchanges had also taken place between Swiss individuals or galleries and the ERR, but these involved fewer paintings, normally only two or three. Among these transactions was an exchange between the Galerie Neupert of Zurich, representing Alfred Boedecker, an art dealer in Frankfurt, and the ERR, acting on behalf of Hitler. The gallery supplied *Painter Seated on Bough of Tree* by Ludwig Knaus (estimated value SwFr10,000) and received *Girl with a Fishing Net* by Renoir (estimated value SwFr35,000), one of the large number of paintings confiscated from the Paul Rosenberg collection. The actual exchange took place at Basle railway station, on the German side of the frontier, on 7 April 1943. In due course the Renoir was sold to the Galerie Tanner, also of Zurich, which in turn sold it to a Swiss collector.[23]

Cooper discovered that paintings had also changed hands in a number of cash transactions involving the Galerie Fischer, Hofer and Wendland. Between December 1940 and December 1942, the value of such deals between Fischer and Hofer totalled SwFr1,133,930. Transactions between Hofer and Wendland during the period from 1940 to January 1944 reached a total value of FFr7,420,000 and SwFr258,000.[24]

Throughout the war, both Wendland and Hofer had made frequent use of the German diplomatic bag for the secure transportation of looted works of art into Switzerland. In this they were assisted by the commercial attaché at the German legation in Berne, Helmut Beyer, who conveyed the pictures across the German frontier into Switzerland. Another German official involved in this traffic was Adolf Wüster, the art adviser at the German embassy in Paris tasked with keeping the German elite informed of all major works of art which were for sale in the French capital. Wüster, who had lived in Paris for a number of years and was well known as a dealer and collector, had paid frequent visits to Basle, Zurich, Lucerne and Berne. He handled sales of works of art on behalf of the German foreign ministry, as well as for other government and Nazi party agencies, and acted as agent for the foreign minister, Joachim von Ribbentrop. He had also purchased pictures for German museums from Swiss dealers, offering them looted works of art from France.

He was reported to have offered the Bernheim-Jeune collection, confiscated from the Paris-based firm of art dealers which had been forcibly purchased by the Germans, to the Galerie Tanner in Zurich for SwFr1 million.[25] In October 1944 Wüster was transferred to the German embassy in Madrid where, among other things, he was entrusted with the task of decorating the embassy interior with works of art.

During his investigations Cooper received a considerable amount of assistance from British diplomats in Switzerland, who had previously identified a number of individuals involved in the traffic in looted art. Among them was a Swiss named Steinemann, who lived in Zurich and at the Clinica San Rocco in Lugano. On 6 April 1944 he was reported by the British consulate general in Zurich as having offered for sale five pictures from the Jaffe collection. Four of them were identified as *Portrait of a Lady* by Goya, *Woman Spinning* by Velázquez, *A Doge* by Titian and a landscape by Constable. The fifth picture remained unidentified but was reported to be by van Dyck. Four and a half months later, on 22 August, the British vice consul in Lucerne had reported that Steinemann was offering between 100 and 200 pictures for sale.[26]

As he continued his enquiries, Cooper discovered that high-ranking officials representing German museums had made a number of visits to Switzerland during the war for the purpose of procuring works of art. Among them were Hans Posse and Herman Voss, who took part in transactions involving stolen pictures in Zurich, Basle and Geneva. Voss was reported as having brought into Switzerland a picture by van Dyck which belonged to the Jaffe collection. Dr Kurt Martin, Director of the Karlsruhe Museum and director of all museums in Alsace, and Dr Otto Förster, Director of the Wallraf-Richartz Museum in Cologne, also made appearances on a number of occasions.[27]

From his investigations, Cooper concluded that none of the Swiss museums had acquired looted works of art during the war. However, he had found evidence confirming that considerable quantities of paintings had found their way to Switzerland, although it was impossible to estimate the numbers accurately. He was certain, however, that the majority of the looted works of art from France which he found in Switzerland had been imported from Germany. Official Swiss government figures for the import of works of art during the period 1939–44 showed that imports from France had declined steadily, while those from Germany in 1941 and 1943 had increased dramatically. A report by the US Government Foreign

Economic Administration (Enemy Branch), compiled in August 1945, put the estimated total value of pictures deposited by Germans in Switzerland, together with those looted works of art found in the possession of Swiss dealers, at between SwFr100 million and SwFr350 million.[28]

While he had received several reports from French and Swiss sources that works of art had been smuggled into Switzerland via Geneva, as opposed to being openly imported, Cooper had been unable to obtain firm proof of this other than evidence relating to pictures brought into the country via the German diplomatic bag. However, he learned that individuals other than those principals already mentioned had been involved in smuggling looted works of art from Germany into Switzerland. Among these was a German named Emil Zaunkeller, who lived 25 kilometres from Basle, on the German side of the border, and who was known to have received large quantities of looted works of art from Paris.[29] Another was Carlos Jahn, who lived in Lugano. A German, and known as a fanatical Nazi, Jahn was engaged in the sale in Switzerland of a number of paintings looted by the Germans in Italy, where he had two agents, unfortunately identified only as 'Cornelius' and 'Henrick', who lived in Milan.[30]

Yet another German national involved in similar activity was a woman named Frau Dr Schwegler, who occasionally resided in Zurich and was said to have been a friend of Himmler. She had extensive dealings with a Swiss named Vassali, who was reported to have arrived there in April 1945 from Germany with several trucks containing a large number of works of art, and to have established a partnership with a Swiss named Schmidlin, the owner of the Galerie Schmidlin in Zurich. Schmidlin was subsequently questioned but insisted that the paintings were the property of Frau Dr Schwegler who, he claimed, had imported them into Germany from Italy. However, his story was not believed by Cooper who interrogated him further.[31]

Cooper also discovered that a group of Germans had been engaged in smuggling works of art, along with other valuables and securities, out of France into Switzerland. This group was headed by an individual named Carl Moritz Bunge, who had lived in the Swiss canton of Tessin for six years. Previously based in Buenos Aires, Bunge had been a manager for the Hamburg-America shipping line, and during the war he had travelled frequently between Switzerland, Italy and France. Information about Bunge gathered by the Allied legations in Berne indicated that he maintained accounts at several banks, including the Crédit Suisse in Zurich, the Banca della Svizzera Italiana in Lugano and an unidentified Swiss bank in Buenos Aires. Other members of Bunge's group included Fritz Schmidt, a German living in Lugano, another German named Scheit, also resident in Lugano and treasurer of the local branch of the Nazi party, and the Comte de Mileant, a German national of Russian descent living in Switzerland.[32]

Despite his success in tracking down these and other individuals, Cooper had been unable to determine the fate of the vast majority of the works of art looted by the Nazis, other than those discovered in the possession of Swiss galleries and individuals, once they reached Switzerland. His own opinion was that they were in the vaults of Swiss banks or in the possession of freight forwarding agents. His task as an investigator was made all the more difficult by the fact that any items, including looted works of art, could be exported from Germany into Switzerland and stored in free-ports, known as Zollfreilager, for up to five years under the name of the company or individual to whom they had been consigned, without being classified as imports.[33] Cooper was, however, able to track down a number of looted paintings to one location: the collection of Emil Bührle, the head of the Swiss family which owned the famous armaments company Oerlikon-Bührle whose aircraft cannon and anti-aircraft guns saw service with forces on both sides during the war.

Bührle, a keen and well-known collector, was approached in early 1941 by a Swiss named Kaspar, of the Galerie des Beaux Arts in Zurich, who suggested that he might be interested in an opportunity to acquire a complete collection of Italian, Flemish and Spanish Old Masters of varying quality which belonged to a collector in Berlin. Bührle subsequently bought the collection for SwFr110,000, keeping fifty of the paintings and selling a half-share in the remainder to Theodor Fischer for SwFr60,000. This jointly owned portion was eventually sold for a handsome profit at auction for SwFr180,000, leaving Bührle in credit with Fischer to the tune of SwFr90,000.[34]

In September 1941 Bührle travelled to Paris; here he met the dealer Charles Montag, who introduced him to Roger Dequoy, the head of Dequoy et Cie – the 'Aryanized' Galerie Wildenstein. Bührle made five purchases from Dequoy: a landscape and a portrait of a nude by Renoir, a self-portrait by David, and two portraits of men by Greuze and Titian respectively. These were left on deposit with Dequoy pending arrangements for their despatch to Zurich. During questioning by Cooper, Bührle maintained that it was during his visit to Dequoy et Cie that he met Hans Wendland for the first time.[35]

It was after his return to Zurich that Bührle was visited by Theodor Fischer, who informed him that there were a number of French paintings, obtained from German museums, in the Galerie Fischer which might be of interest to him. Bührle consulted a friend, who had serious doubts about the paintings' provenance, and his lawyer, who warned him that if the paintings were German loot he could face problems in the future over his ownership rights. Bührle chose to ignore this advice, however, and in December 1941 acquired five paintings from Fischer.

In May of the following year Bührle received a visit from Wendland, who told him that Fischer was in possession of more French paintings of even greater quality and importance than those which he had already purchased. Ignorant of the fact that these new paintings belonged to Wendland, Bührle travelled to Fischer's gallery in Lucerne, where he made some further selections. While doing so, he mentioned to Wendland that the five paintings which he had purchased in Paris were still with Dequoy et Cie and that he wanted to bring them to Zurich. A few weeks later Bührle was told that the Director of the Karlsruhe Museum, Kurt Martin, had taken the Titian to a place of safety and that the four other paintings had been moved to Berlin. Later still, to Bührle's great surprise, the Renoir landscape and the self-portrait by David were delivered to his house. Unbeknown to him, they had been brought into Switzerland by train, via the German diplomatic bag, and delivered by Hofer.[36] The other three paintings remained in Germany until Bührle wrote to his lawyer in Berlin and asked him to expedite their despatch to Zurich. In August 1944 the paintings arrived in Basle, accompanied by Bührle's lawyer, where they were impounded by the Swiss customs because there was no import licence with them. Bührle wasted little time in using his influence, contacting Dr Vodoz of the Department of Interior in Berne and a senior officer of the Swiss customs service. Shortly afterwards the paintings were permitted to enter the country and were placed in Zurich's free-port.[37] Bührle's troubles were not over yet, however, and he faced further problems in obtaining the paintings' release. Nevertheless, once again his influence with the Department of Interior, together with an undertaking to present the Titian to the city's Kunstmuseum, paid off and eventually he was able to place the three paintings with the rest of his collection.

Not long before Cooper's return to Switzerland in September 1945 to continue his investigations, Bührle had received a visit from Paul Rosenberg, the owner of two of the collections confiscated by von Behr's ERR and of several of the paintings still in Bührle's possession. So slow was the progress made by the Swiss government in investigating the presence of looted works of art in Switzerland, despite information passed to it by the Allies, that Rosenberg had decided to pursue his own investigations and track down his missing paintings himself. Rosenberg accused Bührle of having acquired the paintings in the full knowledge that they had been looted by the Germans. Bührle offered to return them to Theodor Fischer, from whom he had bought them, on the condition that he was refunded in full. When confronted by Rosenberg, Fischer lied, stating that he had been given the paintings by Hofer as payment in kind and that, having discovered them to be loot, had attempted to return them to Germany but had been unable to do so. Despite a proposal that he should receive payment in full, and subsequently an offer that he should be given back three-quarters of his paintings, Rosenberg insisted that any settlement should be negotiated between the Swiss and French governments.

Not long after Rosenberg's visit, Douglas Cooper also called on Bührle. Under questioning, the Swiss collector admitted that he had purchased paintings from Fischer, to whom he had been introduced by Wendland. He also told Cooper that he had been warned by both his lawyer and his art adviser of the consequences of buying paintings which could have been looted, but had chosen to disregard this advice. Cooper ended the interview by advising Bührle to hand over the paintings to the Swiss government, to whom the Allies would shortly be passing the evidence accumulated on Swiss involvement in the traffic in looted art. Bührle agreed to do so within a matter of days.

Cooper's return to Switzerland also enabled him to interview Hans Wendland in person, which he did on three occasions at the latter's home. Wendland, a German national, had fallen foul of the Swiss authorities because he did not possess a work permit to enable him to conduct his business as an art dealer, and consequently carried out all his transactions through Theodor Fischer and the Galerie Fischer in Lucerne, only selling directly to a few private clients who could be relied upon for their discretion.[38] Under questioning from Cooper, Wendland admitted to selecting looted works of art at a Berlin apartment belonging to Hofer. These were the pictures which were eventually delivered to the Galerie Fischer. He also admitted that he knew they had come from Göring, having been told as much by

Hofer, and that he was aware that they were items which had previously formed part of confiscated collections. Wendland told Cooper that none of the works of art which he had brought into Switzerland had been officially imported.[39]

During these interviews, Wendland gave Cooper details of some of the deals which he had made in Paris during the war, and in doing so revealed some of his main contacts. Among these had been the French industrialist and collaborator Achille Boitel. A fluent German-speaker, Boitel had acted as an interpreter for the Germans during the initial stages of the occupation of the French capital in 1940 and had enjoyed excellent relations with them – as witnessed by his ability to obtain any permits he might require from the German authorities. Wendland told Cooper that he was almost certain Boitel had worked for the Gestapo.[40] Boitel had financed several of Wendland's deals and kept most of the latter's funds in France for him, often buying and selling gold on his behalf. By the end of the war he had disappeared; as mentioned in chapter 3, he was later said to have been killed by the Resistance. According to Wendland, Boitel should have been in possession of FFr10 million belonging to him; however, when a friend of Wendland's made enquiries on his behalf, he was told by Boitel's son-in-law that there was no trace of the money. Wendland considered this to be highly unlikely.

When questioned by Cooper as to his relationship with Hugo Engel, the Paris-based art dealer who had assisted Karl Haberstock to rescue the Wildenstein collection from the clutches of the ERR, Wendland claimed that he did not know him at all well. Under further questioning, however, he admitted that he had commissioned Engel to retrieve money and further pictures from eight individuals in Paris who were keeping them for him.[41]

One unwelcome surprise for Cooper on his return to Switzerland was the discovery that, since his previous visit in March, no steps had been taken by the Swiss authorities to seize any of the looted works of art notified to them by the Allies. Nor, as mentioned previously, had they implemented the decree freezing German assets in Switzerland or carried out the promised census. This was in despite of the fact that they had, along with representatives of the British, French and American governments, signed an agreement on 8 March stating:

> The Swiss government on its behalf and that of the Principality of Lichtenstein affirms its decision to prevent the territory of Switzerland and of the Principality from being used for the disposal, concealment or

reception of assets which may have been taken illegally or under duress during the war. It declares furthermore that, in the framework of the Swiss legislation as it stands today, or as it will be completed in the future, every facility will be given to the dispossessed owners to claim in Switzerland and Lichtenstein their assets found there.[42]

The Allies understood this agreement to mean that the Swiss would take measures to prevent the disposal or concealment of loot in Switzerland, and that owners of such items would be permitted to claim them. The Swiss, however, did not regard the agreement in the same light, arguing that Articles 934, 935 and 936 of the 1907 Swiss Code of Law, augmented by a special decree concerning restitution of objects looted in German-occupied territories, provided full facilities for dispossessed owners to recover their possessions. The three articles in question stated that a dispossessed owner could, during a period of five years from the loss, submit a claim against the holder of the lost items concerned if the latter had acquired them in bad faith. However, if the items had been acquired at auction, in a market or from a dealer specializing in that category of goods, the claim had to be accompanied by payment of the sum for which they had been purchased. The special decree, signed on 20 August 1945, stated that a dispossessed owner could apply to a cantonal court, in the canton in which the looted items had been located, for a temporary sequestration pending the preparation of a legal case in which a claim would be submitted. However, the dispossessed owner had to show proof of dispossession and no sequestration would be granted without a defence being heard. A period of six months was permitted to elapse between the demand and the commencement of proceedings but, if no lawsuit was commenced within that period, the sequestration was automatically suspended.[43]

In effect, this meant that dispossessed owners of looted paintings were responsible for making separate claims against those individuals holding their possessions and had to bear the costs of such proceedings. Moreover, the implication was that owners had to prove that purchasers had acquired items in bad faith, and that they would be liable to pay compensation. In all probability, any claims would be met by endless legal delays while the holders of the disputed paintings exercised their rights of appeal. Moreover, it appeared that the Swiss federal government itself would play no role in respect of claims for the restitution of looted material.

This situation was unacceptable to the Allied representatives on the joint delegation conducting negotiations with the Swiss. Accordingly, they asked Cooper for his assistance in negotiating a solution to the problem. At their request, he prepared an official list of seventy-six paintings, belonging to eight different collections looted by the Germans, which were known to be in the hands of nineteen galleries and individuals in Switzerland.[44] On 12 October 1945 copies of the list were sent to the Swiss Federal Political Department by representatives of the British, French and American delegations. They were accompanied by letters requesting immediate action by the Swiss government to seize and impound looted works of art in accordance with the agreement of 8 March 1945. On the following day, further letters were sent to the Federal Political Department, requesting that the businesses of sixteen Swiss individuals connected with the traffic of looted works of art be suspended forthwith, pending investigation of all works of art which had passed through their hands since 1940.

Almost immediately Cooper, through the Director of the Kunstmuseum in Berne, Max Huggler, was asked to attend an informal meeting with the Federal Political Department to discuss what action could be taken by the Swiss government with regard to restitution of looted works of art which had found their way into Switzerland. The meeting was chaired by Dr Vodoz of the Department of Interior – the official who had previously assisted Emil Bührle to import his looted works of art into Switzerland. His department was at that time dealing with the whole question of loot and restitution as it affected the Swiss economy. It was announced that the Swiss government had produced a draft constitution for a special commission, to be established under the aegis of the Department of Interior, but that no decision had been made as to the extent of its powers or on whether it would deal with German assets as a whole or only looted works of art.[45]

At Vodoz's request, Cooper briefed those present on looted works of art in Switzerland. He gave details of the seventy-six identified works on the list sent to the Federal Political Department, emphasizing that the list had to be considered incomplete as he had already discovered other paintings which he suspected to have been looted. Asked whether he possessed documentary evidence, he assured the Swiss that he did indeed and produced some sample reports for them to inspect.

The first of these named a Swiss sculptor, André Martin, who lived in Zurich. Cooper possessed evidence that Martin had been in possession of three looted pictures which he had acquired from the dealer Max Stöcklin, who had obtained a number of paintings from the ERR in Paris and from Gustav Rochlitz. The three paintings concerned were *M. et Mme Ramel* by Ingres from the Rosenberg collection; *Eventuellement* by Janino; and *Liseuse* by Simon Bernard Lenoir. The Ingres and Janino had subsequently been put on sale by the Galerie Neupert in Zurich.[46] Cooper then produced evidence incriminating Dr Willi Raeber, a dealer who was also treasurer of the Federation of Swiss Art Dealers. Raeber had handled four looted paintings: *Stilleben* by Braque; *Liseuse* by Corot; *Fleurs dans un Vase* by van Gogh, from either the Rosenberg or Bernheim collections; and *L'Homme au Chapeau Haut de Forme* by Ingres, from the Rosenberg collection.[47]

Another individual named by Cooper was Dr Alexander von Frey who, as mentioned in chapter 2, was a German with Hungarian nationality. Living in Lucerne, von Frey had been involved in frequent transactions with the Germans and had been in regular contact with Karl Haberstock and Adolf Wüster. He had acquired four paintings from the ERR: *Portrait of a Lady* by Goya, from the Jaffe collection; *Portrait of Grafin N. Pilsach-Soln* by Anton Graff; *L'Homme au Chapeau Haut de Forme* by Ingres; and *Man with a Pipe* by van Gogh.[48] Cooper also produced evidence implicating another Swiss, George Schmidt of Zurich, who had received a Matisse, *Intérieur à Nice*, from a bank in Suisse Romande and subsequently had put it up for sale through the Galerie Aktuaryus. This painting had been one of a large number which had been exchanged between the ERR and Gustav Rochlitz, but Cooper had been unable to discover how it had entered Switzerland.[49]

Cooper also named three galleries. The first was the Galerie Neupert in Zurich which had received, among a number of looted paintings, *Paysage en Hauteur avec Arbres* by Lenoir from the Germans on behalf of an unidentified dealer, taking delivery of it at Basle railway station. When subsequently selling it on to the Galerie Tanner, Neupert himself gave a guarantee stating that he had purchased the painting from a Swiss private collection before the war. Cooper had also found Neupert to be in possession of photographs of a number of nineteenth-century French paintings which had passed through the gallery's hands after 1940.[50]

Having heard Cooper's evidence, Vodoz summarized the Swiss position. While it accepted the joint Allied approach, the Swiss government was not prepared to use its powers for the sake of seventy-six paintings. In other words, it was not prepared to amend the 1907 Code of Law, or to circumvent it in any way. Vodoz suggested that the Allies appoint a Swiss lawyer to represent all the dispossessed owners in the cantonal courts to which they would have to apply for sequestration of the paintings in question. If this were granted, the Allies' lawyer would then submit a list of pictures to the newly established commission which would act as a mediating body. In the event of the commission failing in its task of negotiation, the Allies' lawyer would have to take legal action against the Swiss galleries and individuals in possession of the paintings.

Cooper raised the question of the five-year time limit for claims, bearing in mind that the pictures had been confiscated from their owners by the Germans in 1940. Vodoz admitted that this had caused his government some concern but pointed out that, under Article 936, there was no limitation of time in cases where items had been acquired in bad faith.[51] Cooper also asked about future research in respect of pictures whose identities and locations in Switzerland were still unknown to the Allies. Vodoz informed him that the special commission would have powers to pursue enquiries on its own and at the request of the Allies. If looted items were discovered, the information would be passed to the lawyer representing the Allies who would then have to take action as already discussed. At this point Max Huggler expressed his misgivings, saying that he believed that only a central commission with full powers of sequestration, adjudication and restitution could deal with the problem effectively. Vodoz replied that such an arrangement would be impossible and that sequestration had to be applied for by the Allies through the cantonal courts. The special commission was intended to play the role of an intermediary in order to avoid a large number of lawsuits.

On 22 October the Swiss government replied to the Allies' letters in terms which more or less mirrored those used ten days earlier. On 2 November, however, M. Petitpierre, federal counsellor of the Federal Political Department, handed an aide-memoire to the French ambassador and the British and American ministers.[52] It appeared from this document that the Swiss had experienced a sudden major change of heart in their attitude towards the problem of looted works of art in Switzerland. On 7 November, accompanied by the commercial counsellor of the British legation, Cooper attended a meeting at the Federal Political Department called to present a full explanation of the Swiss proposals and to discuss in general terms the investigation that the Allies were insisting should be undertaken by the Swiss.

This meeting was chaired by Dr Daenicker, who announced that the Federal Political Department would henceforth be making every effort to persuade those Swiss individuals and galleries in possession of the looted seventy-six works of art traced by Cooper to surrender them voluntarily for storage in the Kunstmuseum in Berne, pending legal proceedings by the Allies for restitution. Indeed, his department had already written to those concerned. Daenicker emphasized, however, that his department had no legal powers to enforce the handing over of the paintings. However, the Swiss government had decided to exercise special powers available to it and to establish a special commission to investigate the matter and to adjudicate on claims. The Allies would meanwhile be required to provide proof of ownership on behalf of those from whom the paintings had been confiscated by the Germans.[53]

Cooper recommended that the Federal Political Department carry out serious investigations into Theodor Fischer, Hans Wendland and the Galerie Schmidlin, and that certain other individuals be submitted to further questioning, including Willi Raeber, André Martin, Alexander von Frey, and the owners of the Galeries Aktuaryus, Tanner and Neupert.[54] On request, Cooper provided documentary evidence against those he named and a summary of questions which should be put to them.

Shortly after that meeting Emil Bührle wrote to the Swiss authorities, maintaining in a lengthy statement that, until the visit from Paul Rosenberg a few weeks earlier, he had not known that the paintings he had purchased from Fischer had been looted. The Swiss official to whom Bührle wrote was Dr Vodoz of the Department of Interior, who not only had chaired the meeting attended by Cooper in October but had assisted Bührle to import into Switzerland the paintings which he had purchased from Roger Dequoy in Paris.[55]

Douglas Cooper returned to England in mid-November 1945; shortly thereafter Lieutenants James Plaut and Theodore Rousseau of the OSS ALIU arrived in Switzerland to continue the Allied investigations. They discovered that the Swiss government had still not taken effective measures to solve the problem of looted art in its country and that the French embassy too was making little effort to pursue the matter. Undaunted, the two OSS officers proceeded with their work, carrying out further questioning of the now cooperative Hans Wendland. During the course of their enquiries they discovered that classified Allied documents had been passed to Theodor Fischer by Swiss officials and that the Swiss Federation of Art Dealers had advised its members not to cooperate with any enquiries concerning looted art.[56]

In early December the Swiss government passed legislation

covering the return of property looted from countries occupied by the Germans during the war, but went no further: no special commissions were established, nor were any further investigations into looted works of art in Switzerland carried out, despite its several undertakings to do so. In short, the Swiss played for time. They were well aware that the Allies had more pressing problems elsewhere. Any effective investigations into missing works of art would require resources which were rapidly becoming unavailable as the specialist MFA&A branches were disbanded and those individuals with the requisite knowledge and experience were demobilized and returned to civilian life. Once Cooper, Plaut and Rousseau had departed, the pressure for further action went with them, and the Swiss were well aware of this.

Paul Rosenberg, however, refused to give up his fight for an official settlement, and in 1948 his case eventually came to court in Lucerne. Besides Theodor Fischer, seven others faced charges of having bought looted paintings. Of these, four decided to settle out of court and surrendered the paintings in their possession. The remaining four, including Fischer, appeared in court and, far from denying the charges, based their defence instead on the premise that the paintings had been confiscated from their original owners with the agreement of the French government in power at the time. Fortunately, short shrift was made of this disgraceful and dishonest argument by Rosenberg's lawyers, who were well equipped with documentary evidence supplied by the Allies. Consequently, the tribunal decided in Rosenberg's favour. In the event, the paintings remained in Switzerland: for, having won his case, Rosenberg then agreed to sell the paintings to Bührle, who also purchased several others. These remain in the famous Bührle collection, of which part is private and the rest open to the public in the Swiss National Gallery of Art in Berne.

Thus the investigations into looted works of art in Switzerland petered out into a somewhat unsatisfactory conclusion. Douglas Cooper summed up the situation in his report, dated 10 December 1945, in which he stated that he had been unable to complete the task of tracing looted works in the limited time allotted to him and that he had left Switzerland with many questions unanswered and a firm belief that a large number of missing works of art still lay concealed in the vaults of the country's banks and in the warehouses of its free-ports. Also in December 1945 an OSS report estimated that the value of looted art lying in Swiss bank vaults, forwarding agencies, depositories or private hands was between US $29 and $46 million.

But Switzerland was not the only neutral country of which the Germans made frequent use as a conduit for looted works of art. While Douglas Cooper and his counterparts in the OSS ALIU concentrated their efforts on Switzerland, the search for assets smuggled out of Germany and the formerly occupied territories was also being directed towards certain other neutral countries, notably Spain and Portugal.

7

A WILD GOOSE CHASE

Throughout the war and after it the Allies were well aware of the financial value to the enemy of looted property, including works of art. Quite how vast the sums involved were is best illustrated by estimates drawn up at the time. The British Ministry of Economic Warfare calculated that the value of art treasures looted by the Germans was US$144 million; but Francis H. Taylor, the Director of the Metropolitan Museum of Art in New York, subsequently reported that the correct figure was between $2,000 million and $2,500 million.[1] Obviously, then, the Allies were keen to restrict as far as possible German access to assets concealed in neutral countries; and it was for this reason that a particular resolution was drawn up at the United Nations Monetary and Financial Conference at Bretton Woods in July 1944. Known as Resolution VI, it made the following statement with regard to looted property and enemy assets:

> That all governments of countries represented at this conference take action consistent with their relations with the countries at war to call upon the governments of neutral countries to take immediate measures to prevent any disposition or transfer within territories subject to their jurisdiction of any . . . looted gold, currency, art objects, securities . . . and other assets looted by the enemy; as well as to uncover, segregate and hold at the disposition of the post-liberation authorities in the appropriate country any such assets within territory subject to their jurisdiction.[2]

This resolution was signed by forty-four nations, which in turn requested the governments of the neutral countries of Eire, Portugal, Spain, Sweden, Switzerland and Turkey to cooperate with the United Nations in the securing and safeguarding of property looted by the Germans, including works of art. Despite this measure, however, the Germans achieved almost unhindered success in using neutral countries as conduits for trafficking in looted property for the purpose of raising much-needed foreign currency.

The Allies had been aware of the German plundering of Europe as early as 1939 when, as related in chapter 4, confiscated works of art were auctioned in Switzerland. The following year, as the Wehrmacht swept through Europe, its formations were followed by representatives of almost every part of the Nazi party machine, whose depredations encompassed not only the artistic and cultural assets of their victims but also their economic and industrial wealth. As the war progressed and the tide gradually turned against Hitler, the Allies learned of measures being taken by senior Nazis to protect the results of their thieving, as reports reached them of large quantities of works of art being smuggled out of Germany and the occupied territories to secret repositories in neutral countries, where they could be hidden before being offered for sale.

The principal architect of this operation was Hitler's private secretary, Martin Bormann. After the defeat of the Wehrmacht at Stalingrad in January 1943, Bormann had realized that Germany would inevitably lose the war and had started to lay plans to disperse the country's most priceless assets to locations where the Allies would find it difficult, if not impossible, to lay their hands on them. Throughout 1943 and 1944 Bormann held a series of secret meetings with the individuals who controlled such assets: bankers, industrialists and senior civil servants. These culminated on 10 August 1944 with a conference at the Hotel Rote Haus in Strasbourg, at which he was not personally present but at which his orders were made abundantly clear by his representative, an SS obergruppenführer named Scheid. Bormann directed that assets such as gold, precious stones, valuable works of art, industrial blueprints (including weapons designs), securities and large amounts of American and Swiss currency were to be smuggled abroad. Furthermore, those industrialists present, who included representatives of Krupp, Messerschmitt, Volkswagen and Rheinmetall among their number, were instructed to commence making plans to establish themselves and their respective commercial concerns overseas. It was Bormann's intention that by the time the Allies arrived in Berlin, there would be nothing of any major value left there for them to seize.[3] These instructions were followed to the letter, and by 1946 an overseas industrial empire of 750 companies had been established in neutral countries. Of these, 214 were located in Switzerland alone, while Spain and Portugal harboured 200 between them. A large number were also established throughout South America, including 98 in Argentina.[4]

At the end of 1942 the Allies had discovered that during the previous year Germany had shipped to Switzerland amounts of gold totalling far in excess of the country's known reserves. Further investigations uncovered the fact that a large proportion of this gold had been looted from the occupied countries, including the Netherlands and Belgium, which lost $200 million and $223 million respectively to the thieves of the Reichsbank.[5] Much of it was melted down and recast as gold coinage. The Allied response was to restrict Swiss imports of food and essential items for a period of three months while extracting an undertaking from the country that trade with Germany would be reduced by 40 per cent. The Swiss agreed to comply but in the event failed to do so. In the meantime, the Germans continued to move their assets covertly abroad with virtual impunity. In 1943, as noted in chapter 6, the Allies established the Safehaven Programme in an attempt to impose an economic blockade on neutral countries. In practice, although extensive monitoring and investigation of the covert movement of enemy assets was carried out by the Allied intelligence services and other agencies, such as the British Ministry of Economic Warfare and the US Foreign Economic Administration, Safehaven proved largely ineffective in stemming the flow of assets to neutral countries.

While Switzerland was strategically the most important of the neutral states, maintaining and in some respects even intensifying its strong links with Germany throughout the war, Spain came a close second as a repository for German assets, including looted works of art; and it was to Madrid that Alois Miedl, the German banker who acted as an agent for Göring in procurement of works of art for the latter's collection, made his way in May 1944 with the purpose of disposing of a large number of paintings on behalf of the Reichsmarschall.

Accompanied by his family, Miedl travelled by car across France to the town of Hendaye on the Franco-Spanish frontier. There he made his way to the house of Jean Duval, a Corsican who specialized in smuggling paintings, jewellery and cars into Spain and whom Miedl had met in Paris in June of the previous year. Married to a Russian woman, Duval was also known to Allied intelligence agents in Spain as an agent of the Sicherheitsdienst and to have connections with a body of criminals in Marseilles known as the Spirito Carboni gang.[6] Miedl handed over to Duval a large number of paintings, later reported to number some 200, packed in wooden crates, and also most of his luggage. The latter included a large bag containing securities, among which were a number which had not been cleared with the German authorities. As security for the loan of a large sum of Spanish pesetas, Miedl also handed over one of the two American Mercury cars in which he and his family had made the journey. With the assistance of Duval, the Miedls successfully crossed the Franco-Spanish frontier and made their way to the town of San Sebastian and the Hotel Continental, where they took up temporary residence.

Shortly after his arrival in Spain, Miedl attended a meeting at the Bar Basque with an acquaintance of Duval's, a Belgian named Charles Georges Koninckx. Koninckx had been recommended to Miedl because of his connection with a Spaniard named José Uyarte, the former private secretary to the Spanish minister of colonies and a friend of the Director of the Prado in Madrid whom Miedl wished to approach with a view to interesting the museum in the purchase of some of the paintings owned by Göring. Living in San Sebastian, Koninckx was employed as a buyer by a Belgian company, the Groupement Confiturier de Belgique. He was known to have made a fortune dealing with the Germans on the black market and to have close associations with another Belgian, Adrian Otelet, who also lived in San Sebastian. Like Duval, Otelet was known to be involved in smuggling operations between Spain, France and Belgium.[7]

Koninckx duly arranged a meeting for Miedl with Uyarte and this took place in Madrid in the bar of the Palace Hotel. Miedl broached the subject of a possible sale of some sixty paintings to the Prado Museum. After some discussion, Uyarte asked if the paintings were looted from Jewish collections. Despite Miedl's assurances to the contrary and insistence that he had documentary proof of their legitimate origin, however, the Spaniard was not convinced and declined to assist Miedl further. Undismayed by this setback, Miedl returned to San Sebastian from Madrid during the following month and informed Koninckx that he had succeeded in arranging for a consignment of twenty-two paintings to be smuggled over the frontier into Spain and that these would be placed in bond in the free-port of Bilbao. On 24 July, the paintings arrived as planned.[8] A month later, on 20 August, Miedl crossed back into France and made his way to Biarritz for the purpose of bringing out another American car and some more luggage, which was later reported to include a further case of paintings. He was accompanied on this occasion by Jean Duval and a German named Otto Gräbener, ostensibly a businessman who lived in San Sebastian and travelled extensively throughout the Iberian peninsula, but in reality no mere commercial traveller: he was known to the Allied intelligence services as a member of the Gestapo.[9]

Miedl and his two accomplices had planned to return to Spain on the same day but were delayed. Travelling in two cars, they reached Hendaye on the following day, the 21st, and found that the frontier had been closed by members of a Resistance unit of the Forces Françaises de l'Intérieur (FFI), who promptly arrested them. Gräbener, in whom the FFI showed great interest, was immediately isolated from Miedl and eventually transported to Paris for interrogation by Allied investigators who were interested in his activities on behalf of the Gestapo. Miedl was placed in a cell where he found the Belgian Koninckx, who had arrived in Hendaye on the same day and had also been arrested. Miedl was subsequently interrogated at length by the FFI about Gräbener and told them what he knew of the latter's business activities. Early on the following morning he was suddenly released without explanation and escorted across the frontier bridge at the town of Irun by two FFI officers. He later explained that his release was due to the intervention of his Jewish wife, who had apparently heard of his arrest and had made her way to Irun to intercede on her husband's behalf with the French, explaining that she was Jewish and that her husband had done much to help Jews in the Netherlands during the German occupation. According to Miedl, she had succeeded because one of the French officers to whom she had spoken was himself a Jew. However, although Miedl later denied it, there was subsequently a report that the German military and air attaché at the embassy in Madrid, Generaloberst Eckhardt Kramer, had also interceded with the Spanish authorities and that it was his influence that had resulted in the Spanish officer in charge of security at Irun, a Colonel Ortega, using his good offices with the French to persuade the FFI to release Miedl.[10]

Having escaped the clutches of the French, Miedl returned to San Sebastian and his family. By this time, however, his activities had come to the attention of the Allied intelligence services. On 14 September the MFA&A Branch at SHAEF received a report of Miedl's presence in Spain. Enquiries revealed that he was attempting to negotiate an agreement with the Spanish authorities for permission to bring a number of paintings into the country. Suspicions were aroused and the Madrid station of the Secret Intelligence Service (SIS), located in the British embassy, was asked to investigate. At the same time, the Dutch government and the American embassy in London were informed. On 28 September the SIS reported that it had located Miedl's whereabouts – he had left the Hotel Continental and was staying in the Pension Ursula – and that he had deposited a consignment of paintings in Bilbao. Further reports from the British embassy in Madrid stated that the paintings were suspected to be

part of the Dutch Goudstikker collection, which Miedl had purchased on behalf of Göring in 1940, and that they included works of
eighteenth-century Dutch origin by Rembrandt, van Dyck, Rubens,
Jan Steen and Cranach the Elder, as well as a number by Cézanne.[11]

Further information on Miedl and his activities was obtained from
interrogation of Koninckx, who had since been transferred from his
cell in Hendaye to a detention camp near Bayonne, where he was
questioned on 7 October by Allied investigators. He revealed that
Miedl had succeeded in smuggling the paintings into Spain with the
assistance of a company called Baquera Kutsche y Martin SA,
located in Irun, which had stored them in the free-port area at Bilbao
on Miedl's behalf.[12] One of the owners of the company, a German
named Martin, was known by the Allies to be an agent of the
Sicherheitsdienst. Further investigations revealed that this consignment comprised twenty-two paintings contained in three cases, and
that it had started its journey in Paris in July 1944. It had been
consigned to a Spanish customs agent named Ramon Talasac who
had acted on behalf of a firm of insurance and shipping agents,
Hoppe & Cia. Based in Bilbao, this company was owned by two
partners who were believed to have been involved in German
intelligence operations in Spain. The consignment had arrived in the
bonded warehouse in Bilbao on 24 July 1944 and had been
deposited in the name of Alois Miedl. Allied investigators started to
widen the scope of their enquiries even further, and it was not long
before they discovered that Miedl had already smuggled 200
paintings into Spain. They also learned that these had come from
Göring's collection.[13]

Attention was concentrated on uncovering the method by which
Miedl had contrived to bring such a large number of pictures into
Spain. Suspicion centred on a group of smugglers, well organized and
sufficiently well equipped to handle such a large consignment, led by
the Belgian Otelet, who was known to have worked constantly with
the Germans. A German group also came under suspicion, headed by
an individual named Heinrich Bauer who travelled throughout Spain
and frequently crossed the Franco-Spanish frontier. Collusion was
also suspected on the part of the French commissaire spécial at
Hendaye, Antonio Lopez, who was known to have connections with
several of the gangs of smugglers in the region.[14]

On 26 October Miedl appeared in Madrid, bringing with him two
works by Goya which he claimed had been 'stolen by the Reds
during the Spanish Civil War'. Shortly afterwards, he proceeded to
publish a catalogue of the 200 paintings which he declared were for

sale, all being the so-called property of Göring. Among those listed were works by Rembrandt, Rubens, van Dyck, Jan Steen, Ter Borch, Brouwer, Vermeer, Cranach the Elder, Goya, van Gogh and Cézanne. It was reported at the time that the Prado Museum was interested in purchasing one of the works by Vermeer, a *Magdalen*, for the sum of Pta2 million.[15]

Publication of the catalogue incurred the wrath of the German attaché Kramer who, no doubt on Göring's orders, admonished Miedl for setting about the disposal of the paintings in such a high-profile manner and urged him to withdraw the catalogue, a copy of which had apparently found its way to the British embassy. Further Allied investigations revealed that the paintings had been concealed inside the German embassy. Much to the annoyance of Miedl, responsibility for their disposal was now assumed by Kramer, again undoubtedly on the authority of Göring, who handled the matter in a somewhat more circumspect manner. At the beginning of December the catalogue of the 200 paintings was withdrawn.[16] Relations between Göring and Miedl deteriorated as a result of this affair and eventually the latter broke off all contact with the German embassy.

Early in the following year, 1945, a list of some of the paintings being offered by the Germans in Barcelona was published by the British Ministry of Information. Unfortunately, no copy of this list can now be found and details of only a small number of the paintings concerned are available. Even this limited information, however, reveals several Old Masters among those put up for sale: *The Virgin, The Child and St John* by Rubens; *Portrait of a Gentleman of the Epoch* by Goya; *Portrait of an Old Man and an Angel* by El Greco; *Portrait of Two Romans* by Titian; and a painting of the Italian school of *The Adoration of the Three Kings*.[17]

Realizing that there was little or no chance of laying their hands on any of the 200 paintings advertised in Miedl's ill-advised catalogue, the Allies thereafter concentrated their efforts on the consignment being held in bond in Bilbao. They feared that this might be removed by Miedl and his various accomplices from the free-port and transferred to Portugal, where there was an active market in which good prices were being paid at the time, or to South America where it would be almost impossible to keep further track of the paintings. They thus decided that the highest priority had to be given to gaining access to the paintings and identifying them as belonging to the Goudstikker collection in order to provide irrefutable proof to the Spanish authorities that they were Dutch property.

The Dutch legation in Madrid had already initiated diplomatic action in December 1944 in an effort to gain access to the paintings in Bilbao. Offers of assistance from the British and American embassies, in the form of bringing pressure to bear on the Spanish authorities, were politely rejected by the Dutch who believed that a low-key diplomatic approach was more likely to produce the desired results. Furthermore, they were also anxious that Miedl might be in possession of psuedo-legal documentation proving his title to the paintings. Initially, however, the Spanish Foreign Office proved somewhat uncooperative in its response to the Dutch request for access, saying it needed proof of the fact that the paintings were of Dutch origin. This was forthcoming in the middle of March, when the American embassy produced firm evidence in the form of details of three of the paintings which confirmed them as being from the Goudstikker collection. In the absence of the Dutch head of legation from Madrid, this evidence was presented by the counsellor at the American embassy, W. Butterworth, on the occasion of the first visit by the newly appointed American ambassador, Armour, to the Spanish foreign minister, Lequerica. A few days later the Spanish foreign ministry acceded to the Dutch request, instructing the free-port authorities in Bilbao to give access to the paintings to a delegation from the American embassy and Dutch legation.

Shortly afterwards the head of the Dutch legation, accompanied by an American diplomat, was permitted to inspect and photograph the twenty-two paintings in bond at Bilbao. Ten of these were identified as being from the Goudstikker collection: *The Penitent Magdalen* by van Dyck, a work which had formerly belonged to the Grand Duchy of Oldenburg; *Portrait of a Lady* by J. B. Perroneau; *Portrait of Three Children* by Sir Thomas Lawrence; *Eleazer and Rebecca at the Well* by Cornelis Buys; *Magdalen in the Wilderness* and *Jesus on the Mount of Olives* by Corot; *Portrait of a Man* by El Greco; *Portrait of a Woman at a Table* by Gerard Dou, formerly in the de Wild collection; *Portrait of a Man Seated at a Table* by an unidentified artist; and a landscape by Thomas Creswick.[18] The other twelve paintings were *Madonna with the Child and Angels* by Mainardi, from the A. J. van Aalst collection; *Portrait of a Man in Armour* by Ferdinand Bol; *Portrait of a Lady in Red* by Jean Louis David; *Madonna and Child with St Catherine and St Nicholas* by Palma Vecchio; a seascape by J. Porcellis; *Christ Teaching in the Temple* by Aert de Gelder, which had previously been in the Cassirer collection; *Portrait of a Man* by Frans Hals; a Jan van Brueghel school painting of a landscape; an English school portrait of a woman; a Dutch school painting of a landscape; a Venetian school portrait of a man; and a Dutch school portrait of a man.[19]

It was some time, however, before the Spanish could be persuaded to hand these works of art over to the Dutch. When the paintings eventually did return to the Netherlands, the question arose as to whether the sale of the Goudstikker collection had been forced and thus whether the works from it could be considered in the same category as others which had been compulsorily purchased or looted by the Germans. Jacques Goudstikker's widow, Desirée, failed to convince the Dutch authorities that this was indeed the case and eventually gave up her claim to the elements of the collection which had been purchased by Göring. She did, however, succeed in recovering the property purchased by Alois Miedl, namely Nyenrode Castle, three houses and the offices of her late husband's company in Amsterdam. Subsequently, in order to resolve financial problems, she sold the castle, one of the houses and the office property.

The final chapter to the Miedl affair unfolded in 1945 when Alois Miedl himself was interviewed on a number of occasions during April by officers of the OSS ALIU in Madrid where he was by then living, having successfully avoided attempts by the Dutch government in 1945 to have him extradited from Spain to the Netherlands. When questioned, Miedl denied having brought any paintings into Spain except for the twenty-two held in the free-port in Bilbao and a further three small works which he had concealed in his luggage when entering Spain in July 1944: a landscape by Adrien Brouwer; a portrait of a head by Jacob Jordaens, formerly part of the Goudstikker collection; and a small landscape by Essentlents. Miedl further disclaimed any involvement with dealing in confiscated or forcibly purchased works of art and any connection with Generaloberst Kramer at the German embassy.[20] To this day there are no records available which tell of the ultimate fate of the 200 paintings smuggled into Spain by Alois Miedl and subsequently disposed of by the Germans in Madrid.

Throughout the war the Secret Intelligence branch of the OSS maintained a covert presence within an American embassy residence in Madrid. In January 1945 it was informed of a Nazi operation to smuggle works of art and other looted assets to South America by a route which took them via the Netherlands and Belgium to France and the port of Bordeaux, from where they were shipped to Spain and the free-port of Bilbao. The OSS was also advised that the smuggling was being controlled from Madrid.[21] An operation was mounted immediately to uncover the identities of those involved in the smuggling and to trace the route through Spain. However, the efforts of the OSS proved fruitless for six months until, in June 1945, after the end of the war in Europe, two looted paintings by Cézanne came to light after one was purchased from a dealer in Madrid by a friend of an OSS agent to whom he proudly displayed his new acquisition. The agent concerned, an American woman named Aline Griffith, also learned that the dealer was offering other paintings of the same ilk, notably French Impressionist works. Although she was swift to follow up the lead, she was too late: the dealer had sold the entire stock of paintings to another dealer from Barcelona and all efforts to discover the identity of the latter proved unsuccessful.[22]

In the meantime, however, Aline Griffith had learned from an informant that two large crates of paintings had been deposited for safe keeping by the German embassy in the Japanese legation in Madrid. The informant had heard the head of legation mention that the paintings had been imported from France via Bilbao and that arrangements were being made for their onward despatch to South America. These paintings, however, did not remain in the legation for long. In August, still reeling from the cataclysm at Hiroshima and Nagasaki, and anxious about further concealing and giving diplomatic protection to Nazi assets, the head of legation had the crates removed to a small apartment near Madrid's Plaza Santa Barbara, thus giving the OSS an opportunity to gain access to them. However, the attempt was foiled at the last moment. Aline Griffith, heavily disguised as an elderly Spanish woman, gained entry to the apartment and was in the process of opening one of the crates when she was discovered and attacked. Fortunately she succeeded in disabling her assailant and narrowly escaped with her life.[23]

A second attempt was planned during September; but, before it could be put into action, the OSS received orders from Washington to cease all operations in the Iberian peninsula and for all personnel to return to the United States. Indeed, the decision had been taken to disband the entire organization, now that the war was over, and to replace it with a much smaller body called the Central Intelligence Group. It was this group which, in 1947, formed the nucleus for the Central Intelligence Agency.

The identities of the individuals responsible for this particular smuggling operation would have remained unknown had those heading the newly established Central Intelligence Group not decided to ignore orders from the State Department and to leave some agents in place without the knowledge of the American ambassador. Among them was Aline Griffith. Ostensibly working in Madrid for a company of cotton fibre importers established by the Central Intelligence Group, she continued her intelligence work in Europe until 1947 when she married a Spanish nobleman, the Count of Quintanilla, who later assumed the title of Count of Romanones on the death of his father. A few years later, in the mid-1950s, the Countess of Romanones resumed her intelligence career; and in February 1963 two events took place on the same day that would lead to the eventual unmasking of the individuals behind the wartime Nazi smuggling ring.

On that particular day, the Countess received a visit from her former chief in the OSS, who had by then risen to senior rank in the CIA. He asked her to undertake a mission to help uncover a Soviet mole known to be working in the headquarters of NATO in Paris. As a result of intelligence received from one of its own highly placed agents in Moscow, the CIA suspected that the mole held a senior position and thus was likely to move at high levels in Paris society. It was for that reason that the decision had been taken to involve the Countess. She and her husband were well known among the Parisian elite and counted among their friends the Duke and Duchess of Windsor, whom they had met in the United States while on honeymoon in 1947. That evening, the Countess and her husband held a party at their home in Madrid in honour of the Duke and Duchess, who were paying them a visit. During dinner, the Duke mentioned a painting which he and the Duchess had seen in a shop in the Calle Leon that day and had decided to buy for their collection. The description of the painting fitted that of a work by Cézanne known to have been looted and observed in 1944, by an OSS agent in the Netherlands, being packed with a large number of other Impressionist works for despatch to Spain. The description had been given to those OSS agents involved in the hunt for Nazi assets, including Aline Griffith, and the Countess was quick to remember it when it was mentioned by the Duke.[24] The following day, on leaving Madrid to return to Paris, the Duchess of Windsor asked the Countess to collect the painting on her behalf and bring it to Paris, where she and her husband were shortly due to visit. However, on calling at the shop, the Countess was informed that the picture had already been purchased by another customer. Once again, it had eluded her grasp.

Shortly afterwards, an operation to hunt down the Soviet mole was mounted by the CIA and the Direction de la Securité du Territoire (DST), the French security service. The Countess, along with other CIA and DST agents, and assisted by the Duchess of

Windsor whose aid she enlisted, played her part and contributed to the identifying of the mole. Also unmasked was his KGB 'handler' – who by sheer chance was also revealed as one of the masterminds behind the Nazi smuggling operation during the war. To the Countess, these revelations came as something of a shock: for the KGB agent and the Nazi smugglers were all acquaintances of her and her husband in Paris and Madrid.[25] Although she later gave a detailed account of these events in her memoirs of her wartime days with the OSS, *The Spy Went Dancing*, the Countess chose to conceal the identity of the man who controlled the smuggling operation in order to protect his children and grandchildren, who she felt should not suffer from the exposure of him and his misdeeds. She continues to do so even today, but has confirmed that to the best of her knowledge his family, who live in Madrid, is still in possession of a large amount of the looted art which he smuggled into Spain.[26]

It was only after the arrest and trial of the unidentified Soviet agent and the 'mole' that details of the Nazi operation some two decades earlier, to smuggle looted works of art through Spain to South America, came to light courtesy of the DST. It transpired that during the period 1938–45, one of the other ringleaders of the operation had been employed as an adviser to Göring on major art collections in France, Belgium and the Netherlands. He had subsequently become involved in the smuggling of Nazi assets out of the German-occupied territories to neutral countries and had made use of a fleet of fishing boats belonging to the father of one of his fellow ringleaders who was also a collaborator.[27] Large numbers of works of art were transported by train across France to Bordeaux, from where they were shipped to the free-port at Bilbao. They were then smuggled to a warehouse in Seville to await despatch to South America.

Although there was no conclusive proof, investigators suspected that the ringleaders had many of the paintings copied, sending on fakes in place of the originals. This was an extremely dangerous practice, as by 1945 several Nazi organizations were already in existence outside Germany with the sole purpose of looking after Nazi interests in the post-war world. Chief among these was the Organization der Ehemaligen SS-Angehörigen (Organization of Former Members of the SS), better known as the ODESSA, which in those days had its European headquarters in Madrid.[28] Headed in Europe by Otto Skorzeny, an SS obersturmbannführer and commander of the wartime SS special forces unit, the Jagverbande 502 (502 Special Service Battalion), the ODESSA was established in 1945 to oversee post-war Nazi interests worldwide and in particular to safeguard the interests of former members of the SS, whom it sought to infiltrate into positions of influence in the post-war West German administration. It also supervised the operations of other more specialist Nazi organizations, such as *Die Spinne* (The Spider), known as the 'Arana' in Spain, which operated escape routes for former SS personnel wanted for war crimes by the Allies.[29]

Organizations such as the ODESSA were swift to visit retribution on those who thwarted their aims or interfered with their operations. One such was a Russian Jew living in Madrid. Michael Sokolnikoff appeared to his friends in the Spanish capital to be a man of considerable means, living as he did with a German Jewess known as Mme Sansom in a suite in the Ritz Hotel and enjoying all the trappings of wealth. On 11 June 1945 his body was found lying on a road some thirty miles from the city. Subsequent investigations by the Spanish authorities revealed that Sokolnikoff had in fact been a principal Nazi procurement agent in Spain, responsible not only for conducting transactions in basic commodities such as the purchase of huge consignments of food but also for organizing the smuggling of large amounts of looted property, including works of art, from France and Switzerland into Spain.[30] Sokolnikoff was also reported to have dealt in large quantities of diamonds and precious stones of high value on behalf of his Nazi masters, and it was these which apparently led to his death. Spanish investigators learned that at the end of the war he had been in possession of £5 million worth of diamonds and other stones, a huge sum at that time. For some unknown reason, he had refused to hand the stones over to his employers and the latter had punished him accordingly. The stones were subsequently found by the Spanish police; the safe containing them also held two other passports in Sokolnikoff's name in addition to his own, one confirmed as Argentinian and the other unconfirmed but reported as British. Investigators subsequently learned that Sokolnikoff had paid the sum of £20,000 to unidentified foreign officials for these passports.[31]

Another individual allegedly involved in the smuggling of looted works of art from France to Spain has been named as André Urbanovitch who, according to information from the DST, first appeared in France in 1940 in the town of St Pandoux-La-Rivière, in the Dordogne. He has been reported as being of Serbian nationality but Michel Gardère, a French journalist and author who has spent several years investigating Urbanovitch, says that no trace of him or his family was found when staff of the French embassy visited the village in Serbia where he had reputedly been born and brought up; indeed, his given address did not exist. At the time of his appearance in the Dordogne, Urbanovitch claimed to be a Jewish refugee and to have previously served in a French army unit of foreign volunteers until demobilized at Caussade in the district of Tarn et Garonne. An address in Paris he gave at the time to police was later found to be non-existent.[32]

Although there is little information available on his activities during the following four years, according to DST files Urbanovitch is reported as having collaborated with the Germans on a number of occasions. He apparently also became involved in trafficking in looted works of art, using contacts in Switzerland. In early 1944, however, he obviously realized that the tide of the war had swung firmly against the Germans and decided to change sides, joining the Francs Tireurs et Partisans (FTP), the French Communist Resistance organization. In June 1944 he took part in an attack on a large German convoy, and thereafter participated fully in FTP operations.[33] On 10 August 1944 Urbanovitch led an FTP operation to round up French collaborators in the newly liberated town of Périgueux. It was as a result of his activities there that he gained a reputation for ruthlessness: over fifty executions and cases of torture were attributed to him, some of them involving members of the FFI, the Gaullist underground army of which the FTP did not form part. Ultimately, and somewhat ironically, his activities earned him the highest Resistance decoration.

By the end of the war Urbanovitch was a wealthy man, having acquired large amounts of money, works of art and jewellery by various means. Not long afterwards, however, the more dubious of his wartime exploits looked like catching up with him. There had for some time been increasing unease about the torture and executions carried out by him in 1944, ostensibly under the auspices of the FTP, and eventually the French authorities decided to investigate, convening a tribunal in 1946. The writer André Malraux, who had commanded a large FTP Resistance group which had operated in the area of Tulle, in the département of Corrèze, spoke in Urbanovitch's defence. Malraux's influence as a respected former Resistance leader was undoubtedly of some consequence, because Urbanovitch was cleared of all charges. It was later claimed that the two men had known each other before their days in the FTP, having met during the Spanish Civil War. Malraux would later, in 1959, become minister of culture and arts in the government of President de Gaulle. Urbanovitch and Malraux continued to see much of each other and it was subsequently reported, but never confirmed, that they went into business together. Urbanovitch bought an art gallery in Paris, in front of the Porte de l'Elysée, as well as interests in galleries in Zurich, Madrid and in Japan.[34] According to one unidentified source, he was reported to have been involved in sales of looted paintings in each of these countries.

Allied intelligence reports list a number of other individuals as being involved in smuggling looted works of art into Spain. Among these was Hugo Barcas, a wealthy member of the right-wing Falange who lived in Barcelona's Paseo de Colon; he travelled frequently to France, Chile and Argentina and was suspected of smuggling large numbers of paintings to the latter two countries. Another was a Frenchman named André Gabison who was also suspected of being involved in the amassing of funds in Spain for post-war German use. Living in Madrid and travelling extensively between Paris and Hendaye, he was reported as dealing solely in French art treasures.[35] Others on the list include a number of dealers known to have been involved in the trade in stolen art. Among them was a Frenchman named Pierre Lottier, who admitted his involvement when questioned in 1944 by the Spanish police.[36] Lottier, who had previously worked for the Gestapo in France, owned an antique shop, Muebles Manonellas, in the Avenida Jose Antonio in Barcelona, as well as others in Nice and elsewhere in France. He specialized in smuggling porcelain and Sèvres china into Spain, where it was offered for sale in his shop in Barcelona which had been established for this purpose. Lottier was assisted in his smuggling operations by a German named Erich Schiffman who also lived in Barcelona and was identified as a member of the Gestapo working undercover: Allied agents discovered that the Germans had gone to the extent of withdrawing his identity papers and revoking his German citizenship in order to give him a more convincing cover.

The route along which looted works of art were smuggled also passed through Portugal. One Allied intelligence report stated that a considerable number of works of art had been placed in a large vault in the German embassy in Lisbon.[37] Others identified a bookshop in Lisbon as a principal conduit for looted works of art finding their way through Portugal. Called the New German Bookshop and located in the Avenida da Liberdade, this business had been established in late 1943 by a German named Buchholz in partnership with a Portuguese called Lehrfeld. Buchholz had brought with him from Germany half a million reichsmarks' worth of paintings, sculptures and books which he had proceeded to sell at very high prices. Investigations by British officials revealed that he had been involved from 1938 onwards in the selling of works of art from confiscated Jewish collections and that Swiss dealers had been in contact with him in 1944.[38]

Another German identified as being actively involved in the Portuguese traffic was a woman named Margarethe Eisen, also known as Mrs C. Duarte. One work of art identified as having passed through her hands was *Salome* by Titian, reported to have been subsequently smuggled to England.[39] Portuguese businesses named as being involved in the handling of looted works of art included the Galeria de Arte, located in the Rua Nova da Trinidada in Lisbon and owned by two partners, a Portuguese named Conrad John and a Romanian called Leon Josipovicci. The latter worked closely with a woman named Elfrida Marques Pereira who had also been implicated in trafficking in looted paintings.[40]

A figure who loomed large in the trade in works of art from confiscated Jewish collections, having previously worked for the ERR in France, was a Frenchman living in Lisbon named Jean Rolland Ostins. Until 1940 Ostins had been a prominent antiques dealer on the Quai Voltaire in Paris. Immediately after the armistice between France and Germany he had declared himself a committed collaborationist and thereafter had experienced few problems when travelling on business between France and Portugal. In 1941 he arrived in Lisbon and approached the commercial attaché, Henri Bouchet, at the French legation, ostensibly on behalf of the French Red Cross and another rescue organization called Secours National. The real reason for Ostins' approach is unknown but he subsequently proved so difficult and uncooperative that all dealings with him were eventually terminated by the legation and he resumed his activities as an antiques dealer.

Ostins had a bad reputation and was known to be entirely unscrupulous in his business dealings. He was also known by the Allies to be involved in the smuggling of diamonds, using the Vichy diplomatic bag to move the stones. In this he was assisted by the wife of Colonel René d'Amade, the notoriously pro-German military attaché at the French legation in Lisbon. Ostins also made use of fishing boats which sailed regularly between Lisbon and Marseilles. He and his mistress, a Mme Lidoine with whom he lived when in Lisbon and who handled his affairs when he was absent in France, were also very active in the black market. They frequently entertained Germans and French officials of the Vichy regime who came to Lisbon to purchase antiques.

Like all those known or suspected to be involved with trafficking in enemy assets and loot, Ostins was placed on the Allied 'Watch List'. On one occasion, in June 1943, his apartment in the Avenida Place Hotel was entered by Allied agents who removed documents for photocopying; unfortunately, although the papers were later replaced Ostins noticed that they had gone missing and realized that he was under surveillance. Shortly afterwards, he moved to a private apartment. The Allies had another reason for keeping a close eye on Ostins: they suspected that he was working for German intelligence. One of his contacts was a German lawyer, Dr Wolfgang Krehl, who was known to have connections with the Abwehr; furthermore, Ostins was also known to be acting as a paid intermediary for the Germans and the Vichy regime. Allied agents learned that he regularly received considerable sums of money from France and that he transferred large amounts to Argentina, although on whose behalf it was never discovered.[41] Ostins held a 50 per cent share in the Lisbon-based company Laos Ltd, which specialized in exporting goods, including works of art, from Portugal to the United States. Ostins' correspondence was regularly intercepted by the Allies, and an extract from a letter to him from his New York partner Mrs Nat Smolin gives an indication of the kind of business they were conducting:

The only way to carry out successfully the business in question is as follows: Let me know what fine pictures you can get. Only very well known ones, museum pieces and known throughout the world, can be sold in the way you suggest. If I find a buyer, you must be ready to send me documents, and photographs, expert opinions etc. No one will buy a picture for payment before delivery unless he can be certain that what he buys is really incontestably good and that he is not running any risk. How can you arrange to give those guarantees?

Among the moderns, Rouault and Picasso are easily sold, provided they are famous pictures of very good quality. Photographs are essential – we can do several million dollars worth of business if what we can offer is suitable and if the payments present no dangers. It is up to you now to find out and to keep me informed. I warn you in advance that my country won't give me a visa to go to Lisbon in any circumstances. It will perhaps be easier for you to come here.[42]

By 1948, the Safehaven Programme had achieved little in tracking down and securing looted works of art in neutral countries. Only limited success had been achieved by Wing Commander Douglas Cooper and members of the OSS ALIU in Switzerland and virtually none at all by the OSS and SIS in Spain and Portugal. Little assistance was accorded to Allied investigators by the authorities of the countries concerned, who were well aware that the following year would see the formation of the first post-war government in Germany and were anxious not to incur its wrath.

Indeed, almost immediately after it was established in August 1949, the new West German government approached all the neutral governments and made it abundantly clear that the handing over of any wartime Nazi assets would be regarded as 'theft' and that compensation would be expected for any such losses. The Germans were already displeased that the Swiss government had in 1946 handed over SwFr250 million to the Allies in compensation for gold bought from Germany during the war (suspected by 'Safehaven' investigators to have been looted, some of it from Belgium), having been persuaded to do so by the Americans' offer to free some of their assets which had been frozen in 1941. For the most part, German intimidation had the desired effect. In Spain, Safehaven negotiators found themselves making no progress at all with the authorities, who were openly unwilling to make any moves against Germans living in Spain and known to be in possession of looted property. The Portuguese were equally uncooperative and at times even more brazen, announcing that they would only hand over property looted from the wartime occupied countries in exchange for German-owned assets in Portugal. No doubt the latter were then quietly handed back to the Germans.

Thus it was that Allied efforts to retrieve looted works of art from neutral countries failed almost completely. Thousands of works of great value remained concealed in the vaults of banks or in the well-guarded homes of former senior members of the Nazi regime who had fled Germany and escaped Allied retribution to live under the protection of supposedly neutral regimes in safe enjoyment of their stolen treasures.

8

TO THE VICTORS THE SPOILS

The beginning of 1947 found MFA&A staff in post-war occupied Germany continuing the work of restitution: returning works of art to those whose title to them had been proved beyond doubt. A large number of items, mainly the property of Jews, had to be declared heirless as countless complete families had perished in the Holocaust leaving no one to claim them. By this time, however, the majority of the original MFA&A officers had returned to their respective countries and their former careers in the worlds of art and academia. Those personnel who remained – some replacement MFA&A officers, some civilian staff in the post-war administration of the Allied zones of occupation – were faced not only with continuing the process of restitution but also with the task of tracing and recovering large numbers of works of art which had been looted since the cessation of hostilities and had subsequently found their way on to the black market. Furthermore, there was the problem of looting by members of the occupation forces.

It is an unpalatable but inescapable fact that Allied troops did indulge in large-scale looting of works of art in Germany during the immediate post-war period. The majority of such was carried out by personnel of the US Army – largely because most of the Nazi repositories were located in the areas occupied by American forces – and involved officers and men of all ranks from general to private. Examples of the looting of Germany's art treasures by American military personnel have been publicized on occasion in the past, as for example in accounts of the Quedlinburg Treasure, but the full story was published only in 1994, when Kenneth Alford, having researched the subject for fourteen years, produced *The Spoils of World War II: The American Military's Role in Stealing Europe's Treasures.*[1] Such was the extent of the looting by Allied occupation forces revealed by Alford, and by newly available archival material relating to American MFA&A operations in post-war Germany studied by the authors, that there is room here only to cover selected major instances in which works of art were spirited away to the home countries of the victors, the majority of them never to be recovered.

One such theft took place in September 1945 at the Schloss Hohenaschau, near Rosenheim in Bavaria, which had been used as a repository for the collection of the Städtische Galerie im Lenbach-haus, better known as the Lenbachhaus Museum, in Munich.[2] The collection had been deposited in the castle, which belonged to Freiherr Ludwig von Cramer-Klett, during 1941. Later that year the castle was requisitioned by the German government, which used it as a naval rest centre until September 1944 when it was converted into a hospital for the Kriegsmarine. Throughout this time the works of art remained undisturbed in the castle's cellars under lock and key. The keys to the cellar were held by the wife of the former director of the rest centre, Hans Lebel, who had been conscripted into the army.

In August 1945 the castle was occupied by a US Army medical unit which was stationed nearby at Fischach. Security was, however, the responsibility of another unit, Battery C of the 58th Field Artillery Battalion under the command of Lieutenant Glenn E. Calloway. On 31 August James Shields, an English representative of the United Nations Relief and Rehabilitation Administration (UNRRA), arrived at the castle accompanied by his assistant Zarko Pavlovich, a former officer of the Yugoslav army. Together with other UNRRA person-nel, the two men had come to the Rosenheim area at the head of an advance party tasked with commencing the establishment of an UNRRA displaced persons camp. On the following day, Frau Lebel handed the keys to the cellar and the art repository to Pavlovich. This act was witnessed by another German, Fridolin Göser, the Mayor of Hohenaschau, who saw Pavlovich put the keys in his pocket.[3]

Ten days later, on 11 September, Shields and Pavlovich left the castle and the keys were handed to Sergeant Leno V. Bonat of Battery C of the 58th Field Artillery Battalion. On 24 September Bonat's unit left Hohenaschau for the town of Bad Aibling, and the same day, the keys were given to Private First Class Delbert Ripley, a member of the US Army military government detachment based at Rosenheim. On 1 October Company A of the 1st Battalion 39th Infantry Regiment, commanded by Lieutenant Stratton, arrived and occupied the castle, and that same day Lieutenant Jonathan Morey, the MFA&A officer responsible for Bavaria, asked the acting director of the Lenbachhaus, Herr Schüssler, to carry out a complete inventory of the paintings in the castle's cellars – nine months since this had last been done in December 1944 by Frau Lüttgens, the restorer at the Lenbachhaus. To the dismay of all present, it was discovered that 116 paintings were missing, among them works by Franz von

Lenbach, Philipp Sporer, Josef Wopfner, Wilhelm von Dietz and other German masters.[4]

For some reason, no immediate action was taken concerning the theft and it was not until four weeks later, on 28 October, that MFA&A officer Lieutenant Walter Horn began his investigations into the matter. On the same day, it was discovered that the massive wooden door to the cellars had been forced open; indeed, whoever was responsible had torn it off its hinges. Whover had done this – presumably between 1 and 28 October – could not have avoided making a great deal of noise; but somehow they had apparently contrived to avoid causing any disturbance and alerting nearby guards. Already overloaded with work, Horn found himself hampered by lack of information as to the possible whereabouts of the missing paintings and by the absence of personnel whom he wished to question but could not because they had been redeployed elsewhere in Germany. He commenced his investigation by pinpointing the period during which the paintings had been stolen. By questioning closely those who had entered the cellars, he was able to deduce that the theft had taken place during September. During that period, the keys had been in the possession of only four people: James Shields, Zarko Pavlovich, Leno Bonat and Delbert Ripley.

Horn proceeded with interrogating these four individuals. Of these, two subsequently became the main suspects: James Shields and Zarko Pavlovich. The latter initially denied ever having been in possession of the keys to the cellar but, when confronted by a sworn statement by Frau Lebel, eventually admitted that he had entered the repository in the company of his superior, Shields. On being questioned by Horn, however, Shields denied that he had held the keys to the cellar or that he had visited the cellar with Pavlovich. Despite lengthy interrogation of both these men, Horn was unable to establish the guilt of either of them. At one point he had Pavlovich placed under close arrest in solitary confinement without food for four days. Despite the discomfort of a very cold cell, exacerbated by sciatica and rheumatism, Pavlovich maintained his innocence and eventually was released. Horn was not convinced, however, and suspected that he was covering up for Shields, in Horn's view the primary culprit. Horn also believed that Bonat was also implicated in the theft, as he had custody of the keys during the period 1–24 September during which Horn believed the theft had taken place.[5]

Horn was convinced that the theft of the Lenbachhaus paintings had been well organized and was the work of someone with a knowledge of fine art. Only the most valuable works had been taken, making it highly unlikely that the paintings had merely fallen prey to marauding troops entering the cellar in search of loot. Furthermore, some of the works stolen were so large that a truck would have been required to transport the entire consignment of 116 paintings away from the castle. A careful watch was kept on the black market in the hope that some of the paintings might surface, but this proved fruitless. Those involved in the investigation believed that the entire consignment was being kept together in concealment. On 4 September 1946 the investigation into the theft of the Lenbachhaus paintings from the Schloss Hohenaschau was terminated for lack of evidence and the file closed. During the years since then, a total of seventy-three paintings from the collection have been recovered; but forty-three are still missing, including *Gabriele Lenbach* and *Studie aus Kairo* by Franz von Lenbach; *Holzfischer im Bodensee* by Josef Wopfner; *Raufende Landsknechte* by Wilhelm von Dietz; *Dr Voltz als Artillerist zu Pferde* by Louis Braun; and *Faust und Gretchen* by Michael von Echter.[6]

Another example of a major theft involving personnel of the occupation forces is that which took place in 1945 in the German province of Büdingen, part of the area occupied by the US Army's XIX Corps. Under the control of elements of the 2nd Military Government Regiment, the province comprised the small town of Büdingen itself and approximately 100 villages. Near the town was the Schloss Büdingen which belonged to Prince Otto Ysenburg, whose family had owned it since 1250. The castle contained a large collection of antique firearms which, under the military law forbidding the possession of weapons by Germans at the time, were due to be confiscated by the US army.[7] The military government detachment was commanded by a junior officer, Lieutenant Robert K. Bryant, assisted by Lieutenant Sinclair Robinson. The latter's responsibilities included those of MFA&A officer along with those of legal officer, finance officer and public health officer.

Not long after his unit's arrival on 31 March 1945, Lieutenant Robinson had paid a visit to the castle which was surrounded by an estate of some 17,000 acres of forests and countryside. He had made the acquaintance of Prince Ysenburg, who subsequently became a frequent visitor to the offices of the military government detachment. Shortly afterwards, Robinson had asked the prince if he knew of any repositories containing works of art in the area. Ysenburg knew of none but had introduced the American to his cousin, Count Solms, who lived in Laubach and possessed his own collection. Furthermore, the Count was a director of the Städelsches Kunstinstitut und

Städtische Galerie, better known as the Städel Museum, in Frankfurt. Solms had in turn introduced Robinson to the museum's curator, Dr Albert Rapp. Robinson learned that Rapp was due to visit the town of Amorbach, some 65 miles south of Büdingen, for the purpose of inspecting a collection of works of art belonging to the museum. It had been stored in a castle there since the end of July 1944, having been moved from the museum because of the risk of damage from Allied bombing raids; and indeed, not long after the removal of the collection the museum had been partly destroyed by several direct hits.

Robinson volunteered to drive Dr Rapp to Amorbach, although it was outside his area of jurisdiction. His offer was accepted and on 17 April the two men, accompanied by Prince Ysenburg, set off for the Schloss Amorbach. On their arrival at the castle, which they found occupied by a US Army unit, they discovered that it had fallen prey to troops of the 2756th Engineer Construction Battalion, who had looted the repository. The scene was one of mayhem, with paintings damaged or cut from their frames and removed, statues smashed and the contents of crates lying strewn all over the floors of the rooms in which they had formerly been securely stored.[8]

One of those who took part in the looting stole several items, including a thirteenth-century illuminated manuscript, two casts of Egyptian cylinders, twenty-five Japanese shadowgraphs, a Napoleonic briefcase, a small chest and some medieval documents. He later made the following statement which briefly describes what had taken place:

> There were other boxes there I could have gotten and I didn't take them – there were so many trying to take things, but I sent the valuables I took home one at a time. The officer told us that if we got caught sending it he would be fined $70. We knew we were not supposed to steal valuable things like that; still, if a fellow can get it he takes it. Some fellows were going round smashing things just for spite. When I went into the storage room you couldn't move in there there were so many fellows in the place. They broke open the crates and took out the things. It went on for a day or two.[9]

Robinson wasted little time in securing what remained in the repository, which he immediately declared out of bounds to all troops. Borrowing a truck from a nearby unit, he enlisted the aid of some troops and loaded fifty-five paintings of major value on board the vehicle and into his own car, saying that he would take them back to Büdingen where they would be stored securely. Dr Rapp attempted to compile a list of what the officer was taking away but Robinson overruled him, saying that it could be done later. During the return journey, Robinson quizzed Dr Rapp as to the value of the nineteen paintings on the back seat of his car. The latter responded by pointing out just one, *Pan and Nymphs* by Rubens, and saying that it was worth about US $220,000.

On arrival at Büdingen, the paintings in the truck were unloaded and stored in a secure room in the castle. Robinson, however, drove his car to his quarters in the town and, with the assistance of two female servants, unloaded two paintings, Rubens' *Pan and Nymphs* and *Two Saints* by Joos van Cleve, securing them under lock and key before returning to the castle and unloading the remainder. There, together with Prince Ysenburg and his family, Robinson inspected the remainder of the paintings. It soon became apparent that he had no knowledge of art, and Dr Rapp quickly realized that the American was interested only in the paintings' monetary value. Robinson left shortly afterwards, and it was only then that Rapp noticed that the Rubens and a number of other paintings were missing.[10]

Three days later Robinson paid another visit to the castle and, having obtained the key to the repository, removed a further four paintings: *Motiv aus Tivoli* by Nicolaes Berchem; *Orphan House in Amsterdam* by Max Liebermann; *Landscape with Cattle* by Constant Tryon; and *Venetian Redoubt* by Canaletto. Loading these into a trailer attached to his jeep, he drove to his quarters where he stored them with the rest of his loot, which by then included a collection of silverware which he had also pilfered from the castle. That evening, however, Dr Rapp returned to the castle and, on being told of Robinson's visit, immediately carried out an inventory of the paintings in the repository. He found that six were missing.[11]

Robinson's greed was such that a few days later he insisted on accompanying Rapp and Ysenburg on a visit to the town of Bad Wildungen, 90 miles north of Büdingen, to inspect another collection belonging to the Städel Museum. On their arrival the three men discovered that the repository was guarded by a US Army unit commanded by a captain who had the keys in his custody. Rapp decided not to enter the building, for fear of Robinson catching sight of the paintings inside, and so he and his two companions returned to Büdingen without further ado.

On 21 May the 978th Field Artillery Battalion arrived in Büdingen and the commanding officer, Lieutenant Colonel James F. Wood, decided to locate his battalion headquarters in the castle. At about the same time Prince Ysenburg was arrested by the US Army's Counter Intelligence Corps because of his connections with the Nazi party, and was interned in a detention camp at Schwarzenborn. Shortly after his arrival, Wood was informed about the six missing paintings and asked Dr Rapp to produce a report on the matter. The latter did so, at the same time submitting a copy to Lieutenant Robinson and requesting a receipt for the six works of art in question. Robinson refused to accept the report and returned it to Rapp, ordering him to change the last sentence which stated that the paintings had been 'taken into custody by the Military Government'. Rapp acceded to Robinson's demands under duress; fearing harm either to himself or to the Ysenburg family, he altered the report to state that the paintings were 'under control of the Military Government'. Wood, meanwhile, had reported the matter to the Criminal Investigation Section of the 518th Military Police Battalion.[12]

A few weeks later Lieutenant Robinson departed for Wiesbaden to collect a load of champagne. Driving his own car, an Opel commandeered from some luckless German civilian, he was accompanied by a truck which he led to the place from which the consignment was to be collected. He did not, however, return to Büdingen immediately: having supervised the loading of the champagne, he disappeared for a few days. His whereabouts during that time were never ascertained; shortly afterwards, however, it was discovered that certain important items were missing from the Städel Museum repository at Bad Wildungen, namely the Willehalm manuscripts and the priceless *Liber Sapientiae* which contained the *Song of Hildebrand*, a heroic poem written in AD 800. It was later discovered that Robinson was at the time in possession of documents authorizing his travel to Liège in Belgium, which had already gained some notoriety as a black marketplace for sales of looted works of art. The Willehalm manuscripts turned up in the autumn of 1945 in New York, where they were sold to a book dealer.[13]

On 29 June a military police Criminal Investigation Division agent interviewed Prince Ysenburg in the detention camp at Schwarzenborn and obtained a statement from him concerning the six missing paintings. Shortly afterwards, he also questioned Robinson's two female servants who had helped him unload the paintings and carry them into his quarters. On 4 July, Robinson was arrested and his quarters searched. Although the collection of silverware stolen from the Schloss Büdingen was recovered, and subsequently returned to its rightful owners, no trace of the six paintings was found. Despite pressure from Lieutenant Colonel Wood, Robinson's immediate superior, Lieutenant Bryant, refused to bring charges against him and after only one day under close arrest Robinson was released and returned to his duties.[14]

Robinson was well aware, however, that the matter would not end here, and set about protecting himself against the inevitable further enquiries. On 7 July, accompanied by two fellow officers, Lieutenants Leonard H. Harrison and Hans Witten, he drove to Frankfurt and the offices of the partially destroyed Städel Museum. There they ransacked the filing cabinets in their search for the original of the report written by Dr Rapp concerning the six paintings missing from the repository at Büdingen. Unable to find it, they summoned the museum's administrative assistant, Doris Schmidt; as she would not permit them to remove the report itself, they proceeded to intimidate her into typing a summary of it.[15] The following day Robinson, this time accompanied by Lieutenant Juan J. Beotegui, drove to the Schloss Laubach where Dr Rapp was living. Despite the fact that the unfortunate man was ill, Robinson and Beotegui roused him from his bed and drove him to an area of forest outside the town. There Robinson, who was armed with a pistol and carbine, proceeded to threaten Rapp, telling him that he would have him gaoled for falsely accusing an American officer of theft.

Robinson also pressurized others who could bear witness against him. On 6 July, Princess Ingrid von Sayn-Wittgenstein had given a statement to the Criminal Investigation Division, saying that she had seen four of the missing paintings in a trailer attached to Robinson's jeep parked in the courtyard of the Schloss Büdingen. Three days later, Robinson and Beotegui drove to her castle at Kreus Wertheim and forced her to make another statement contradicting her previous one.

Four days later Robinson summoned Prince Ysenburg, who had by then been released from detention with the assistance of Lieutenant Colonel Wood. He threatened him with confiscation of his entire estate, which had been frozen by the US authorities, unless he produced a retraction of his earlier statement concerning the six missing paintings. Robinson claimed that he controlled Ysenburg's assets and that he had already liberated the sum of RM50,000 from them. He also made the point that he had an influential 'friend with a much higher rank than Colonel Wood'. Despite these threats, however, Ysenburg refused to give in to Robinson's demands.[16]

In the meantime, the investigation into Robinson's activities continued. In late August 1945 the Assistant Inspector General of

XXIII Corps, Lieutenant Colonel Charles A. McLean, carried out an inquiry into the affair, and at the end of the month, Robinson was questioned at Bad Homburg. He took refuge behind the Twenty-Fourth Article of War, which equates to the American civil law's Fifth Amendment, and thus avoided self-incrimination. He did, however, categorically deny having removed the six paintings. Lieutenant Colonel McLean was not convinced by Robinson's sworn testimony and recommended that the latter be court martialled for theft and for misuse of military transport. All documentation concerning the case was studied by a pre-trial investigating officer, Lieutenant Colonel C. J. Merrill, who also interviewed Robinson and all the witnesses. It was perhaps at this juncture that Robinson's 'friend with a much higher rank than Colonel Wood's' intervened, because shortly afterwards Merrill decided that, notwithstanding the irrefutable evidence against the lieutenant, all charges against Robinson should be dropped forthwith.

It appears that even this brush with the military authorities may have failed to dissuade Robinson from further indulgence in his larcenous pursuits. Shortly after the termination of the inquiry, 134 paintings disappeared from the Städel Museum repository at Bad Wildungen.

In 1948, the majority of the missing works mysteriously reappeared in the basement of the Städel Museum. Twenty-five, however, were still missing, though four were subsequently recovered. Seventeen years after the theft, on 16 and 23 February 1962, ten paintings reappeared briefly when they were auctioned in London and bought by dealers who subsequently sold them on. These had apparently been acquired previously by private collectors living in London.[17] Two more paintings, *A Traveller Resting at a Well in the Forest* by Carl Friedrich Lessing and *Mariners Loading Freight in a Southern Harbour* by Johannes Lingelbach, surfaced in the United States in 1963 when they were acquired from a private owner in New York by the art dealers French & Co. of Fifth Avenue, acting on behalf of a collector, Mrs Gay Robinson, also of New York. Both paintings are, however, still listed as missing.[18]

In 1980, the Städel Museum located another missing painting, *The Fainting Fit* by Quiringh Gerritsz van Brekelencam, which had been acquired by an individual named Thorhauer living in the German town of Hofheim in the area of Taunus. Negotiations took place with the aim of recovering the painting but these were apparently unsuccessful as the painting too is still listed as missing from the collection.[19] Four years later the museum was offered another of its missing works, *Sunny Path at the Forest Edge* by Théodore Rousseau, which had been acquired by the New York art dealer E. J. Landrigan. The latter approached the museum which declined to purchase the painting, and it was subsequently sold.[20]

In 1965, 110,000 files of the US Army's Criminal Investigation Division, containing information relating to the post-war looting in Germany, were destroyed. It has never been ascertained who was responsible. As Kenneth Alford surmised many years later, 'Now we understand why the high command did not want Robinson investigated. Some high-ranking officer was out to make a killing in looted art, but who was it?'[21]

Germany was not the only area in which elements of the US Army took the saying 'to the victor the spoils' very literally indeed. In August 1947 a civilian MFA&A officer, Evelyn Tucker, was appointed to the staff of the American headquarters in Vienna. This was as a result of increasing pressure from the other Allies, who suspected that a large number of works of art were still concealed in Austria and that the Austrians were attempting to integrate them into their own national collections. The Dutch had, for example, discovered that a large number of their works of art were still stored in the repository in the salt mine at Alt Aussee which, contrary to popular belief, had not been emptied of its contents.[22]

The Allies had insisted that all the contents of the mine should be transferred to the American collecting point at Munich, where they would be properly processed for eventual restitution. The Austrians, however, had protested on the grounds that the transfer of the mine to their authority in 1946 meant that its contents were under their control. Not surprisingly the Americans, represented in this dispute by James A. Garrison, Chief of Reparations and Restitution at the headquarters of the US military government in Austria, dismissed this claim and insisted that the US Army would continue to exercise control over the mine and its contents.

On 26 August 1947 Evelyn Tucker, whose principal role was investigation into missing works of art and their restitution, carried out her first task: a visit to the repository in the mine at Alt Aussee. She was accompanied by another MFA&A officer, Herbert Leonard, and Dr Gottfried Kreutz, a representative of the Austrian Bundesdenkmalamt, the Federal Office for the Preservation of Monuments. Also present was the administrator of the mine, Max Eder. As she toured the mine, Miss Tucker learned that the Austrians had moved all the works of art still stored there into the two large chambers known as the Springerwerke and the Kammergraf, measuring 6,000 and 5,625 square feet respectively. She and her companions carried out an inventory of the contents of the mine and it soon became apparent that a number of items still in the mine had been designated Austrian when in reality they were Dutch property. There were also large numbers of items labelled as Dutch, French and Belgian. One very large painting, hitherto unidentified and stored in the Springer-werke, was recognized as *Caterina Cornarvo* by Hans Makart, belonging to the National Art Gallery in Berlin.[23]

Evelyn Tucker reported on what she had discovered at Alt Aussee, with the result that on 28 August, despite strong protests from the Austrians, the contents of the mine were loaded on to a convoy of US Army trucks and despatched to the American collecting point at Munich. Included in the shipment was Hitler's personal collection, comprising mostly paintings acquired from private collections by the staff of the Dienststelle Mühlmann during their looting operations in the Netherlands.[24]

Some weeks later Evelyn Tucker visited the US Military Government Property Control Warehouse in Salzburg where all Nazi loot captured in Austria by the Allies, including works of art, was stored. While there, her attention was drawn to a supposedly worthless collection of some 200 paintings which had been stored in a small room in the warehouse for the past two years and had been given a nominal total value of $10. On 6 November, she entered the room and found it crammed to the ceiling with paintings which she proceeded to remove, realizing that they were far from worthless. Transferred to the Carabinierisaal in the Residenz Palace in Salzburg, the collection was found to be of major value: numbering some 1,181 works in total, it included paintings by Rembrandt and Van Ruisdael.[25]

During the rest of 1947 Evelyn Tucker visited repositories throughout Upper Austria, and it was at this time that she began to encounter evidence of looting and dubious acquisition of works of art by US occupation forces. On 30 October, accompanied once again by Dr Kreutz, she arrived in the town of Linz which had featured so prominently in Hitler's ambitions. It was now the location of the headquarters of the 42nd US Infantry Division. Her first port of call was the monastery of St Florian, located in the village of the same name. There she inspected a large quantity of looted furniture, paintings and antique musical paintings, brought to the monastery by the Germans during the war, some of which she was able to identify as being French or Dutch property. The abbot of the monastery was less than cooperative in letting her view these items and referred caustically to the Americans as 'the looting Amis'. Miss Tucker was somewhat mystified by this remark and on the return journey to Linz quizzed her companion as to its significance. Dr Kreutz explained that earlier in the year five truckloads of the most valuable items had been removed from the monastery by troops of the 83rd US Infantry Division for use in furnishing the quarters of senior American officers in Upper Austria.[26]

The following day Miss Tucker and Kreutz visited the Kremsmünster monastery, which is located on the top of a mountain not far from Linz. There she found further evidence of theft, albeit thwarted, this time by an officer of the 26th US Infantry Division. One of the monks recounted how he had spotted two small cases lying in the hallway with other baggage, awaiting loading aboard vehicles on the day of the departure of officers who had been billeted in the monastery. The monk had succeeded in removing both cases and on opening them had found inside twenty-two small paintings, mainly of Bavarian origin, which had obviously been looted during the American advance through southern Germany. Despite the ensuing commotion once it was found that the paintings were missing, the Americans had departed without their loot and the monk handed over the paintings to Miss Tucker.

Soon after her return to Salzburg, Evelyn Tucker had occasion to interview Frederic Wels, the owner of a gallery who in 1939 had been given by the Austrian Nazi party the task of establishing a large art gallery in Salzburg, which did not possess one at the time. High on Wels' list of prospective purchases for this project had been a large number of the paintings and tapestries looted from Salzburg by Napoleon Bonaparte in 1813; and, much to the delight of the burghers of Salzburg, he had indeed been successful in buying several of the items concerned. During her conversation with Wels, Evelyn Tucker learned that a large amount of property belonging to him and his wife had been stolen by an American officer, whose identity was known to him, and that little effort was being made by the US military authorities to investigate the affair. She also learned that works of art belonging to him had been confiscated and were hanging in the American officers' club at the Cavalierhaus in Salzburg. This building had been constructed during the war by the Germans and furnished with looted items from France and Holland; in 1945 it had been taken over by the Americans and all previous attempts by MFA&A personnel to carry out an inventory of its contents had been frustrated. Evelyn Tucker's request to enter the club was likewise denied.[27]

Her interest aroused, Miss Tucker started to investigate looted works of art in other American officers' clubs and senior officers' quarters. She visited the US Army rest centre at Gmunden, where she found French, Dutch and Hungarian paintings as well as a large amount of valuable French period furniture. A visit to the Gugelhof Officers' Club in Linz revealed that it was furnished almost entirely with works of art and furniture looted from the Schwarzenberg Castle in Czechoslovakia, among which was the painting *Pastoral Scene* from the school of François Boucher which comprised part of a French claim.[28] Access to other establishments, however, eluded her. Among those were the Traunblick Villa which had been commandeered as the quarters of General Geoffrey Keyes and which was known to contain a large number of valuable works of art including one by van Dyck and another by François Millet. Unfortunately, Evelyn Tucker was somewhat naïve in not realizing that her zealous pursuit of works of art purloined by the American military establishment was attracting attention at the highest levels of the US military government in Austria. Her actions were considered most unwelcome among those senior officers involved in the illicit trade and export of looted works of art, and it would not be long before they took action to put a stop to her investigations.

One of the establishments to which she attempted to gain entry was the Villa Warsburg in Salzburg, the quarters of Major General Harry J. Collins, officer in command of the 42nd US Infantry Division. Among the looted paintings hanging on the walls of the villa were *Harvest in Maxglan* by Anton Doll; *Laufen Near Ischl* by Anton Schiffer; and *Bad Gastein and Waterfall* by Thomas Ender. All three had been looted by the Nazis from German collections. Eight other paintings in the villa – one by van Dyck; another work by Anton Schiffer, *Mountain Ridge on Radstaetter*; and six Hungarian works of major value – had been removed by the Americans from the Residenz Palace in Salzburg. The Schiffer would subsequently disappear after the villa was handed over by Collins to his successor, Major General Kendall, who was later suspected of having purloined it.[29]

Such was Evelyn Tucker's disregard for authority that in December 1948 she went so far as to investigate the works of art hanging in the offices of General Mark Clark, the commander of US forces in Austria, and those of his staff. In the office of James Garrison, Chief of Reparations and Restitution, she found five valuable Hungarian paintings, and in that of Veron Kennedy, the property control officer, she discovered more of the same – all the subjects of claims by the

Hungarian government.[30] In the apartment of another member of the headquarters staff, James Langer, she espied a painting from the collection of Frederic Wels, *Cows in a Stable* by Verboekhoven, together with two Hungarian paintings: *Sunset with Peasant House* by Komarum Kanz and *Head of a Man* by an unidentified artist. Also in the apartment was Rembrandt's portrait of his mistress, *Hendrije Stoffels in Bed*, which she succeeded in having released to her by Langer's wife.[31]

Needless to say, this foray by Evelyn Tucker into the very heart of the US military government in Austria caused consternation and concern at the highest levels. The final straw was a report she wrote immediately afterwards, recommending that an investigation be mounted into the removal of looted works of art and other items to Vienna by General Clark himself. Shortly after submitting this report she was notified that her employment was terminated with effect from 1 February 1949.

In her final report Evelyn Tucker gave details of the looted works which had disappeared while in American custody. Among those she identified were paintings from the collection of Dr Alphons de Rothschild, stored in the salt mine at Alt Aussee, which were stolen from the repository between early 1945 and early 1946 along with four drawings by Dürer: *Knight, Death and Devil*; *Madonna with Grasshopper*; *Adam and Eve*; and *Hubertus and Rowlandson*. Two pen and ink drawings by Dürer from the same collection also went missing: *The Man Sick with Palsy* and *Unexpected Visit*.[32] Another repository, located in the Lauffen salt mine at Bad Ischl, near Alt Aussee, suffered thefts of a landscape by Berchem; *Hope* and *Faith* by Heermskerck; a portrait of a woman by Rubens; *Portrait of a Gentleman* by van Dyck; and *Sketch for a Ceiling of the Venetian School* and *Christ* by Antonello de Messina.[33]

Nor were thefts from repositories confined to those in Austria. The collection centre at Munich had also suffered losses, some of which subsequently surfaced for sale outside Germany. In 1948 a painting by Wilhelm Liebl, *Boy's Head with Hat*, was bought from a Swiss bank by Dr Robert Nathan, the owner of a gallery in St Gallen, Switzerland. This painting had been purchased in 1941 by Göring's agent, Hofer, from the Galerie Schmidlin in Zurich. Its provenance prior to that is not known.[34] This was not the first stolen painting purchased by Nathan: he was already in possession of fourteen works by Spitzweg which had also been taken from Munich, one of which, *Das Lieblingsplätchen*, he was known to have sold. When informed of the origin of his acquisitions, he refused to hand them back; and there was no way that he could be forced to do so under Swiss law.

An inventory carried out by the collection centre staff revealed that over 100 paintings and a quantity of jewellery belonging to the Rothschild family had been illicitly removed from the supposedly highly secure centre, and subsequent investigations revealed no clue as to who had been responsible. Indeed, the matter remained a mystery until August 1948, when information obtained by the Kriminalpolizei in Munich led to the unmasking of the culprit as one of the centre's guards, a German named Albert Krinner. Subsequent investigations by an American MFA&A investigator, Edgar Breitenbach, revealed that Krinner had stolen over 100 paintings as well as considerable amounts of silver, jewellery and porcelain.[35] In addition to the two paintings already mentioned in connection with Robert Nathan, others stolen by Krinner – mainly by German artists – included *The Town Crier*, *Hermit Reading*, *The Dragon Charmer* and *Landscape at Sunset* by Carl Spitzweg; *Girl with Rake* by Franz von Deffreger; *Portrait of a Man* by Wilhelm Busch; *Marine* by Eugène Louis Boudin; *Monk Tasting Wine* and *Falstaff* by Eduard Grützner; *Peasant and Girl in a Kitchen* by Frederichs Friedlander; *Portrait of a Woman with Hat and Red Flower* by Hans Makart; and *Bridge in Prague* by Auguste Mathieu. The remainder included works by Eduard Schleich, Dirk von Berghem, Wilhelm Trübner, Fritz August von Kaulbach, Paul Weber, Heinrich Bürkel, Buchner, and Anton Braith.[36]

Krinner would have had little difficulty in finding customers, given the flourishing black market in works of art that existed in Germany at this time. Among the wealthy Germans known to be active in the trade was Georg Hoffmann, who lived in Munich and was reputed to have cornered the art market in the city. His spending power was notorious: in one of his reports on Hoffmann, Breitenbach mentions that he had heard that Hoffmann was planning to spend some RM3.5 million on purchasing works of art.[37] According to a report written by Breitenbach in February 1948, Hoffmann had made a number of considerable acquisitions. In 1946 he had purchased from a woman in Hamburg a collection of fourteen paintings, comprising French Impressionist and post-Impressionist works, German expressionists and at least one work by Munch. In January 1948 he bought another collection which included *Dancer* by Degas, *Port of Rotterdam* by Signac, *Lady with a Mirror* and another unidentified picture by François Boucher, and works by Manet and Monet.[38]

Breitenbach subsequently discovered that Hoffmann was in possession of looted works which he claimed he had purchased in all
innocence. Among those confiscated from him and taken to the
collection centre were the unidentified work by Boucher, a painting
of ducks by Charles Jacques and a landscape by Johann Barthold
Jongkind.[39]

Much of Breitenbach's information concerning Hoffmann was
obtained from an informant, a German named Wido Schliep who
lived in Hamburg. Schliep was a restorer of paintings and had acted
as an agent in several art deals; it was through him that Hoffmann
had purchased the Jongkind landscape. It appeared that Schliep
knew Hoffmann reasonably well and was familiar with his activities
in the art black market. He told Breitenbach of several paintings in
Hoffman's possession, including a work by Jan van Goyen and
Merry Company by Goya, and a number of Dutch and Spanish Old
Masters. One of these was *Bohnenfest* by Jan van Steen, which
Schliep had glimpsed as it was being loaded into a car belonging to a
friend of Hoffmann's, Karl Obermaier. Hoffmann had been very
annoyed when he realized that Schliep had caught sight of the picture
and, after allowing him a brief glance at it, demanded that he forget
ever having seen it. From Hoffmann's behaviour, Schliep had
suspected that the painting was looted, but did as he was asked and
never mentioned it thereafter – until his interview with Breitenbach.[40]

Breitenbach was particularly interested to hear Schliep name Karl
Obermaier in connection with Hoffman. Obermaier was the wealthy
owner of a very large firm of contractors called Moll, from whom
two years previously Breitenbach had confiscated a number of
paintings, some of which had been purchased from Hoffmann. These
had turned out to be Dutch property and had subsequently been
returned to their rightful owners in the Netherlands.

On 14 February 1948, Hoffmann appeared at Breitenbach's office
to offer himself for interview. He was obviously concerned that
Breitenbach should be making searching enquiries about him and
insisted that all his wealth stemmed from his businesses, and that
these were entirely legitimate. The biggest of his industrial concerns
was Stahl und Metallbau AG, the second largest steel production
plant in Bavaria which had previously formed part of the Messerschmitt empire; his three other companies were involved respectively in
publishing, the production of instructional aids for the teaching of
physics, and the manufacture of special furnaces for the production
of gypsum and synthetic sandstone. Breitenbach questioned Hoffmann closely on his art acquisitions and the latter listed a number of

them, including a winter landscape by Goyen, a Dutch landscape with cows, another Dutch landscape in the manner of Hobbema and a Spanish painting depicting a man and woman with a lute in the manner of Goya. He made no mention whatsoever of the painting by Jan Steen about which he had been so secretive in front of Schliep.

When Breitenbach checked with Schliep, the latter maintained that he had learned from a conversation with Hoffmann's secretary, Eva Kern, that the industrialist was in possession of a large number of paintings, and insisted that these included two works by Goyen and a Goya depicting three people. Furthermore, he had heard Hoffmann say to an individual named von Dallwitz, 'I too have a few Schloss paintings.' Schliep was convinced that Hoffmann was in possession of a Hobbema landscape from the Schloss collection, No. 94 in the collection's catalogue, and *Madonna* by Ambrosius Benson.[41]

Breitenbach decided to interrogate Hoffmann further and to question others with whom he was known to have dealings – among them Martin Schneider, who was already in trouble with the US military authorities after being found with a looted painting by Ruysdael and who had fallen out with Hoffmann, whom he blamed for his troubles. Unfortunately, the records available do not recount whether Breitenbach ever took such further action.

Wido Schliep also provided Breitenbach with information concerning a group of former Wehrmacht officers who were in possession of a large number of paintings looted from the monastery at Monte Cassino and subsequently stolen again from the Munich collection centre where they had been deposited. He had initially passed this information to a contact in the British military police in Hamburg, but no action had been taken; so Breitenbach decided to pursue the matter himself. In early 1948 he discovered that an art dealer in Hamburg, Felix Roman Jagielsky, had been offered two Tintorettos from Monte Cassino by a former Kriegsmarine officer, Kapitän zur See Klaus May. Further investigation revealed that the paintings were now in Bavaria in the possession of a group of former Luftwaffe officers living in Berchtesgaden under assumed names. Schliep's contact was a member of this group, which was headed by a man named Dieckfeldt who claimed to have been a high-ranking officer and to have been awarded the Knight's Cross with Oak Leaves and Swords, one of the highest German decorations. Dieckfeld had described some of the paintings in the group's possession, which included two by Jan Miensz Molenaer, *Festivities on the Holy Day of the Magis* and *Scene in an Inn*; *Portrait of a Gentleman* by Rubens; *Portrait of the Queen of Naples* by Franz von Lenbach;

Pietà by van Dyck; *Landscape with Herd* by Nicolaes Berchem; *Landscape with Still Life* by van Strij; *Landscape* by De Ryck; *Landscape* by Neyts; and *Diana and Acteon* by Adriaen van der Werff. Dieckfeldt had claimed that the latter five paintings were from the Göring collection. Breitenbach passed this information on to the MFA&A authorities in the British zone, in which Hamburg was situated, but there is no information available to show whether they took any further action.[42]

Other information passed on by Breitenbach to the British concerned a painting from the Schloss collection, *Portrait of a Lady* by Moreelse, and four works from Hitler's collection: *Portrait of Baroness von Heymberg* by Rayski; *Portrait of a Young Man* by Wilhelm Leibl; *Landscape* by Kökök; and *Christ and the Adulteress* by Franken. All five paintings had been looted from the Führerbau in May 1945 and were being offered for sale in 1948 by dealers in Hamburg.[43]

Further evidence of trafficking in paintings looted from the Führerbau came to light in September 1948 when two women being questioned by Breitenbach in the course of his investigations identified a third woman, whom they had known while living in one of the three Berlin anti-aircraft towers known as *Flaktürm*, which were used to store works of art, as being responsible for the removal of twelve paintings from the repository in May 1945. Breitenbach set out to trace the woman, named as Magdalene Wienecke, and eventually tracked her down to an address in the town of Felmoching. On being questioned, Frau Wienecke and the man with whom she lived both admitted to having been in possession of the paintings, all twelve of which were apparently from the Schloss collection. Unfortunately, however, Breitenbach was too late to recover them: in June 1945, an American officer, accompanied by a German civilian, had appeared at their home and confiscated the paintings. Breitenbach checked the records of the collection centres but there was no record of the paintings ever having been received by them.[44]

Despite the size of the task facing them, MFA&A investigators in Germany did enjoy some success. On 4 November 1948 Breitenbach recovered five paintings from Hitler's collection which had been looted from the Führerbau in 1945 by a German named Karl Boser: *Portrait of a Gentleman* by Hendrick Gerritsz; *View through the Porta Sant Angelo in Naples* by Frans Vervloet; *Portrait of a Girl with a Basket* by Heinrich Weber; *The Repentant St John Chrysostomos* by Hans Baldung Grien; and *Landscape with Ruins, Shepherds and Cattle* by Jan Siebrandsz Mancadam.[45] Of greater note, however, was the recovery made by French MFA&A officer E. J. B. Doujinsky, who on 3 May 1949 visited a farm some 90 miles from Munich in the company of a Kriminalpolizei officer named Waldhor. There the two men found fifteen major works by French artists which formed part of a hoard concealed by a senior SS officer named Brandl who had been responsible for a considerable amount of looting in France during the German occupation. Brandl had apparently sent the hoard to the farm, which was owned by an elderly relative, for safe keeping until his return. He had, however, committed suicide in 1946 and some of the hoard, mainly valuable jewellery, had subsequently been removed by his mistress, Elisabeth Pertl, who had already been questioned by MFA&A investigators and at whose home a large amount of looted silver had been discovered.[46] Under threat of deportation to France, Pertl had revealed the whereabouts of the paintings, which comprised *Still Life, Apples and Nuts*, *Woman near a Well* and *Roses in a Vase* by Renoir; *Forest along a River* by Corot; *Village along a River* by Lépine; *Fishermen and Boats on the Beach* and *Sketch of a Child with a Drum* by Boudin; *Gathering of People* by an unknown artist; *Landscape with Waterfall* by Courbet; *Still Life, Dead Bird on a Table* and *Landscape* by Monet; *Head of an Old Man* by Cézanne; and *Landscape, Village on a River* and *Landscape with Lake* by Sisley.[47]

One major problem facing the US authorities in Germany was the question of restitution of some of the works of art claimed by the government of Italy which, as one of the Axis powers, had fought alongside Germany against the Allies. The return of looted works of art was a simple matter as they had been acquired in an illegal fashion. A large number of items, however, had been purchased by Hitler and Göring on the wartime Italian art market, and to these the German authorities could also be deemed to have a legitimate claim – which, indeed, they were not slow to pursue. Opinions on the legitimate ownership of these works were divided, and among those who supported the Germans' claim was Stewart Leonard, the chief MFA&A officer and director of the Munich collection centre.

The Italians maintained that their claim should be considered in the same light as that of Austria, which had also supported Germany during the war. Indeed, considering that the Italians signed an armistice in 1943, after the overthrow of Mussolini, and thereafter supported the Allies, there were perhaps grounds for their claim on this basis. The US authorities, however, refused to consider Italy in this light and initially rejected its demands. The Italians refused to accept this and became extremely vociferous in their campaign for the return of their art treasures.

The Italian spokesman in these negotiations was Rodolfo Siviero, the former official of the Uffizi Palace Gallery who, as recounted in chapter 1, had formed the secret organization set up to protect Italy's treasures during the German occupation after the collapse of Mussolini's Fascist regime. Since the end of hostilities in Italy, Siviero had dedicated himself to tracking down Italy's missing art treasures, and such was his devotion to that cause that he was not prepared to allow anything to divert him from it – certainly not American obduracy. Eventually, his persistence paid off and General Lucius Clay, the Deputy Military Governor in Germany, gave orders for the looted and confiscated Italian works of art, which numbered over 100 in total, to be returned to them.

This decision was greeted with dismay by some of the staff at the Munich collection centre and Stewart Leonard, refusing to obey Clay's order, resigned. Clay, dismayed at the furore caused by his decision, agreed that only some of the art works would be despatched while further investigations were carried out into the remainder. Among those returned to Italy were *Leda and the Swan* and Corsini Memling's *Portrait of a Gentleman*, both from the Spiridon collection.[48]

Siviero continued to be a thorn in the Americans' side, relentlessly pursuing his goal of restitution of all Italian art treasures still in the possession of the Munich collection centre. In the end, his vociferous behaviour proved his undoing. In 1949 he was barred from visiting the centre and indeed from entering the American occupation zone in Germany, and subsequently the Italian government removed him from office because he was proving a threat to relations between Italy and the United States. Siviero was not, however, deterred from pursuing his cause and in 1953 was rewarded with the return to Italy of most of the items for which he had so ceaselessly campaigned.

By this time, General Clay was in fact keen to dispose as quickly as possible of all the art works remaining in the care of the US military government in Germany. On 15 July 1945, during the Potsdam conference attended by the Allied heads of state, he put forward proposals to Secretary of War Henry Stimson and Secretary of State James Byrnes among which was a suggestion that all works of art owned by Germany should be transported to the United States for 'safe keeping'. His grounds for this were dubious: that there were neither enough qualified personnel nor sufficient facilities to take proper care of all the works of art currently being stored by US occupation forces. This was patently not the case: both the collection centres at Munich and Wiesbaden were sufficiently staffed and well equipped for their roles. Nevertheless, three days later Clay received tacit agreement from President Truman and shortly afterwards approval was received from Secretary of State Byrnes, who wrote to his Allied opposite numbers and informed them of the plan. However, in a letter of 1 August 1945 to Ernest Bevin, the British Foreign Secretary, Byrnes revealed that there was no definite commitment to return the works of art to Germany by stating that their 'eventual disposition will be subject to future decisions'.[49]

When news of Clay's proposals became public there was consternation. The American MFA&A staff at the two collection centres and throughout the US zone of occupation made plain their hostility to the plan by drawing up a letter, signed by twenty-five of their number, which was sent to their chief, Lieutenant Colonel Bancel Lafarge, for submission to General Clay as an official protest. Lafarge, however, while sympathetic to their feelings, was fearful of the consequences for his subordinates should the letter be sent, and thus retained it in his possession. One MFA&A officer, Captain James Rorimer, felt so strongly that he submitted his resignation, but it was refused. Others wrote letters of protest in which their feelings were only too plain. Opposition was also forthcoming from America's allies, who objected so strongly that Byrnes was forced to state in writing that 'this government fully intends to return all art objects of bona fide ownership as soon as conditions ensuring their proper safekeeping have been restored'.

Even in the United States itself the reaction had in the main been one of disapproval, despite government assurances that the works of art would be returned to Germany in due course. Hostile articles appeared in the press, including accounts of the strong opposition of the MFA&A officers in Germany, and a petition signed by a large number of art experts was sent to the President. Despite all the opposition, however, the transfer to America of 202 German-owned works of art, almost all of them the property of the Kaiser Friedrich Museum, went ahead, and on 6 December 1945 the US Army transport ship *James Parker* arrived in New York.[50] In its hold it carried forty-five crates containing 202 paintings which included works by Dürer, Botticelli, Brueghel, Rembrandt, Velázquez, Vermeer, Titian and van Eyck. After being unloaded, the precious cargo was transported to the National Gallery of Art for secure storage.

There were undoubtedly elements within the American art and museum establishment who hoped that the paintings would remain hidden in the gallery's vaults until such time as all thought of their being returned to Germany had conveniently been forgotten. This is reflected by sentiments expressed at the time by Theodore Rousseau, a former member of the OSS ALIU and after the war the Director and Curator of Paintings at the Metropolitan Museum of Art: 'America has a chance to get some wonderful things here during the next few years. German museums are wrecked and will have to sell. I think it's absurd to let the Germans have the paintings the Nazi big-wigs got, often through forced sales, from all over Europe. Some of them ought to come here, and I don't mean especially to the Metropolitan, which is fairly well off for paintings, but to museums in the West which aren't.'[51]

Unfortunately for Rousseau and those of a like mind, however, the US Army was the official custodian of the paintings and wished to relinquish its responsibilities at the earliest opportunity. In 1946 the army requested that arrangements be commenced with regard to returning the collection to Germany. There was much prevarication, however, and no decision was taken by the government until 1948, when it was decided that the paintings would be put on public display at the National Gallery of Art before being returned. The exhibition opened on 17 March 1948 and continued until April of the following year, when some of the paintings were shipped to Germany. The remainder were taken on a tour of the United States before they too were returned to the collection centre at Wiesbaden.

The decision in 1948 to return works of art to Italy had prompted a furious response from Austria, which had never ceased to insist on retaining all looted art found there in 1945 and on the return of works of art taken from repositories such as Alt Aussee. Dr Otto Demus, the Director of the Bundesdenkmalamt, had succeeded in enlisting the aid of Evelyn Tucker, by then totally disillusioned and disgusted by the large-scale looting and forcible confiscations she had encountered during her period of employment as an MFA&A officer in Austria. With Dr Demus, Miss Tucker had visited the collection centre at Munich where she had raised the subject of restitution of works of art to Austria with Herbert Leonard, who was in charge of the centre. Leonard's response had been negative, going on to inform her that General Clay had directed that all unclaimed and unidenti-fied works of art and other items would be handed over to the government of Bavaria by 31 August 1948, in recognition of Bavaria's assistance in bearing all the costs of maintaining and operating the collecting centre. In fact, this decision was based on an agreement between the government of Bavaria and the Office of the

United States High Commission for Germany, on the basis of which Bavaria had agreed to finance the cost of the collection centre.

Evelyn Tucker's strong representations on Austria's behalf had initially obtained agreement that items identified as being of Austrian origin would be returned. However, in December 1948, when she and Dr Demus returned to Munich and met the new head of the collection centre, Steven Munsing, who was blunt and to the point: no works of art would leave the centre without irrefutable documentary proof from the United States Forces in Austria (USFA) that the items concerned were Austrian. Despite Miss Tucker quoting the relevant USFA directives governing all works of art removed from Austria after 13 March 1938, Munsing had remained obdurate.[52]

This problem was not resolved until June 1951, by which time the Munich collection centre's stock of unclaimed works of art had been reduced to a total of 4,608 items (from a total of 23,117 placed there by 1 April 1946) which, if remaining unclaimed and unidentified, would be handed over to Austria. It was at this point that the US authorities turned for assistance to Professor Stuart Lane Faison, a former member of the OSS ALIU who had taken part in the interrogations of those principally involved in the Nazi looting of Europe's art treasures, and to former MFA&A officer Thomas C. Howe, who had been an assistant to another illustrious member of the wartime MFA&A community, George Stout. Faison and Howe set to work and within a few months had succeeded in reducing the number of unclaimed items which could be considered restitutable to Austria to a total of 960 paintings. The Germans protested strongly against any works of art being returned to Austria, but their objections were overruled by the US High Commission for Germany which on 20 January 1952 gave orders for the transfer of these 960 works to Austria. Shortly afterwards, the entire consignment was moved in two convoys by road from Munich to Salzburg, where it was placed in the Residenz Palace, together with the collection of 1,181 paintings rescued by Evelyn Tucker in November 1947, and a large number of works of art and books also stored there.[53]

In May 1952 West Germany ceased to be an occupied country and, as the Federal Republic of Germany, became a nation in its own right. All remaining items in the Munich and Wiesbaden collection centres were handed over to the newly formed Division of Cultural Affairs of the German Foreign Ministry which was headed by Count Wolff Metternich, the former head of the Kunstschutz of the wartime Wehrmacht. These comprised works of art supposedly still to be returned to Austria; Jewish property; and works of art which had belonged to senior members of the Nazi regime. Thereafter, the collection centres were closed.

The story of Austria in relation to looted art, however, did not end here. In 1955 a large consignment of approximately 6,000 Hungarian-owned works of art and other items – antiquities, porcelain, glass, silver, furniture and furnishings, books and manuscripts, coins and medals – was transferred from the former American zone of occupation in West Germany to Austria, where it was stored in a fourteenth-century monastery in the town of Mauerbach, near Vienna. There it was joined by the 960 items returned from Munich in 1952, and the 1,181 paintings salvaged by Evelyn Tucker. The US military authorities charged the Austrian government at the time with the responsibility of making every conceivable effort to identify the previous owners of such items and to return them at the earliest opportunity. Furthermore, on 15 March 1955, the State Treaty of Austria (Federal Law 152/1955) came into force, which stated in Article 26 that Austria had a duty to restitute property which had been looted or confiscated during the Second World War. But the Austrian authorities subsequently ignored any undertaking given in response to the Americans, and it was not until June 1969 that a list of these works of art, 8,423 in all, was published and claims of ownership invited up to a closing date of 21 December 1972. Although a few claims were submitted, none was taken seriously; and later in 1969 a statute of limitations was published declaring that all unclaimed items would become the property of the state.[54]

In December 1985, as a result of continuing worldwide pressure, the Austrian government grudgingly agreed to an eight-month period, from 1 February to 30 September 1986, during which further claims could be submitted. Thousands did so, but faced considerable difficulties and official intransigence at every step. One woman claiming a painting which had been the property of her father had her claim rejected because her statement of the painting's width was incorrect by one inch. She subsequently discovered that the painting had been put into a larger frame. Another had her claim rejected because she was unable to recall the exact combination of colours used in a landscape which had belonged to her father.[55]

By 1993 only a small number of paintings, books and other items had been claimed successfully by their rightful owners. The rest remained in the clutches of the state, which proceeded to make use of the collection to decorate government offices and embassies throughout the world. One priceless work, Vermeer's *Artist in his Studio*, which belonged to the Czernin family, was hung in the Kunstmuseum in Vienna despite a request from the family for its return. Their claim was defeated in 1952 when the courts ruled in favour of the government.[56]

The international Jewish community refused to let the matter rest and continued to put pressure on the Austrian government to allow claims for restitution to be submitted. Eventually, in 1995, the Austrian government gave in to world opinion and agreed to auction the collection and donate the proceeds to Jewish charities for the benefit of the victims of the Holocaust and their families. In July that year the entire collection was handed over to the Federation of Austrian Jewish Communities; a committee of prominent Jews was subsequently established to oversee the organization and conduct of the auction and to preside over the disposal of the proceeds thereafter. Among its members were Simon Wiesenthal, Lord Weidenfeld, Sir Georg Solti and five members of the Rothschild family.

Nevertheless, there were still misgivings in some quarters about the auction. Although the government confirmed that it had been 'looking after' a total of 8,423 works, previously stored at Mauerbach but more recently secured in the huge chambers of the Schönnbrunn, the huge former imperial palace of the Habsburgs, only 1,045 lots were listed in the auction catalogue published by Christie's of London prior to the auction, which was to be held at the end of October 1996. Among the paintings featured were Botticelli's *Florentine Lady*, a Rembrandt self-portrait and works by Canaletto and Peter von Cornelius, all of which were formerly from one family's collection. Missing from the list, however, were a number of sketches by Leonardo da Vinci which were believed by some to have been in the Mauerbach collection. This omission gave rise to suspicion, despite repeated assurances from the government to the contrary, that the Austrians had retained the best of the collection for themselves.[57]

Shortly before the auction, two nineteenth-century seascapes and nine Japanese Imari plates were spotted in the catalogue by a woman living in Tel Aviv. Greta Fattal recognized them as being from the collection which had belonged to her parents, who had lived in Vienna until 1938 when they had fled to Israel, leaving behind all their possessions. With the help of the Jewish community in Vienna she submitted a claim; it was successful, and the two paintings and plates were handed over to her before the auction. These items were, however, only a very small fraction of her family's collection, which had included a work by Rembrandt.[58]

Greta Fattal was not alone in recognizing former family possessions displayed in the profusely illustrated catalogue: other similar claims resulted in a total of 167 lots being withdrawn from sale before the auction eventually took place in Vienna on 29 and 30 October. Potential buyers numbered some 1,000 and bidding was strong throughout. The sale comprised 878 lots of Old Master paintings and drawings, nineteenth-century pictures, tapestries, textiles, carpets, sculptures, ceramics, glass, silver, arms and armour, furniture, coins and other items. A number of works were bought by private collectors who subsequently presented them to museums. These included Ronald S. Lauder, Chairman of Estée Lauder, the cosmetics conglomerate, who bought several items for the Yad Vashem Holocaust Museum in Jerusalem.[59]

Highlights of the sale included two still life works by Abraham Mignon, *Peonies, Roses, Tulips and Poppies in a Glass Vase* and *Peaches, Grapes, a Gourd, Cherries and a Corn Cob*, which sold for $1,190,182 (the highest price achieved throughout the auction) and $570,442 respectively. Among other paintings sold for high prices were *Carafe* by Alexander Archipenko, which fetched $425,836; *In the Schtetl*, a nineteenth-century village scene by Ludwig Knaus ($343,204); *The Madonna and Child with Saints* by Petro di Francesco Degli Orioli ($312,217); *The Oriental* by Friedrich von Amerling ($301,889); *The Flower Arrangement* by Otto Scholderer ($260,572); and *A Young Woman Arranging Flowers in an Urn* by Abraham Brueghel and Guillaume Courtois ($219,256). The total sum raised for victims of the Holocaust and their families was $14,567,193.[60]

Austria is not alone in having retained looted works of art until forced by moral pressure to surrender them. The finger of accusation can also be pointed yet again at Switzerland which, as recounted in chapter 6, was markedly reluctant until recent times to cooperate in the restitution of looted works of art found within its frontiers. A case in point is that of two paintings which currently remain in Switzerland despite strenuous efforts on the part of their owners to recover them; another concerns a picture over which negotiations between a Swiss museum and the owners have dragged on for over forty years.

The two works by Camille Corot, *Odalisque* and *San Giorgio Maggiore*, were among a number taken from the Paris home of the Bernheim-Jeune family in 1941 when their entire collection was confiscated by the ERR. In 1945, during his investigations in Switzerland, Wing Commander Douglas Cooper discovered that the family's collection had been offered for sale in Switzerland at a price of FFr1 million by three individuals: the German collector and dealer Adolf Wüster, the Paris-based dealer Etienne Bignou and a Swiss dealer named Charles Montag.[61] As mentioned in chapter 6, Montag had connections with the notorious Roger Dequoy of Paris, to whom he had introduced the Swiss collector Emil Bührle in September 1941.[62] Cooper subsequently discovered the two Corots in the possession of Klara Veraguth of Zurich, together with two others by the same artist, *Femme Grecque* and *Lac d'Oberland*, from another unidentified collection: it transpired that all four had been acquired from the Galerie Tanner in the city's Bahnhofstrasse, one of the Swiss galleries named by Cooper as dealing in looted art. The owner, a Swiss of the same name, was reported as having acquired all four works in 1941 and to have exhibited *Femme Grecque* and *San Giorgio Maggiore* in Zurich during the following year.[63]

It transpired that Tanner had sold the paintings to one of Frau Veraguth's sons-in-law, a Frenchman named Engbert Janninck who lived in Paris in the rue St Georges. They had subsequently been deposited in the bank of her other son-in-law, a Swiss named Schultess. When subsequently questioned by the French authorities, Janninck had claimed that he had bought the paintings in France in 1940 and had subsequently taken them to Switzerland. This lie was, however, easily exposed when it was pointed out to him that the paintings had been in the possession of the Bernheim-Jeune family until they were confiscated in early 1941.[64]

Armed with this information, the Bernheim-Jeune family issued a writ in Switzerland for the return of their two Corots.[65] Representatives of the family travelled to Switzerland, where they confronted Tanner. During a telephone interview from his gallery in Paris, Michel d'Auberville said: 'My father and uncle went in 1945 to speak with the owner of the gallery who had sold the paintings. But he told them that if they did not desist asking questions, he would have them run out of Switzerland. It was a clear threat. To make it worse, they were told in 1947 by the Swiss authorities that it was too late to pursue the claim.'[66]

The prolonged and persistent efforts on the part of the Bernheim-Jeune family have proved fruitless. To this day Michel d'Auberville remains unsuccessful in his attempts to recover the two paintings, the Swiss authorities continuing to maintain that it is too late for him to submit a claim. Fortunately, however, his efforts to recover a third painting in Switzerland appear to be bearing fruit. In chapter 4, brief mention was made of a work by Bonnard, *The Venus of Cyrène*, which had been given by the artist himself to his friend Josse Bernheim-Jeune. A still life portraying a vase of flowers on a table with a pile of books, one bearing the title of a novel written by the latter, the painting hung above the door in the dining room of the family's Paris town house, in the rue Desbordes-Valmore, which was commandeered initially by Vichy forces, and subsequently by the Germans, in 1941. Josse Bernheim, who had written the love story which gave its name to the painting, and his two sons, Jean and Henri, had fled the French capital for Lyon the year before. It was not until the family recovered ownership of the house at the end of the war that the theft was discovered, the painting having been crudely removed from its frame.

The mystery of its whereabouts persisted for a dozen years, despite intensive investigation by the Bernheim-Jeune family. Then, in 1957, while they were compiling a catalogue raisonné of works by Bonnard, the family were contacted by officials at the Kunstmuseum in Basle. Their letter enclosed a photograph of a Bonnard in their collection: the very same work which had been taken from the family's town house in Paris. Two years of delicate negotiations followed: but they failed to bring the painting home.[67]

Nearly forty years later, there appeared to be a change of heart by those running the Basle museum. Late in 1996 Katerina Schmidt, director of the Kunstmuseum, wrote to Michel d'Auberville, Josse Bernheim-Jeune's grandson, and the contact opened the way for possible restitution. Monsieur d'Auberville explained: 'It is clear from the museum's 1957 letter, and from what Madame Schmidt has told me, that they simply did not know the work was stolen. After all, why bother to let us know that they had the painting in the first place? The negotiations with the Kunstmuseum are at a delicate stage but we both believe that we can arrive at a settlement favourable to the museum and the family'.[68]

Meanwhile thirty more Bernheim-Jeune paintings, lost during the sacking of the Château de Rastignac, remain missing despite the family's efforts to trace and recover them.

Despite the efforts on the part of the wartime Allies to carry out restitution of works of art looted by the Nazis to their rightful owners, hundreds of thousands of items are still missing. While it is known that a large number have found their way to the West, countless others were trapped in 1945 in the Soviet zone of occupation in Germany, where they were found by the Red Army and removed by aircraft or train to the Soviet Union. It is only in recent years that the fate of some of this huge quantity of art treasures, many of them priceless, has been revealed.

9

TROPHIES OF WAR

The arrival of Soviet forces in Germany in January 1945 was heralded by the largest offensive launched by the Red Army in the entire war. A total of 180 divisions thrust south-westwards into Germany, and on 21 April Marshal Georgy Zhukov's armies reached the outskirts of Berlin. Already reeling from the effects of Allied bombing by day and night, the city was now subjected to further pounding by Soviet artillery while tanks and infantry fought their way through the streets. In the last few days of bitter fighting for the city, before the guns at last fell silent at 3 p.m. on 2 May, several thousand Soviet and German soldiers died. In the devastation of Berlin, the museums and treasurehouses of the capital lay open to the invaders, who wasted little time in plundering them.

Plans for the looting of Germany had been laid by the Soviet government some six months previously under the auspices of a body with the unwieldy title of Extraordinary State Commission on the Registration and Investigation of the Crimes of the German-Fascist Occupiers and their Accomplices and the Damage Done by Them to the Citizens, Collective Farms, Public Organizations, State Enterprises and Institutions of the USSR. Formed in November 1942 by the Council of People's Commissars, this body was charged with a variety of tasks related to the German occupation of parts of the USSR, including estimates of the value of works of art looted, damaged or destroyed by the Nazis.

The Extraordinary State Commission in turn established a panel of experts who were required to draw up lists of works of art equivalent in cultural and monetary value to those lost by the USSR during the German invasion. These were based on evaluations of losses produced by museums and other institutions throughout the Union, parts of which were still occupied by German forces. The panel comprised Igor Grabar, a painter and respected art historian; Viktor Lazarev, formerly Curator of Paintings at the Pushkin Museum; and Sergei Troinitsky, the former Director of the Hermitage Museum. The idea of the panel had originated with Grabar, who had suggested it to Nikolai Shvernik, the head of the Extraordinary State Commission and Secretary of the Communist Party Central Committee. It had received support from the head of the Commission's Culture Department, Vladimir Makarov.[1] The actual compiling of the lists was further delegated to a number of academics who had extensive knowledge of art collections in Germany and other countries (the lists covered Germany, Austria, Italy, Hungary and Romania).

The nominations for Italy included five paintings in Florence's Uffizi Gallery: *Madonna with a Pomegranate* by Botticelli; two *Madonnas* by Filippino Lippi; *Adoration of the Magi* by Ghirlandaio; and Piero di Cosimo's *Perseus and Andromeda*. Others included Brueghel's *The Blind Leading the Blind*, from the National Gallery in Naples, and Velázquez's *Portrait of Innocent X* belonging to the Dora Pamphili Gallery in Rome.[2] In Austria, thirty-five paintings were selected from Vienna's Kunsthistorisches Museum, including works by Velázquez, Brueghel, Tintoretto, Rubens, Giorgione and Bosch. Hungary's National Gallery in Budapest was also a target, with works by El Greco, Titian, Goya, Rembrandt and Velázquez earmarked for confiscation. Romania escaped with just one of its art treasures, El Greco's *Adoration of the Magi*, designated for removal.[3]

The major part of the list drawn up by Grabar's panel consisted of works belonging to Germany's galleries and museums. The Old Pinakothek in Munich was to lose a total of 125 paintings, including Titian's *The Crowning with Thorns*; Jacob Jordaens' *The Satyr and the Peasant*; Botticelli's *Lamentation*; Tintoretto's *Mars and Venus Surprised by Vulcan*; Tiepolo's *Adoration of the Magi*; Velázquez's *Young Spanish Nobleman*; Poussin's *Lamentation*; five works by Goya; three *Madonnas* by Raphael; almost all of the collection's paintings by Rubens, including his *Fall of the Damned*; and Roger van der Weyden's *Columba Altarpiece*. Others on the list were Hans Holbein the Younger's *Portrait of Sir Bryuan Tuke*; Adam Elsheimer's *Rest on the Flight into Egypt*; Albrecht Altdorfer's *Danube Landscape*; and the Master of the St Bartholomew Altar's *St Bartholomew with St Agnes and St Cecilia*.[4]

The Kaiser Friedrich Museum was also singled out for confiscation of 179 major works, among them Rembrandt's *Hendrickje at an Open Door* and *Man with the Golden Helmet*; Petrus Christus' *Portrait of a Young Girl*; van Eyck's *The Virgin in a Church*; Raphael's *Colonna Madonna*; Giotto's *Entombment of Mary*; Luca Signorelli's *Pan*; and others by van Dyck, Titian and Rubens.[5] The Dresden Gallery was to forfeit the majority of Old Masters in the collection, including Raphael's *Sistine Madonna* and Rembrandt's *Portrait of a Man in a Hat with Pearls*; Velázquez's *Old Man*; and a number of nineteenth- and twentieth-century French paintings which included Puvis de Chavanne's *The Fisherman's Family* and Courbet's *Stonecutters*.[6] Many other German cities, too, were on the lists: Frankfurt, Kassel, Oldenburg, Potsdam, Augsburg, Darmstadt, Braunschweig and Karlsruhe. They were destined to lose not just paintings but also collections of drawings, sculptures, antiquities, tapestries, arms and armour, furniture, jewellery and complete libraries of rare books and archives.

The task of physically confiscating art treasures from museums and galleries in Soviet-occupied areas fell to small units of the Red Army known as 'trophy brigades', groups of art experts under the overall authority of the Arts Committee of the Council of People's Commissars. The first trophy brigades were despatched from Moscow to join their respective Red Army 'fronts' towards the end of February 1945, thereafter travelling in the van of the advancing troops. They were to be supported in their work of locating and securing listed works of art, gathering them together at collection points and arranging their transportation by train to Moscow by special units of the Red Army designated as 'trophy battalions', which would provide guards, labour and vehicles. Day-to-day control of the trophy brigades was vested in trophy commissions, each appointed to a specific front. These in turn came under the authority of the Special Committee on Germany, which reported to the State Committee of Defence.

The first major German art hoard discovered by Soviet forces was the repository in the underground factory of the Focke-Wulf aircraft company near the village of Hohenwalde, some 80 miles east of Berlin in the area of Meseritz. When inspected by the First Belorussian Front trophy brigade under Lieutenant Colonel Andrei Belokopitov, it was found to contain the collections of the Kaiser Friedrich Museum as well as those of the museums of Tallinn and Riga, which had been looted previously by the Germans. Unfortunately, although troops had been sent to secure and protect its contents, considerable damage had already been inflicted. Paintings had been cut from their stretchers, porcelain and glass smashed, wooden items used as fuel for fires and tapestries pressed into service as makeshift bedclothes. Furthermore, as discovered by one of Lieutenant Colonel Belokopitov's officers, Major Sergei Sidorov, unofficial looting was being carried out by troops acting on behalf of senior Soviet officers keen to lay their hands on items of value. These looters were expelled from the repository with the assistance of troops of the 20th Trophy Battalion. At the end of March, Sidorov received orders to despatch the entire contents of the repository to

Moscow, and everything was duly loaded aboard a train; then, just before it set off, a convoy of trucks arrived with the contents of the Schloss Pansin near Stargard, some 80 miles north-east of Berlin. These were also loaded aboard, without any form of inventory. A few hours later the entire consignment departed for Moscow. It was the first of many.

The Soviet command had prior knowledge of two major repositories in Berlin and these should have been high on the list of priorities of the trophy brigade assigned to the city. As mentioned in chapter 8, Berlin possessed three massive anti-aircraft towers, known as *Flaktürm*. One of these was situated in the district of Friedrichshain, another in Tiergarten, adjacent to the city's zoological gardens, and the third at Humboldthain. Near each was a *Leitturm*, a smaller gunnery control tower equipped with radar and radio communications. The Friedrichshain *Leitturm* and the zoo *Flakturm* had been used as repositories since late 1941, when collections from Berlin's major museums and galleries had been moved into them for protection against Allied bombing. All the towers were heavily defended by well-equipped garrisons and were stocked with sufficient food and water for several months.

On 26 March 1945 Squadron Leader Douglas Cooper, by then the Assistant Director of the MFA&A Branch of SHAEF, wrote to Lieutenant Colonel Sir Leonard Woolley at the War Office in London informing him that intelligence sources had revealed the existence of repositories in the *Flakturm* and *Leitturm* and that they contained not only the larger and more important works belonging to the Berlin state museums but also the archives and records of the German Kunstschutz in France. Cooper suggested that the Soviet authorities should be informed about these repositories immediately.[7] Two days later Woolley wrote to a Mr C. O'Neill at the Foreign Office, advising him of these facts and asking him to pass the information on to the Soviet allies.[8]

The intelligence from Cooper's sources was accurate. Among the works of art on the first floor of the Friedrichshain *Leitturm* were 411 large paintings from Berlin's Picture Gallery. Among these were 160 Italian works, including paintings by Fra Angelico and Luca Signorelli's *Pan* which, as mentioned previously, was on the Soviet list of works to be seized. These were stacked together with works by Murillo, Francisco de Zurbaran, Chardin, Reynolds and Rubens, alongside crates containing antiquities from the Berlin state museums, 400 sculptures and other treasures. But it appears that either the information never reached the forward headquarters of the Soviet forces advancing into Berlin or it was disregarded. On 25 April the Friedrichshain *Flakturm* and *Leitturm* came under attack from artillery and armour, resulting in considerable damage to the smaller tower and the destruction of some of its contents, which included collections belonging to the Museum of Decorative Arts. Two days later the zoo *Leitturm* and *Flakturm* came under fire from tanks of the 8th Guards Army; although the *Flakturm* withstood the shelling, its garrison surrendered on 1 May.

During that final week of fighting, from 25 April to 3 May, other repositories were discovered by Soviet troops as they fought their way through the streets of Berlin: the New Mint, whose cellar contained hundreds of works of art; the Schlossmuseum and the Museum of Decorative Arts, both located in the Kaiser Wilhelm Palace on Museum Island; the Kaiser Friedrich Museum; and the Pergamon Museum, to mention just a few. The cellars of all of them were packed with treasures which awaited the arrival of the Red Army's trophy brigades.

On the night of 5–6 May disaster struck when a fire broke out on the first floor of the Friedrichshain *Leitturm*, followed a few days later by a second, damaging or destroying much that had been left untouched by the first. A few days later Belokopitov visited the tower and found a scene of utter destruction: priceless sculptures reduced to piles of dust, smashed fragments of porcelain intermingled with charred remnants of paintings, melted glass and bronzes, and everything covered in a thick layer of ash. Shortly after the fire, American MFA&A officers visited the *Leitturm* and recovered a small number of items, which they handed over to the staff of the Kaiser Friedrich Museum. Subsequent investigation revealed that the fire had been started deliberately, but it was never established who was responsible. It was not until January 1946 that any effective efforts were made by the Soviet forces to excavate remaining items from the ash and rubble-filled chambers of the *Leitturm*. Some 10,000 damaged items were eventually sent to the Pushkin Museum and the Hermitage for evaluation as to possible repair and restoration.

There was an interesting postcript to this episode. In February 1946 a painting was confiscated from a German art historian, one Dr Winkler, who was valuing it for a Count Kamensky, the owner of an antique shop in the American zone, who claimed to be a Soviet-born person of no nationality. The painting was identified as Dieric Bouts' *The Donor with St Augustine and St John the Baptist*, last seen stored in the Friedrichshain *Leitturm*. Under questioning by the

Americans, Kamensky stated that he had bought the painting from a Soviet officer named Captain Evdokimov. Initially arrested for violating regulations prohibiting the movement of works of art between zones of occupation, he was subsequently released on bail. However, he was not at liberty for long, being rearrested after the Americans learned that Dr Winkler had been questioned by the Soviet authorities and ordered to hand over the painting to them. Freed on the request of the Soviets, who claimed that he was a Soviet citizen, Kamensky subsequently disappeared. American demands for information about Captain Evdokimov, and how he had acquired the painting, elicited no response.[9]

Meanwhile, the zoo *Flakturm* was the scene of much activity. The largest of the three towers, it had been the repository for a large number of collections, mainly of antiquities and Far Eastern art. Also stored there, however, were the larger paintings belonging to the National Gallery. Shortly after the surrender of the garrison on 1 May, Soviet troops entered the *Flakturm* and discovered Dr Wilhelm Unverzagt, the Director of the Museum of Pre – and Early History, standing guard over the Trojan Gold, the priceless treasure of King Priam excavated in 1873 from the site of the city of Troy, on the north-west Anatolian coast of Turkey, by the German archaeologist Heinrich Schliemann. Soon afterwards, the *Flakturm* was secured by troops of the Soviet military counter-intelligence service.[10] On 13 May the first consignment of works of art left the zoo *Flakturm*, and six days later its first level was virtually empty. On 26 May a senior delegation of Soviet officials led by the deputy head of the Arts Committee, Andrei Konstantinov, visited the tower and inspected the crates containing the Trojan Gold, which shortly afterwards was loaded aboard a Red Army truck and driven away. On 30 June a Soviet military aircraft took off from Berlin for Moscow, carrying not only the Trojan Gold but also seven crates containing a collection of paintings which included Daumier's *Woman with Child*; a garden scene by Monet; a Cézanne view of Mont Sainte-Victoire; a sleeping nude by Courbet; a portrait of a woman by Velázquez from Hitler's private collection; Degas' *A Walk*; Renoir's *Woman on a Stairway*; and a *St Bernard* by El Greco. Other works in the same consignment included eighteen paintings from two private collections, those of Köhler and Gerstenberg, among which were Manet's *Portrait of Rosetta Mauri*, El Greco's *John the Baptist*, Goya's *Lola Jiménez*, Daumier's *Revolution* and *Laundresses*, a landscape by Courbet and a *Ballerina* by Degas. The aircraft's priceless cargo also included the sixth-century BC Eberswalde treasure, the fifth-century Kottbus treasure and the eleventh-century Holm treasure.[11]

The largest item in the *Flakturm* was the Pergamon altar, the massive marble edifice from the ancient Greek city of Pergamon which had previously been housed in its own building on Museum Island. Moved to the zoo *Flakturm* for protection in the latter part of 1941, it had been stored on the third level of the tower. With the *Flakturm* situated in the zone of Berlin shortly to be occupied by British forces, there was concern among Soviet trophy brigade personnel that American forces, who were already nearby, might remove the repository's contents. Having been refused access to the tower by the guards, members of Soviet counter-intelligence, Beloko-pitov appealed to the commander of Soviet forces in Germany, Marshal Zhukov, who ordered that the *Flakturm*'s contents were to be evacuated without delay. Soviet sappers and trophy brigade personnel began work the same evening, under the dismayed eyes of observing American MFA&A officers, and within two days the Pergamon altar had been removed and sent on its way, with other Greek antiquities, to Russia.

Elsewhere in Berlin the Soviet trophy brigades had a race against time on their hands to remove the collections of the Ethnographic Museum, the Museum for Pre- and Early History and the Art Library from their repositories, for all these were in the areas designated for future occupation by other Allied forces. The institutions on Museum Island were systematically stripped of their treasures by the trophy brigade acting with the authority of Marshal Zhukov. By the end of June 1945 all paintings from private collections, as well as those looted from Poland by the Germans and stored on the island, had been removed: over 250 in all, including Goya's *Maypole* and works by Ercole Roberti, Andrea Mantegna and Lorenzo di Credi. Among other works assembled at one of the trophy brigade's collection points before being despatched by train to Moscow were elements of the Siemens collection, including a nude by Ferdinand Hodler, a floral work by Delacroix and Manet's *Two Women in Black*.[12]

Another trophy brigade had discovered a major repository containing collections from the Dresden Gallery. The city of Dresden, laid waste by firestorms caused by British and American bombing in the middle of February, fell to Soviet forces on 8 May 1945. Its museums and other major buildings had been been reduced to ruins, but the Dresden Gallery's collections were safe, having been removed to a number of repositories, the most important of which was in a mine near the village of Gross Cotta near Pirna, some 10 miles south-east of Dresden. Conflicting claims to having discovered the Gross Cotta repository and its priceless contents were subsequently made by various individuals keen to take the credit for having done so. The most credible story is that the presence of the repository was revealed to Soviet troops who occupied the Schloss Weesenstein prior to the fall of Dresden by the director of the Dresden Gallery himself, Hermann Voss – who, as recounted in chapter 1, had succeeded Hans Posse as the Sonderbeauftrager of Sonderauftrag Linz in March 1943. However it came about, as soon as the information was obtained the castle and the mine were immediately secured by troops of a trophy battalion and the Arts Committee was notified of the discovery. Shortly afterwards trophy brigade officers arrived to inspect the repository and its contents. Among the approximately 400 paintings of the Dresden Gallery collection secreted there, of which the most important was Raphael's *Sistine Madonna*, were Dürer's *Dresden Altar*, Rembrandt's *Rape of Ganymede* and *Self-Portrait with Saskia*, Giorgione's *Sleeping Venus*, Titian's *Young Woman in White*, Rubens' *Diana*, José de Ribera's *St Agnes*, and landscapes by Watteau and Canaletto.[13] The evacuation of the repository began on 26 May and was completed in two days, the entire contents being transported to the Schloss Pillnitz about fifteen kilometres from Dresden, where a collection point had been established. Such was the eventual importance and value of the castle's contents that the NKVD, the Soviet state security organization, immediately took over responsibility for its security from the army.

Attention was then turned to the Schloss Weesenstein and its contents – not only some 500 more paintings of the Dresden Gallery collection but also the Koenigs collection of drawings, the collection of prints and drawings of the Kupferstichkabinett, part of the graphics collection acquired for the Führermuseum in Linz, the Sonderauftrag Linz records, a unique collection of German nine-teenth-century drawings, forty etchings by Rembrandt and the Palmier collection. Difficulties experienced in packing and loading the numerous prints and drawings of the Kupferstichkabinett collection prolonged the evacuation here over a period of two weeks.

A third major Dresden Gallery repository was discovered in a mine near Pockau-Lengefeld, not far from the border with Czechoslova-kia. Among the 350 paintings which had been secreted here were Titian's *The Tribute Money*, Rembrandt's *Self-Portrait* and a *Madonna* by Botticelli. On arrival at the mine a trophy brigade officer, Major Natalia Sokolova, and two of her colleagues found more paintings in a nearby barn, one of which was Rubens' *Bathsheba*. They also found two empty frames, identified from their labels as belonging to portraits by van Dyck, from which the paintings had been stolen. The contents of this repository were also despatched to the Schloss Pillnitz collection point. More of Dresden's riches were found in a further repository at the Schloss Meissen, north-east of the city: twenty-three paintings from the Dresden Gallery and three panels, Correggio's *Holy Night*, *Madonna with St Sebastian* and *Madonna with St George*. Another repository was discovered at Barnitz, containing works by Max Liebermann, Lovis Corinth, Constantin Meunier and Gauguin.[14] Another important discovery was a repository at the Schloss Königstein, some 35 kilometres from Dresden. During May it was occupied and searched by a trophy brigade largely consisting of NKVD officers, one of a number of such units active in Vienna, Budapest and Berlin, where they sought out banks and emptied their vaults and safes of currency, jewellery and works of art. Currency removed from German banks by them was subsequently used to finance purchases of works of art, gold, jewellery and other items of value by the Soviet Commissariat of Foreign Trade in the Allied zones of occupation through a network of companies established for that purpose. Having secured the Schloss Königstein, this particular NKVD trophy brigade expelled the castle's occupants and set about plundering its contents. In the cellars were found the collection of the Green Vault, Dresden's jewellery museum; a thorough search of the rest of the castle uncovered items from the city's Historical Museum and paintings from the Dresden Gallery. The latter included Vermeer's *Girl Reading a Letter by a Window*; Dürer's Dresden Triptych and *Portrait of a Young Man*; Rubens' *Mercury and Argus*; the van Eyck triptych; Hans Holbein's *Portrait of Morette* and *Double Portrait of Sir Thomas Godsalve and his Son*; and Lucas Cranach's central panel of the St Catherine altarpiece and *Portrait of Duke Heinrichs des Frommen*.[15]

These items had already been recorded as missing by the trophy brigade at the Schloss Pillnitz, by then under the command of Lieutenant Colonel Alexander Rototayev, who had previously been the assistant to the head of the Arts Committee. The NKVD brigade refused Rototayev's officers entry to the Schloss Königstein and despatched its loot direct to Moscow rather than sending it to join the rest of the Dresden collections at Pillnitz. When the consignment arrived in Moscow, several important works were found to be missing. Despite orders being issued for searches to be carried out, it was not until the following year that the majority of the missing items were located in Ukraine, as described later in this chapter. The van Eyck triptych was also subsequently found in July 1946 by staff of the Hermitage in Leningrad as they unpacked crates received from the Pushkin Museum. It apparently had been overlooked when the consignment had first been received in Moscow from Germany the previous year.

Such was the increasing importance of the Schloss Pillnitz repository that the removal of its contents to Russia became a matter of some urgency. On 12 July 1945 the commander of the First Ukrainian Front, Marshal Ivan Konev, received orders signed by Stalin himself to provide all necessary assistance to the trophy brigade of Lieutenant Colonel Alexander Rototayev in arranging the transportation of the Dresden collection to Moscow. Two weeks later, three experts arrived to select the works of art to be despatched to the Soviet capital. These were Professor Mikhail Dobroklonsky, the Deputy Director of the Hermitage; Professor Vladimir Blavatsky; and Boris Alexeyev, who had been a curator at the Kuskovo Museum in Moscow before the war and was an expert in porcelain. From a total of some 1,250 paintings found in the three repositories containing the Dresden Gallery collections, over 600 were selected for removal together with large quantities of drawings, prints, sculptures and other works. On 30 July a train bearing the entire consignment departed for Moscow. The remaining items were left in the Schloss Pillnitz, which was in the charge of the military administration governing the area.[16]

Soviet forces did not, however, have things all their own way in their pursuit of Germany's art treasures. On arrival at the Kaiseroda mine near Merkers, they found that the repository had already been emptied of its contents: works of art belonging to Berlin state museums, and the major part of the gold reserves of the Reichsbank. As described in chapter 4, these had fallen to the Americans, who by the cessation of hostilities had advanced some 100 miles inside the zone designated for occupation by Soviet forces.[17] American troops had also removed works of art from a mine at Ransbach and other repositories in the region of Thuringia and the Harz Mountains, areas within the designated Soviet zone of occupation. On one occasion Lieutenant Colonel Belokopitov and members of his trophy brigade arrived at the salt mine near the village of Bernterode to find themselves unable to enter it, as it had caught fire beforehand and was shortly afterwards demolished by German explosives which had been stored there. Even had they been able to gain access, however, they would have found nothing of value: the contents of the mine, namely 250 paintings, several tapestries and other treasures belonging to Prussia, had been removed in May by the Americans.[18]

The bitterest pill for the Russians to swallow, however, was the discovery that their erstwhile allies had found the principal German repository at Alt Aussee in Austria, which lay not far from the border dividing the American and Soviet zones of occupation in Austria, subsequently securing and removing its contents as recounted in chapter 5. Soviet forces had arrived in Vienna on 13 April 1945. Had Stalin known of the fabulous treasure hidden in the depths of Alt Aussee, there is little doubt that he would have ordered the Red Army to advance further into Austria and seize it.

Alt Aussee was not the only repository in Austria discovered and emptied by the Americans before the arrival of Soviet forces in the country. Others included the Lauffen salt mine at nearby Bad Ischl in the American zone of occupation, where the Vienna Kunsthistorische Museum collections had been secreted. When the US troops arrived, however, a number of works had already been removed by a detachment of SS troops on the orders of the Gauleiter of Vienna, Baldur von Schirach. A convoy of trucks had taken away a total of 184 paintings, all of them belonging to the Kunsthistorisches Museum, among which were works of major importance by Rembrandt, Velázquez, Titian, Dürer and Brueghel.[19] The Americans were also first into the Schloss Rossbach, north-east of the town of Bad Bruckenau, which contained works of art belonging to the Städel Museum including a number of French Impressionist paintings and Old Master drawings, some by Rembrandt. Across the Austrian border into Czechoslovakia the Hohenfurth Monastery, whose contents included furniture and sculpture looted from the Rothschild and Mannheimer collections, as well as a lifesize marble statue of *Polyhymnia* by Canova, was emptied only days before the arrival of Soviet forces in the area.[20]

The Americans did, however, miss one important repository in the Soviet-designated zone which contained an important collection of Impressionist and Post-Impressionist paintings and sculptures. The property of an industrialist named Otto Krebs who died of cancer in 1941, the collection comprised a total of ninety-eight Impressionist works by Degas, Picasso, Renoir, Manet, Gauguin, Cézanne, van Gogh, Matisse and Signac and had been hidden in the cellar of Krebs' country home on the estate of Gut Holzdorf near Weimar, the capital of the region of Thuringia which lay within the Soviet occupation zone. In April 1945 American troops were briefly billeted in the house, but did not discover the collection; nor did it come to light in the repeated pillaging of the house after their departure. Then, during the early part of 1946, Gut Holzdorf was occupied by the commander of the Soviet military administration in Thuringia, General Vasily Chuikov. He was advised of the presence of the collection by the director of Weimar's Fine Arts Museum, Walter Scheidig, who asked that it should be handed over to the museum. Permission to remove the collection was initially granted in the following year by Chuikov's deputy, but this was subsequently rescinded by the general himself. It was not until over a year later that the matter was drawn to the attention of Major General Leonid Zorin, the head of the Department of Reparations, Supplies and Restitution of the Soviet military administration in Germany, who wasted little time in sending two of his staff to carry out a search of Gut Holzdorf. The collection was removed and shortly afterwards spirited away to Leningrad and the Hermitage Museum. However, twenty of the paintings disappeared at some point en route, and today the Krebs collection in the Hermitage comprises only seventy-eight works of art.[21]

As they advanced into Germany and Austria, Soviet forces made good use of the assistance they were getting from the British, who continued to provide them with information concerning known repositories in Austria and Germany. In a letter of 3 April 1945 to Mr C. O'Neill of the Foreign Office, Lieutenant Colonel Sir Leonard Woolley had asked that the Soviets be informed of a major repository in the Schloss Nickolsburg, belonging to Prince Dietrich-stein and situated on the Austrian–Czech border, and of others in north-east Austria located by a British MFA&A officer, Wing Commander Jack Goodison. The latter included the Jagdschloss Rothschild near Langam, the Schloss Feldsburg and Schloss Ebsgrub near Dundenburg, the Schloss Gaming and the Stift Klosternenburg. Three other repositories identified by the British to the Soviets were in Vienna: the Liechtentensche Galerie and the Liechtensteinscher Somer-Palast, both in the city's Furstengasse, and the Liechten-steinsches Majorats in the Bankgasse.[22]

Furthermore, on 27 April 1945 the British embassy in Moscow had written to Mr A. J. Vyshinski of the People's Commissariat for Foreign Affairs, informing him of the location of a repository concealed in the Forsthaus Glambeck, a forester's lodge on the estate of the Schloss Görlsdorf near Angermünde, some 100 kilometres north-east of Berlin.[23] This contained part of the collection of

Chinese art belonging to Baron von der Heydt, a Swiss national; the remainder of the collection was stored in the August Thyssen Bank in Berlin, where the Foreign Office decided that it would be the responsibility of the MFA&A Section of the British element of the Control Commission for Germany once British forces reached Berlin. In due course the Soviet reply came, stating that the collection had disappeared from the repository by the time they reached it.[24] Whether they were being economical with the truth, or had been beaten to the draw once again by the Americans, has yet to be revealed.

In early May 1945 the Red Army's 38th Field Engineer Brigade occupied the area of the village of Kyritz, some 60 miles north of Berlin, and commandeered the nearby Schloss Karnzow for use as accommodation for the brigade's senior officers. During their three-month stay, the castle's new occupants learned of the existence of a secret cache in the cellars and, on breaking into it, discovered that it contained a large number of works of art. Unbeknown to them this repository, one of four belonging to the Bremen Kunsthalle, contained fifty paintings, over 1,700 drawings and some 3,000 prints, including works by Cézanne, Goya, Van Gogh, Titian and Rembrandt.[25]

Among the junior officers in the brigade was Captain Viktor Baldin, an architect in civilian life with a considerable knowledge of fine art. On hearing of the find he went to the castle where, examining the large number of drawings littering the floor, he found a number of works by Dürer, Goya, Rembrandt and Rubens, as well as a study by van Gogh for his *Starry Night*. He also discovered that the repository had already been emptied of much of its contents. Realizing the importance of the collection, he attempted to draw his commanding officer's attention to the matter, but – unsurprisingly, given that all the senior officers of the brigade were in possession of loot from the castle – met with an unsympathetic response. Baldin thus proceeded to conduct his own rescue operation, removing over 300 drawings from the cellar and, during the next few weeks, as the brigade withdrew from Germany and made its way back to the Soviet Union, adding further to his collection by trading some of his own possessions for drawings looted by troops and fellow officers in his unit, one of which was a *Head of Christ* by Dürer. He eventually amassed a total of 362 drawings and two small paintings, Dürer's *Salvator Mundi* and a portrait by Goya. In 1947, having already fallen foul of the authorities after being found in possession of other looted items, he donated the collection to the Shchusev Museum of

Architecture in Moscow, where it would remain for the next forty-three years. The rest of the works of art looted from the Schloss Karnzow had meanwhile vanished without trace elsewhere in the Soviet Union.[26]

In 1946, however, a Berlin art dealer approached an official of the city's civil government organization, established by the city's Soviet military administration in the immediate aftermath of the war, and asked him to check on a work by Cranach which he had been offered. The painting bore the stamp of the Bremen Kunsthalle and formed part of a collection of 135 items all similarly marked. Investigations subsequently revealed that a further 218 items from the Bremen collection were in the possession of another dealer. These were recovered and questioning of the dealer revealed that all these items had originated from Kyritz. A visit to the village resulted in the recovery of many more paintings and drawings, and a further search of the repository storeroom in the Schloss Karnzow uncovered yet more works, including a *Nativity* by Altdorfer and *St Onofrius* by Dürer, among the rubbish which littered the floor.[27] Items from the Bremen Kunsthalle collection would continue to appear on the Berlin art market over the next twenty years. Some were recovered during the 1950s, including a *Madonna and Child* by Masaccio and another Cranach; two watercolours by Dürer reappeared in 1962.

The Soviet pursuit of plunder in Germany continued remorselessly. During the latter part of 1945, trophy brigade operations began in Leipzig. The collection of over 1,200 paintings belonging to the city's Museum of Fine Arts was removed from fourteen repositories; of these, 111 were subsequently selected for despatch to Russia, including Lucas Cranach's *Portrait of Gerhart Volk*; van Eyck's *Portrait of an Old Canon*; Tintoretto's *Resurrection of Lazarus*; Martin Schongauer's *Madonna among the Roses*; and Hals' *Mulatto*. Large parts of the contents of the Grassi Museum of Applied Art and the Leipzig University Egyptian Museum were also removed and packed for despatch to Moscow. In Gotha the Friedenstein Palace was stripped of its treasures, as was the Schloss Reinhardsbrunn, which lost not only its own collections but also those of the Danzig and Gotha museums. Among the fifty-three paintings appropriated were two important works by Rubens depicting Saints Basil and Athanasius. All these items were removed to a collection point at Leipzig which eventually contained over 50,000 works of art. On 11 March 1946 they were despatched by train to Moscow, where they were divided up and distributed to various Soviet museums, institutions and libraries.

The early part of 1946 saw many more trains heading for Moscow from Germany heavily laden with loot, their unheated wagons filled almost to overflowing. On 15 January forty-one wagons full of works of art left Lichtenberg, followed by others throughout the rest of that month and February. The journey could take as long as a month, and it was not until March that trains arrived bringing the contents of the Berlin Friedrichshain and zoo *Flaktürme* and of the Schloss Weesenstein. Several Moscow institutions received items removed from Germany. The State Historical Museum, Museum of the Revolution, Museum of Literature, Darwin Museum, Polytechnic Museum, Historical Library, Library of Foreign Literature and Academy of Sciences shared 12,500 crates of documents, books, arms and armour, antique furniture, gold and silver coins, textiles, ceramics, silver and other treasures, the majority being allocated to the State Historical Museum.[28]

The Hermitage in Leningrad also received a major share of the spoils. On 31 July 1945 it took delivery of 196 crates of paintings from the Polish National Museum in Warsaw. Discovered in a house in the Polish town of Kynau, some 40 miles south-west of Breslau, by a sapper unit of the Ukrainian Front's 21st Army, they had originally been looted from the museum by the Germans and had subsequently fallen into the hands of a senior officer in whose billet they had been concealed. The 21st Army despatched the consignment, along with seventy crates of books removed from the Schloss Klein Öls, to the Hermitage, where staff found that it contained 212 paintings by European masters and 290 by Polish artists, the latter including Jan Martejko's *Joker Stanchik*. In October 1945 a train arrived in Leningrad having been diverted from its original destination of Moscow, where the Pushkin Museum found itself unable to accept any more of the influx. Comprising thirty-four wagons containing 1,154 crates of works of art, their contents including the Pergamon Altar reliefs, this consignment followed close on the heels of the Hermitage's own collection returning from Sverdlovsk, to which it had been evacuated during the war. It was followed in turn by three other trains, each bringing vast quantities of works of art. The task of registering this flood of items fully occupied the staff of the Hermitage during the coming months of 1946.

Elsewhere in the Soviet Union, Kiev's Museum of Western and Oriental Art also received a major share of the treasure in the form of 456 paintings from the Dresden Gallery, while the city's Historical Museum was given a further forty-one from the same collection. These had been sent direct to Kiev, without the knowledge of the

Arts Committee, by the trophy brigade of the Council of People's Commissars of the Ukraine, which had removed the paintings from the repository at the Schloss Pillnitz after the departure of the consignment for Moscow. Among them were major works which had obviously been overlooked by Lieutenant Colonel Rototayev and his experts when selecting items for the Pushkin Museum. These included Dürer's Dresden Triptych – seriously damaged by damp, the consignment having been left lying on a snow-covered airfield before being collected and taken to the museum – Cima da Conegliano's *Christ*, Lucas Cranach's *Nativity*, Veronese's *Finding of Moses* and *Portrait of Duke Heinrichs des Frommen*, and Rubens' *Old Woman with Brazier*.

The massive influx of huge quantities of works of art and other items inevitably placed a strain on resources available in Moscow for unloading, transportation and storage. At times, chaos reigned at the stations where the trains ended their long journeys, the situation being exacerbated by inaccurate manifests listing the items loaded at points of embarkation. In some instances consignments were left unguarded and a number of thefts took place. The organization initially responsible for receiving and registering all works of art removed from Germany was the Commission on Reception and Registration of Trophy Valuables, established in April 1945. It was headed by Pyotr Sisoyev, who had previously been in charge of the Arts Committee's Department of Visual Arts. In addition to registration, the commission was also tasked with distribution of works of art to museums and institutions throughout the Soviet Union, sending complete trainloads as far afield as Tajikistan and Turkmenia. The commission's life, however, was a short one. Having processed the first consignments at a leisurely pace, it soon found itself under pressure when a succession of large trainloads arrived in Moscow. Shortly afterwards, the Arts Committee disbanded it and transferred responsibility for registration and distribution to the Pushkin Museum.[29]

The task was an enormous one, bearing in mind that by the close of 1945 the Pushkin Museum alone had received 2,991 crates of works of art. The actual number of looted items delivered to the museum eventually totalled over half a million; by the end of the following year all but 100 crates had been opened and their contents inspected. The major problem facing the museum's staff was one of storage: every inch of available space in the museum was occupied, and some of the temporary storage areas were far from suitable. The problem was exacerbated by the urgent need for repairs and restoration work on a number of paintings, including forty-one from the Dresden collection, after their lengthy journey for which the canvases had been rolled up. The hard-pressed Pushkin staff were unable to cope, and art students were eventually called in to assist in opening the crates and listing their contents.

At the Hermitage, the staff encountered similar problems with items which had been damaged in transit. Fifteen of the Pergamon Altar reliefs were in need of repair, as were a painting by Marco Zoppo, *Enthroned Madonna with Saints*, some etchings by Rembrandt, a quantity of prints by Dürer and Hendrik Goltzius, and a number of Old Master drawings; all had been found to be soaking wet when unpacked. Indeed, out of over 800,000 looted items delivered to the Hermitage, more than 20,000 were in need of restoration.

In the autumn of 1946 an exhibition of looted works of art took place in the Pushkin Museum, to which only high-ranking political and military figures were granted access. It was held in two closely guarded galleries whose contents were kept secret and to which entry could be gained only on production of a special pass. Among the many paintings on display were the *Sistine Madonna*; Ribera's *St Agnes*; Giorgione's *Sleeping Venus*; Frans Hals' *Mulatto*; Vermeer's *Girl Reading a Letter*; Paris Bordone's *Woman with a Rose*; Rembrandt's *Old Woman Weighing Gold*; van Dyck's *Apostle Matthew*; and *Presentation in the Temple* from the school of Cranach.[30]

In that year, allegations of long-suspected corruption and dishonesty involving the unofficial looting of works of art and other items of major value finally came to the surface. During the campaign in Germany looting had been endemic among senior officers of the Red Army, who had removed the entire contents of castles and large houses throughout the areas occupied by their troops. Convoys of trucks, trains and even aircraft were pressed into service to bring back works of art, furniture and other trappings of wealth and luxury which subsequently disappeared into homes and dachas. Nor was such looting confined to the Red Army; it extended even to the Arts Committee itself and its deputy head, Andrei Konstantinov, who amassed a large amount of booty during a number of visits to Germany. Unfortunately for him, however, this came to the attention of the authorities in March 1946 when he shipped a wagonload of works of art, furniture, crystal, two pianos, carpets and other items by train to Moscow. Discovered by customs officers, the entire consignment was confiscated and turned over to the Pushkin

Museum along with the contents of the rest of the train. Konstantinov was dismissed from his post shortly afterwards.

In July of that year investigations into unofficial looting were commenced by the Ministry of State Control. Lev Mekhlis, who headed the enquiries, saw them as a way of currying favour with Stalin by providing evidence of corruption among senior Red Army officers who the dictator feared were too popular after their triumphs in Germany. When misconduct on the part of members of the Arts Committee was uncovered, senior officials were quick to shift the blame on to their subordinates among the former members of the trophy brigades. The commander of the Berlin brigade, Andrei Belokopitov, and one of his assistants, Alexander Voloshin, were accused of having included the paintings which had accompanied the Trojan Gold on its flight to Moscow in the consignment for their own ends, and in late 1946 were summarily dismissed from their posts. This was despite pleas that their sole motive had been to get the paintings to Moscow as soon as possible and thus prevent their being left for the Germans. Other trophy brigade personnel deemed guilty of misconduct suffered similar fates.[31]

It was the investigations into the looting by Marshal Georgy Zhukov which revealed the extent of looting and pillage by some senior Red Army officers in Germany. In late August 1946 a trainload of antique furniture, despatched to Moscow on Zhukov's orders, was discovered by customs officials, who informed the MGB secret police, the successors to the NKVD. A lengthy inquiry was launched and in early January 1948 the MGB searched Zhukov's dacha outside Moscow as well as his apartment in the capital. There they found a veritable Aladdin's cave of treasures: paintings, bronzes, antique furniture, silver, porcelain, glass, books, carpets and tapestries, fabrics, furs, curtains and jewellery. All were immediately confiscated.

Zhukov had already fallen from grace with Stalin, and had been despatched to Odessa as the commander of the military district there. Now he was sent even further into exile, to complete obscurity in the Urals. Other senior officers, including those of the NKVD, suffered worse fates. General Konstantin Telegin, political commissar to Zhukov during the campaign in Germany, was arrested and accused of various crimes, including looting. A confession extracted under torture resulted in a search of his Moscow apartment which revealed silver, porcelain, tapestries, works of art and other items, all of which were confiscated. Telegin was sentenced to twenty-five years' imprisonment.[32] Also arrested in 1948 on suspicion of looting was Major

General Alexei Sidnev, a senior former NKVD officer. He was found to have in his possession a large number of items of gold and jewellery taken from the safe deposit boxes of German banks, as well as a quantity of tapestries looted from Berlin's New Mint repository; a search of his apartment in Leningrad produced a large quantity of furniture, silver and other items.

The investigations even reached as far as former senior officers of the dreaded SMERSH counter-intelligence service, finding evidence of large-scale looting along with improper use of Soviet military aircraft to fly large consignments of loot to Moscow. Ironically, these revelations resulted in the dismissal of Viktor Abakumov, the former chief of SMERSH and head of the MGB, whose officers had been conducting the investigations. His treasures confiscated, he was arrested and subsequently executed. Abakumov's demise was primarily the result of information given to Stalin by the former's arch-rival General Ivan Serov, who had been in command of NKVD operations to confiscate gold, currency and items of major value from banks and other institutions in Germany. Serov too had succumbed to temptation and, with the assistance of his subordinates, had purloined large amounts of money, gold and jewels; for some reason, however, he was spared any punishment and remained in the Soviet intelligence apparatus, eventually being appointed head of the KGB under Nikita Khrushchev.[33]

In December 1949 it was announced by the Central Committee that the Pushkin Museum would henceforth be dedicated to an exhibition of gifts given to Stalin the previous year on the occasion of his birthday. This ludicrous decision was naturally met with dismay by the Pushkin staff, who were still struggling to cope with the enormous workload caused by the massive influx of trophy art from Germany. Nevertheless, two weeks later the exhibition opened. Its exhibits in some instances were simply laughable: boxes of chocolates, bottles of wine and other items of a similarly undistinguished nature were sumptuously displayed while collections of priceless looted treasures were crammed into halls and galleries elsewhere in the museum in deteriorating conditions. There they remained until May 1953, two months after the death of Stalin, when the farcical Exhibition of Gifts was brought to a merciful end and its contents removed to the Museum of the Revolution. Almost immediately work began on returning the Pushkin's treasures to their former places in the museum's exhibition halls and galleries, and the registration of trophy works of art was resumed.

In early 1955 the decision was taken to return the Dresden

collection to East Germany as a gesture of goodwill, and on 31 March an announcement appeared in newspapers to that effect. A Ministry of Culture summary of items belonging to the Dresden Gallery listed 738 paintings, seven miniatures and ten tapestries as being in the possession of the Pushkin Museum, with a further eleven paintings in the Hermitage. Shortly afterwards, this list was supplemented with a further 501 paintings and two pastels in the Museum of Western and Oriental Art in Kiev. It was decided, however, that there should be an exhibition of the collection prior to its return to East Germany, with the attendant propaganda emphasizing the role of the Red Army and the Pushkin Museum in its so-called 'rescue' and restoration. The exhibition, whose star exhibit was Raphael's *Sistine Madonna*, was an outstanding success, over a million visitors passing through its halls before it closed and the collection returned to its home in the Dresden Gallery.[34]

Further returns of works of art and other items to their rightful owners followed in 1956. The Soviet Union retained all works belonging to West Germany and to private collections found in German repositories by the Red Army, but Poland regained works of art looted by the Germans, including Hans Memling's *Last Judgement*, while Romania was given back collections evacuated to Russia for safe keeping during the First World War. (These did not, however, include the crown jewels of Queen Marie, icons and archives sent to Russia for protection in July 1917, just before the occupation of Bucharest by German troops. Three months later the Bolshevik Revolution had effectively removed all guarantees of the return to Romania of these national treasures, which remain to this day hidden in Russian depositories.) East Germany pressed for further items to be returned, including a large number from museums in East Berlin, Leipzig and Gotha, as well as works of art still missing from the Dresden collections.

It was at this point that the somewhat chaotic and incomplete state of Soviet registration procedures came to light, as it rapidly became obvious that insufficient information was available to trace the items in question. Further investigations produced a breakdown of items held by the Soviet Union's two principal museums: 536,357 were in the possession of the Pushkin Museum, 1,051 being paintings of which 480 were of unknown provenance; the Hermitage held the vast total of 829,561 items, 2,724 of them paintings, as well as a number of large archives belonging to the cities of Berlin and Brandenburg. Additional information was provided by government departments, and eventually the Ministry of Culture produced a comprehensive set of statistics for items looted from Germany. According to this, a total of 2,614,874 individual objects, together with 534 crates of archaeological works, had been removed. This figure included 108,338 works of art from private collections, 915 of which were paintings. Over 50,000 items were of unknown provenance.[35]

A major problem facing those dealing with further returns to East Germany and other Soviet satellite states was the very poor condition of large numbers of works of art. Numerous restorers were enlisted as the massive task of restoration began in Moscow and Leningrad. Eventually, however, the task became one of such herculean proportions as to absorb all available restoration resources, to the detriment of both museums' own collections. In view of this, the Ministry of Culture announced that badly damaged items would henceforth be returned to East Germany. However, 561 items in the Hermitage and 1,277 in the Pushkin Museum deemed beyond repair were to be destroyed rather than returned, in order to avoid allegations of mistreatment which the Soviet regime feared might provide its enemies with useful propaganda.

Having handed back the major parts of the Dresden collections, the Soviet authorities assumed that a similar show of generosity would be forthcoming in return, and had given the East Germans lists of those works of art looted by Germany during its occupation of territories within the USSR. It received a rude shock when the German Democratic Republic announced in October 1957 that no works of art from the Soviet Union had been found in searches of German repositories. This bleak response was a reflection not of dishonesty or intransigence, but of the mixture of incompetence, bureaucracy and secrecy governing relationships between various ministries within the Soviet government apparatus.

The organization responsible for tracing and recovering Soviet works of art looted by the Germans was the Committee on Cultural and Educational Institutions. In 1947 a team of its experts had conducted searches in the Soviet-occupied area of Germany, while the other Allies handed over items found in their zones of occupation. Among the latter were 534,120 items from the museums of Minsk, Kiev, Pskov, Smolensk and Novgorod received from the Americans during the period 1945–8. These were delivered to the Red Army's Department of Reparations, Supplies and Restitution of the Soviet military administration in Germany, whose records were highly classified and thus not made available to the committee.[36] Eventually a vast quantity of Soviet-owned works of art was amassed in a repository in East Berlin, remaining there undisturbed until 1947 when they were returned to the USSR by train. The situation was made even worse when the Committee on Cultural and Educational Institutions was closed down in 1953 and its records consigned to obscurity in the archives of other government departments. Thus, although the items concerned had in fact been returned to the USSR, there was no record of their repatriation.

The consequent apparent intransigence of the East Germans only served to harden attitudes in the Soviet Union, where some officials demanded that there be no further returns to East Germany until the latter reciprocated. Others proposed that those items belonging to West Germany should be retained until Germany was eventually reunified, knowing full well that reunification would never be permitted by the Soviet leadership. In the event, all objections were overruled by the Chairman of the Central Committee, Nikita Khrushchev, who in May 1958 gave orders for the further return of works of art and other items to East Germany. A delegation from the GDR arrived towards the end of the following month and in early August exhibitions of the principal items from the collections to be returned were mounted at the Pushkin Museum and the Hermitage for their benefit. Among the paintings, drawings and sculptures were works by Munch, Picasso, van Eyck, Brueghel, Rodin and Maillol. The East Germans were not, however, shown the secret repositories containing large quantities of looted works from private collections and other countries.

During the rest of 1958 a total of 1,569,176 works of art, filling some 300 railway wagons, were returned to East Germany. The process was deemed completed during January of the following year,[37] and in May 1960 the GDR signed an accord to that effect. However, further low-profile returns to East Germany took place during the late 1960s, 1970s and 1980s, when works including Lucas Cranach the Elder's *Portrait of the Elector Johann des Beständigen* and Rubens' *Monument to King Albrecht II* and *Landscape with the Christ Child and John the Baptist* were restored to their former owners. Nevertheless, over one million looted items belonging to West Germany or taken from repositories of Nazi loot remained concealed in secret storehouses or in the possession of Soviet ministries.

The existence of the repositories within the Soviet Union, and indeed much of the story related in this chapter, would have remained unknown but for the efforts of three art historians during the 1980s. In 1984 a Ukrainian named Konstantin Akinsha working in the Museum of Western and Oriental Art in Kiev stumbled across a number of books and manuscripts from German collections, including the Berlin Academy of Arts. Shortly afterwards, one of the museum's curators showed him a depository in the museum containing portfolios of red chalk drawings by Rubens, etchings by Marc Chagall and Alexander Archipenko, gouaches by Emil Nolde and prints by Piranesi; all these sported labels on the back showing them to be from the collections of the Dresden Kupferstichkabinett and Berlin Academy of Arts. These and other items had arrived at the museum only a few months previously from the archives of a government ministry in which they had been discovered by chance, having been deposited there soon after the end of the war.

During the same period Akinsha became a member of a commission carrying out research into the fate of Russian Orthodox churches and their property, including works of art, in the Ukraine. Travelling around the country in the course of his work, he was on several occasions offered works of art which were all too clearly items looted from Germany by members of the Red Army. This, coupled with his discoveries in the museum, rapidly led him to the conclusion that in all probability considerable numbers of looted works of art were concealed in the Soviet Union.

Two years later, in 1986, he moved to Moscow to study for a doctorate at the Research Institute of Art History. This was the period of *glasnost* and *perestroika* under Mikhail Gorbachev, and in 1987 the young art historian felt sufficiently confident to broach the subject of 'trophy art works' to a newly established independent organization called the Culture Fund. His qualifications and membership of the Research Institute established his credentials and he was appointed to the Commission on the Return of Cultural Heritage subsequently formed by the Culture Fund.

At this time Akinsha was reunited with a fellow art historian named Grigorii Kozlov with whom he had studied at Moscow State University in the late 1970s. Kozlov had subsequently worked for the Ministry of Culture before moving in 1987 to the Pushkin Museum. His duties here included providing information to members of the public who brought works of art to the museum for an expert opinion; on many occasions he was shown items which had clearly been looted from Germany by former members of the Red Army.

In the autumn of 1987 Kozlov chanced upon documents in the process of being destroyed by some of his colleagues. Offering to assist in their destruction, he was able to spirit away a quantity of them. Subsequent study revealed some to be records of transportation of trophy art works from Berlin to Moscow, while others documented the return of works of art to East Germany during the 1950s under the Khrushchev regime. Others still were inventories of works of art hidden in secret repositories throughout the Soviet Union.[38] Kozlov confided in Akinsha, who in turn revealed his discoveries in the Ukraine. The two men joined forces and continued their investigations, amassing an archive of information as they did so. The problem facing them was how to publish their discoveries and bring them to the world's attention. Two years later the opportunity presented itself with the arrival in Moscow of Milton Esterow, the editor of the American publication *ARTnews*, who was to speak at a conference on the Western art market. Akinsha succeeded in introducing himself to Esterow and, at a meeting which lasted almost an entire day, recounted the story of the secret repositories.

Having checked carefully on both Akinsha and Kozlov, Esterow eventually agreed to publish the story. The piece which eventually appeared in the April 1991 issue of *ARTnews* focused on the Koenigs and Bremen Kunsthalle collections as well as the Trojan Gold; this was followed by further articles relating the operations of the Red Army trophy brigades, the removal of works of art from Germany, and the art treasures still hidden in repositories in the USSR. These stories were also published in the newspaper *Izvestia* and other Russian publications.

Although the regime of Mikhail Gorbachev was somewhat more liberal than those of his predecessors, Akinsha and Kozlov nevertheless showed remarkable courage in persisting with their campaign to publicize the existence of the secret repositories. Kozlov not only faced the wrath of the director of the Pushkin Museum, Irina Antonova, but was also questioned by the KGB. He refused, however, to be intimidated; and, fortunately for him, his arrest had been forbidden by the Minister of Culture, Nikolai Gubenko, concerned about the reaction of the Western media who were by then taking an increasing interest in the subject of the secret depositories.[39]

One Westerner who succeeded in penetrating the Soviet veil of secrecy was Helen Womack, a freelance journalist based in Moscow. In an article published in April 1991 in the *Independent on Sunday*, she described a depository of trophy art treasures in a sanatorium belonging to the Academy of Sciences at Uzkoye, on the southern outskirts of Moscow. Her account was based on an unauthorized visit to the sanatorium by an unnamed individual who had gained entry to the building and filmed its interior with a video camera, identifying a landscape by the French seventeenth-century artist Gaspard Dughet and two other works which appeared to be by Antoine Pesne. Another painting was deemed to be from the school of Rubens, while others were suspected as having been taken from Sans Soucis, Frederick the Great's palace at Potsdam.[40]

Helen Womack subsequently visited the sanatorium herself but was refused entry. Questioning the manager about its contents, she was denied any further information; but she did learn that the Church of St Anne, next door to the sanatorium, contained a huge collection of books which had been removed from Germany. This was later confirmed by a Russian journalist, Yevgeny Kuzmin, who had previously visited the church on two occasions. He had found huge quantities of German books stacked in piles alongside Russian publications withdrawn from circulation by Stalin's regime. He later estimated that the church contained several hundred thousand books, all suffering from the appalling conditions in which they were being kept.[41]

Two months later Helen Womack finally gained entry to the sanatorium at Uzkoye when she attended a wedding reception held in its clubhouse. Two landscapes hanging on the walls caught her eye, and on enquiring about them she was informed that they were trophy art works. She later visited the club again and, with the permission of its manager, photographed the two paintings; they were subsequently identified by Akinsha and Kozlov as Wilhelm Schirmer's *Vespasian's Temple in Rome* and *The Narni Valley*, both belonging to the Schlossmuseum in Berlin from which they had been looted in 1945.[42]

Shortly after Womack's articles were published, the Soviet Academy of Sciences announced that the collections of German books in the church at Uzkoye were to be handed back to Germany. In July 1991 a senior official of the German Ministry of Interior, Horst Waffenschmidt, visited the repository and identified the collections of a number of German libraries in Berlin. Not long afterwards, the newly independent Central Asian republic of Georgia declared that it would return to Germany some 200,000 books removed by its trophy brigade in 1945.[43]

Within Russia itself, the first stories about secret repositories had begun to surface early in 1991. On 18 January an interview with Alexei Rastorgouev appeared in a Paris-based Russian-language newspaper, *La Pensée Russe*, which revealed how Schliemann's

Trojan Gold had been hidden away in a secret store in the Pushkin Museum. Rastorgouev was a lecturer at Moscow State University whose father, Leonid, had served with the Red Army in Germany at the end of the war. 'He was a metallurgist,' said Alexei, speaking to one of the authors on the telephone from his home in Moscow. 'Being a postgraduate student, he was given the senior rank of colonel. He managed to see the Berlin Friedrichshain flak tower before and after the fire there and he saw quite a lot of what was happening to the art that was discovered. Those in my profession, art history, and also in the museums in the post-war years also saw a lot. They would sometimes see works of art being brought into the museums which were thought to have been destroyed. You have to remember that in 1946 or 1947, these processes were organized not as top secret. The government had control and these things were normal. A select few people were invited to an exhibition of *Place de la Concorde* by Degas and works of trophy art in the Hermitage.'[44]

Rastorgouev's article initially made little impact; but shortly after its original publication it was reprinted by the German newspaper *Die Zeit*, and in April 1991 it appeared in Russia's main national newspaper, *Izvestia*, the same month that Akinsha's and Kozlov's own revelations had made headlines in their home country. Some eight years after the piece first appeared in print, Rastorgouev appreciates the not insignificant risk he took by broaching such a sensitive subject. 'There was already a moderate government by that time,' he continued, 'but I still had some people call me, telling me that I was putting my head in a noose.' Whatever the risk may have been, it was compounded by further revelations he made in an article, entitled 'Art as a Prisoner of War', which appeared in the magazine *Literaturnaya Gazeta* on 23 June 1991. The effect was almost immediate and, for Rastorgouev, adverse. 'Certain museum directors, including Irina Antonova at the Pushkin, turned against me,' he claims. 'Doors were closed to me and invitations to museum conferences withdrawn – all of which made it harder for me to do my job. I suppose they tried to turn me into a non-person in professional terms.'

The result of all this publicity was further pressure on the Ministry of Culture by elements of the Soviet cultural establishment, including prominent art historians and the Soviet branch of the International Association of Art Critics, to acknowledge the existence of the secret repositories and reveal their contents. Eventually, despite resistance from some museums, Minister of Culture Nikolai Gubenko officially admitted the existence of the repositories at a press conference in October 1991 and announced that a Commission on Restitution was to be formed. These announcements were, however, tempered by a statement that the USSR would only return works of art in exchange for items of equivalent value looted from its territories by the Germans.[45]

Two years previously, in 1989, the Director of the Bremen Kunsthalle had received a surprise visitor in the form of Viktor Baldin, the former Red Army engineer officer and architect who had by then been appointed Director of the Shchusev Museum of Architecture, which housed the collection of 362 drawings and two paintings rescued by him from the looted repository of the Schloss Karnzow in Germany, as described earlier in this chapter. Baldin recounted his story to his fellow director and told him of his several unsuccessful appeals to the Soviet hierarchy to have the collection returned to Bremen.[46] Despite the absence of any response to these requests, the following year Baldin tried again, appealing directly to Boris Yeltsin, who had by then succeeded Mikhail Gorbachev as President. Yeltsin's reaction was a positive one, but the Ministry of Culture's was otherwise: Nikolai Gubenko personally confiscated Baldin's collection, which was handed over to the Hermitage Museum in St Petersburg (no longer Leningrad). At the instigation of the Ministry of Culture, the luckless Baldin was subsequently vilified in the Soviet press as a thief.

It was as a result of having met Baldin and listened to his story that Konstantin Akinsha and Grigorii Kozlov set out on the trail of other parts of the Bremen Kunsthalle collection, discovering two caches of Bremen works in a secret depository in the Pushkin Museum. The first comprised thirty-four drawings taken from the Schloss Karnzow by Vladimir Balabanov, another officer in the same engineer brigade as Viktor Baldin. Balabanov had taken them with him at the end of the war when he returned to the Soviet Union and his home in Samarkand. In the 1960s he had donated them to the local museum, but the Ministry of Culture learned of the gift and the drawings were confiscated and handed over to the Pushkin Museum. The second cache contained fifty drawings which had appeared in Siberia at the end of the 1960s and, having been given to a museum in Novosibirsk, also eventually ended up in the Pushkin.[47]

In late 1992 Russia announced that it was considering the return of the Bremen Kunsthalle collection to Germany, but that in the meantime parts of it would be unveiled to public view. In December an exhibition of 138 drawings opened at the Hermitage: 131 of the 362 recovered by Viktor Baldin from the Schloss Karnzow and a further seven, all by Dürer, from those acquired by the Hermitage from elsewhere. Among those exhibited were Rembrandt's *Landscape with Three Windmills*, Boucher's *Study of Diana Bathing*, Delacroix's *Oriental Warriors*, van Gogh's *Starry Night*, van Dyck's *Carrying of the Cross*, van Scorel's *Transfiguration*, di Cosimo's *Transfiguration* and Guercino's *Toilet of Venus*. The seven works by Dürer included *The Cavalcade*, *View of Nuremberg*, *View of Kalkreuth Village*, *Lamentation* and *Self-Portrait as Suffering Christ*.[48] Early in 1993 the exhibition moved to Moscow and the Pushkin Museum; it subsequently returned to St Petersburg, but all optimism about its possible return to Germany eventually evaporated, as there was thereafter no mention of it again by the Russians.

Also in 1992, the reappearance of another collection of works belonging to the Bremen Kunsthalle resulted in Akinsha and Kozlov carrying out their most courageous and undoubtedly risky act in their campaign to restore looted art to its rightful owners. Kozlov had been told of a man who had approached the Ministry of Culture, claiming to be in possession of a collection of Bremen paintings and drawings looted after the war. He had been fobbed off by officials who had dismissed him out of hand as a lunatic. Kozlov, however, took the report seriously and after some weeks succeeded in tracing the old man to his home in a Russian provincial city. Having made contact, Kozlov and Akinsha visited the man, who proved to be an art historian acting on behalf of a former soldier who had removed a quantity of works of art from the Schloss Karnzow repository in May 1945. Shortly after their arrival at a dilapidated one-room apartment in the desolate, poverty-stricken outskirts of the city, the two art historians found themselves looking at a collection of drawings, prints and paintings which included Dürer's watercolour *Landscape with a Castle near a River*; Toulouse-Lautrec's lithograph *La Goulu*; Adrian von Ostade's *Tavern Scene*, Hans Baldung Grien's drawing *Two Heads*; and Jacob Jordaens' drawing *King David*. The collection also included works by Tintoretto, Manet and Rubens.[49]

In March 1993 Kozlov and Akinsha accompanied the art historian as he delivered his friend's collection to the German embassy in Moscow. There the treasures were taken into the safe custody of diplomats who, sceptical when first approached, could hardly believe their eyes as works by Dürer, Tintoretto, Jordaens, Rubens, Manet, Delacroix, Goya, Toulouse-Lautrec and others were laid out before them and checked off against a Bremen Kunsthalle list. However, the collection remains there to this day as the German government feels that its return to Germany via the diplomatic bag would only serve to imperil negotiations with Russia over the return of looted art in general and the rest of the Bremen collection in particular.[50]

Other elements of the Bremen Kunsthalle collection also reappeared during the 1990s. In 1993, three drawings were offered for sale to a number of dealers in New York. Although none of them was deemed to be of any great value – indeed, one ostensibly by Poussin was said to be a forgery – all bore the stamp of the Bremen Kunsthalle and were subsequently seized by the Federal Bureau of Investigation. In December of that year drawings by Rembrandt and Dürer, all also bearing the stamp of the Bremen Kunsthalle, were offered for auction at Sotheby's in New York but were turned down.[51] In 1996 a painting from the Bremen collection, Hans von Marées' *Self-Portrait as a Young Man*, was returned, followed in 1998 by several further works. In February, the Ukrainian government returned three drawings: *Heidelberg Castle Tower* by Carl Philipp Fohr; *Head of a Girl* by Johann Heinrich Tischbein the Elder; and *The Ruffian* by Joos van Craesbeeck; during the same month another drawing, Caspar David Friedrich's *Boy Resting on a Tree Stump* was returned anonymously; and in May two more were also returned by persons unknown: *Head of a Young Saint* by Johann Friedrich Overbeck and *Stage Scene* by Arthur von Ramberg.[52]

Akinsha and Kozlov meanwhile continued with their endeavours, writing further articles which were duly published in *ARTnews* and the Russian émigré press. Eventually they decided to produce a book. *Beautiful Loot: The Soviet Plunder of Europe's Art Treasures*, published in 1995, provides a comprehensive account of the Soviet Union's wholesale looting of Germany and the Nazi repositories. Among its revelations are details of some of the hitherto secret depositories in the Pushkin Museum, which houses some 200,000 items including the Koenigs collection, and the Hermitage, which numbers among its trophy art works the Krebs, Köhler and Gerstenberg collections, minus eighteen paintings which in July 1945 were placed on the same aircraft as the Trojan Gold and despatched to Moscow. Another major depository lies within the Holy Trinity–St Sergius monastery in the city of Sergiev Posad, some forty-odd miles north of Moscow.[53]

Through their exposure of the secret depositories in the former Soviet Union, Alexei Rastorgouev, Konstantin Akinsha and Grigorii Kozlov rendered an immense service to the world of art and culture. The considerable risks that they took in doing so are illustrated by the murder in 1994 of a Ministry of Interior official, Anatoli

Sviridenko, whose body was found lying by a railway line near Kaluga. At the time of his death, Sviridenko was investigating a series of thefts of works of art from the depository at the Holy Trinity–St Sergius Monastery.[54]

The pressure on Russia to provide further revelations about the contents of its secret depositories continued, and in February 1995 the Pushkin Museum unveiled some of its hidden treasures in an exhibition bearing the somewhat unwieldy title: 'Twice Saved: Masterpieces of European Art of the Fifteenth and Sixteenth Centuries Removed to the Territory of the Soviet Union from Germany as a Consequence of the Second World War'. The sixty-three works displayed included paintings by El Greco, Lucas Cranach and Renoir; others were Goya's *Lola Jiménez*, Daumier's *Revolution* and *Laundresses*, all three from the Gerstenberg collection, *Madame Chocquet at the Window* from the Bremen Kunsthalle and Manet's *Rosita Mauri* from the Köhler collection. For some reason, notwithstanding the title of the exhibition, works by Corot, Cézanne, Degas, Gauguin, van Gogh, Monet, Pissarro and Toulouse-Lautrec, some of which belonged to the Hatvany and Herzog collections, were also featured. Among paintings from the Herzog collection known to be in Russia are *Carnival* and *Bullfight* by Goya, *St Andreas* by El Greco and *Portrait of a Lady in a White Dress* by Renoir.[55]

Shortly afterwards, on 30 March, the Hermitage opened a rival exhibition. Called 'Hidden Treasures Revealed', it comprised seventy-four Impressionist and Post-Impressionist paintings from the Gerstenberg, Krebs and Köhler collections. These included Degas' *Place de la Concorde*, van Gogh's *White House at Night*, Gauguin's *Two Sisters from Tahiti* and a seascape by Seurat, with other works by Cézanne, Courbet, Gauguin, van Gogh and others.[56]

Six months later a major exhibition of the 307 drawings from the Koenigs collection still held in Russia was put on show in the Pushkin Museum. It opened on 2 October 1995, almost three years to the day since the then Minister of Culture, Yevgeny Sidorov, gave the first official confirmation that his country was in possession of the drawings. Among the works displayed were Tintoretto's *Study of Head of Emperor Vitellius*, Fragonard's *Park with a Foundation* and a black and red chalk *Portrait of Sebastiano Lombardi da Montecatini* by Fra Bartolomeo. Other exhibits included five sheets of sketches by Rubens and a *Recumbent Lion* by Rembrandt, matching a similar picture which had been taken from the main body of the collection during the war but returned thereafter to the Netherlands.[57]

The staging of the exhibition was plagued by the same sort of problems which have hampered Dutch attempts to recover the drawings. An offer by the Netherlands to loan the Pushkin some of its own Koenigs works was turned down by officials in Moscow. Consequently, the Dutch announced their own rival exhibition. Called 'Counterparts', it was staged in the Dutch Institute in Moscow between 30 November 1995 and 21 January 1996. The accompanying catalogue explained how celebrations to mark the end of the Second World War highlighted 'the urgency to solve the pending issue of the return of the Koenigs collection to the Netherlands'. 'The Netherlands Government', it continued, 'expresses the hope that both exhibitions will contribute to this. Our countries, two befriended wartime allies, should be able to cooperate with a lawful solution of this matter.' The catalogue's editors added pointedly: 'The cooperation of the Russian Ministry of Culture in this cultural project is gratefully acknowledged.'

In December 1996 the Hermitage staged another exhibition from the Gerstenberg, Krebs and Köhler collections, this one comprising eighty-nine works by van Gogh, Goya, Cézanne, Delacroix, Signac and Daumier. Among those on display were van Gogh's *Boats on the Beach at Saintes-Maries*, Daumier's *Gare Saint-Lazare* and Signac's *Boats in a Harbour*.[58]

Another significant result of the revelations in 1991 about Russia's secret repositories was the start of negotiations between Germany and Russia over restitution of looted works of art. The end of that year saw the final collapse of the Soviet Union, to be replaced by the Confederation of Independent States. During the following year the German–Russian Cultural Agreement was signed by President Boris Yeltsin and Chancellor Helmut Kohl, and a joint commission was established to deal with the problem of restitution of works of art belonging to both countries. Headed jointly by Mikhail Piotrowski, Director of the Hermitage, and Germany's Dr Werner Schmidt, then Director of the Print Room of the Dresden Museum and subsequently Director of the museum itself, the commission aimed to establish a framework to advance the possibility of a joint handing back of each nation's art treasures. Three prominent academics from the recently reunified Germany and three from Russia met in Berlin at the end of October 1993 and in Moscow in June 1994.[59] Lists of missing works of art were exchanged. The German delegates were keen to press for details on pieces from the Staatlichen Museum in

Berlin and the Weimar Museum, which prior to reunification was in the old East Germany, as well as from the Dresden Museum and the Krebs collection. However, the negotiations were hampered by lack of information on the Russian side, particularly with regard to the large quantities already returned to them by the Americans in the aftermath of the war. Irina Antonova, the bullish and fiercely defensive director of the Pushkin Museum, gave her justification for Russian obduracy, saying, 'In American museums there is a mass of stuff from Russia. They don't reveal anything.'[60] The Cold War may have been dead in theory, but the mistrust of the last fifty years was obviously hard to shake off. Russian officials also demonstrated their fondness for filibustering, the delaying tactic of 'talking out' matters until the expiry of set deadlines. Contrary to the belief of both Yeltsin and Kohl in 1992, it did not prove possible for even a small number of works of art to be returned. Attempts to relaunch the foundering discussions were halted by the argument that no further meetings should be held until after the celebration of the fiftieth anniversary of Hitler's defeat in 1995. Then came delays during which Russian constitutionalists contended that war loot seized from Germany should be considered as reparations for the wholesale damage and losses suffered by Russia during the war. Such a suggestion marked the beginning of the end of the talks between the two countries. It also proved to be the origin of the 'trophy law' which followed.

The Russian parliament, the Duma, sought to push through legislation nationalizing the 'trophy' art works which had not managed to make it back to their pre-war homes. The rejection of the scheme by an embattled President Yeltsin – on grounds arguably just as patriotic as those of the measure's proponents – made no real difference; the nationalizing bill became law in late April 1998. He later denounced the act, backed by a ruling of Russia's Constitutional Court, as 'a slap in the face', adding, 'there are many more Russian artefacts in foreign lands. We cannot touch them under this law.' An appeal was announced by his aides but it was clear that with other, more immediately pressing problems, such as the perilous state of a Russian free market still in its infancy, the plight of war loot might not be at the top of his list of priorities.

The warning signs about the possessive intentions of senior Russian officials were clear almost a year before Yeltsin was forced reluctantly to put his signature to the 'trophy art' bill. In June 1997 the Hermitage mounted yet another major exhibition of works from the Krebs and Gerstenberg collections, along with a selection of works from the Bremen collection. Dr Anne Röver-Kann of the Bremen Kunsthalle claims the exhibition marked a depressing development in the whole saga of 'trophy art'. 'When I went to see it,' she told one of the authors, 'I found that for the first time the pictures had all been given Russian inventory numbers. Previously they had retained only their Bremen numbers. I thought to myself that this was a worrying move. It appears to strengthen the claim of the Russians to the works, it formalizes their grip on them. It was not something I wanted to see and it goes without saying that I was sad.'[61]

It has not all been sadness, though, for German museums in the recent past. In September 1998, the High Court in London ruled that the Gotha museum should receive back a tiny Old Master painting stolen in 1946. *The Holy Family with Saints John, Elizabeth and Angels* by the Dutch artist Joachim Wtewael was painted in 1603 on a copper plate measuring just 20cm by 15cm, yet is worth an estimated £700,000. It had been owned since the early nineteenth century by the Saxe-Coburg family, from whom Prince Albert, Queen Victoria's consort, was descended. In 1918, under an arrangement which saw the transfer of many of the family's assets to the control of the region of Thuringia, the painting was moved to the custody of a Grand Ducal museum. In 1946 it was seized from the museum, together with many other precious items, by a Red Army trophy brigade commanded by a Major Alexeyev and spirited away to Moscow. Successive German governments, including that of East Germany which took control of part of Thuringia, always maintained that the painting had gone to Russia, but nothing certain was known of its whereabouts until it appeared on the black market in Moscow in the mid-1980s. In 1985 it was sold by the son of a Soviet colonel named Kozlenkov who had acquired it soon after its disappearance from Germany. Two years later it was taken out of the Soviet Union by Mariouenna Dikeni, the wife of the Togo ambassador in Moscow. Mrs Dikeni, the London court heard, specialized in smuggling religious icons out of Russia and had agreed to smuggle the painting on behalf of an unnamed Russian to another black market art dealer, Helmut Furst, based in Berlin. Whether it reached him remains unclear, as Mrs Dikeni subsequently returned to Moscow claiming that she had deposited the painting with a relative.

From Germany this tiny treasure continued its journey, ending up in London. It subsequently came into the possession of a collector named Mina Breslav, who sold it in 1989 to a Panamanian-registered finance company called Cobert. This company in turn attempted to sell the work at auction through Sotheby's. However, it was withdrawn when questions were asked about its provenance, at which point the German government stepped in to stake its claim. Attempts by Cobert to fight the claim, on the grounds that the German thirty-year statute of limitations had expired, were dismissed by the presiding judge, Mr Justice Moses. In awarding custody of the painting to German officials, he said: 'To allow Cobert to succeed when, on its own admission, it knew or suspected that the painting might be stolen . . . does not touch the conscience of the court.' And, in a judgment which could have far-reaching implications for other claims on looted art, he added: 'The law favours the true owner of property which has been stolen, however long the period which has elapsed since the original theft.'[62]

The case of the Wtewael painting, and other successes, have provided encouragement and hope for German museum officials, such as Dr Röver-Kann, about the chances of further recoveries of works missing from their collections. In May 1998 the Bremen Kunsthalle was fortunate enough to regain another of its missing works after Paul Bril's drawing *Roman Ruins* appeared in the Stockholm saleroom of the Swedish auction house Auktionswerk. It was spotted by German art dealer Marcus Marshall who, in a telephone interview with one of the authors from his Munich office, told how he had come across it. 'I know as an art historian that one must be careful of this stolen art all the time. I only noticed this drawing because I'm quite a generalist. Although I don't specialize in paintings or drawings, I take a fair interest in them as an enthusiast. I saw this drawing high up on the auction room wall and thought it seemed familiar, so I got a ladder and went up to take a closer look. I saw that it bore not the Kunsthalle stamp but that of the Kunstverein, a sort of social club which preceded it. If someone didn't know the history, they wouldn't have recognized the stamp.

'I telephoned the museum and eventually they agreed to buy it. I bought the drawing for about £2,000 at auction and had them reimburse me the cost of the painting and my own costs for the trip. I certainly wasn't looking to make money on the deal which I had made. I thought I was helping the museum out, doing it a favour. However, I didn't get a thank you, not even that courtesy. It is symptomatic of the culture in Germany. There is a prejudice by the museums and universities, and the academics, against the art trade. Although I am not happy at the treatment I received here in Germany, it doesn't surprise me.'[63]

Nor is it surprising that a missing work of art, looted by Red Army troops in 1945, should have turned up in Sweden. Although it was supposedly neutral during the Second World War, according to wartime Allied intelligence reports Swedish free-ports were used as havens and clearing houses by Nazis who later despatched their loot to the major world art markets of the United States and Britain, or hid them as 'nest eggs' elsewhere around the globe. According to Dr Röver-Kann, Sweden today features as part of the route for looted art secretly exported from Russia and sold in Finland, subsequently finding its way through Scandinavia to art markets in Europe and the United States.[64]

IO

THE LAND OF THE FREE

It was very clear to all those involved. In early 1946, with experience and information gleaned from months of detailed enquiry into Nazi art theft in Europe still fresh in their minds, Allied MFA&A specialists had little doubt about the destinations for which much of the still-missing material was headed. A final report in May from the the OSS ALIU analysed the presence of stolen material in the safe havens of neutral countries such as Switzerland, Sweden, Spain and Portugal, and in almost every case concluded that there was 'some evidence . . . but more detailed investigation needed'. Despite the weight of evidence indicating the movement of art to the cantons of Switzerland and the Iberian peninsula, as described in previous chapters, the ALIU expressed significantly more concern about the illicit traffic to the Americas. 'From information obtained,' read the report, 'there appear to be three significant problems of containing transfer [to the United States]. Relaxation of wartime controls on former collaborationist dealers, presence of assets being held for the benefit of collaborationist dealers by their American colleagues, importation because of the relaxation of wartime controls on works of art of questionable origin.'[1] The ALIU's anxiety about Latin America was even stronger. 'It is likely', the report continued, 'that a considerable volume of loot may have reached the South American continent. Further investigation will be required with particular reference to movement from South America of looted works of art.'

It was natural that much art should head to America. As the one true superpower in 1945 and the largest post-war economy, the United States had a voracious appetite for art. Moreover, it had proven to be a sanctuary for many prominent and wealthy Jewish families fleeing the Nazi Holocaust. Many had major art collections, some of which accompanied them. Art dealers, eager to maintain business as usual, simply moved their operations to the United States. Furthermore, such was the sheer weight of loot moved around Europe, it became very simple for returning military personnel to send or bring home rare and valuable 'souvenirs'. However, at the time hardly anyone bothered to listen to the advice from those in a position to know. Now, more than half a century later, a large part of the fabric of the American art market is in danger of unravelling – and is fighting hard to avoid it.

On 4 June 1998, the directors of American museums were forced to take an unprecedented step. Needled by adverse publicity following revelations about war loot in some of the most reputable galleries in the United States, and following a report by a group of their most senior colleagues, they announced a 'comprehensive review' of their works to ensure that all were of reputable provenance.[2] It was a measure clearly designed to restore confidence. Having been put on the defensive by media coverage of a number of high-profile claims against members, Philippe de Montebello, Director of the Metropolitan Museum of Art in New York, launched the initiative in direct and positive fashion. 'America's museums', he said, 'place themselves on record as committed to acting swiftly and proactively to conduct the necessary research that will help us learn as much as possible about works for which full ownership records have not been available previously.' Mr de Montebello, as chairman of the Association of Art Museum Directors (AAMD), also gave details of a new set of guidelines designed to ensure that any new acquisitions by any of the association's 170 members, whether permanent or on loan, bought or donated, would be thoroughly vetted. The two initiatives were the result of five months of deliberation by an AAMD 'task force' which also recommended settling claims in a 'mutually agreeable manner'. In effect, for all its attempts to appear 'proactive', the association was indulging in crisis management.

Ironically, the events which arguably obliged the museums and significant other bodies in authority to take action had little to do directly with the objects permanently in their custody. Between October 1997 and January 1998 the Museum of Modern Art in New York staged an exhibition of works by the Expressionist Egon Schiele. All the paintings were owned by a foundation set up by the Viennese ophthalmologist and collector Rudolph Leopold. The retrospective had already been shown in six cities in four countries, including London, Tokyo, Zurich and Düsseldorf. All had passed off without incident. However, on Christmas Eve 1997 an article appeared in the *New York Times* which administered a sudden jolt to the smooth progress of the tour. Entitled 'The Zealous Collector', it was written by the newspaper's art correspondent, Judith Dobrzynksi, and although not the first reference to war loot by American journalists that year it had perhaps the greatest impact.[3]

It told the story of Lea Bondi Jaray, an art dealer who had fled from Austria and the Germans in 1937. Before her departure, Mrs Bondi had been coerced into handing over one of her paintings, *Portrait of Wally*, a depiction of Schiele's mistress, to a German art dealer by the name of Friedrich Welz. The *New York Times'* article included extracts from a letter Mrs Bondi wrote a decade before her death, recounting how Leopold had got his hands on the painting. 'I asked him to pick up my picture . . . and send it to me immediately,' she wrote. 'The next thing I heard was that my picture was . . . owned by Dr Leopold.' Described as having 'badgered and manipulated owners until they sold him their treasures', Leopold himself was reported as offering a justification for his approach to acquiring art: 'If you don't pay the best price because you are not a Rockefeller, you have other ways to get your collection.'

When the story hit the news stands, the response was immediate. The Bondi family wrote to the Museum of Modern Art asking for the painting to be returned not to Dr Leopold, via the exhibition's next stop in Barcelona, but to them. The museum received a similar appeal regarding a second work held in New York for the exhibition: *Dead Cities*, it was claimed, had been owned by Fritz Grünbaum, a comedian who had died at Dachau concentration camp in 1940. Despite the requests, museum officials prepared to return the paintings under a contract governing the loan which had been signed with their Austrian counterparts at the Leopold Museum in Vienna. But then, with the 150 paintings in the exhibition already crated up and ready for despatch, the Manhattan District Attorney Robert Morgenthau intervened, serving the museum with a subpoena to ensure the two Schiele works did not leave the country while the delicate matter of ownership was being resolved.

This move by Morgenthau, better known for his ability in tackling organized crime than for dealings with the art trade, quickly escalated the matter from a tug-of-war into an international incident. Reaction in Vienna was predictably hostile. Citing the 'warlike mentality' of the District Attorney's office, Klaus Schroder, managing director of the museum which now owns the 5,400 works in the Leopold collection, was under no illusion as to the gravity of the situation. 'This', he said, 'could rise up to a very big scandal.'[4] His Museum of Modern Art counterpart, Glenn Lowry, was equally concerned. As part of the museum's submission to sidestep the ban on handing back the Schieles, Mr Lowry gave a sworn statement in which he voiced a forecast of dire consequences if the Morgenthau injunction stood. 'Issuance of the subpoena has a potentially devastating effect,' he argued. 'The problem is not restricted to a pair of paintings in the Museum of Modern Art. Museums . . . are deeply concerned about the prospect that lenders will keep their works at home rather than risk sending them to New York.'[5] Arguing that a 1968 New York state law offered an 'unqualified' immunity from sequestration, Mr Lowry continued: 'Any diminution of protection erodes lenders' confidence; every shade of gray suggests that lenders to New York museums do so at their peril . . . To be effective the New York law must mean just what it says: that loans of art in New York may not be seized by anyone, for any reason.' However, there was one important fact that both Austria and the Museum of Modern Art had overlooked: while the New York law may have been on the statute book, it had not been tested in a court of law. The Schiele affair was a test case, and all the more important for that.

After four months of deliberation, Supreme Court judge Laura Drager agreed with the museum. However, at the time of writing the deadlock continues. The paintings remain at the Museum of Modern Art while the state's justices consider an appeal by Morgenthau. The Bondi family is preparing to file a lawsuit formally registering a claim for ownership of *Portrait of Wally*. And the debate over the proper approach to the question continues to rage. Glenn Lowry warned of the difficulties which might come to light through scrutinizing the origins of the Leopold collection, saying, 'One must be very careful about applying the standards of today to things that happened in the past.' In the art world, however, and in America in particular, it has proved almost impossible to divide the present from history.

Francis Taylor was one of Philippe de Montebello's predecessors as Director of New York's Metropolitan Museum. Described by his peers as a man of 'animation and dramatic flair', he was, as noted in chapter 4, one of the senior American figures responsible for the establishment of the MFA&A organization within the wartime US armed forces. Taylor helped contribute to a report, published two days before Germany's unconditional surrender to General Eisenhower at Rheims on 7 May 1945, which spelt out the immediate dangers facing the art world following the cessation of hostilities. While the British had seriously underestimated the value of the plundering on mainland Europe, putting the figure at $144 million (£36 million), Taylor claimed 'that the Nazis had stolen European art treasures valued at $200,000,000 to $2,500,000, more than the total value of all the works of art in the United States'. The collections belonging to various members of the Rothschild family alone were worth 'several tens of millions of dollars'.[6]

By the time this report was written by an official at the Foreign

Economic Administration in Washington (the equivalent of the British Ministry of Economic Warfare), the United States had had several years to observe the intentions of those in charge of moving the loot, while Britain had made severely flawed efforts to stem the flow of ill-gotten art treasures out of Europe – indeed, a study of the traffic penned in February 1945 explained that British MFA&A staff listed as one of their top priorities 'preventing the export of enemy "valuables" particularly to the Americas'.[7] However, it can be argued that on this front the Allies were always going to be fighting a losing battle. They were effectively in a position of permanently trying to catch up with their Axis counterparts when it came to tracking events, policies and objects. Until they liberated Europe, they could do little but amass the maximum possible amount of information on the Nazi looting of occupied territories and lay plans for recovery and restitution once the war was over. By the cessation of hostilities in May 1945, however, the Nazis had, as described in earlier chapters, systematically spirited away huge amounts of loot, including considerable quantities of art treasures. Measures were taken in the form of the Safehaven Programme to monitor the movements of Nazi loot from Germany through neutral countries, but interception was almost impossible.

Import controls were imposed by the United States early in the war: but just when it seemed the necessary measures might be in place to frustrate the attempts of the European art community to move its business to a country where it could flourish unaffected by the war, the Allies dropped their collective guard. Faced with a deluge of demands from those who had fled the Germans to be allowed to have their possessions sent on from the occupied territories, Washington introduced special permits for those who could argue an exceptional case 'on compassionate or similar grounds'. There was, not surprisingly, a rush for these documents, and 213 applications came from people wanting to move works of art to the United States. Of those, 144 requested permission to move works by almost every artist in the canon – from da Vinci to Monet, Teniers to Bonnard – to New York, after London the largest pre-war art market. Having granted the export passes, the US authorities admitted that they might have blundered. 'In a large number of these cases,' one February 1945 report explained, 'what purported to be proof of ownership and of lack of enemy interest was supplied before the application was granted.' However, the strong possibility remained, the report continued, that 'some works of art which had in fact been looted from occupied territories were included in these consignments'.[8]

Among those who fled to the United States was Georges Wildenstein, whose name featured prominently among dealers investigated by Allied MFA&A officers. As mentioned in an earlier chapter, during the German occupation of France in 1940 he had been a victim of Nazi avarice, with 302 of his paintings listed as having been seized by the ERR,[9] while also allegedly being a beneficiary of the wartime upsurge in art trade in Paris. Before the war Wildenstein, both a collector and a dealer, had lived 'over the shop', in grand apartments above his gallery in the rue de Boetie, near the Elysée Palace. As a Jew, he had to be vigilant in order to avoid arrest. However, it has been claimed that once France fell under the German yoke, Wildenstein was not entirely the victim he has been portrayed. As described in chapter 3, he apparently succeeded in striking a deal with Hitler's chief agent, Karl Haberstock, in which his business was 'Aryanized', keeping some of his possessions safe from confiscation and himself and his family out of the concentration camps.[10] Wildenstein himself was allowed to move to the United States in 1941, where it was later claimed that he had arranged with Haberstock to take receipt of a number of Impressionist paintings in exchange for a Tiepolo from his Paris gallery. During his absence from France, his business was left in the care of Roger Dequoy, the man later described by the Allies as 'the worst of the collaborationists among the dealers' in France.[11] Soon after the war's end, Wildenstein allegedly returned to collect some of the profits of his company's trade while an 'Aryanized' business.

In April 1941 Wildenstein, who was noted by British MFA&A officer Douglas Cooper to have offices in both New York and London in addition to his premises in Paris, apparently received in the United States a shipment of seventeen paintings, including two landscapes by Corot and Renoir and others by the likes of Watteau and Fragonard.[12] According to a British intelligence report, the consignment evaded Allied controls and succeeded in making its way from Marseilles across the Atlantic on board the French ship SS *Carimare*. Yet Wildenstein was not among those who, as detailed Allied accounts claimed, had obtained the required documentation permitting him to move his art to the United States.[13]

In the same month that Wildenstein reportedly received his cargo, a more audacious plot was taking shape. As recounted in chapter 6, the German art historian and dealer Hans Wendland played a key role in Nazi acquisitions of art. A German-born art historian and dealer, he maintained strong business relationships with other dealers in Paris and Switzerland who were equally untroubled by the moral implications of working with the Nazis; indeed, he was judged by the Allies to be 'an adventurer and ready to make any deal, however shady, if he thinks it will bring money ... An investigation of his financial status would probably reveal that he knows much about the concealed German assets both in Switzerland and France.'[14] In April 1941 Wendland was discussing the logistics of smuggling art from the Louvre in Paris through Switzerland to New York for sale. The details of the plan emerged from letters mailed to Paul Graupe, a former associate from Paris. Graupe was a Jewish dealer who, fearing arrest, had fled the French capital and made his way to New York in December 1940 via Switzerland. Unaware, like Graupe, that his every word was being monitored by United States government agents, Wendland proposed a joint venture with Graupe involving the movement of some of the world's greatest paintings to America on board 'neutral' Swiss ships sailing out of the northern Italian port of Genoa.[15]

According to Allied documents, Wendland assured Graupe that the plan had the full support of Hitler's top aides, with whom he maintained an excellent rapport. Graupe, however, decided not to become involved, and no subsequent evidence can be found in the now declassified wartime files to suggest that the scheme was ever put into action. It is intriguing, given the scope of German attempts to smuggle art and senior Nazis to the American continent (as described later in this chapter), that at the end of the war Wendland's desire to evade prosecution for his part in the disgraceful events of the occupation led him to apply for an Argentinian passport. When that failed, he attempted to transfer a large part of his amassed fortune to his niece, who held a Mexican passport. In the event, despite repeated attempts to bring him to book, he eluded retribution and lived out his last years in Paris, where he died in modest circumstances, most of his assets having been seized by the Swiss authorities.

Other dealers joined the likes of Wildenstein in flouting American import restrictions. In July 1941 Paul Rosenberg – whose departure to the United States from France is examined in the next chapter, along with the fate of his collection – stated in a letter, intercepted by the American authorities, that he had successfully received sixteen paintings by the Surrealist artist André Masson, sent to him in New York. Four paintings from other collections – *Portrait of the Bellelli Family* by Degas, a watercolour by Toulouse-Lautrec and two pictures by Forain – had also been sent to the 58th Street offices of

Perls Galleries, having begun their journeys in Nazi-occupied France and successfully evaded US movement restrictions en route.[16] The gallery's proprietor, Klaus Perls, had been born in Berlin in 1912 and moved to America at the age of twenty-three, opening his New York dealing house just two years later. In 1941, the year his undetected shipment arrived, he became a naturalized American citizen. The Bellelli portrait which had been sent to him was later acquired by the Musée d'Orsay in Paris.[17]

It was just as easy for Bucholz Galleries in New York to lay their hands on prints and drawings by Kathe Kollwitz, Picasso's *Absinthe Drinker* and two woodcuttings by Edvard Munch: *The Kiss* and *Man and Woman*.[18] Curt Valentin, the gallery's director, had been among those taking part in the notorious Fischer sale in Lucerne in 1939, when 126 art works from German state collections considered 'degenerate' by the Nazis were sold off.[19] Anyone who had bothered to take note would have recognized the Picasso offered by Bucholz's office in Berlin to its counterpart in New York as one of the paintings which had gone under the hammer at Lucerne. And yet, although the American authorities were aware, through mail intercepts, of the gallery's dealings in the smuggling of looted art, no action was taken against it.

Not every smuggling episode went the way of the art trade. In June 1941 three paintings by the French Expressionist artist Georges Henri Roualt, sent to the United States from Montreux in Switzerland, were impounded by US Customs in New York on grounds of 'evidence of enemy interest'.[20] However, the failure of this operation seems from the available documentation to be something of an exception rather than the rule. The exporters were obviously pandering to an established appreciation of Roualt's work. Three of the painter's pre-war pieces are currently owned by major American museums which, interestingly, have found themselves at the centre of looted art scandals in recent years. *Three Judges* and *Christ Mocked by Soldiers* both hang in the Museum of Modern Art in New York, while *The Old King* resides in the Carnegie Museum in Pittsburgh. No suspicions have so far come to light, however, that these works were illegally acquired.

It is important to realize that the art trade between America and Europe in these years was not just a matter of European dealers making commercial incursions into the United States. It was a two-way traffic. Even during the war there were art firms in the United States prepared to do business with the Nazis. Having learned of

Hitler's preferences for the Führermuseum, Schneider-Gabriel Galleries in New York approached German embassy officials in the city to announce that they had five paintings by Franz Lenbach for sale.[21] Four of them were portraits of the Iron Chancellor, Otto von Bismarck, and all belonged, according to the gallery, 'to an old New York family'. On 10 December 1940 news of the offer was conveyed, with accompanying photographs, to Berlin and Martin Bormann who, in turn, informed Hans Posse, the head of Sonderauftrag Linz. The latter authorized the purchase eight days later, but the deal was never closed, even though Posse wrote, 'The price of about 25,000 reichsmarks for all five items seems to me to be a very reasonable one.'

Unsurprisingly, perhaps, given their wartime activities, certain dealers later fell foul of the law. Both the Wildenstein and Perls galleries subsequently featured in court cases about looted art which should have defined the policies of American museums towards works acquired under duress by the Nazis and helped New York's Museum of Modern Art and others avoid the controversies which have attended them in the late 1990s.

Erna Menzel was a Belgian Jew who, in the early part of the war, lived in Brussels with her husband. On 31 March 1941 representatives of the ERR called at the couple's apartment just weeks after they had fled for the safety of the United States, leaving behind them a number of paintings, including *The Peasant and the Ladder*, a work in gouache (known over the years by a number of other names, including *Jacob's Ladder*) by Marc Chagall, an artist classed as 'degenerate' by the Nazis. Records show that the picture had been purchased in 1932 for $150, or BFr3,800, through the Brussels gallery of Georges Giroux, where it was among a number of pieces in the collection of Walter Schwarzenberg.[22] Those who confiscated the painting helpfully, as it turned out, left behind a receipt explaining that it had been taken away for 'safe keeping'.

After the war the Menzels searched perseveringly for their lost art works, a task interrupted only by Mr Menzel's death in 1960. The Chagall was found, in November 1962, to be in the possession of Albert List, a prominent New York art collector.[23] List had bought it from the Perls Gallery on Madison Avenue on 14 October 1955 for $4,000, claiming the dealer had told him that the gallery had full title and authority to sell the painting. When asked by the courts to explain how he had acquired the Chagall, Klaus Perls testified that he had bought it from the Galerie Arte Moderne, 'one of the leading, most representative, reputable galleries in Paris', for $2,800 in July

1955. Try as they might, lawyers involved in the case in 1966 could not establish where the work had been in the fourteen years after it was seized by the ERR. There was little doubt who the owners had been, although Perls attempted to defeat the claim on the grounds that the confusion over the name of the work meant the widow Menzel could not be sure the painting she sought was the same painting sold to Mr List. That argument failed, as did Perls' alternative contention that the artist had in fact prepared two versions of exactly the same work. Mrs Menzel, however, did not receive the picture she had been seeking for twenty-five years, but was instead awarded a cash sum from Albert List equivalent to its market value, fixed at $22,500.[24] List in turn successfully sued the Perls Gallery for the money that he had been forced to pay out.[25]

It is interesting to ponder why the result of this case has apparently been so easily overlooked by museums and art dealers, bearing in mind that Klaus Perls and his wife, Amelia, became such well-known and immensely rich individuals. Klaus Perls has been a trustee of the Metropolitan Museum in his adopted home town of New York since 1992. He and his wife were estimated to have donated $60 million to charity in 1996 alone, placing them in the American benevolence stakes behind only the billionaire financier George Soros and the department store tycoon family, the Skaggs.[26]

Sixteen years after the Menzel case was resolved, an elderly German woman, Gerda Dorothea de Weerth, found one of a number of art treasures which had been missing since being looted by American troops almost forty years before. Claude Monet's *Champs de Blé à Vetheuil* had been bought by her father in Berlin in 1908. On his death fourteen years later ownership of the Impressionist masterpiece passed to her, and it remained in her home in the German capital until 1943, when the likelihood of the Nazis' defeat and the threat of the painting being lost in the Allied bombing blitz on the city prompted her to send it to her sister's castle in the south of the country. When the forces of the Reich surrendered in 1945, the castle was used to billet American troops; and when they left, de Weerth's sister noted that some of her family's property, including the Monet, had disappeared. Complaints to local American senior officers brought no redress.

Thirty-seven years later, Gerda de Weerth discovered that the painting was now owned by a Mrs Edith Marks Baldinger of New York. Mrs Baldinger had bought the work in 1957 'in good faith' from the city's legendary Wildenstein Gallery, which had purchased the painting from a dealer in Switzerland during the previous year.[27]

Naturally, Mrs de Weerth asked for the Monet to be returned to her. Her request was refused, and the matter subsequently went before the courts. In April 1987 a federal judge decided that Mrs Baldinger should return the painting. Again she refused. It was not until 1994 that the case was finally settled, and unsatisfactorily so for Mrs de Weerth. Although there was no dispute that she had owned the Monet or that it had been looted from her family by American troops, the highest appeal court in New York ruled that she had fallen foul of the 'statute of limitations', stipulating the time allowed to bring a prosecution, in their jurisdiction by taking her claim to a federal court first.[28] Mrs Baldinger held on to her Monet, and yet more questions were asked about the role of the Wildenstein Gallery.

However, neither the Menzel nor the de Weerth case prompted a response on the scale of that associated with the controversy surrounding the Schiele paintings in 1998, with its greater perceived threat of legal action by the authorities. Some museum directors, it appeared, simply did not take notice of the possible implications of these disputes for their trade, just as their predecessors had ignored the continued vigilance suggested by warnings issued before the end of the war. A forty-eight-page US government report completed on 5 May 1945, two days before the Germans' surrender in Europe and a full three months before the atom bombs were dropped on Hiroshima and Nagasaki, spelt out the future dangers.[29] 'It must be noted', wrote the paper's author, H. M. Crooks,

> that the Nazi policy in regard to the looting of art pieces was a long-range one, and part of the plan envisaged in case of defeat. They realized the importance of securing for themselves stable foreign currency and the greatest possible finances abroad. But, alarmed by economic crises throughout the world, they must have felt that works of art are negotiable assets, that they represent stable international value, and are a safe investment. This long-range planning will make more difficult the task of identification and the eventual recovery of looted art.

Crooks was explicit about the source of the problem. Even before the Japanese attack on Pearl Harbor brought the United States into the the war, 'attempts were made to transport works of art through Spain and Portugal, for sale in the United States and the Latin American countries'. The funnelling of treasures into the Iberian peninsula, as documented in chapter 7, had been investigated by agents of the OSS and Britain's SIS working out of Lisbon and Madrid. The objective of moving material to the United States was well known, and by the time Crooks was writing his report he may well have been aware of evidence that works of art, some of which had passed through supposedly neutral countries, had already arrived on the American art market. However, his document is also useful in its consideration of other destinations for looted art.

Latin America was a well-known refuge for leading Nazis fleeing retribution – and for some of the art dealers who had assisted their wartime acquisitions of looted art. Their behaviour entirely accorded with Crooks' long-term theories. 'Hermann Goering has millions invested in Argentina,' reported one US agent. 'I personally saw paintings, sculpture, etc, looted by the Nazis on sale in Buenos Aires since late 1943, receipts from which were being held for Goering.' A letter from the US Consul in Vienna dated 16 December 1946 added that Göring had transferred 'more than $20 million of his personal fortune' to Argentina in diplomatic pouches.[30]

Argentina's role as a haven for senior Nazis was confirmed more than fifty years after the war by a US State Department report of 1998 which told how the country had 'become the center of Axis espionage and propaganda activities in South America'.[31] More than just a local breeding ground for fascism, the country was home to subsidiaries of major German companies such as I. G. Farben, the chemical giant which manufactured Zyklon B, the poison used in the gas chambers of Nazi concentration camps. It was estimated that Germany had $200 million worth of assets in Argentina. However, attempts to close down the two-way supply line between Berlin and Buenos Aires foundered because of British hunger: Prime Minister Winston Churchill decided that good relations with Argentina had to be maintained in order to keep shipments of beef arriving to feed his ration-starved citizens during the bleakest days of the war.[32] Argentina's support for the Nazis did not effectively come to public attention until 1960 and the dramatic arrest and prosecution of Adolf Eichmann by the Israelis. The architect of the so-called 'Final Solution' for Europe's Jews, Eichmann was captured at his Argentinian hideaway and taken to Israel, where he was hanged for crimes against humanity two years later. It was Eichmann who had been instrumental in increasing the volume of treasure at the disposal of the Nazis by confiscating the art and property of 80,000 Austrian Jews in return for issuing them with exit visas.[33]

Tracking the whereabouts of fugitive Nazis was not the only reason why Buenos Aires featured in Allied enquiries. During the latter part of the war and its immediate aftermath art dealers, including some from the United States, were setting up branches in South America to take advantage of the spoils the Nazis had accumulated and subsequently smuggled abroad. Subjected to lengthy surveillance by the US Federal Office of Censorship, which intercepted their mail, such dealers were monitored in their contacts with clients and associates. The New York-based dealers de Königsbergs had established connections in Argentina, Mexico, Chile and Uruguay. Crooks' report concluded: 'We found no proof that looted art was involved, but a study of another art dealer, Nicholas Karger, doing business in Venezuela, seemed to indicate that the South American art market is being flooded with pieces of doubtful authenticity, which makes the task of tracing authentic and valuable looted art objects even harder.'[34]

Ties between South American galleries and their European counterparts came in for close scrutiny by the Allies, who were keen to find evidence to back up what they were learning of the smuggling plots. Francisco Cambo had dealt 'almost exclusively' with Swiss dealer Theodor Fischer in Lucerne before moving from Barcelona to Buenos Aires only months after the start of the war. Cambo's links to Fischer made his affairs a target of Allied investigations, along with those of dealer and collector Thaddeus Grauer who lived at Sao Paulo in Brazil.[35] That city's connections with Nazi loot were further highlighted in mid-September 1998 when four paintings, including one each by Monet and Picasso, turned up in the hands of local wealthy families. The pictures, valued at $3.5 million collectively, had been smuggled out of Europe at the end of the war. Negotiations between their last owners and the World Jewish Congress ended with the works being surrendered to the Brazilian Justice Department while research continued to trace heirs of the Europeans from whose pre-war collections the works had been taken.[36]

Countries not immediately involved in the conflict were also subjected to the attention of the Allied investigators. Conscious of the role played by Germany in the installation of the puppet Norwegian premier Vidkun Quisling in 1942, an investigation similar to that targeted on South America commenced in Scandinavia. Its discoveries, summed up in a memo dated February 1943, were indisputable. It read: 'Certain members of the Nazi party . . . are beginning to send their valuables from Germany to Sweden, where they are to be sold to form a capital investment in Sweden. Bukowski's, the well-known Stockholm auction rooms, have received two cases of valuable pictures from Germany during the last two weeks but the consignor is unknown.'[37] There was no mystery about works which arrived the following year. Only five months after the memo from Stockholm, Allied forces landed in Sicily. As they massed for an invasion of the Italian mainland just across the Straits of Messina, treasures from the Naples Museum were moved from several repositories where they had been placed at the start of the war. The task of packing up hundreds of precious objects began in August. On 6 September, 187 crates left the monastery at Montevergine and were transported to another, larger and more secure, at Monte Cassino, fifty miles to the north of Naples.[38] However, the German forces used Monte Cassino, which stood atop a mountain, as a fortress. The damage it sustained during the ensuing siege was substantial, with some of the stored works of art being destroyed and the remainder disappearing. One of these, Jan Brueghel's *Blind Leading the Blind*, thought to have perished, was reported by the Allies to have reappeared in Sweden in September 1944. Six months later, an American agent reported that 'large crates believed to contain carefully packed pictures were lying in the Free Port of Stockholm. One was addressed to Dr H Koux, a personal friend of many Nazis, which led one to believe it might contain looted art.'[39]

Suspicion of Swedish involvement in the movement of smuggled Nazi loot even touched a family revered worldwide since 1945. Raoul Wallenberg was a Swedish businessman and diplomat who used his wartime posting to Budapest to save tens of thousands of Hungarian Jews. He disappeared in the months after the war and was widely presumed to have been captured by Soviet intelligence as a suspected spy. In 1989 the Soviet authorities, while admitting no responsibility for his disappearance, returned some of his personal belongings including his diplomatic passport and diary. However, wartime Foreign Economic Administration documents throw a somewhat less glorious light on the activities of Raoul's relatives. They illustrate how, at the same time as he was risking his life to save Jews, members of his family were actually profiting from their persecution: their Enskilda Bank in Stockholm received substantial quantities of looted gold from the Nazis for safe keeping, and retained 7.6 tonnes of it after the war.[40] One of the bank's directors, Marcus Wallenberg, was also suspected by Britain of receiving plundered paintings, and though the charge was never proven, the whiff of suspicion persisted. The same doubts hung around an art dealer in central Stockholm. Early in 1945 the Gallery Saint Lucas staged an exhibition of Flemish and Dutch paintings. When questioned by the Allies, the gallery's director 'refused to indicate how he obtained possession of them but stated simply that a number of them were obtained from "poor Jewish refugees" '.[41]

Intercepting looted art being imported from abroad was not the only aspect of the problem facing the American and British authorities in the years after the war. A more significant activity which, though smaller in volume, had the potential to cause greater damage was looting by American and British troops based in Europe. Even before the proof became convincing, the rumours were enough to be a matter of serious concern. In July 1945, both British and American military commanders were having to address Dutch allegations that their national art treasures were being taken home 'as souvenirs'.[42] However, the manner in which they followed up their enquiries did not inspire confidence. In August 1945 thousands of crates of objects found in areas under British control were moved to a castle at Celle, near Brunswick. They included the valuable Gans collection, from Berlin, of golden Roman artefacts. Attempts by museum officials from the German capital to gain entry to the repository, to establish which of their treasures were stored there, were rebuffed. An inventory of the castle's contents in September 1947 revealed that thirty-two Gans pieces were missing. The German art dealer who had been placed in charge of administration at the repository was immediately sacked and an investigation launched by embarrassed British officials. Search warrants were executed at the English homes of some of the soldiers who had served at Celle. Two months after the thefts first came to light, the British concluded that none of their men had been involved. As a result, no one was ever brought to justice and the objects were never recovered. The Foreign Office was informed on 20 April 1949 of the decision to hand the remaining items at the Celle collection point over to the local German authorities. Major General K. G. McLean, commanding British troops in the area, commented 'that the sooner this is done the better'.[43]

As mentioned in chapter 8, a book published in the United States in 1994 illustrated the extent to which Allied personnel had engaged in looting. In *The Spoils of World War II: The American Military's Role in Stealing Europe's Treasures*, Kenneth Alford tells of numerous cases involving American troops and the theft of precious objects from repositories under US Army control, including the collection point at Munich. One of the results of Alford's years of research on the subject was to show that the penalties meted out to those guilty of pilfering were often not consistent with the gravity of their offences – though there were exceptions. In August 1946, Captain Kathleen Nash stood trial accused of stealing a $3 million collection of jewels belonging to Countess Margarethe of Hesse, the granddaughter of Britain's Queen Victoria. The gems and other items, including a Rubens portrait of a small boy and a personally inscribed bible given by Victoria to her daughter the Empress Frederica as a marriage gift, were taken from the castle at Kronberg, near Frankfurt, where Captain Nash had worked in June 1945 as a hostess in the officers' mess. Many were mailed home to relatives in the United States. Despite official denials of a cover-up, details of the looting at Kronberg only came to light in an article in the magazine *Newsweek* two months before the trial began, and senior US Army officers later attempted to persuade the magazine to retract its story.[44] Nevertheless, on 30 September, after a six-week trial, Captain Nash was sentenced to five years in a civilian prison in the United States and her husband, Colonel Jack Durant, to fifteen years' hard labour for his part in the theft. Nash's lawyer, Alford notes, claimed that 'thousands of others' had done the same thing; and the case prompted further investigations which led to the demotion of a general and the discovery of a 'garage crammed with jewelry and other valuables' at the home of a former senior member of General Dwight Eisenhower's staff.

Captain Norman Byrne, meanwhile, received a much less severe punishment for his part in looting. Facing seventeen charges of embezzlement and larceny at his trial in February 1947, he escaped with a mild censure and dismissal. The case had centred on the theft of Meissen china and a large number of paintings which included Dürer's *Big Horse* and Teniers' *The Smoker*. Like Kathleen Nash, Byrne attempted to make allegations about other senior figures involved in stealing valuables, but was prevented from doing so by the prosecution – for reasons which have never been revealed. During his research, Kenneth Alford interviewed Lieutenant Colonel John P. MacNeil, a prosecution witness at the trial. 'I burned my notes', MacNeil told the author, 'as soon as this report was written. I didn't just throw them in the wastebasket, I burned them.' Another document that went into the fire was a dossier on American post-war looting: burned in 1965, the year it should have been made available to the public.[45] However, if the US Army had hoped that the issue would disappear with the destruction of all references to looting by its own troops, it was wrong. Two major court cases featuring the theft of precious art objects by GIs during the war brought the topic back to life.

The first ran for thirteen years and had wider political significance: for the claim issued by the Weimar museum, the Kunstsammlungen zu Weimar (KZW), against Mr Edward Elicofon of Brooklyn, New

York, for the return of two Dürer portraits, led to the legal recognition of the communist state of East Germany by the United States.[46] The KZW's complaint was finally resolved on 5 May 1982, sixteen years after Elicofon originally owned up to possessing the two paintings and only twelve months after the United States government destroyed crucial documentation which would have revealed details of other incidents of looting by members of the US Army which had failed to reach the press.

Elicofon's revelation that he had the two portraits of Hans Tucher and his wife, Felicitas, was the front-page story in the *New York Times* of 30 May 1966. The find was described by an official from the city's Metropolitan Museum, obviously in a state of considerable excitement, as 'the discovery of the century'. Edward Elicofon was already known to some as an art collector of note. Before the Second World War he had roughly 2,000 pieces of oriental art in his home. When a young American ex-serviceman called at his house in the spring of 1946, Elicofon thought nothing of paying $450 for the two paintings which the soldier claimed he had bought while on active service in Germany. He had the pictures framed and hung on his living-room wall. It was not until early May 1966, when a friend showed him a book detailing German works of art missing since the war, that Elicofon realized he had two paintings by one of Hitler's favourite artists.[47]

Immediately his story was made known, both West and East Germany made claims on the works. A protracted and complex legal battle ensued, involving, according to court summaries, 'a labyrinthine journey through 19th-century German dynastic law, contemporary German property law, Allied military law during the post-War occupation of Germany, New York State law and intricate conceptions of succession and sovereignty in international law'. Though the US administration was not a direct party to the case, government officials in Washington sought to strike out the socialists' claim on the paintings by noting that 'the GDR was barred from suing since it was still not recognized by the United States'.[48] Nevertheless, the case went ahead and the pictures' full history was revealed. The works had been owned by successive Grand Dukes of Saxony Weimar since 'at least Goethe's time in 1824' and formed part of the grand ducal art collection which was put on display in 1913 at their museum, the forerunner of the KZW. The collection was ceded to the newly established Territory of Weimar in 1921 by a settlement which granted the family an annual income of 300,000 marks in return, as well as a one-off 'special compensation of three million marks'. They remained in Weimar until 1943 when they were moved to a nearby castle, Schloss Schwarzburg, in Thuringia, to escape the anticipated bombardment by the Allies. They were stolen during the week of 12–19 June 1945 as American troops withdrew from the area, to be replaced by Soviet forces. The Director of the Weimar museum, Dr Schiedig, complained about the theft and subsequently tried to locate the paintings but without success.

Official obstacles to East Germany's recovery of the two Dürers were formally removed on 4 September 1974 with the decision by President Richard Nixon to recognize the communist state and its leader, Erich Honecker, and eight years later the paintings were returned to East Germany – leaving Elicofon out of pocket.[49] Elicofon had argued that under a principle of German law (*Ersitzung*) he was entitled to claim the paintings as his own because no one had claimed them in the previous decade. That suggestion was swiftly dismissed by a New York court which concluded that 'a purchaser cannot acquire good title from a thief'. That comment did not achieve its full resonance until the late 1990s, when the true number of looted works of art in American hands, both public and private, began to emerge.

The second case concerned a theft by Lieutenant Joe Tom Meador from Texas of items from the town of Quedlinburg in eastern Germany. In October 1943 SS officers had taken the most precious objects belonging to the local church of St Servatius and hidden them for safety in a cave at nearby Altenburg. The treasure included gold and silver medieval reliquaries inlaid with gemstones and ivory, and the Samuhel Gospels: illustrated manuscripts bound in a magnificently decorated cover, set with jewels. The items had remained together for nearly 1,000 years. However, the hoard was accidentally discovered in April 1945, after which the American troops posted as guards at the entrance to the shaft, instead of maintaining absolute security as ordered, allowed their friends to inspect the treasures. Meador was overawed by what he saw and, falling prey to temptation, stole a number of pieces, later mailing them back to his family in the United States via the army's postal service. When he returned home he made no particular secret of his souvenirs but did not, apparently, try to sell them. He died in 1980 and his brother and sister inherited the booty.[50]

Two years later attempts to value the objects led to part of their brother's haul, the gospels, being offered for sale to a Berlin cultural institute for $9 million. This alerted the German authorities to the presence of the other articles. However, locating their missing treasures in the vault of a bank in a small Texas town was one thing; getting them back was another, and not necessarily simple. Lawyers representing the Germans had to take out an injunction to prevent Meador's heirs from taking the objects to Switzerland while negotiations about their possible return continued. Eventually, the thief's family handed over the Quedlinburg treasures for $3 million. This, stressed one official, 'was not a price, but a finder's fee'.

Until the University of Kassel issued a lawsuit against a carpet salesman in Massachusetts, William Braemer had no idea of the value of the objects he had taken, also from a German mineshaft. Braemer is now elderly and ill, nursed by his wife at their home in Connecticut. At the end of the war he had been sent to Europe by his employers, an American aircraft manufacturer, to gather information on their German rival, Messerschmitt. He returned with seven miniature paintings, which sat on a bookshelf in his home for thirty years before he decided to sell them for $100.[51] They changed hands once more, being purchased in the early 1970s by Thomas Chatalbash, a dealer in antique oriental rugs, for double the sum Braemer had received. Chatalbash kept four of his acquisitions in a drawer and displayed the others on the back wall of his shop. They were still there in 1989, when they were noticed by Alan Shestack, the then Director of the Boston Museum of Fine Arts, who believed they might be originals. He called in experts, who revealed the startling truth about the seven works. Not only were they indeed originals from the early sixteenth century, they were worth in the region of $500,000. They had been part of a set which made up a nobleman's prayer book; four of the seven were by the Flemish artist Simon Bening, a major influence on the German Renaissance.

This sounded like good news for Chatalbash. However, there was another side to the story which he was not so keen to hear: the paintings had been stolen at the end of the Second World War. In addition to having the works dated and authenticated, Chatalbash was advised to return them. He refused. One of the historians who appraised the works, Richard Linenthal of Bernard Quaritch Ltd, a London firm specializing in antiquarian manuscripts, threatened to inform the German authorities where they could find the missing paintings. Having learned their true value, however, Chatalbash was in no mood to surrender them, and lawyers acting on his behalf claimed he had bought them in good faith and was thus entitled to keep them.[52] Kassel University, however, was no more inclined to relinquish its right to the paintings, and called in the team of lawyer and historian Willi Korte and attorney Thomas Kline to help. As we will see in chapter 11, both Korte and Kline have been instrumental in pursuing claims of families to their own property looted or confiscated during the war.

Korte and Kline managed to trace William Braemer and confirm that the seven paintings which Chatalbash was refusing to surrender were the same pieces he had taken home from Germany.[53] Faced with the undeniable truth of their origins and the prospect of a trial regarding allegations that he had 'fraudulently concealed' his possession of the paintings, Chatalbash caved in. However, he did not walk away empty-handed. In addition to the formal, somewhat frosty thanks of German officials, Chatalbash, like the family of Joe Tom Meador, received a 'finder's fee'. Although the exact sum was not revealed, it was described as 'substantial' and far outweighed the pittance he had paid for the treasures.[54]

An interesting postscript to the Chatalbash case pointed to the wider role and moral stance of museums in dealing with war loot. Alan Shestack, the Boston Museum director who had first established the miniatures' significance, had refused to take the matter further once he realized that Chatalbash had dug in his heels. At the time the case became the subject of a writ eight years later, he expanded on why he had allowed the matter to drop. Writing in the *Art Newspaper*, Shestack contended that museum officials had no obligation to report their own suspicions about works not belonging to their institutions. This attempted justification of a passive approach merely underlined the concerns of many observers since the war that the American art establishment did not take the problem of plunder seriously enough.[55] These concerns were not new, but had grown in intensity over the years since the first looted works had appeared on American soil. However, they were apparently not shared by those with the money to acquire major works of art, be they public institutions or private citizens.

In 1944 the US Treasury Department watched as the irregular sale of a painting by Vincent van Gogh unfolded in a series of intercepted letters. Agents tracked *The Man is at Sea* from France to New York and the temporary custody of the Nazi collaborator Paul Graupe. It finally ended up in the hands of none other than the actor Errol Flynn. During the process of monitoring the voluminous correspondence between the parties to the transaction in Europe and the United States, one of the department's officials, James F. Scanlon, was able to observe at close quarters the efficiency of German methods of appropriation. In a memo dated 18 January 1944 he noted: 'The term "looting" is hardly applicable to German practice of acquiring art objects in France. It was quasi-legal acquisition.'

Hollywood had been a major target for US government surveillance as early as 1940, when the first reports of items of Nazi loot reaching the United States reached the responsible authorities. In October that year a letter on its way to Hollywood was intercepted; posted in Rome, but thought to have originated in Switzerland, it gave notice of five important paintings for sale. The letter contained photographs of the works concerned: Titian's *Death of Cleopatra*, *Baptism of Ethiopian Eunuch* by Rembrandt, *St John with Lamb*, one of the works which had established Bartolomé Murillo's fame, a Corot landscape and Jacopo Palma's *Virgin and Child with Apple* which, it was ascertained, had earlier been taken to Geneva.[56] Eleven months later more Old Master works were on offer, including *Death of Our Lady* by Cranach the Elder and three Bismarck portraits by Lenbach.[57] So great was the concern of the American authorities about the penetration of Hollywood by the Nazis that they enlisted the aid of certain film stars as agents. Cary Grant, born in Bristol as plain Archibald Leach in 1904, received the King's Medal from Britain after the war for his part in keeping an eye on those at the studios, including Errol Flynn and Gary Cooper, who were perceived as Nazi sympathizers.[58]

While some stars had an appetite for the works of the Old Masters, it was the Impressionist works which were most sought after by the West Coast art connoisseurs. The trend was notably typified by actor Edward G. Robinson.[59] Born Emmanuel Goldenberg in December 1893, Robinson, made famous by his 1930 role as a gangster in *Little Caesar*, owned a large number of Impressionist paintings; so large, in fact, that he had them housed in a purpose-built gallery at his Hollywood home. A renowned collection at the time, the gallery was even opened to the public for several days each year. In 1953 forty works, including Robinson's personal favourites, *Black Clock* by Cézanne, *Entombment* by Picasso and Matisse's *Dinner Table*, were exhibited at the Museum of Modern Art in New York between 4 March and 12 April. The exhibition catalogue listed other movie stars as having similar artistic inclinations, with the roll of the museum's sponsors including Tyrone Power, Joan Fontaine, Stewart Granger and Rita Hayworth.[60] While all were collectors and aficionados of modern art, there has been no suggestion that any acquired looted works from the Nazi caches. However, among the museum's other sponsors was Georges Wildenstein, whose alleged connections with those at the heart of the German looting in France have been referred to previously.

One of the works exhibited by Robinson at the Museum of Modern Art, *Jane Avril Dancing* by Toulouse-Lautrec, was later purchased by the Musée d'Orsay in Paris.[61] The van Gogh acquired by Errol Flynn was put up for auction after his death. *The Man is at Sea* went under the hammer on the morning of 29 April 1964 at Sotheby's saleroom on New Bond Street in London and was bought by the New York gallery Acquavella.[62] A quarter of a century later, it was purchased by Aska, a Japanese investment bank, for $7.2 million.[63] As explained in chapter 12, it was joined in Japan a year later by another van Gogh with a chequered history: *Portrait of Dr Gachet*, which had at one time formed part of the ill-starred Koenigs collection. It is interesting to note that even during the war looted works of art were heading for the Far East. American agents making routine mail intercepts of those connected with the cultural rape of Europe came across a letter from one Austrian dealer in Vienna to another in New York, informing him that 'fifty Goya etchings were on their way to Japan, apparently via Russia'.[64]

At the time the two van Gogh paintings were making their way to Japan in the early 1990s, much of the Western art world still claimed to be in the dark about the plunder of the war years. In the 1950s the US National Archives had begun selectively releasing files containing information gleaned from months of interrogating those who had organized the Nazi theft, confiscation and forced sales of an estimated fifth of the world's art treasures. Yet it appears the message had not got through. Jonathon Petropoulos, an author and art historian from Loyola College in Baltimore, believes he knows part of the reason why. He explained: 'In the 1950s, I think there were a number of museum directors who implemented a "don't ask, don't tell" policy and consciously or semi-consciously didn't undertake the research into provenance that would have been appropriate. By the 1960s, people just weren't thinking very much about looted art. There were certainly a few museum officials who knew that they were buying dicey things. There has never been a dearth of unscrupulous people in the art world. But I think that with a vast majority of people, when they acquired art with a problematic provenance, they didn't know what they were doing.'[65]

Despite the publication of a score of newspaper and magazine articles and books, court cases and even a film about the Nazis' carefully orchestrated programme of spoliation, several more years were to pass before looted art was widely recognized as a problem with a potential impact on American institutions. The impetus came from abroad. Seven years after journalists' revelations in 1984 about Austria's continued retention of war loot, historians in Russia made similar discoveries. Major art works were quietly taken off sale lists at top auction houses in London and New York when doubts were expressed about their provenance.[66] However, it was not until 1994 and the publication of Lynn Nicholas' *The Rape of Europa*, a highly detailed and comprehensive account of the Nazi looting of Europe, that the American art establishment sat up and took serious notice. Publicity generated by the book precipitated a major academic conference in New York the following year. For the first time government representatives, academics, historians, lawyers and, more importantly, figures from the American art world engaged in a discussion of the problems at hand. The points raised by the experts at this gathering were eventually published two years later, by which time the ground had begun to shift even further under the feet of museum directors worldwide. French museums, including the esteemed Louvre, had been criticized for retaining items stolen from Jewish collections. Perhaps most significantly of all, the momentum behind enquiries into the whereabouts of gold looted during the Holocaust led to similar questions being asked about other properties which the Germans had confiscated, including bank accounts, insurance policies and works of art.

The shock waves breached the defences of America's premier museums and galleries early in 1997. As the pressure had built up from Europe, it was not surprising that they were felt first on the eastern seaboard. A series of stories in the *Boston Globe* lifted the lid on the scale of the stolen art problem in the United States. The correspondent who broke the stories was Walter Robinson. 'I had been in Europe that spring,' he says, 'writing and researching a piece about France coming to terms with its role in World War II. I learnt about the art which had gone missing during the war. People kept telling me that I should pay attention to the American connection. What I found surprised me.'[67] What Robinson discovered was seriously to undermine the complacency of those in charge of America's art trade. Starting in April, he filed a number of articles which grew in authority and impact as he followed the footsteps of Lynn Nicholas and a handful of others in combing the archives, chasing the leads which the wartime reports fed him.

Local museums came in for particularly unwelcome attention. Boston's Museum of Fine Arts was found to have continued buying prints from one New York-based dealer Richard Zinser, even though it knew he had been imprisoned in Germany for smuggling art.[68] After arriving in Forest Hills, Long Island, Zinser did not keep a low profile. Archive documents show that he had dealings with the art trade in South America and discussed the sale of a $250,000 picture by Pisanello, known as both *The Flower Girl* and *The Pink Lady*, the original of which had been in the Louvre. Zinser's picture was, according to French officials who themselves were involved in art deals with the Nazis, only a good copy.[69] The purchases ceased only when the FBI paid a visit to the museum, which had also bought a Monet, *Woodgatherers at the Edge of the Forest*, and a Picasso, *Standing Figure*, that had passed through the hands of dealers among the many featured in Allied wartime reports as having extensive links with the Nazis.[70] Other newspapers followed where the *Boston Globe* led and subjected their local establishments to enquiry. Museums in Philadelphia, New York, Cleveland and Chicago were subsequently found to have looted works of art in their inventories.

Meanwhile, despite the wealth of loot already in the United States, imports continued to arrive. On 8 September 1997 a sixty-year-old Japanese businessman, Masatsu Koga, was apprehended by US customs officers in a hotel room in New York attempting to offer for sale a dozen Old Master drawings worth an estimated $10 million. One of the drawings, *Woman Bathing* by Dürer, was alone worth $6 million. Koga later pleaded guilty to the smuggling charge.[71] The drawings had been removed in 1945 from a repository containing the collection of the Bremen Kunsthalle and had eventually found their way to the Museum of Fine Arts in Baku, the capital of the republic of Azerbaijan. There they remained until July 1993, when they were stolen together with hundreds of other items in a major robbery. The two Azeris arrested along with Koga, one a lawyer named Natavan Aleskirova and the other a former champion wrestler, were accused of hiding the stolen goods and were due to be sentenced with him in February 1999.[72]

The customs officer who helped mastermind the sting which netted Koga and his accomplices was Bonnie Goldblatt. From her office beneath the gigantic twin towers of the World Trade Center in New York, she leads the US Customs' art squad. Having spent a total of twelve years tracking stolen art, including Second World War loot, she has been witness to the recent movement of Nazi and Soviet plunder. 'And I have to say', she comments, 'that the instances I have become aware of are more and more frequent. I first noticed the trafficking of war stuff about four years ago. Since then we have had a number of cases indicating that the illegal importation of such material is more commonplace. It's not rife, but it's growing. I think there are three reasons why we are noticing more cases. Firstly, the art market is very good, very healthy at the moment. Secondly, survivors from the war and their heirs are dying off and those with the stolen art in their hands feel more comfortable about their abilities to move it without being found out. Finally, everybody is a bit more sensitive to the subject now than when we initially became aware of it. It's certainly got a higher profile and that is meaning more people are on the look out for questionable materials.'

Agent Goldblatt is charged with ensuring that the next generation of customs officers is well aware of this particular type of contraband. She oversees training seminars for staff on the art unit and is constantly updating her own knowledge of what stolen art objects are around by meeting with other experts in the field. 'That's where I get a lot of my cases,' she explains. 'There's a network of other people in law enforcement and attorneys. We go to conferences on the subject and they may ring me up if they hear of something interesting. There are a lot of leads which go nowhere but sometimes they take us somewhere interesting.' She is quick to dispel suggestions that the trade is all down to organized crime. 'Certainly the cases which we have seen appear to have been organized by individuals and that is the only pattern we have detected. We do believe, however, that there is a lot of stolen war art out there and I don't think people will stop moving it until the art market starts to dip a little. Even then,' she adds, 'the people who have had it until now may get a little desperate and try to sell.'[73]

While Bonnie Goldblatt and her colleagues in United States law enforcement and art circles have been put under the spotlight by a rash of cases, Britain has not remained insulated from the scandal of plundered art. In November 1997 Sotheby's in London called off the planned sale of *A Dune Landscape with Two Figures by a Fence* by the seventeenth-century Dutch artist Jacob van Ruisdael after Walter Robinson of the *Boston Globe* pointed out, none too subtly, that the work had been confiscated by the Nazis.[74] The auction catalogue had actually listed the painting as 'acquired in 1941 for the Gallery in Linz', but Sotheby's apparently had previously not regarded the information as being worthy of concern. The decision to halt the sale was saluted by Jewish groups as a 'linchpin moment'. One spokesman said: 'It will be impossible from now on for any auction house not to take a thorough second look at artworks that arouse the vaguest suspicion.'[75]

The Tate Gallery was found to be in possession of a painting by Edvard Munch, *The Sick Child*, a deeply personal work representing the childhood death of the artist's sister from tuberculosis.[76] The painting had been donated by a Norwegian philanthropist who had purchased it at the auction of 'degenerate' art held by Theodore Fischer in Lucerne in 1939. Museum officials later attempted to defuse the potential damage from discovery of the work's origins by pointing out that it had been removed from a German museum by Hermann Göring and not confiscated from a Jewish family by the Nazis. Ironically, the British Museum has a drawing by Hans Baldung Grien, *The Rape of Europa*, which gave its name to Lynn Nicholas' exposé of Nazi looting and was itself taken by the Germans from the Ukrainian city of Lvov in 1941. The sketch was given to the museum in 1993 by a wealthy German family, the Schillings.[77] A drawing by Dürer, *Man with an Oar*, which formed part of the same haul, was bought in 1953 by Birmingham's Barber Institute, part of the city's university, for £2,000 from the London dealer Colnaghi's. The Institute's director, Richard Verdi, is frank about the acquisition. 'Our records indicate that at the time we purchased it, the dealer did not give us a full account of provenance. We all know now, of course, what happened with this drawing and the others from that collection,' he says, 'it's very simple. But we are not alone in having a work of this nature. There is scarcely a museum in the world that does not harbour some plunder taken under various circumstances at various times from various places around the world.' As to whether the drawing will be returned, he adds: 'We are going to wait and see what happens and what the appropriate advice or requests are before we do anything.'[78]

Yet another Dürer taken from Lvov by the Germans, the watercolour *The Emperors Charlemagne and Sigismund*, was bequeathed to the Courtauld Institute by one of its major benefactors, Count Anthony Seilern, in 1978.[79] Count Seilern's bequest also included three paintings from the enforced sale of the collection of Dutch-German banker Franz Koenigs, as will be recounted in chapter 12.

The evidence presented to the museums was irrefutable, the pressure on them to respond immense. A conference held in London in November 1997 to examine the Nazi looting of gold resulted in plans by the US State Department to stage a similar meeting in Washington during the following year, this time with looted art at the centre of the debate.

Senior American museum directors attempted to jump the gun by setting out their stall at a sitting of the Senate Banking Committee on 12 February 1998. The principal members of the committee, including Republican Senator James Leach and his Democrat counterparts Nita Lowey and Charles Schumer, had previously announced that they were considering introducing a bill to tighten the restrictions governing the checking of the history of art at the time of sale. The Association of Art Museum Directors was, according to its chairman Philippe de Montebello, fully committed to a programme of research and to resolving claims from victims of the war fairly in a manner 'reconciling the interests of individuals or their heirs who were dispossessed of works of art with the complex legal obligations and responsibilities of art museums to the public for whom they hold works of art in trust'.[80] Seconding for the association, Glenn Lowry outlined how 'over the years . . . we have formed strict collecting policy guidelines which we adhere to when conducting provenance research'.[81] Unfortunately, the revelations of the previous twelve months clearly showed that the research had simply not been thorough enough, or else establishments like New York's Metropolitan Museum would not have found themselves facing the problems that beset them.

In the summer of 1997 the museum, the largest in the Western hemisphere with a collection of more than two million items, admitted it was facing two claims for paintings in its custody. It was alleged that one work by Claude Monet, *Le Repos dans le Jardin Argenteuil*, had been stolen from a bank vault in the Russian zone of Berlin in 1945, long before it was donated by one of the museum's trustees, Jayne Wrightsman.[82] Her late husband had purchased the work in 1954 from New York dealer Alexander Ball, another of those whose wartime pursuits and connections are so clearly brought to life by documents available in British and American archives.[83]

Glenn Lowry's assertion that museum historians were in the dark because documents enabling them to check the true history of a piece of art were not available 'until the last few years' was undermined by the case of the second piece at the Metropolitan Museum to be the subject of a claim. The work was among twenty paintings which Belgian collector Emile Renders was forced to sell to Hermann Göring in August 1940 after a threatening letter from the Reichsmarschall. Ten of the pictures were later recovered; *Man of Sorrows*, a Dutch painting of Christ dating from the fifteenth century, was later listed in a Belgian government catalogue, published in 1994, as one of the ten Renders pieces still missing. Nicolas Vanhove, a spokesman for the Belgian Ministry of Economic Affairs, said it was 'hard to believe' that the Metropolitan Museum had not known of the losses.[84]

The AAMD's protestations of innocence and proclaimed commitment to rectify any failings took concrete shape with the creation by the directors of the Metropolitan Museum, the Museum of Modern Art and nine other top-ranking museums across the United States of a 'task force' just a month before the Senate hearing. It reported in June 1998 and put in place tough new guidelines on research and acquisition. Similar action was taken in Britain with the setting up of a special group of the country's most senior museum directors to address the problem. Headed up by Alan Borg, the Director of the Victoria and Albert Museum, it met for the first time in mid-August 1998 following consultations with those orchestrating the United States' response to concerns about war loot. Assurances have been given that this body is not going to merely mimic American actions. A spokeswoman for the National Museum Directors' Conference (NMDC) explained: 'It is crucial that any guidelines for museums in the United Kingdom are based on the experience of museums over here. But it is also important that we learn from what the United States has done and will continue to do. We recognize that this is an issue which may well be of concern to those people who visit museums in Britain and we also acknowledge that we cannot address these problems in isolation. We are faced with a rapidly evolving set of circumstances and do not yet know the full scale of the problem. We need to hear from groups who can make a useful contribution to the discussions on the subject.'[85]

The first consideration of the problem in Britain came after a request to the National Heritage Secretary, Chris Smith, from Lord Janner of the Holocaust Educational Trust for information on what the country's museums were doing about it. Smith passed the request on to the NMDC. Unlike his proactive American counterparts, however, the British Secretary of State merely asked to be 'kept informed of developments'. His private office confided to the authors of this book that he had no plans to travel to Washington for a major international conference on the subject due to be held there in November 1998;[86] and indeed he did not attend.

According to Thomas Hoving, himself a former Director of the Metropolitan Museum, the attempts by American museums in the run-up to this conference to plead ignorance of looted art are simply not plausible. The knowledge of what took place during the war, he argues, was within the museums' easy reach all the time. 'My boss when I was a curator was James Rorimer, who was at the [Munich] collecting point and wrote a book in the late 1940s about Nazi looting. He was punctilious. My chief curator, Theodore Rousseau, was also at the collecting point and was Göring's interrogator and interpreter. Nothing would have passed their scrutiny. We young curators were steeped in the Nazi [loot] possibility because of Rorimer and Rousseau.'

Hoving, who wrote a book entitled *Making the Mummies Dance* about his time as a museum director, added that the extra burden of research announced by the AAMD is also uninspiring and unoriginal. 'For any professional curatorial staff in any museum worth its salt, painstaking provenance searches were and presumably are always conducted for, say, works over $5,000 in value. The Met acquisitions form has a section which goes into all information on a work's history including "street rumour and speculative talk". I wrote the form which is still being used these days. Of course, Rorimer and Rousseau had in their minds a rolodex of German and Swiss names that alerted them to Nazi connections. It really doesn't matter if a young curator has never heard of the Holocaust or the Cold War, he or she should delve into everything involving the past history of a prospective purchase, gift or bequest.'[87]

I I

BLOOD ON THEIR HANDS

Of all the accusations made in the post-war years, that of collaboration with the enemy was considered among the most grievous. Thousands of pages of Allied testimony, together with documents left behind by the retreating Nazi forces, illustrate the extent of complicity between the art world and the German marauders. Museums, private collectors and, primarily, art dealers in Europe and overseas jockeyed with each other to benefit from Hitler's looting of Europe. As will be clear from the various episodes recounted in earlier chapters, their conduct during the war years was based not on the quest for survival, as they would later argue, but on the desire for profit.

Their behaviour was not radically altered by the end of the conflict. Preservation of themselves and their gains, financial or material, was paramount. Nor was it much affected by the enquiries of the Allies into art confiscation. While retribution was visited on some of the Germans involved in looting, few among the scores of dealers who assisted them all too willingly were even fined for playing a similar part. After the war had ended, Allied prosecutors concentrated on those guilty of mass murder, and most of those involved in the cultural genocide which followed merely slipped into the shadows and continued their business as if nothing had happened. If there was any great change after the end of hostilities, it was that the trade in stolen art was freed from the shackles of wartime containment to the Continent and became a truly global, multi-billion-dollar business. To many art dealers, the details of what had happened to collectors such as Friedrich Gutmann and their families became a mere footnote in history.

Friedrich Gutmann was born into wealth, the youngest son of one of Germany's banking barons. Eugen Gutmann had founded the famous Dresdener Bank and was a member of the country's elite. Friends with royalty, he owned a large house on the Friedrichstrasse in the very heart of Berlin, a city at the very heart of Germany. His desire to secure high social status for himself and his family was such that, reportedly acting on advice from Bismarck, he even renounced his Jewish religion in favour of Protantism because the Iron

257

Chancellor had warned him that being a Jew might hamper any further progress. The future of young Friedrich and his two sisters seemed assured. While he was packed off by his father to run the London branch of the family bank, both girls married ambassadors to the German court. Not even the outbreak of war in 1914 appeared capable of halting his rise – although he, like many other Germans in Britain, was held for the duration of the conflict as an enemy alien, in his case in a camp on the Isle of Man.[1] After the war was over, Friedrich went to the Netherlands with his German wife, Louise, to start an Amsterdam branch of his father's banking concern. They took with them their son, Bernard, born during the couple's time in England; a daughter, Lili, was born in 1919. The business was a success and Friedrich, or 'Fritz' as he became known, installed his family in an elegant seventeenth-century property on an estate at Heemstede, near Haarlem.

Having emulated his father in his business success, Gutmann now followed him in acquiring an art collection. Friedrich shared to a degree Eugen's passion for precious metals, particularly silverware, but his real enthusiasm was for paintings. Initially he favoured the Old Masters, acquiring *Samson and the Lion* by Lucas Cranach the Elder and *Portrait of a Young Man* by Sandro Botticelli, as well as works by Guardi, van Goyen, Holbein and others. These masterpieces, hung around the three-storeyed house at Heemstede, were joined in the late 1920s and early 1930s by Friedrich's first Impressionist purchases, including a couple of works by Degas – himself born into a banking family. One of these, *Landscape with Smokestacks*, would prove to be of much significance to his heirs more than sixty years later. By the time the dark forces of the Third Reich began to spread out across Europe at the end of the decade, Gutmann had some forty-five paintings in all and his collection had acquired a measure of renown, with a catalogue of its contents prepared by a noted German art expert, Otto von Falke.

Even before the activities of Hitler's looting squads became widely known, Gutmann attempted to keep his treasures one step ahead of the German forces. Dismissed from his job at the Dresdener Bank after the Nazis seized power in 1933, he responded by starting another bank, Proehl and Gutmann, with some success; refusing to relinquish his professional career without a fight, he was equally determined to avoid losing his property to Germany's new masters. In April 1939 he decided to split up his collection. Some paintings were sold privately to an art dealer and collector named Kurt Walter Bachstitz, who ran offices in Munich and The Hague. Bachstitz's brother-in-law was Hermann Göring's principal art agent and adviser, Walter Andreas Hofer, although the connection was of little benefit to him. When Bachstitz's Jewishness threatened to compromise Hofer's business, the latter paid for his sister to divorce her husband. Hofer did obtain an exit visa to Switzerland for Bachstitz, but it came at a price: *Samson and Delilah* by Jan Steen and two ancient Greek necklaces, passed to the Reichsmarschall in return for granting Bachstitz permission to leave Germany.[2]

Some of the paintings in the Gutmann hands were despatched to New York;[3] a dozen other canvases, among them two Degas, one Renoir, a Memling and a Dosso Dossi, together with a selection of antique furniture, including some sofas dating from the reign of Louis XIV, were sent to Paris and the care of dealer Paul Graupe and his colleague, Arthur Goldschmidt. Graupe, a German-Jewish dealer with offices on the Place Vendôme,[4] was anxious about the prospect of invasion. In 1940, less than a month after receiving the consignment, he placed it in storage at Mme Wacker-Bondy's warehouse at boulevard Raspail, on the other side of the Seine, and headed for the sanctuary of Switzerland. Rather than leave it in the conspicuous name of its real owner, it was registered under the pseudonym of 'Muir', the surname of one of Graupe's English friends.[5]

Graupe's precautions were soon justified. Not long after the invasion of the Netherlands, the carrion of the art world, dealers revelling in the boost which the Nazis had given to their trade, began to circle. It came as no surprise when they revealed that they had their eyes on the Gutmann collection. On 12 September 1940 Dutch dealer Eduard Plietzsch wrote to Kajetan Mühlmann, State Secretary for the Arts under Reichskommissar Arthur Seyss-Inquart, Hitler's representative in the Netherlands. Plietzsch's letter was 'for your private information' and amounted to a briefing paper on the prime art collections in the Netherlands and the extent to which their contents fulfilled the Führer's requirements for Sonderauftrag Linz. After first trying to explain that there was precious little classic Dutch art which had not been removed from the country already, he moved on to a number of collectors and gave details of where they lived and the contents of their collections. He mentioned that 'a few important German masters can be found in the possession of Fritz Gutmann (portraits by Cranach, Burgkmaier and Baldung)'.[6] By the time Plietzsch had finished his letter, other predators had already touched down at the Heemstede house. Hofer had called on Gutmann in the company of Alois Miedl and both persuaded him to sell to them items from his collection of bronze and silverware. They took three pieces: a large double cup gilded in silver and two smaller, decorative cups, one featuring a figure of the Goddess Diana, the other a centaur.[7]

Miedl and Hofer were assisted in their endeavours by the changing circumstances in which the Gutmann family lived. The Netherlands was by this time subject to Hitler's anti-Semitic laws governing the treatment and property of Jews in Nazi territories. Even though Friedrich's father had changed his religion, the family was still classed as Jewish; as a result, Gutmann had been banned from working and was forced to wear the yellow star. Under these obscene laws his collection could have been confiscated. A sale at least allowed him to make some money to help his family survive.[8] Hofer later told those probing his wartime activities that Gutmann had also told him where he had moved his collection of paintings.

The unwelcome and avaricious attention to his collection moved Gutmann to write warnings to his children. He told Bernard, who had initially gone to England to study at Cambridge University and by the outbreak of war was working for the Red Cross, to stay in Britain. Conscious of his father's classification as an alien during the First World War, Bernard had anglicized his name by deed poll to Goodman in an attempt to avoid being singled out in the same way. Also in 1940 he wrote to Lili, who within three years would be living in Florence, having (like her aunt) married an Italian diplomat. Friedrich's letter to his daughter was brief, touching and to the point. 'Very Important', it began. 'For your information later, remember that ... some important objects of art in New York with [the dealers] Stern Drey ... further the firm Paul Graupe in Paris ... has also valuable pieces.' Friedrich went on to provide a list of objects, with short descriptions, before closing the letter 'P', for 'Papa'. In the years after the war, that letter was to prove very important.[9]

The information which Hofer had gleaned from Gutmann about the scale of the collection did not take long to reach those coordinating the acquisition of materials for the Führermuseum, including Karl Haberstock, arguably the most senior of Hitler's coterie of leading art advisers. Retracing Hofer's footsteps, Haberstock called on Gutmann at Heemstede in February 1941. He had a proposition: a sale of some of the banker's art works held at his home and in the Paris warehouse, and of the remaining gold and silverware, including objects by Jamnitzer, a Nuremberg goldsmith, dating from the time of the Renaissance. Given the disadvantage under which Gutmann laboured as a consequence of his Jewish ancestry, it was hardly a fair proposal, but Haberstock was at pains to give the deal at least a veneer of propriety by having an inventory drawn up and Friedrich sign a letter consenting to the sale.

Haberstock eventually came away with several paintings from the Wacker-Bondy warehouse, including a *Madonna* painting by Hans Memling and four which were later sold to Hitler for the Führermuseum at a price of RM100,000: Adriaen Isenbrandt's *Madonna and Child*, *Samson and the Lion* by Cranach the Elder, *Carts on the Dune* by Jan van Goyen and *Portrait of a Man* by the German fifteenth-century painter Jacob Elsner. Gutmann was also forced to part with one painting which would reappear, much to the delight of his heirs, more than fifty years later: Sandro Botticelli's *Portrait of a Young Man*.[10]

Haberstock's visit proved to be the last straw for Friedrich and Louise, who began requesting permission to leave the Netherlands in order to join Lili in Italy. Meanwhile, ERR staff in Paris were busily appraising the rest of the Gutmanns' works of art, which they had by then tracked down in the French capital. Hans Wendland had also used the Wacker-Bondy warehouse to store some of his paintings and came to know what else was being kept there. According to Mme Wacker-Bondy, the Germans visited the warehouse on a number of occasions during 1942 and 1943 and took everything the Gutmanns had sent for safe storage.[11] Wendland himself made off with a 'whole railway van full of art from Paris'. Some works headed immediately for Germany, having been identified as suitable additions to the Linz project. One of Gutmann's, a small *Portrait of a Man* by Dosso Dossi, was selected by Göring for his own private collection at Karinhall. Impressionist works, however, which were classed as 'degenerate', were sold or swapped by the Nazis among their network of friendly dealers. Two such works from the Gutmann collection were to resurface with calamitous results for the art world more than fifty years later: Degas' *Landscape with Smokestacks* and a painting by Pierre Auguste Renoir, *Apple Tree in Bloom*, also known as *Le Poirier*. All three had been removed from the Wacker-Bondy warehouse by Wendland.[12]

Friedrich and Louise were led to believe they would fare better than their collection. In June 1942 no less a figure than Himmler had written what appeared to be a personal guarantee of the couple's safety, exempting them 'from any kind of security police measures'. Eleven months later, however, two SS officers turned up at Heemstede and instructed the Gutmanns to pack immediately as they had finally been granted their wish to go to Italy. They were put on a train heading to Florence via Berlin. On the day they were due to arrive, Lili turned up at the railway station, but they did not. For the next three days she waited in vain for her parents. Understandably worried, she made enquiries about her parents' whereabouts through her husband's highly placed friends, but to no avail.[13] She later discovered that when Friedrich and Louise arrived in Berlin they were diverted not towards Tuscany but to Theresienstadt, a concentration camp in Nazi-occupied Czechoslovakia where, in April 1944, Friedrich was found beaten to death after repeatedly refusing to sign over the remaining pieces of his collection to his captors. Days later, his widow was put on a train out of Theresienstadt, but again was not bound for safety. This time Louise was sent to Auschwitz, where she died in a gas chamber.

Friedrich's death in particular epitomized the awful powers that those helping to shape Nazi art looting wielded, consciously or otherwise, and why the current trade in wartime loot is regarded with such distaste. The very pieces of silver for which Friedrich lost his life had been coveted by Karl Haberstock on his trip to the Heemstede estate. When Friedrich refused to sell, as he continued to do later with such tragic consequences, Haberstock wasted no time registering his displeasure. Of course, now that the Gutmanns were dead the remainder of their possessions could be disposed of without any difficulty. An order issued by Göring in Paris on 5 November 1940 had made the acquisition of 'ownerless' Jewish collections a primary objective of the ERR.

At the war's end, Lili and Bernard realized that not only had they lost their parents in horrific circumstances but the Germans had laid waste to the family fortune, their home at Heemstede having been completely emptied of anything valuable. Furthermore, they faced major problems in trying to establish what was missing as they had no record of what the Nazis had stolen. A list of precisely which works had been sold or stored and where was also lacking. The letter Friedrich had sent Lili in 1943 suddenly became relevant in trying to assess what had been taken.[14]

Independently of her brother, Lili submitted a claim based on her own memories of what had been in her childhood home and, of course, the information her late father had given her. Details also began to emerge from Allied interrogations of central figures in the Nazi looting programme. Shocking in their revelations of the extent to which dealers in both Europe and the United States had engaged in wartime art trade with the Germans, the reports were also useful to the younger Gutmanns in assessing the probable fate of their father's collection. They included the fact that both Paul Graupe and Arthur Goldschmidt were known to have traded works of art with the Nazis. The American dealers to whom some Gutmann objects had been consigned were also discovered to have been in business with another collaborator, the Munich-based dealer Walter Bornheim.[15]

Some of the family's missing paintings turned up among the cache of art earmarked for the Linz museum which had been stored at the Alt Aussee salt mine; others at Allied collection points; yet more in the hands of private dealers. By the early 1960s, when the German government paid Bernard and Lili compensation for the family silver and paintings which were still missing, some twenty-five works of art had been recovered. However, the precarious financial predicament in which they had been left gave Bernard and Lili no choice but to sell whatever treasures they had managed to recover.[16]

By the time of Bernard's death in 1994, sixteen paintings were still missing from the collection. They included two views of Venice by Francesco Guardi and the two works by Degas, as well as male portraits by Hans Baldung Grien and Dosso Dossi, a van Goyen landscape and the Renoir, *La Poirier*. Despite his efforts spanning nearly half a century, Bernard considered himself to have failed the family by not completing the task of piecing back together the collection his father had so carefully assembled. His two sons, Simon and Nick, remained largely unaware of their father's obsession during their childhood in London. Nick, who was born in 1945, said: 'It surprised us both that he didn't talk about the subject. On reflection, we know that he spent his available time and our school holidays looking for things. He even took a job working as a travel agent to enable him to get about more easily on his research trips. On one occasion he took us to San Diego and found a Frans Hals which had been in his father's collection and sold before the war. He avoided all reference to the Holocaust. It came to a point where he would turn off television documentaries if they mentioned it. He was a broken man.'[17]

So reticent had Bernard Goodman been, indeed, that his sons only learned of his personal crusade during a chance conversation with their Aunt Lili at Christmas 1994, several months after his death. 'We had been talking about the recent discovery of caches of looted art in Russia and she mentioned that she hoped ours would be among them,' said Nick. 'We, of course, asked what she meant and she told us the story of the collection and as much as she knew about what had happened to it. Soon afterwards we received Father's papers and came across all these documents in French, German and Russian which filled in more details. We decided to carry on his research. We wanted to do something for the sake of justice for the family and our father's memory. The last twenty years must have been so hard for him, not making much progress. He went to his grave not having found the paintings, yet his work has allowed us to do just that.'

Nick had moved to Los Angeles in 1984 to marry and work as a film production designer. His Hollywood home bears witness to the additional work he and his brother have done to further their father's efforts, and to their success. A study desk is piled with books, faxes and files on the paintings they have tried to hunt down. Under it lie several large cardboard boxes, each crammed to bursting point with photocopied documents from archives in the United States, Britain and Europe and bound legal briefs.

Given the potential volume of work involved in investigating every one of the missing pieces, Nick and Simon decided to concentrate on the best-known, the three Impressionist works. Shortly after they began researching, they picked up the trail of one of the two missing Degas. The discovery in a local library early in 1995 was to prove momentous not just for the Goodman family but the entire art world. *Landscape with Smokestacks* had, they discovered, featured in a 1994 exhibition at the Metropolitan Museum in New York and the Museum of Fine Arts in Houston, Texas. A programme catalogue even listed the name of its new owner: Daniel Searle, the septuagenarian heir to a multi-billion-dollar pharmaceutical fortune. Searle had donated the work to the Chicago Art Institute, of which he was a trustee.[18] However, while tracking down the Degas may have proved relatively easy, the process of trying to recover it has been lengthy, frustrating and expensive.

Mr Searle responded to a letter from the Goodmans' lawyer, Thomas Kline, with a stern rebuff of the family's claim. The brothers then called in Willi Korte, a German lawyer and historian, now based in the United States, who has come to be recognized as one of the foremost experts on the subject of Nazi art loot and the post-war trafficking in it. By checking archives in America and Europe, he was able to plot the painting's history back from the point in 1987 when it had been bought by Searle for $850,000. His work removed any lingering doubts about Nick, Simon and Lili Goodman's right to the painting, producing an auction sale catalogue from 1931 which showed that Friedrich Guttman had bought the Degas from an art dealer in Berlin.

Confirmation of the Goodmans' connection to the work prompted a settlement offer from Searle, which was immediately turned down. Upset at being snubbed, Searle's attorneys and experts went on the offensive with some evidence of their own. Instead of being merely stored in Paris, they claimed, the Degas had been sent to the French capital for sale and was duly bought, legally, by Hans Wendland.[19] Thereafter, the painting had been sold on to Wendland's brother-in-law, Hans Fankhauser, and subsequently to a New York collector, Emile Wolfe, from whom Searle had made his purchase via a dealer, Margot Schab.[20] It had also appeared in exhibitions in museums at the prestigious Harvard and Yale universities before being bought by Searle. Surely, his lawyers contended, the Goodmans had not shown 'due diligence'. Had the family paid closer attention to the art markets and museums, they suggested, then the painting's whereabouts would have become known far earlier. Using such an approach against a family seeking restitution was novel. Previously, this argument of 'due diligence' had always been put forward by Holocaust heirs to claim that art dealers, collectors and curators had not done enough checking of their own. Now the phrase had been turned into a defensive weapon against the claimants.

With Korte's help the Goodmans dismissed Searle's objections, following the voluminous paper trail left behind by German wartime art looters and OSS ALIU investigators who had dissected their operations in 1945 and set them down in cold, concise yet highly detailed 'Consolidated Interrogation Reports'. That the finger of suspicion pointed at nearly all of Hans Wendland's deals was due in part to the work of British wartime MFA&A officer Wing Commander Douglas Cooper. As described in chapter 6, Cooper had established the nature of Wendland's business through interviews with the Swiss-based dealer and his expansive network of associates across the continent, and examination of countless documents and account books illustrating how he had operated. Investigations by Cooper and his American colleagues showed how Wendland had despatched the Degas from Paris to Fankhauser, who at that time was living in Basle.[21] In 1951 Fankhauser, who had paid Wendland's legal bills in his successful attempt to evade justice for trading with the Nazis, sold the landscape to Wolfe. Margot Schab, who bought the painting from Wolfe in 1987, suggested to contacts at the Chicago Art Institute that it might be a worthwhile investment. Short of the necessary funds, the Institute persuaded Mr Searle to dig into his substantial wealth to purchase the Degas on its behalf.[22]

Still Searle refused to bow to the weight of fact ranged against him, though his case seemed weak by comparison. Two of the Chicago Institute's curators, who had advised on the purchase, testified that they simply did not know about any wartime art looting by Germany, despite the publicly available government documents, newspapers and magazines and at least three English-language books published during the previous decade and a half.[23] The plea of ignorance not only undermined the argument that the Goodmans had not paid enough attention to the comings and goings of the art world but, coming from senior figures, was a lamentably feeble excuse. Lloyd Goldenberg, managing director of Trans-Art International, a Washington art history database, is scathing. 'It would have taken me only five minutes to establish that both of those paintings had been looted during the war. There are plenty of materials which could be checked. Some papers may have been confidential during the war but they're freely available now.'[24] Thomas Hoving, a former Director of the Metropolitan Museum in New York, is equally critical. 'If two trained curators', he says, 'state in a sworn affidavit that they didn't know the Nazis looted art . . . well, frames is the extent of their expertise.'[25] When reminded of the Chicago Art Institute's defence, Willi Korte, whose detective work comprehensively outgunned its experts, merely raises his eyebrows and asks with incredulity: 'And these people have PhDs from Harvard?'[26]

Faced with an imminent federal trial, Searle finally decided to settle in September 1998, agreeing to terms which Nick Goodman had proposed twelve months previously in an attempt to avoid an unseemly legal battle. In recognizing the Goodmans' claim on the painting, the tycoon would donate his half-share to the museum, which would pay the claimants' half of the painting's full value. Neither side commented on the exact payout; although the settlement was believed to be worth $500,000 to the Goodmans, this sum was almost completely absorbed by legal costs. Ironically, the fees for Searle's own lawyers topped the amount he had originally paid for the work. 'It was a terrible waste,' says Nick Goodman. 'Both sides spent a lot of money and effort, but we felt we had to because we hoped it would be a landmark case and point out to both claimant families and the collectors the many pitfalls in trying to sort something like this out.'[27]

The significance of the case cannot be overstated. In one of the most high-profile disputes of its kind, it established the right of heirs to art looted during the Holocaust. From the point of view of others with claims to pursue, it had only one weakness: the Goodmans' authority had not been asserted by a federal court. However, even without the establishment of that formal, legal precedent, the episode had still outlined key issues and given hope to others. 'We know that we will never have a Degas or a Renoir hanging over the fireplace,' says Nick. 'We're resigned to that fact. But what we were hoping to do and still hope to do is score a moral victory so that our case really will give support to those other families for their own claims. The business of claims, particularly in the United States, is simply too expensive. There needs to be some sort of arrangement between museums, collectors and families to prevent the need for such a mess again.'

There were, sadly, several other negative aspects to the story, some of which pre-dated the painting's discovery. First, Hans Wendland and his fellow dealers, as we saw in chapter 10, escaped justice for their part in the looting of the Gutmann collection; and, although acknowledging that some meaningful penalty should have been imposed, Nick Goodman can appreciate why they went free. 'The trials of those dealers who actually went before a court mostly ended in acquittals. The trials were taking place at the same time of those of the Nazi leaders in Nuremberg. Compared to those hearings, people weren't it seems too concerned about individuals who had just nicked a few paintings. They were small fry.'[28]

According to a report by Douglas Cooper, Wendland had little to worry about after the war. Hugo Engel, another collaborator and art dealer, had succeeded in being appointed a cultural consultant to the Securité Militaire, the authority running France in the wake of its liberation. Engel, who was married to an Englishwoman, was sent to Switzerland where, protected by the cover of his official posting, he managed to sell some of Wendland's paintings for SwFr300,000. The pair discussed setting up a business in Paris together. Certainly, by the end of 1945, Wendland was back in France with an apparently clean conscience, having been removed from the Black List of collaborators, again with Engel's assistance.[29]

The second drawback to the resolution of the Chicago Art Institute affair is that the recovery of one Degas only accentuates the fact that the other which had been in the Gutmann collection, *Woman Drying Herself*, is still missing.

The *Landscape with Smokestacks* case involved a great expense of time and money; it was far simpler for Nick, Simon and their aunt to achieve a settlement in the case of another lost work: *Portrait of a*

Young Man by Sandro Botticelli, taken from the family collection by Karl Haberstock. Early in 1997, Lili Goodman took a call at her home in Tuscany from Christine Koenigs, the fate of whose father's collection is traced in the next chapter. On the previous day, Ms Koenigs noted, Sotheby's had conducted a sale of Old Masters in New York; and among the works on offer was the Goodmans' Botticelli.[30] The sale catalogue clearly mentioned the Gutmann heritage, yet the painting still went under the hammer and fetched $650,000. The Goodmans' Washington-based attorney, Thomas Kline, was immediately contacted and managed to prevent the painting leaving Sotheby's auction house in downtown Manhattan. The buyer, an elderly Italian gentleman, was contacted. The negotiations were swift, face-to-face and conclusive, taking place in an office with no lawyers involved. The Goodmans were awarded a six-figure sum, believed to be as much as half the value of the painting although, because of a legal agreement drawn up after the meeting, neither the family nor Mr Kline has been allowed to confirm the exact amount. Questions about Sotheby's action in allowing a looted work to go under the hammer were highlighted when it was discovered that the auction house kept its $100,000 commission from the original sale.[31]

Sotheby's came in for fresh scrutiny over its handling of another of the Goodman claims. Soon after the brothers' research began, they were alerted to the presence of their missing Renoir, *La Poirier*, by a friend working at the Getty Museum near their California homes. David Jaffe, the museum's curator of nineteenth-century paintings, discovered that the painting had featured in an April 1969 auction at Sotheby's New York affiliate, Parke-Bernet, where it had been sold for £85,000. When Sotheby's refused to give any information on the painting's past or new owners, Tom Kline was called in to help again. He took the matter before a New York court where Sotheby's was forced, reluctantly, to disclose the name of the buyer. The auction house issued a statement spelling out why it intended to stick to its guns. 'Client confidentiality', it asserted, 'is not unique either to Sotheby's or the auction business. If disclosing the identity of a buyer becomes important, as with the Renoir, we do our best to achieve a satisfactory resolution for both parties.'

In the case of the Goodmans, the disclosure set them off on an another paper trail. The painting, they learned, was owned by the Mallard Corporation of Tortola in the British Virgin Islands. Tracing the thread through company documents, trusts and foundations, the Goodmans eventually discovered that the work had been purchased by one Mrs Brunilde Nuñez de Baeza. The work's poorly documented post-war provenance also takes in Switzerland, the Bahamas and Argentina; but its current location is less glamorous. While Michael Metliss, a solicitor acting for the Goodmans in Britain, and Mrs de Baeza's lawyers try to negotiate a mutually beneficial solution to the problem of ownership, the colourful *La Poirier* remains in a dull, nondescript warehouse in central London.[32]

Two miles across the English capital from the Renoir's temporary home live cousins Count Adam Zamoyski and Prince Adam Czartoryski, heirs to another major European collection sacked by Nazi looters. At the time of the invasion of Poland on 3 September 1939 the Czartoryski family, members of the Polish nobility, owned magnificent properties spread out across the country: several large agricultural estates and castles at Goluchow in the west and Sienewa in the east and, at Krakow, one of the oldest private museums in Europe. A large elegant building in Paris, the Lambert, now owned by part of the European branch of the famous Rothschild family, was another significant part of the family's portfolio.[33]

The massive Czartoryski art collection comprised several thousand individual items, ranging from ancient coins to delicate Limoges enamels. It also contained some paintings of renown, among them a canvas by Raphael that was arguably the most noteworthy of all the pieces housed in the grand surroundings of Krakow. *Portrait of a Young Man*, also known as *Portrait of a Gentleman*, dated from 1515 and was believed to be a self-portrait of the artist. It had been acquired in Venice by a previous Prince Czartoryski for his mother, Isabella, who had herself been largely responsible for the treasures in Krakow, journeying across Europe to find suitable items for the museum. Unsurprisingly, situated as it was in the first territory to be invaded and occupied by the Nazis, and being one of the best-known collections in Europe, the hoard was immediately targeted by those leading Hitler's programme of organized plunder.

Aware of the value of the collection and its attractiveness to an invading force, on 24 and 25 August 1939 the then head of the family, Prince Augustin Czartoryski, sent the most precious articles to his country house at Sienewa, where they were carefully placed in the cellar of an outbuilding used as an office and walled up for safe keeping. As German troops swarmed into the area, however, they learned of the cache from a local miller, a man named Sauer who had been a member of the Volksreich. The first of those to reach the house on 14 December departed with the most portable objects, the enamels, coins and prints, damaging the Leonardo, *Lady with the*

Ermine, in the process. The canvases, it seemed, were too cumbersome to be moved immediately and were left for the attention of other, more specialized looters.[34]

By early October, Kajetan Mühlmann, recently appointed Special Commissioner for the Protection of Art Works in the Occupied Territories by Göring, had taken three of the most significant paintings to his patron in Berlin: *Lady with the Ermine* by Leonardo da Vinci, *Landscape with the Good Samaritan* by Rembrandt and *Portrait of a Young Man* by Raphael.[35] Mühlmann later argued under interrogation that he had received full cooperation from the Czartoryski family in taking their possessions and had been following his job description to the letter in seeking to protect the three works from Soviet forces.[36] At the time, however, during the actual process of looting when there was no need to hide their true intentions, his colleagues made no attempt to disguise the status of the works of art in their possession. Hans Posse wrote to Martin Bormann on 14 December 1939 of his wish to see the three paintings join the contents of the Führermuseum. 'I am not in a position to make any detailed suggestion for distribution before a survey is possible of the entire confiscated material,' he reported. 'But I should like to propose now that the three pictures of the Czartoryski collection by Raphael, Leonardo and Rembrandt, which are at present located in the Kaiser Friedrich Museum in Berlin, be reserved for the Art Museum in Linz.'[37]

The trio of paintings became the subject of a tug of war not merely between Göring and Hitler but also between Berlin and those locally in charge of the forces of occupation. Mühlmann's superior was Hans Frank, Reichskommissar of Poland, who had installed himself at the Wawel Palace, the former home of the country's royal family, and issued instructions that it should be furnished to his taste with exquisite Louis XV and XVI furniture. He was dismayed at the departure of the three paintings to Göring and ordered that they be returned to Krakow to adorn his new home. An apparent newcomer to the pursuit of art collection, Frank failed to hide his ignorance with any success, being scolded by Mühlmann for hanging the da Vinci above a radiator.[38] In early 1941 Mühlmann, torn between his duties to Frank and his loyalty to Göring, attempted to assuage his powerful patron's disappointment at losing the three Old Masters by bringing him Watteau's *Pretty Polish Girl*, taken from another Polish collection, that of the Lazienki in Warsaw.[39] Nevertheless, the Raphael and its two illustrious companions continued their journeying back and forth. The three made another enforced trip to Berlin later in the same year, only to head eastwards again in 1942 as Allied bombing of the German capital was stepped up. On each of their trips between Krakow and Berlin, they were accompanied by Mühlmann, who testified during interviews with Allied interrogators to having carried *Lady with the Ermine* with him on the train.[40] (All Hitler actually received from the Nazi haul in Poland was a group of thirty drawings by Dürer, including twenty-eight from the Lubomirski collection in Lvov and two belonging to Czartoryski, which were sent to him in Berlin. Instead of being passed on to those responsible for Sonderauftrag Linz, the sketches remained to decorate his office.[41])

In autumn 1943 the three Czartoryski pictures, perhaps the most significant items in the Polish booty, were back with Reichskommissar Frank at his official residence in Krakow. By this time Mühlmann had been replaced in his role as protector of the arts by an architect and interior designer, Wilhelm de Palisieux. A young man with family connections to nobility (his mother was a French marquise), he had met Frank on holiday and appears to have leapt at the chance to join the Reichskommissar's staff.[42] Frank's possession of the three Czartoryski paintings was comparatively short-lived. The following year, as the Red Army advanced, Frank and his henchmen were on the retreat. He and Palisieux had already established an escape route and a network of safe houses stretching from Siechau in western Poland through Murau in southern Austria to Frank's Bavarian home at Neuhaus-am-Schliersee. On 17 January 1945, as Soviet troops stormed Katowice, Frank left Krakow for Count von Richthofen's castle at Siechau. Ahead of him was sent a truck containing papers and the three paintings. At Siechau, the works of art were packed in crates while compromising documents were shredded and burnt. The Raphael was sent on to Austria, arriving with Frank on the twenty-first. Three days later a small convoy of vehicles headed for Neuhaus carrying Frank's close aides and their possessions. Three cases of art from the baggage which arrived in Bavaria were left at the offices which Frank shared with his aide-de-camp, Sturmbannführer Helmut Pfaffenroth, but the Czartoryski works were not among them. Instead they were brought by Frank ten days afterwards.[43]

Exactly what happened next has remained impenetrably shrouded in mystery for the past fifty years and has frustrated the efforts of Adam Zamoyski and his family to reclaim their property. When the 10th US Armored Division rolled into Neuhaus on 4 May 1945, Frank was taken into custody by an American officer, Lieutenant

Daniel Kern. A quantity of works of art found in his possession were brought to the central collection point established at the Führerbau in Munich, under the control of American MFA&A officer Lieutenant Craig Hugh Smyth. On 14 June, the collection point's first day of operation, Smyth turned his attention to the crates seized from Frank on his arrest. He later wrote: 'Opened one case, found among other things Leonardo's *Lady with the Ermine*. In the same crate were a Dürer portrait, three Rembrandts including the Czartoryski landscape, six other paintings and several drawings.'[44] The Raphael, however, was missing. Frank was questioned but gave no clues as to where it was – if, indeed, he knew. It was suspected that Palisieux or Pfaffenroth, both of whom had disappeared, might have absconded with the painting. In any event, the former Reichskommissar did not have much opportunity to profit from whatever ill-gotten gains he might have salted away. Found guilty at Nuremberg of war crimes, he was condemned to death and hanged. Palisieux was later arrested and detained in the French zone of occupation and served several years in prison for his part in the looting programme. The Raphael remained unrecovered.[45]

Fortunately, most of the other items in the Czartoryski collection were returned. In November 1945 Major Karol Estreicher of the Polish army finally received permission to take both *Lady with the Ermine* and *Landscape with the Good Samaritan* back to Krakow where they arrived on 30 April 1946, travelling in the same transport as the Veit Stoss altarpiece. After the war Count Stefan Zamoyski, son-in-law of the prince who had been in charge of the Czartoryski family treasures, pursued the missing objects with varying degrees of success. 'Roughly ninety per cent of the stuff from Krakow and sixty per cent from Goluchow has been reclaimed,' says Adam Zamoyski, the count's son. 'Other bits and pieces have come back over time and from various sources.'[46] As the post-war push for restitution continued, the family was awarded cash payments for objects it had tracked down but could not recover. In 1955 Adam Zamoyski's father was given an undisclosed amount in lieu of two medieval enamels which had been sold to a museum in Boston by none other than Georges Wildenstein.[47] It was Wildenstein whose 'Aryanized' firm in Paris, as mentioned in chapter 3, had been strongly criticized by Allied art experts for doing business with the Nazis after the German occupation of France. It was also Wildenstein's magazine, *Gazette des Beaux Arts*, in which Hitler's pet dealer, Haberstock, had placed advertisements in the hope of attracting even more classic works for Sonderauftrag Linz. A cultural affairs official at the State

Department in Washington, Ardelia Hall, notified Count Zamoyski that the objects had resurfaced. The threat of court action was enough to ensure that the matter was resolved speedily. Wildenstein explained that he had found the enamels in Liechtenstein.[48]

While it appeared that the Czartoryski family was succeeding in pressing claims for the outstanding elements of its collection, it was in fact beginning to lose heart. This was due in no small part to the new political situation in Poland. The communist regime had little interest in supporting disadvantaged aristocrats, regardless of how or why their circumstances had altered. It was not until 1989 that the new head of the family, Adam Czartoryski, managed to reclaim the museum at Krakow, which has now been placed under the control of a family foundation to ensure its future. The Czartoryskis' other properties had been confiscated. The magnificent ornate country house at Sienewa, which had once rivalled the famous French palace at Versailles in beauty and appearance, was left to fall into ruin. Attempts at restitution were left in a similar state of disrepair by the new post-war government.

Informal enquiries were addressed to German authorities about compensation for the works which remained lost, but received little if any response as the Iron Curtain descended and the Cold War settled over Europe. A lump sum for reparations had been paid to Poland's new rulers: it was up to them, Count Zamoyski was bluntly informed, to decide if the family was to receive anything at all. In the end, the only cash they received was for several racehorses which had been taken by German soldiers from one of the Czartoryskis' country estates. 'Given the way the leadership in Warsaw had approached things already,' said Adam Zamoyski during an interview with the authors in London, 'it was decided that it simply wasn't worth even bothering making a claim. We knew it would get nowhere.'

Nevertheless, against even so unpromising a backdrop, attempts to trace the missing Raphael continued; but they took the Czartoryski heirs no closer to the lost masterpiece. Hans Frank's assistant, Palisieux, was released from prison in 1954 and agreed to a meeting with Count Stefan Zamoyski in Switzerland. He did not turn up at the rendezvous, and the following day Zamoyski discovered he had been killed in a car crash. Several years later, Frank's art restorer breathed fresh life into the inquiry by giving a statement saying that he had seen the portrait with Palisieux shortly before he was gaoled. Ernst Kneisel had returned to Austria after the war and resumed his trade. In the 1950s his work had taken him to New York, where he was tracked down by the count's lawyers. In 1965 a delighted

Zamoyski prepared to initiate legal proceedings in Germany for compensation. However, when asked to repeat his earlier remarks in the form of an affidavit, Kneisel declined, mysteriously maintaining that he had never seen the Raphael in his life. Frustrated by his lack of progress, Stefan Zamoyski simply gave up. He died twelve years later, distressed at his inability to trace the Raphael.

It is ironic that the very interest shown by lawyers, historians and heirs in the subject of looted art may have added to Adam Zamoyski's difficulties in furthering his father's work. 'Over the last twenty years or so we have been reduced to keeping a weather eye out for pieces of the collection,' he says. 'As a result, small objects have turned up from time to time. But the large pieces still outstanding, such as the Raphael, have continued to elude us and I believe it's partly because of the pressure created by the fact that Second World War loot is a hot topic. There are very few people in the art world who are not sensitive to the subject.

'The family believes that it's simply not worth making enquiries because the stuff which remains to be found is valuable and is probably in the collection of someone who knows just what they have got but is not going to let it surface when there is all this attention. Documentary histories are all well and good but there is only so much that the documents can tell us. The rest is up to dealers or collectors, and when there is a painting like Raphael they are not going to be too forthcoming. There is a mountain of evidence to show that they do not talk if it's not good for them and if they can't make a sale.'[49]

One sale of a Czartoryski heirloom was stopped early in 1998, when the New York auction of a painting by the Dutch sixteenth-century artist Jan Mostaert at Sotheby's on 30 January was sensationally halted. *Portrait of a Lady*, presumed to be Anne of Bretagne, used to hang in the palace at Goluchow but disappeared along with the rest of the family's treasures in late 1940.[50] Interestingly, the German appropriation for the Führermuseum was not the first time the painting had been stolen. Originally the property of the Archbishop of Salzburg, it had been seized by the army of Napoleon Bonaparte and subsequently purchased by Isabella Czartoryska, the woman responsible for enriching the family collection in Paris during the 1860s. Count Adam Zamoyski and his cousin who now heads the Czartoryski family were notified of its presence in an Old Masters' sale in Manhattan and succeeded in having the work withdrawn before it went under the hammer. Its links to the Polish nobility were clearly listed in the sale catalogue,

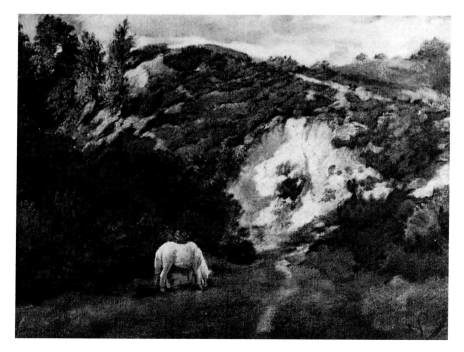

Landscape with a White Horse by Wilhelm Lindenschmit. Looted in September 1945 from the Lenbachhaus repository in the Schloss Hohenaschau in Bavaria, it is still missing. (Städtische Galerie im Lenbachhaus)

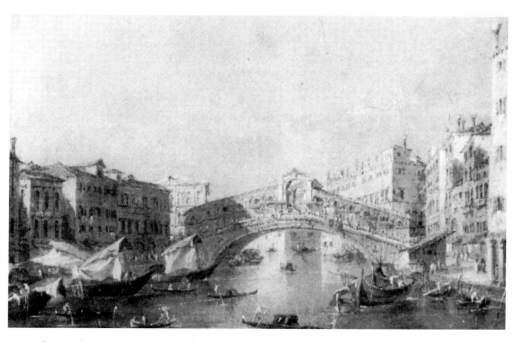

The Rialto Bridge in Venice by Francesco Guardi. This is one of two views of Venice by Guardi, belonging to the Schloss Collection, which were missing until found in the possession of the Lorenzelli Museum in Bergamo in Northern Italy. Negotiations for their return are still in progress. (French Ministry of Foreign Affairs)

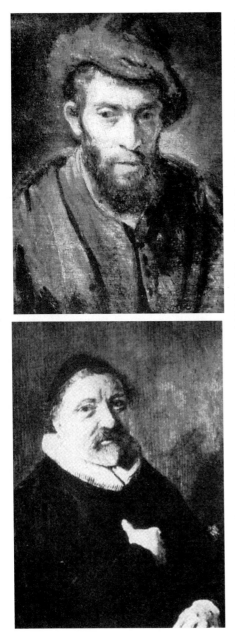

LEFT: *Jew in a Fur Cap* by Rembrandt. Part of the Schloss Collection, this master-piece was missing until found on display in the Carnegie Museum in Pittsburgh, in whose vaults the painting is currently located. The museum has since refused even to discuss the painting. (French Ministry of Foreign Affairs)

BELOW LEFT: *Portrait of Pastor Adrianus Tegularius* by Frans Hals. Missing from the Schloss Collection, this painting reappeared more than once when it was sold at auction on four occasions in New York and London during the period 1967–1979. It was eventually seized from an American dealer during an art fair in Paris in 1990. The painting has since remained in France while ownership is still being contested. (French Ministry of Foreign Affairs)

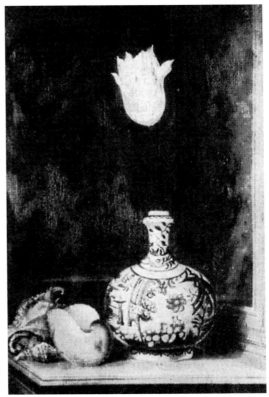

Still Life with Tulip by Dirk van Delen. Part of the Schloss Collection, this work was missing until 1989 when it was exhibited by the Boimans van Beuningen Museum in Rotterdam. Negotiations are currently under way to resolve the issue of ownership. (French Ministry of Foreign Affairs)

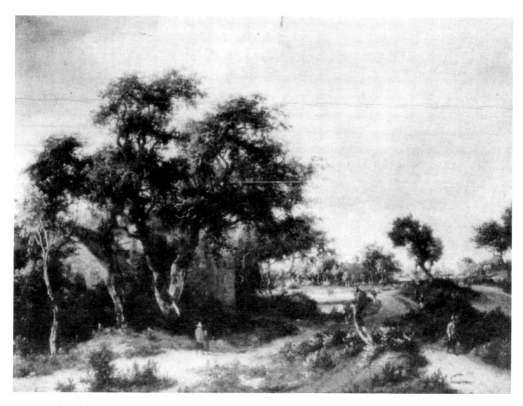

Wooded Landscape by Meindert Hobbema. Part of the Schloss Collection, in 1945 this work was suspected by US MFA & A officer Edgar Breitenbach of being in the possession of a wealthy German industrialist in Munich who was known to have made a number of acquisitions on the post-war black market. It is still missing. (French Ministry of Foreign Affairs)

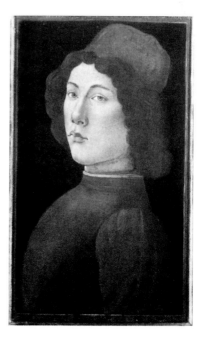

Portrait of a Young Man by Sandro Botticelli. Removed from the Wacker Bondy warehouse in Paris by Karl Haberstock in 1941, it disappeared until 1997 when it was recognized after being auctioned by Sotheby's in New York. Negotiations with the new owner led to acceptance of financial compensation by the Goodman family. (Charles Naylor)

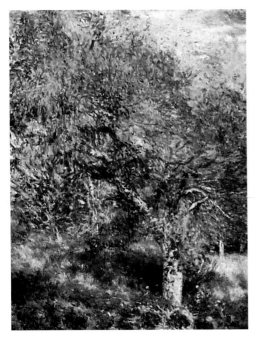

Apple Tree in Bloom or *Le Poirier* by Pierre Auguste Renoir. Removed from the Wacker Bondy warehouse in Paris by Hans Wendland during the period 1942–1943, this painting from the Goodman Collection was missing until 1995 when it was found to have been sold at auction in 1969 by Parke-Bernet in New York. Lengthy investigations revealed the new owners as being a Virgin Islands-based trust. The painting is now in a warehouse in London and currently the subject of lengthy legal negotiations.
(Charles Naylor)

Landscape with Smokestacks by Edgar Dégas. One of two works from the Goodman Collection removed from the Wacker Bondy warehouse in Paris by Hans Wendland during the period 1942–1943, it was missing until found in the possession of the American collector Daniel Searle who had donated it to the Chicago Art Institute. Lengthy legal proceedings eventually led to a settlement between Searle and the Goodman family. (Charles Naylor)

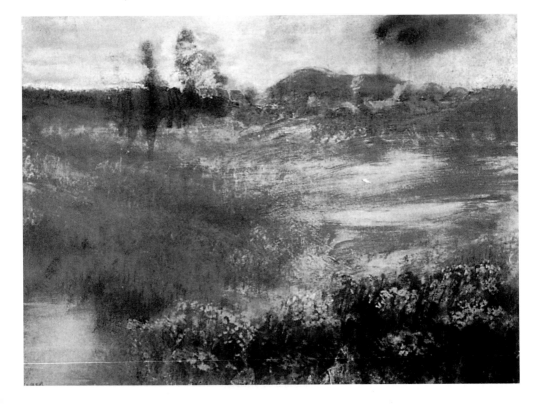

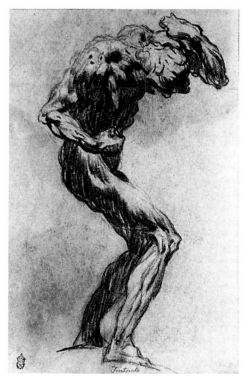

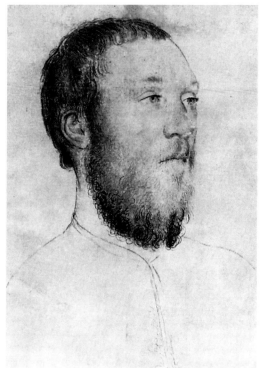

Study after a Bronze Statue by Jacopo Tintoretto. This work is currently in the Pushkin Museum, Moscow, and thus is listed as still missing from the Koenigs Collection. (Boijmans van Beuningen Museum)

Portrait of Sir Charles Wingfield by Hans Holbein. This work from the Koenigs Collection was returned to the Dutch Ministry of Culture by an anonymous West European collector in 1995 and is now in the Boijmans van Beuningen Museum in Rotterdam. (Boijmans van Beuningen Museum)

Portrait of a Man with a Red Beard by Hans Brosamer. Still missing from the Koenigs Collection, this drawing was tracked down and recovered in Russia by art historian Alexei Rastorgouev. It is currently in a vault in the Stolichny Bank in Moscow. (Boijmans van Beuningen Museum)

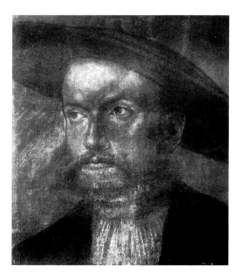

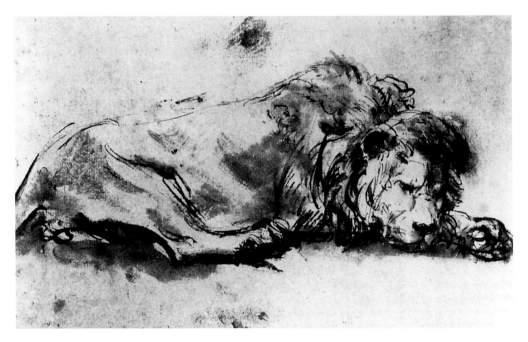

Recumbent Lion Turned to the Right by Rembrandt. One of a pair: one is in the Boijmans van Beuningen Museum in Rotterdam, while the other is in the Pushkin Museum, Moscow, and thus is still listed as missing from the Koenigs Collection. (Netherlands Office for Fine Arts)

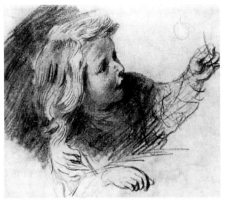

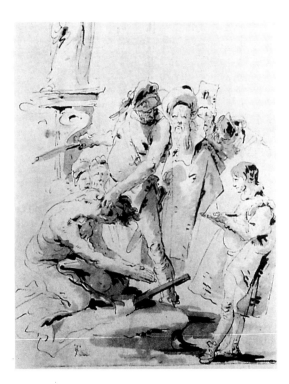

ABOVE: *Half-Length Figure of a Child Turned to the Right, Blowing Bubbles* by Antoine Watteau. Still missing from the Koenigs Collection, it is currently in the Pushkin Museum in Moscow. (Netherlands Office for Fine Arts)

LEFT: *The Beheading of St John the Baptist* by Giambattista Tiepolo. Still missing from the Koenigs Collection, it is currently in the Pushkin Museum in Moscow. (Netherlands Office for Fine Arts)

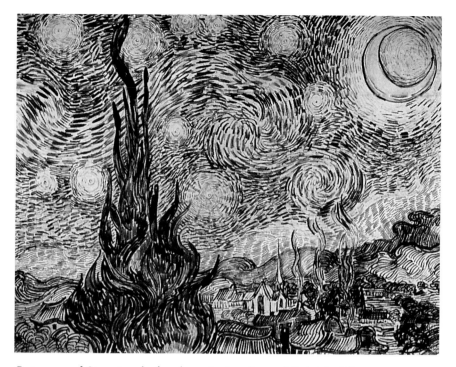

Cypress and Stars (study for the painting *Starry Night*) by Vincent van Gogh. One of the collection of drawings rescued in 1945 from the Bremen Kunsthalle repository in the Schloss Karnzow by Red Army officer Viktor Baldin, it is in the possession of the Hermitage Museum, St Petersburg, and thus is listed as still missing from the Bremen Collection. (Bremen Kunsthalle)

Young Female Nude by François Boucher. One of the collection of drawings rescued in 1945 from the Bremen Kunsthalle repository in the Schloss Karnzow by Red Army officer Viktor Baldin, it is in the possession of the Hermitage Museum, St Petersburg, and thus is listed as still missing from the Bremen Collection. (Bremen Kunsthalle)

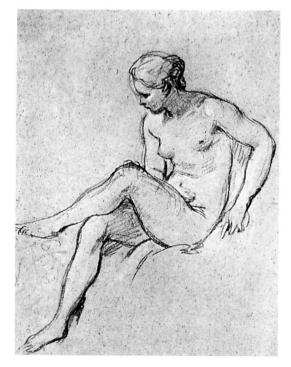

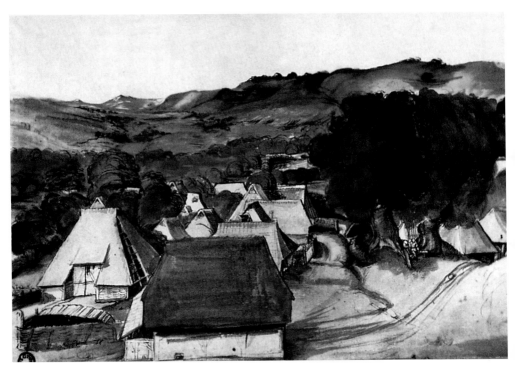

View of Kalchreuth by Albrecht Dürer. One of the collection of drawings rescued in 1945 from the Bremen Kunsthalle repository in the Schloss Karnzow by Red Army officer Viktor Baldin, it is in the possession of the Hermitage Museum, St Petersburg, and thus is listed as still missing from the Bremen Collection. (Bremen Kunsthalle)

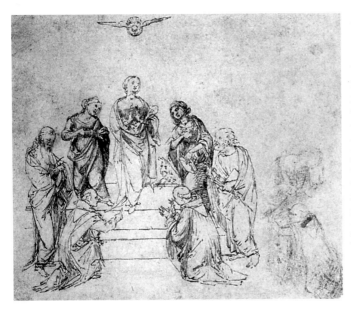

Immaculate Conception by Piero di Cosimo. One of the drawings rescued in 1945 by Red Army officer Viktor Baldin from the Bremen Kunsthalle repository in the Schloss Karnzow, it is currently in the possession of the Hermitage Museum in St Petersburg and thus is listed as still missing from the Bremen Collection. (Bremen Kunsthalle)

along with its estimated value of between $75,000 and $90,000. Having documented their right to the portrait, the Czartoryskis entered into formal proceedings of negotiating a settlement with Knoedler, the New York gallery which had put it up for sale. Those talks continue at the time of writing.

Another element of the Czartoryski collection turned up in a big auction sale, this time in London. In 1990 Christie's announced plans to sell a seventeenth-century Persian silk carpet, known as a Polonaise, which had been stolen from the museum at Krakow and was considered to be worth twice as much as the Mostaert portrait, about $200,000. It was being sold by a Swiss national who rather intriguingly, given the escape route taken by Hans Frank with some of the Czartoryski possessions, claimed to have purchased the carpet in Bavaria. Again, the item's previous ownership was not a great secret, particularly when the auction catalogue was published describing it as 'the Czartoryski Polonaise Rug'. Once more the family intervened and the sale was stopped. Seven years of legal discussions followed before the valuable carpet was finally returned to Krakow and put back on exhibition; and it was not surrendered willingly or cheaply, as Count Adam Zamoyski explained to the authors in July 1998. 'We had to pay the Swiss owner £60,000 to get the rug back. We sent the bill immediately to the German government as their predecessors had been responsible for taking it in the first place. It really illustrates the cost to the family of trying to find and then regain ownership of what was stolen during the war. Occasionally the Polish government steps in with a contribution but the ongoing legal costs are fairly substantial.'[51]

The matter of expense is one concern common to many families who decide to pursue claims, often all the way to the courts. Thomas Kline continues to represent the Goodmans in their attempts to reclaim some of their former possessions. The brothers are still on the trail of the two Guardi landscapes which went missing after appearing in the possession of the Nazi collaborationist dealer Nathan Katz. Three other works from Friedrich Gutmann's sizeable collection have turned up in a sample of 113 items from a total of 3,500 seized by the Nazis and now handed back to the Dutch government but not yet passed on to their pre-war owners. A painting by Michele Rocca, *Mars and Venus*, and another by Angela Schuszler, *Chicken*, went through the Bohler Galleries in Munich in April 1998.[52] The latter, which was reported to have ended up in the hands of Hitler himself, and an earthenware piece which was acquired by Kurt Bachstitz are now the subject of a claim for their return.[53]

Thomas Kline has also worked with heirs to the great Schloss collection, as well as government officials from Belgium and Bremen museum directors, in chasing down looted art works. Speaking at the offices of his law firm in downtown Washington, only a couple of blocks from the White House, Kline appreciates the delicacies involved. 'The families are glad of whatever support they can get in these cases,' he says, 'because it is a terrible drain to bring litigation. Most of the cases I have been involved with in one way or another have involved a high degree of combativeness. I like to take pro bono cases but everyone in private practice has a commitment to their firms to generate revenue. We can't do everything for free, much as we like to help, especially in cases like these.

'There have been suggestions of how we can improve the situation. One was having the art dealers and government fund a pool while the victims would accept less compensation for their lost works and the courts would accept a lower standard of proof. But the comments I have heard about such a proposal have been critical. The dealers don't want to pay a tax to support claims while the families don't want to accept less compensation.'[54]

The compensation in the case of the Czartoryski Raphael would be immense. Some experts assess the value of this painting, which stands only two and a half feet tall, at roughly £5 million. Not surprisingly, efforts to find it continue. Bernard Taper, now a professor of journalism at Berkeley University in California, was an American officer who took part in the interrogation and debriefing of some of the key Nazi looters in Europe immediately after the war finished. 'Of all the investigations I was involved in during those two years,' he has said, 'the one that most preoccupied and tantalized me was the search for the Raphael . . . There were nights when I dreamed of it. I knew the painting only from a small black and white photograph . . . but in my dreams it was always in sumptuous colour.' Writing in 1995, he continued: 'My own present hunch . . . is that the Raphael is not something that Frank would have left behind and that he did bring it along to Neuhaus but quite possibly left it in another residence he owned there that the Americans who arrested him did not know about.' The Raphael, he concluded, 'is possibly the most important painting lost in the war and still missing.'[55]

Polish historian Wojciech Kowalski joined the pursuit during the 1970s but came up against two considerable obstacles. First, all the wartime documents had been claimed by the ruling Communist

Party; second, those in charge of the country were not keen on being too inquisitive about more senior members of the eastern bloc. Kowalski reported having been told by one official: 'You are talking about treasures removed by Nazis but you are also thinking about treasures looted by Russians and in that instance you are a liability not only for us but especially for yourself.' In 1991, after communism lost its grip on power, Kowalski was appointed Commissioner for Polish Cultural Heritage Abroad, an office with responsibility for the restitution of art stolen by Germany during the Second World War. However, in his three years in the post, he came no closer than anyone else to finding the elusive Raphael.[56]

'It has acquired almost mythical status,' said Count Adam Zamoyski. 'Every now and then, I get reports of it turning up somewhere but they always prove to have no substance. They're all third or fourth hand and very vague. There was one suggestion two years or so ago that it had been seen in the house of some film or pop star on an island off the Australian coast. People imagine it's gone far away because they have heard about the escape of Nazis via organizations like Die Spinne and ODESSA, but I think it's more likely to be in Europe still. Someone else said it was sitting in the collection of a retired Russian general. That's much more plausible. Either way the whole business is frustrating but slightly entertaining at the same time.'

The Raphael, though perhaps the most valuable, is to the remaining members of the Czartoryski family only one of more than 150 objects still missing. These include five full-size canvases and a further nine miniatures from the Krakow museum's paintings department, while the whereabouts of nine prints and four east European miniatures are also unknown. The largest single body of material which has not been traced was taken from the museum's antiquities collection: 137 pieces, all of them gold, have not been seen since the German invasion sixty years ago.

Count Zamoyski continued: 'It is not as though every member of the family says daily, "Oh, I wish we had it back." The amount of stuff taken was staggering and we have to keep our eyes open for whatever is about. Recently I had a telephone call that a Swiss dealer and collector of Limoges enamel had offered two pieces from Goluchow for sale. Likewise, I am convinced that the Raphael has not been destroyed and I remain hopeful that it will turn up some day.'[57]

When an oil painting by Henri Matisse turned up in Seattle, it created the sort of threat dealers had feared but so far escaped.

Unlike Daniel Searle, once the owners of *Odalisque* realized it had been stolen they contacted the heirs of the pre-war collector of whose hoard it had once formed part. As described in earlier chapters, Paul Rosenberg was one of many French Jews whose art collections were seized by the Germans. A personal friend of Henri Matisse, Rosenberg had fled France as the Nazis invaded, leaving behind more than 300 major paintings, 162 of which had been deposited in the vaults of the Banque Nationale de Crédit at Libourne near Bordeaux. Twenty-one of them, including *Odalisque* (also known as *Oriental Woman Seated on the Floor*), were by Matisse. The paintings were found by a local police inspector, appraised on 6 April 1941 and sent up to the ERR depot at the Musée du Jeu de Paume.[58] Göring's agent Hofer informed the Reichsmarschall by letter on 26 September that he had selected from the haul thirty-eight works by artists such as Manet, Degas, Sisley, Renoir and Toulouse-Lautrec for the collection at Karinhall.[59] *Odalisque* remained at the Jeu de Paume until July of the following year, when it was bought by the German art dealer Gustav Rochlitz.[60] It then disappeared from view, as one of fourteen works which, as mentioned in chapter 6, were despatched from Paris to Baden-Baden but went missing, reported to have been taken to Switzerland.

The painting next appeared in 1954 in Manhattan's Knoedler Gallery, owned by the billionaire entrepreneur Armand Hammer, having been bought from the Paris firm Drouant-David. The American dealer sold it on to the Seattle-based Canadian timber tycoon Prentice Bloedel. In 1991, like the Degas in the Goodman–Searle case, the Matisse was donated to the new owner's local gallery, the Seattle Art Museum. However, five years later the gift attracted the sort of attention that had not been anticipated when Bloedel's relations recognized the oil painting as one of those stolen by the Nazis from the Rosenbergs. They contacted the collector's heirs who in October 1997 filed suit, demanding the museum return the work. This time it was not the new owners but the museum itself that dug its heels in, insisting in June 1998 that it would prefer the issue to be resolved in court rather than simply hand over the painting, worth an estimated $2 million, to the family. The Rosenbergs accordingly sued at the end of July. Their lawyer, Camden Hall, speaking at the time the writ was issued, said: 'The museum needs to give the painting back. For the museum, the painting is part of its inventory. For the Rosenbergs, it's their heritage.' However, at the same time, Hall was willing to strike a conciliatory tone. 'My feeling is if we get the painting back quickly without a lot of spear-throwing, we'll probably just fade into the sunset.'[61]

Given the example of the Gutmann–Searle battle, which proved so costly to the art establishment in terms both of money and of its image, the question arises why the Seattle Art Museum decided to go to court. Lloyd Goldenberg of Trans-Art International has his own ideas. 'The clear implication', he explains, 'was that the museum was saying to the Rosenberg family that they had to sue in order for the museum directors to go after Knoedler. There is a doctrine under New York law known as equitable indemnification. In simple terms it means that if a party to that transaction was in possession of facts that were material to the sale, such as where this painting had come from, and chose not to make them known, then they have an obligation if something goes wrong somewhere on down the line. This case will alert dealers to the fact that they have a lot of skeletons out there that can come back and bite them on the behind. They are at risk.'[62]

Risks of one sort or another have always been a part of the art business – as illustrated by the case of Göring's purchase of van Meegeren's reproduction of Vermeer's *Christ with the Woman Taken in Adultery*. The former Reichsmarschall learned of the swindle in 1945, as he awaited trial at Nuremberg, from American MFA&A officer Herbert Stewart Leonard. Fifty years later, in 1995, Leonard's colleague Bernard Taper wrote: 'At that moment, Hermann Göring looked as if for the first time he had discovered there was evil in the world.'[63] The irony of the situation was that van Meegeren proved to be one of the few in the wartime art trade who was gaoled for dealing with the Nazis. He was subsequently released after painting yet another 'Vermeer' in his prison cell to rid himself of the charge of selling a Dutch national treasure to the enemy.

TWICE BITTEN

The 1990s have not been kind to the French national conscience. Instead of being salved of any responsibility for some of the tragic consequences of the Second World War, France has been reminded of its culpability. Even the late President François Mitterrand, it has been claimed, had links with officials of the Vichy regime which acted as Hitler's puppet authority. Revelations of collaboration between the country's art establishment and those involved in the Nazi looting of Europe only add to the insecurity. However, for all that heirs of Holocaust victims have sought to exploit the discomfort many feel about the wartime conduct of some of their compatriots, they still find their attempts to find justice obstructed by government and the law.

Jean de Martini is a perfect example of this continuing struggle. Since he retired from the world of banking in 1980, he has dedicated himself to pursuing the elements of the fortune to which he and other heirs of the Schloss family should, in principle, be entitled. It has not been easy; but the fog of bureaucracy has not dimmed his enthusiasm for the task. Instead, on the fifteen-minute car ride from his flat in the Courbevoie district of Paris to the former family home, M. de Martini is energetic in explaining not just how far the family fell but also how much ground they have covered in reclaiming their works of art.

The grand house itself stands on the avenue Henri-Martin, a short distance from the Bois de Boulogne, among other large town houses in the heart of the fashionable sixteenth arrondissement. Now the brickwork is worn and flecked with age, but at the turn of the century the magnificent building was in an excellent state of repair. It was owned by Adolphe Schloss, a German-born businessman who earned a fortune selling stock to department stores across France and overseas. Such was his standing in European commerce of the day that his personal clients included some of the continent's highest elite. He had even sold the Tsar's court in Russia a beautiful silver tea service.[1] From the headquarters of his firm, Schloss et Cie, halfway across the city on rue Martel, Adolphe Schloss amassed a considerable fortune, much of which he lavished on the home he and his wife

Lucie created for themselves and their five children. Enabled by his commercial success to indulge his passion for art, and using a network of friends and informers spread across the continent, he built up a spectacular collection totalling 333 works in all. Dutch and Flemish painters of the seventeenth and eighteenth centuries were his particular favourites. The collection was held in high regard by art experts internationally; and while some considered Adolphe to be only an enthusiastic amateur, many more queued up to hear his opinions of their own prospective purchases.[2]

M. Schloss made no attempt to keep his acquisitions secret. On the contrary, anyone entering his home would be confronted by a selection of the finest works imaginable. Once through the imposing front door, visitors would be greeted by a large Snyders canvas hanging in the entrance hall, while in one downstairs lounge were two primitive Italian works. In the billiard room were exotic paintings by Rembrandt and Rubens, while in the dining room hung a Chardin and a Velázquez. Upstairs were more breathtaking pieces. Arrayed along a gallery were further paintings by Rubens and Teniers, a van Dyck and several works by Frans Hals, including the *Portrait of Pastor Tegularius*. Hung elsewhere around the Schloss home were paintings by Brueghel, van Ruisdael and van der Heyden, *Pietà* by Petrus Christus, *Venus* by Gossaert and works by lesser known, so-called 'minor masters' like Molenaer, Boursse and Brekelenkam. After Adolphe's death in 1910, his wife maintained the collection at the family home until her death, when it passed jointly into the hands of her children: Lucien, the eldest, Marguerite, Juliette, Raymond and Henri.[3]

As war loomed in 1939, anxiety spread throughout France. Following advice from their brother-in-law Dr Emile Weil, Lucien and his siblings took the decision to move their art collection out of the city to the apparent safety of central France. On the morning of 20 August it was despatched by truck, disguised by a false consignment slip, to the Château de Chambon in Laguenne, a village near the town of Tulle in Corrèze. The house was owned by Jacques Renaud, a family friend and director of the Jordaan Bank in Paris to which the security of the works had been entrusted. In 1940, as German troops invaded France, the Schloss family packed up and followed its precious collection south.[4]

However, the reputation of its collection proved to be the family's undoing. Soon after Hitler established plans to stock his Führermuseum in Linz with a glittering inventory of treasures gathered by Sonderauftrag Linz, the ERR and others, he and his experts began to ponder on the whereabouts of the Schloss collection. It was of particular interest to him as it comprised paintings by north European painters whose work he prized so greatly.

The authors of the post-war Allied interrogation reports had little doubt of the collection's appeal to the Nazis. One remarked how Hans Posse, the head of Sonderauftrag Linz, 'was interested in acquiring the Schloss collection, and doubtless told Hitler about it'.[5] Adding to its attractiveness was the fact that as the Schloss family were Jewish, their treasures could easily be seized under strict anti-Semitic confiscation laws. Posse, however, died in 1942 without ever having laid hands on the collection – partly, it has been argued, because of the sheer volume of other material which came his way for the museum. It was some time before his successor, Hermann Voss, was able to proclaim that the works had been secured; and even then the Nazis' triumph was only partial.

The collection's pre-eminence before the war had made its absence in the early part of the conflict all the more conspicuous. Even the chief members of the Parisian art community were baffled as to its whereabouts. Few knew the secret; but meanwhile the Germans were closing in. In the winter of 1940 Hitler's agent Karl Haberstock was staying at the Hôtel Negresco in Nice on the French Riviera while on a business trip. Surprised but clearly delighted, he received an unsolicited visit from a 'fantastic woman with a German-Jewish name' whom he took to be a member of the Schloss family. Would he, she asked, be interested in buying the entire collection, all 333 pieces? She produced, he later told the Allies, a typewritten list with brief descriptions but no photographs. There was, however, one complication, she explained. Haberstock would have to make an offer for the works sight unseen, as they were hidden. If his bid was satisfactory, a deal could be struck. Haberstock told his interrogators that he rejected the offer. However, as his subsequent actions show, he was sufficiently intrigued to set his own agents – the arch-collaborator Roger Dequoy and an associate named Georges Destrem – on the trail of the collection almost immediately.[6] Both men made attempts through art contacts to discover its whereabouts; but it was a policeman in Paris who made the vital breakthrough.

Inspector Lienart had been assigned the task of guarding Reichsmarschall Göring on his trips to the French capital. A smartly dressed man in his early thirties at the time, he had accompanied Göring to the Musée du Jeu de Paume on two occasions and had been made well aware of what he and his fellow Nazis were seeking to add to their collections. Ambitious and eager to please, in the summer of 1941 Lienart learned of the location of the Schloss collection from an informant. Weeks later, he called at 38 avenue Henri-Martin with a search warrant; but he found the property empty, the Schloss family having fled the previous year. The only traces of the paintings were the white marks on the walls to indicate where they had once hung.[7] Disappointed, he began to question those still living nearby and learned of the operation to remove the collection nearly two years before. It took him another three weeks to find the haulage driver who had taken them away and only a couple of hours to discover that the paintings had been sent to Laguenne. In the hope of eventually being able to take credit for the seizure of the entire collection, he did not pass this information on immediately.

Meanwhile Haberstock's agents, Dequoy and Destrem, were having no success at all in their endeavours to find the collection. In late August 1942, nearly a year after Lienart had tracked it down, Dequoy, perhaps still hopeful of securing a large commission from the sale of the paintings, wrote to Haberstock. 'I am', he said, 'at present negotiating the Schloss affair and am about to see one of the heirs in Grenoble.'[8] Four months later, his partner Destrem told Haberstock that the family wanted to sell the bulk of the collection. Haberstock's reply, on 14 December 1942, indicated his desperation with the lack of progress. 'I should very much like to acquire some items of the collection, or even the whole collection, if possible,' he wrote, concluding, 'Try to succeed.' By the time he sent his letter, however, the collection's fate had been sealed.[9]

The Vichy commissioner for Jewish affairs, Darquier de Pellepoix, had met with officials of the ERR's Amt Westen in September 1942, three months before Haberstock's anguished appeal to Destrem, in an attempt to organize a mutually beneficial seizure of the Schloss hoard. De Pellepoix was just as eager to get his hands on the collection for the good of Vichy, but faced competition from Baron Kurt von Behr, the head of Amt Westen. A compromise was reached and both agreed that a secret operation should be mounted to seize the paintings. Von Behr suggested that it required the services of the men he called 'the professionals': the Gestapo.

The operation was put into effect in Nice early the following April. Shortly before midday on the eighth, Henri and Louise Schloss were picked up while queuing at a bus stop. The group which arrested them was led by a man named Jean-François Lefranc, a Parisian art dealer who had been named administrator of the Schloss collection by de Pellepoix even before it had been found. According to Henri, Lefranc produced a search warrant and, claiming he was 'authorized by Laval', the Vichy Prime Minister, stated that he was looking for the collection. Supported by officers from the police in Marseilles, Lefranc escorted Henri and Louise back to their house and demanded to know the whereabouts of Henri's older brother, Lucien. Henri pleaded ignorance, but at that moment the postman arrived bearing a telegram from Lucien and a return address in the Ardèche. Lefranc, needless to say, was overjoyed; and Lucien and his brother Raymond were detained the following day. On 10 April, less than twenty-four hours after their arrests, the collection was seized.[10]

Darquier de Pellepoix informed his ERR counterparts of the seizure, adding that he had been authorized to sell the collection provided certain conditions were met. They included a guarantee against wholesale German confiscation and the right of the Louvre authorities to take their pick of the works. The Germans agreed; but it was not long before the bickering started. De Pellepoix sent a telegram to the prefect in Tulle explaining that he wanted the works brought back to Paris for evaluation prior to their sale. The prefect, after consulting with the Vichy Interior Minister, the notorious scourge of the Resistance René Bousquet, refused. Meanwhile, on 15 April a truck arrived at the Château Chambon containing a squad of French 'police', one of whom spoke with a noticeably heavy German accent. They had come, he said, to take the paintings. An argument ensued with the security official, Jean Petit, who had been ordered by de Pellepoix's men to ensure that the collection was not removed. During the exchange, the 'French policeman' revealed that he was in fact a Gestapo officer called Emile Hess. He told Petit that he and his colleagues were taking the paintings and that Petit and Jacques Renaud were to accompany them.[11] Anxious, Petit's men telephoned the local prefect who ordered that the truck, loaded with the seven large cases containing the paintings, be intercepted near Masseret. Hess responded by calling the Limoges contingent of the Gestapo, and an impasse of several hours ensued. Eventually it was agreed to move the paintings to the police headquarters in Limoges to await further instructions. However, instead of following their French escort, the Germans made for a local house under their control.[12] On the following morning the paintings were moved once more, this time to a German arsenal. Feelings ran high and stern words were uttered by the French to the ERR. Even Göring was dragged into the fiasco; irritated, he ordered that the cargo be transferred to French control. Hess and his men complied and it was shortly afterwards deposited in the vaults of the local branch of the Banque de France.

Finally, on 10 August 1943, the paintings were taken to Paris to be inventoried and priced, ready for sale.

In the basement of the Dreyfus Bank building on the rue de la Banque, officials from the Louvre worked for ten days drawing up a full catalogue. Allied records, compiled immediately after the war, describe how a copy, in large type, was sent to Berlin for Hitler to study. The Führer subsequently instructed his representatives in Paris to buy everything not wanted by the French. While Hitler was keen to purchase, Göring had decided that he would not do so. Allied MFA&A staff later concluded that his 'decision not to have anything to do with the collection was inspired partly by the malodorous rumors attending the affair' and Bruno Lohse suggested during his interrogation that he considered the paintings 'too hot to handle'. However, his reluctance to bid for the collection may simply have been down to his shortage of sufficient cash to pay the very high asking prices.

Even though the Louvre's experts could have decided to purchase all 333 paintings, they decided instead to buy just forty-nine works. These included van Ruisdael's *Woodland Swamp*, Brueghel's *Enchanted Island* and the *Pietà* by Petrus Christus. At the prices they had fixed with the aid of Lefranc, their purchases would cost them FFr 18,975,000. (The pricing system the Germans encountered could be described as flexible at best. They objected to the price given to one religious piece by Roger van der Weyden; the cost was revised downwards and the purchase settled.) The Schloss family received nothing. Nor did it receive any of the FFr 50 million paid by the Germans for 262 paintings earmarked for the Führermuseum. That money went into the coffers of the Vichy regime.[13]

However, Hitler was not pleased. Even though he had acquired the bulk of the Schloss family's treasures, he felt 'resentment' at not having acquired everything.[14] Presumably he would have been equally annoyed had he learned that Jean François Lefranc was given twenty-two paintings for his efforts in bringing the collection to sale. His commission included four Rembrandts, among them the celebrated *Old Jew in a Fur Hat*, two Guardis, a Rubens and one work by Frans Hals. Lefranc later sold these on; in November 1943 they were reckoned to be worth in the region of FFr 340,000.[15] They were bought by an apparently unknown Dutch dealer named Buitenweg; members of the OSS ALIU later concluded the name was probably fictitious, invented by the Germans they were interrogating to conceal who really had taken delivery of the works.

Those paintings destined for the Führermuseum went first to the Führerbau repository in Munich, where they were inspected by Hermann Voss. By 29 April 1945, with the Allies closing in, the Schloss works were among 723 pieces which had still not been moved to the main Linz collection repository at Alt Aussee, even though they had already been allocated a catalogue number, 3108. That evening a German crowd, taking advantage of the guards' desertion of their posts, broke into the Führerbau and engaged in wholesale looting, taking paintings and whatever else they could find.[16] Even after American troops arrived on the scene the following day, the thieving continued. Some paintings were later recovered, but by the end of the war 171 of the 333 works originally in the collection were still missing.

Other pieces of the Schloss collection were found as Allied MFA&A officers combed through Nazi repositories of looted art scattered throughout Germany. By the end of the decade, 138 works had been returned to the Schloss family, among them the forty-nine paintings 'bought' by the Louvre. Out of gratitude, Adolphe Schloss's heirs donated Petrus Christus' *Pietà* to the museum. One wonders if they would have been so grateful if they had known that a wartime director of the French state museum, Henri Verne, had bought a work belonging to the collection, a small painting by Brouwer, for FFr 300,000.[17] However, given the substantial cost of getting the family back on its feet, even what had been recovered could not stay in their hands for long. In 1949, the family sold off seventy of the paintings; a further sixty-one went under the hammer in 1951. Seven more were sold in 1961, one of which had allegedly been retrieved from the daughter of the Vichy Prime Minister, Pierre Laval.

The same year saw the German government settle a claim for damages by the four remaining Schloss heirs. On 3 March the family received DM 3,812,000, an estimated 75 per cent of the value of the 161 paintings which had still not been recovered at that time. Some of those missing were presumed to have been consumed by the fire which engulfed the Friedrichshain *Flakturm* in Berlin. A 1945 list by Otto Kümmel, Director of the Reichsmuseums, claimed that those lost to the flames included *Portrait of Cardinal Albrecht of Brandenburg* by Cranach the Elder, *The Merry Trio* by Frans Hals, some still lifes by Cornelius de Heem and Chardin, and ten works by Rubens, including *The Raising of Lazarus*, *The Coronation of the Virgin*, *Venus and Adonis* and *Bacchanal*.[18] By the time Germany considered it had settled its indemnity, the central figures in the

Schloss affair had also been brought to book. Jean François Lefranc was jailed for five years. Bruno Lohse, Göring's agent in Paris, was sentenced to twenty years before eventually being freed following a pardon by General de Gaulle. Baron von Behr had committed suicide in May 1944. Progress towards finding the remaining missing works, however, would take significantly longer to achieve and only then because of a tax demand.

Guiding the authors around the files which fill his study from floor to ceiling, Henry Schloss's 78-year-old adopted son Jean de Martini allows himself a chuckle. 'After Henry's wife died,' he said, 'I received a letter from the tax authorities demanding to know where the paintings were. In France, you see, a person's tax status is based on his or her assets.

'I hadn't a clue what had happened with them after the sales of those which had been recovered. I thought that was the end of the matter. But the tax people were convinced the family still had them. So I thought I should try and find out what I could. If it hadn't been for that letter, I probably might never have bothered to start looking.'[19] What M. de Martini found not only astonished him but mercifully relieved him of the unwelcome close scrutiny of the French tax authorities. The story involved major auction houses and European nobility, and featured several of the more illustrious elements of the Schloss collection.

Some progress came about coincidentally. In December 1977, *Calm Sea* by Jan van der Coppelle, one of the Schloss works thought to have been looted from the Führerbau in Munich, turned up unexpectedly in the same city in the possession of one Frau Ingeborg Pichl. She told the authorities that her husband Eduard Eckstein, who had died six months before, had brought the painting home with him in spring 1945 – around the time the Führerbau had been sacked. The painting, which is also known as *Ship in Port*, was transferred to the care of curators of the Bavarian state collection, where it has remained ever since. Under the terms of the agreement struck between the remaining Schloss heirs and the German state in 1961, 75 per cent of the painting's value (almost DM13.4 million) was paid in its stead in a deal concluded between French and German officials on 22 May 1980.[20]

Searching through back issues of catalogues from salerooms and museum handbooks, de Martini discovered the whereabouts of other Schloss paintings without too much difficulty. Two views of Venice, *Rialto Bridge* and *Piazza San Marco*, painted by Francesco Guardi, have reappeared in the Lorenzelli Museum in Bergamo in northern

Italy. Negotiations are still under way to have them returned.[21] Monsieur de Martini also noticed that another painting, Frans Hals' *Pastor Tegularius*, had surfaced on more than one occasion without too many people bothering to take notice of its provenance. On 3 November 1967 it appeared in a sale of assets belonging to the late Princess Labia at Parke-Bernet, a New York affiliate of Sotheby's. No one seems to have been unduly worried by the sale catalogue's clear mention that the painting had been in the 'Schloss Collection, Paris'; nor to have been prompted to investigate the dead Italian princess's background. If they had, they would have discovered that, as mentioned in chapter 3, her husband, Count Paolo Labia, had been a Milanese aristocrat and collector of works by Tiepolo who during the Second World War maintained close links with art dealers collaborating with the Nazis, among them Göring's principal art adviser, Walter Andreas Hofer.[22]

Having been bought by a Norwegian art enthusiast, *Pastor Tegularius* was put up for auction again, this time at Christie's in London, in March 1972; and once more no one was the slightest bit inclined to pay any attention to its past. Seven years later the painting, a portrait of a round-faced Dutch minister with a black cap and white frilled collar, was back on the market yet again in London, at Sotheby's; by this time, however, it had acquired a fresh whiff of scandal. American art historian Seymour Slive, now retired as fine arts professor from Harvard University, had in 1970 written a book about Frans Hals' work. In his opinion, the painting had been stolen from the Schloss collection. At the 1979 auction, Sotheby's own catalogue told of how the painting had appeared in an official French government brochure detailing wartime art property losses.[23]

Another ten years on and Frans Hals' masterpiece made a final auction room appearance, again at Christie's in London. It was bought by an American dealer, Newhouse Galleries, for £110,000. Apparently unaware of its past, Newhouse took it to Paris in October 1990 for the Bienniale, a prestigious antiques fair. By now, however, Jean de Martini was in pursuit. Tipped off by a senior French customs official that the painting was back on French soil, de Martini's lawyers had the painting seized by the police. A judicial inquiry was quickly convened and one of the gallery's directors, Adam Williams, was warned that he could face a charge of handling stolen goods.

And yet, however promising its beginnings, the investigation has proved to be long and frustrating for Jean de Martini. In November 1995, more than five years after the seizure of the painting, public prosecutors in Paris added insult to the injury of the confiscation in 1943 by deciding that Newhouse had no case to answer. In a three-page judgment which provided the Schloss heirs with no comfort, they ruled against restitution, concluding that it was not the gallery's fault that the painting had a chequered history. Monsieur de Martini appealed against the decision and won. However, at the time of writing, even his lawyers believe he has another few years to wait before the question of ownership and restitution is finally resolved. While the legal tug of war continues, the painting remains in the hands of the French authorities.[24]

Jean de Martini has been as tantalizingly close to, but ultimately no more successful in recovering, other works which have been located in the United States. One painting, said to be *Old Jew in a Fur Hat* by Rembrandt, which had been at the Schloss home on avenue Henri-Martin, was on display at the Carnegie Museum in Pittsburgh until it was found and claimed in 1996.[25] It has since been put into storage and the museum refuses to discuss it. Another of the Schloss paintings, originally believed to be by Rembrandt, was the subject of a legal claim by Monsieur de Martini in the United States. *Portrait of an Old Jew* was bought by a San Francisco dealer, Sydney Ashkenazie, at Christie's in New York in 1993 during a sale of the paintings from the estate of the notable art collector Ian Woodner for what he believed was a bargain $29,000. It later transpired that the man who sold the painting to Woodner, a Michael Shuman from Montreal, had bought it in post-war Munich, a city which became awash with looted art freshly stolen from Nazi repositories as Allied forces arrived.[26]

Though it had passed through several pairs of hands following the end of the conflict, pre-war ownership was not in doubt. *Portrait of an Old Jew* was clearly listed as number 1282 in an official 1947 French pamphlet of wartime losses. A *catalogue raisonné* of the work of Rembrandt by Abraham Bredius also attributed the painting to the Schloss collection and added significantly that it 'seems to have been lost in World War II'. While firm in its conclusion of who the painting had belonged to, it was less sure who had actually painted it adding fuel to the speculation, no doubt to the disappointment of Messrs Woodner and Ashkenazie, by saying, 'The attribution to Rembrandt is very unlikely.'[27] Nevertheless, it was seized in 1996 by US Customs agents as Mr Ashkenazie was trying to sell the painting to pay off creditors following the collapse of his business.

After more than two years of protracted and tense negotiation, lawyers acting for Monsieur de Martini eventually persuaded a court to return the work to the Schloss heirs in Paris. There was an aesthetic disappointment.[28] Further research during the case had backed up Bredius' claim that the painting was almost certainly not a genuine Rembrandt. That conclusion had led to US Customs officials losing their eagerness to charge Ashkenazie with trading in stolen goods. It also meant that the image he had believed was worth up to $10 million was worth significantly less. But at least from the point of view of Jean de Martini, the painting was on its way back to Paris.[29] As for Sydney Ashkenazie, though he was not made a multi-millionaire by his discovery, he did not come out of the affair totally empty-handed. He had successfully argued that Christie's should have been more thorough in their checks of the painting's history. The auction house agreed to pay $30,000 to administrators handling his bankruptcy.[30]

Just as heated discussions about the ownership of Schloss works proceeded in the United States, Dutch authorities proved similarly unwilling to concede that Monsieur de Martini has a case for getting a Schloss work back. In 1989 the Boymans–van Beuningen Museum in Rotterdam exhibited what it described as a work 'unique in many respects': a still life by Dirck van Delen which is otherwise known as *Tulip in a Kendi*, or vase. A glossy catalogue from the show, entitled *Still Life Paintings from the Golden Age*, used an unintentionally painful choice of words. 'Besides symbolising transience and human frailty,' wrote author Fred Meijer, the painting 'could now equally well represent the vanity of worldly riches.'[31]

The van Delen had been part of the Schloss collection and was confiscated along with all the rest in 1943. The exhibition catalogue said as much, containing a brief provenance for the work which acknowledged that it had indeed been owned by 'Adolphe Schloss' but had been acquired by a 'Vitale Bloch'. On learning of the painting's whereabouts, Jean de Martini swiftly despatched a letter to the museum. Its rebuttal of his claim on 16 March 1989 was as bluff as it would have been easy to correct. The museum's director, Professor J. H. Crouwel, replied: 'We knew of course that the painting came from the collection of Adolphe Schloss of Paris, but we have no reason whatsoever to assume that Bloch acquired this work illegally. By the way, our conclusion with regard to Vitale Bloch is that we do not agree with your remark that he was a war time collaborator of the Nazi occupation forces in the Netherlands.'[32]

Professor Crouwel's confidence was ill-founded. Wartime Allied MFA&A officers were only too well aware of Bloch's background. A Russian-born Jew whose business was based in The Hague, he was most certainly one of a number of dealers who did collaborate with the Nazis. He acted as chief adviser to Dr Erhard Göpel, the main buyer for Sonderauftrag Linz in the Netherlands. Furthermore, his name crops up in countless post-war assessments of Nazi art acquisition activities. One report states: 'Goepel had protected him from the anti-Semitic laws and in return received first refusal on whatever Bloch discovered on the market.' It continues: 'Bloch also bought at auction for Goepel on commission. He was highly regarded as a connoisseur.'[33] This information came as a shock to the Boymans, which is now negotiating with Jean de Martini's lawyers to resolve the issue. Unfortunately, however, there is every precedent for not expecting too much. Boymans and Dutch cultural ministry officials have given short shrift to the restitution claims of another family seeking art works seized by Nazi looting squads.

The collection of the Dutch-based German banker Franz Koenigs claimed the headlines in 1992 with its reappearance more than fifty years after its acquisition in a forced sale during the Nazi occupation of the Netherlands. Like Adolphe Schloss, Koenigs was a German, having been born at Kierburg in 1881, and a successful businessman, with interests across Europe; a director of banks in Berlin, Cologne and Haarlem, he even had a stake in two companies in England: textiles giant Courtaulds and Moratti, a knitwear machinery manufacturer.[34] Koenigs' wealth brought him a noble wife, Anna, Countess of Kalckreuth, as well as a castle on the Rhine at Sinzig near Bonn, a eucalyptus plantation just outside Seville in Spain – and an enormous collection of prestigious art treasures. He had begun collecting at the age of seventeen, having purchased works by Toulouse-Lautrec, and by 1935 had amassed forty-seven paintings, including twenty by Rubens, other works by Bosch and major Impressionist artists, and nearly 3,000 Old Master drawings. According to experts sifting through the evidence of the misfortune which later befell the Koenigs family, the collection of drawings comprised some 'of the finest Rubens in existence' as well as sketches by Dürer, Rembrandt, van Dyck, Tintoretto and other leading artists. Perhaps the most significant element of his collection, though, was a large body of work by the artist Baccio della Porta, also known as Fra Bartolommeo: 505 drawings in all, in two volumes bought in 1923 from Grand Duke Karl-Alexander von Sachsen-Weimar.

Like Adolphe Schloss, Franz Koenigs kept his collection at home, at Flora Park in Haarlem. His precious drawings had been carefully put in drawers, but his paintings were visibly, though not always joyfully, on display. While Rubens' *Pinakothek* hung above his wife's writing desk, *Christ on the Cross* by Lucas Cranach was hidden away behind curtains on a dining room wall because the scene of Jesus' decomposing corpse was considered too distressing to have in constant view.

Franz Koenigs was a contradiction. First, although not Jewish, he was fervently anti-Nazi. Indeed, so strong was his opposition to Hitler's policies that he became a Dutch citizen, fearful that his outspoken views would lead to the confiscation of the property he still owned in his native country. In the earliest days of the war, he acted as an agent for the British, reporting to the Foreign Office on German economic strength. One of a sheaf of documents in the Public Record Office in Kew shows that his first contact with British agents took place in Amsterdam's Hotel Doelen on 23 September 1939, three weeks after war was declared on Germany. A letter to officials in London described Koenigs as 'immensely rich' and outlined how he supplied information about the scale of German mobilization and plans for an invasion of Luxembourg and France.[35] The conversation even touched upon Hitler's drive to develop an atom bomb, a topic which 'goes beyond the technical intelligence of the writer'. In short, his Foreign Office handlers concluded the information was 'just the sort of report that would be so useful to us'. As the files testify, more was to follow in the eighteen months before his death.

Koenigs' family shared his distaste of fascism. Anna Koenigs herself came from a staunchly anti-Nazi background. Her relatives were members of a small group called the Kreisauer Kreis, consisting of disenchanted German aristocrats, artists and intellectuals who plotted against Hitler from the small village in Silesia from which their group took its name. One of the Koenigs' six children, Ernst, even died in 1937 fighting General Franco's forces in the Spanish Civil War. Another son, Franz junior, was jailed for three years in the Netherlands during the war for being in possession of anti-German pamphlets.[36]

However, Koenigs was also a major speculator and entrepreneur, always open to a business opportunity. He added to his collection in 1938 with the purchase from the Berlin Nationalgalerie of two works by van Gogh, *Daubigny's Garden* and *Portrait of Dr Gachet*, and one by Paul Cézanne, *La Quarrière de Bibemus*, as Göring sought to capitalize on the clearance and disposal of so-called 'degenerate' art from German collections to raise foreign currency with which to help fund Hitler's war machine. *Portrait of Dr Gachet* alone cost Koenigs

$53,000, in a transaction effected via one of Göring's agents, Sepp Angerer.

Notwithstanding his readiness to trade, Koenigs himself had need of cash. The Great Depression of 1929 had not only curtailed his art acquisitions but had made a hole in the finances of his business. The situation was exacerbated by Hitler's 1935 moratorium stemming the flow of money from German businesses abroad. The effect on the two banks of which Koenigs was a director, Delbruck Schickler and Delbruck von der Heydt, was severe. Consequently, in 1935 Koenigs had taken out a loan of Fl 1.3 million with an Amsterdam bank, Lisser & Rosencrantz. His collection, valued at Fl 4.5 million for insurance purposes, was put up as security. Under the terms of the loan, instead of languishing in a bank vault, the drawings were to be housed in the newly constructed Boymans Museum in Rotterdam under the care of its director, Dr Dirk Hannema.

The Nazis had already struck at the German branch of the Koenigs family before they turned their attention to those in the Netherlands. In 1938 Franz's second cousin, the diplomat Ernst von Rath, who like Koenigs was suspected of having anti-Hitler sentiments, was shot dead outside the German embassy in Paris. It was claimed by the Nazi propaganda machine in Berlin that the killing had been carried out by a seventeen-year-old Jewish terrorist from Poland, Herschel Grynszpan, and this was used as a pretext for the horrors of Kristallnacht, which ensued almost immediately and saw the destruction and seizure of cultural property from Jews and Gentiles alike.[37]

In late summer 1939, Franz Koenigs' situation changed drastically. The invasion of the Low Countries was expected at any moment. A bill of lading shows that in August he sent several works, including van Gogh's *Portrait of Dr Gachet*, to the United States, ahead of the family of Siegfried Kramarsky, a director of the bank which had advanced him the loan, who were also heading for America.[38] On 9 November Dutch dykes were flooded as a means of slowing any invasion; the Netherlands was equally awash with rumour. In the light of their increasingly precarious circumstances, the Jewish directors of the Lisser & Rosencrantz bank told Koenigs they would have to flee the country. Kramarsky, a long-standing friend of Koenigs, was a German Jew who had sheltered others of his creed who thought that by leaving for the Netherlands they would be safe from Hitler's brutal anti-Semitism. Kramarsky had tried three times to gain Dutch citizenship but was refused on each occasion. He and Koenigs agreed that the collector should sell his drawings only to cover his debt, which with interest had grown to Fl 1.7 million.

Koenigs was now in an awkward situation. He had, as Allied experts were only too well aware, 'never been known to sell anything before'. Yet he needed money and quickly, in an environment where the sudden desire to liquidate assets before they became German booty meant the value of his property had plummeted virtually overnight. He contracted another friend, the art dealer Jacques Goudstikker, with a commission to sell his drawings for Fl 2.2 million, offering Goudstikker Fl 120,000 if he did so speedily. At the Boymans Museum, Hannema wanted to keep the collection in his hands. 'It would be a disaster', he wrote, 'if it [the collection] was allowed to leave Rotterdam.'[39] He suggested, however, that the asking price was out of his range. He enlisted the help of industrialist Daniel van Beuningen to purchase the works on the museum's behalf, aware that Kramarsky and Koenigs had laid plans to take the collection to the safe haven of Lisbon for the duration of the war if a sale proved impossible.

Van Beuningen opened with an audacious bid of only Fl 1 million for both the paintings and the drawings. The offer, less than a quarter of the collection's true worth, was understandably rejected. However, his opportunism paid off because of a clause in Koenigs' loan contract which stated that, were the bank to go into liquidation, his collateral would become its property. On 2 April 1940 the bank folded. So paranoid were administrators handling the collapse that they avoided all mention of the seemingly inevitable German invasion. Instead, shareholders were told the liquidation was due to 'obvious reasons we do not have to say here'. A week later, the bank's directors agreed to sell van Beuningen the entire set of 2,671 drawings plus twelve paintings, four by Bosch and eight by Rubens, for his speculative bid of Fl 1 million. (It is an irony of the sale that van Beuningen might not have been able to meet even the vastly reduced price for the collection Koenigs had painstakingly pieced together had he not just received a large insurance payment for one of his ships, sunk by a U-boat of the Kriegsmarine.) Dr Max Friedlander, the former director of the Kaiser Friedrich Museum in Berlin, conducted an appraisal of van Beuningen's prospective purchases and, for his pains, was given several drawings, including one by Tiepolo, *Holy Family*. On the day the van Beuningen purchase went through, German aggression was clearly demonstrated with the invasion of Norway and Denmark. A month later, it was the Netherlands' turn.

Koenigs did not discover that a deal had been struck until he returned from a business trip in mid-April. On the seventeenth he wrote to Hannema on behalf of himself and his wife saying, 'It gladdens us that the collection is staying in Holland and the Boymans Museum is of course our place of preference for it.' Believing his collection now rested safely and permanently in Rotterdam in public hands, he donated two further drawings, both by Carpaccio, to the museum – unaware that, at the time his gift was made, his art works had been bought not by Hannema but by van Beuningen.

The conditions of the sale have had important modern-day ramifications. The Netherlands government, as we will see later in this chapter, claims the drawings for itself, maintaining that Koenigs parted with his collection without any pressure to do so and that he knew full well to whom he was selling. However, correspondence between the Boymans Museum, Goudstikker and Koenigs himself shows clearly that he was obliged to offload the only true collateral in his possession under considerable duress and that he was kept in the dark, deliberately or otherwise, about who ultimately had purchased his collection. The fine detail and the context of the sale militate against Dutch government repudiation of a claim by Koenigs' heirs for his collection to be given back.

Shortly after German tanks began to roll across the Netherlands, van Beuningen took advantage of the interest of Hitler himself to make a tidy profit. On 28 June 1940 he was visited by Hans Posse, who even before the invasion had been keen to acquire the Koenigs collection for the Sonderauftrag Linz. Four months later, on 14 October, he wrote to Hitler's private secretary, Martin Bormann, to outline his progress. 'In principle the Führer agreed to the acquisition ... the price for the part of the Koenigs collection now on sale is 1,500,000 gulden' (about $750,000). The deal was completed on 3 December 1940. Five weeks later, Posse informed Bormann by letter that arrival of the drawings in Dresden was imminent. Posse had bought 526 drawings from van Beuningen for half a million guilders more than the Dutchman had paid for the entire set of drawings and a dozen paintings. The remaining drawings stayed at the Boymans Museum.

Van Beuningen was happy to sell for reasons that went beyond the profitable disposal of some works of art. He wanted to ensure that one of his businesses, supplying coal to Germany from the Netherlands, would continue unaffected. He was not the only one who benefited from Nazi involvement with the Koenigs collection. Dr Dirk Hannema, who wrote of Posse as 'my colleague' and peppered letters during the van Beuningen sale with references to 'the honourable Führer', would get his reward: he was later appointed to the Cultuurraad, or Dutch Culture Council, under Hitler's representative in the Netherlands, Reichskommissar Arthur Seyss-Inquart. But he also got his punishment for siding with the occupying force: described by the Allies as 'the principal collaborator in the Dutch art world', he was jailed at the end of the war; his conduct earned him the displeasure of his fellow citizens in Rotterdam, who were said to be 'extremely violent' towards him.[40]

After the collapse of Lisser & Rosencrantz, Koenigs' remaining paintings were sold off in several lots. Jacques Goudstikker, whose job it was to help the bank sell off its assets, sold three Rubens, including the famed *Conversion of St Paul*, to Count Anthony Seilern on 6 and 8 May 1940 for a total of $24,000. On his death in 1978 they were donated to the Courtauld Institute in London. Another Rubens, *Seed of Cadmus*, was sold to a Mr I. de Bruyn, whose wife was a major shareholder in the coffee firm Douwe Egberts, for Fl 14,500. Nineteen works were purchased for the sum of Fl 700,000 on behalf of Göring by Alois Miedl who, as mentioned in chapter 3, had taken over the Goudstikker firm on the proprietor's death in 1940. Among these were eleven paintings and sketches by Rubens which included *Portrait of Helen Fourment, Crucifixion, Diana at the Bath, Venus and Calisto* and *Achilles and the Daughters of Lycomedes*. The other works were by Titian and the celebrated Dutch landscape artist Henrik Avercamp. Miedl also acquired Goudstikker's central Amsterdam dealing house as well as a castle at Nyenrode, a large town house at Ostermeer and thirty-one paintings for Fl 750,000 guilders ($375,000). In typically efficient fashion Göring's personal secretary, Gisela Limberger, responded by letter to Miedl on 10 June to acknowledge receipt and list the paintings which formed the consignment.[41] Equally efficiently organized were the papers found in 1944 in the safe and filing cabinet at the Goudstikker dealing house after Miedl departed for Spain with a cache of paintings, including Rubens' *Portrait of Michael Opovius*, selected from the twelve Koenigs works he had acquired.

The drawings which Posse bought for Sonderauftrag Linz had been sent to his offices in Dresden before being forwarded to the city's Staatliche Gemaldegalerie. In 1942 they, along with other works gathered by Posse, were moved again, to the Schloss Weesenstein twelve miles east of Dresden, as a precaution against heavy Allied bombing. By this time, the man who had given his name to the collection was dead. On 6 May 1941, Franz Koenigs died under the wheels of a train at Cologne railway station while on his way to meet a cousin for lunch. Although the official version of events stated that he was crushed after climbing under a train to avoid an air raid, suspicions persist that the Gestapo were involved, having found out about his anti-Nazi activities. His wife, Anna, died in November 1946 after suffering a stroke.[42]

Red Army trophy battalions captured Weesenstein and its contents on 10 May 1945. The details of their evacuation of the castle are referred to in chapter 9. For nearly half a century thereafter, precise knowledge of what had befallen the elements of the Koenigs collection in their haul lay obscured by the fog of fear and bureaucracy which settled over communist eastern Europe. In the confusion which immediately followed the conflict, rumours circulated that the works had been damaged or even burnt. German art officials who inspected the former Red Army trophy brigade collection point at the Schloss Pillnitz found that pictures had been ripped from their frames.

The gloom was punctuated by occasional chinks of light. In 1946 Dürer's *Holy Family* was put on display in the Museum für Bildenden Kunst in Leipzig, having been donated by the Red Army. Other drawings from the Koenigs collection ended up in the Print Room at the Dresden Museum. Another Dürer, found by American MFA&A officers in the depths of the Alt Aussee salt mine, was returned to the Dutch in 1953. A dozen years later, a *catalogue raisonné* of Adam Elsheimer's work concluded that two drawings were in the hands of a Moscow art historian and professor, A. A. Sidorov.[43] It was claimed he had purchased them from 'various collectors in Russia'. A further three later also came into his possession, apparently from similar sources. The Pushkin Museum acquired eleven from the widow of a Russian artist who purported to have bought them in Berlin just after the war. Others began to appear in circumstances which suggested their new owners were attempting to ascertain if it was possible to sell. One was deposited at the British Museum in London by the Russian diplomat and sometime KGB agent Viktor Louis in October 1987 for inspection and evaluation. John Rowlands, who was Keeper of the museum's Department of Drawings and Paintings, recognized it as the work of Ambrosius Holbein. Rowlands later commented: 'He came to me for expertise and I told him immediately that it was from a collection that had been missing since the war. He left the drawing for further study, even though I also told him I would have to inform the Dutch authorities about it.'[44] Rowlands did indeed tell the appropriate officials in The Hague almost immediately. Six months after the drawing had been left at the museum, a Dutch application to the

High Court in London to have the work returned to the Netherlands was successful. Unfortunately, Viktor Louis did not appear in court to reveal how it had come into his possession.

The return of another Holbein from the Koenigs collection, *Portrait of Sir Charles Wingfield*, was far more straightforward. It was simply handed back, in good condition, to officials from the Netherlands Cultural Ministry in August 1995 by its anonymous 'West European owner'. And fortune favoured the Dutch a second time in Britain in late 1987. Albert Elen, an art historian appointed by the Netherlands' Fine Arts Office to help track down art works looted during the Second World War and still missing, was in London researching the case of Viktor Louis' Holbein. He visited an exhibition at the Royal Academy of Arts featuring pieces from the collection belonging to Ian Woodner, a property tycoon from New York. Suddenly, Elen found himself staring at *The Virgin and Child*, a drawing by Hans Baldung Grien.[45] This sketch had already acquired an air of some mystery among those trying to reclaim art stolen from the Netherlands. In 1981 an art dealer in Cologne, well aware of the drawing's past, had offered it for sale to the Boymans Museum on behalf of a Russian émigré. The museum's curator, Bram Meij, left the trader in no doubt. 'I told her', he said, 'that the Netherlands had a valid claim against it and that we were not in the habit of buying our own property. She only rang once.' Two years later, though, Meij was offered the same work, this time by a lawyer in Berlin who also suggested more Old Master drawings could be purchased from the same source, apparently in Russia. Again, the approach was strongly and formally rebuffed. So Albert Elen's chance discovery was a welcome surprise.

Elen further discovered that, after being bought by the American in 1984, the drawing had been displayed as part of Woodner's own collection at Harvard University. When contacted by the leading cultural magazine *ARTnews*, Woodner stated that he had bought the drawing 'in good faith'. However, his collection's curator gave an interesting insight into the moral stance of the art world as far as looted art is concerned. Dr Konrad Oberhuber claimed he and the expert who advised Woodner to buy it, Walter Strauss, knew who had owned the Baldung Grien but were not necessarily deterred thereby from making the acquisition. 'At the time, we knew it was a Koenigs' drawing,' said Oberhuber, 'but not that it belonged to Holland. The Dutch claim came later to my ears. I don't think Strauss would have advised Woodner [to buy it] if he had known.' In other words, the rights of an individual to a painting were not a source of anxiety, but the potential of government action was enough to make a buyer and his experts think twice before purchase.

Perhaps the most spectacular reappearance of an element of Franz Koenigs' collection came in 1990. As described above, the banker had purchased *Portrait of Dr Gachet* by van Gogh in 1938 and, as war approached, sent it to America with Siegfried Kramarsky – not, his relatives insist, to settle Koenigs' bank debt, but simply for safe keeping. The painting had been acquired a full three years after Franz Koenigs took out the loan, to repay which he would later be obliged to sell part of his collection. As such, it was not included in the inventory of assets which provided security for the Fl 1.3 million advanced to him by Kramarsky's bank.[46] Yet the safe-keeping arrangement turned over time into something more permanent. In March 1941 *Portrait of Dr Gachet* was put on show in the United States, its owner listed in the exhibition catalogue as 'Anonymous'. Only a few months later, and a short time after Franz Koenigs died under the wheels of a train, the owner was listed as 'Kramarsky'.

The purchase of the work by Koenigs is not in question. There is plenty of supporting evidence. Strangely, however, for individuals who were used to documenting almost their every deed, there is none so far available to illustrate the circumstances under which it was acquired by the Kramarsky family. Even the otherwise supremely detailed book published in 1998, *Portrait of Dr Gachet* by the American journalist and art historian Cynthia Saltzman, fails to pin down the deal. In touching upon how the work came to be owned by the family of the banker who managed to escape to the United States, she reasons: 'It is likely that Koenigs discussed the paintings, *Portrait of Gachet*, *Daubigny's Garden* and *La Quarrière*, with Kramarsky before he bought them,' and that 'most probably, Koenigs used the three Post-Impressionist pictures to pay off part of his debt.'[47] As we have seen, the latter was certainly not the case. No paperwork is reproduced or quoted from to establish with any certainty at all at what point and for how much *Gachet* and the other two pictures changed hands. It is an omission which only adds mystery to that which followed.

In 1960 a discreet mention was made of the work, painted in the artist's Paris studio exactly ninety years before, when it was offered for sale at a price of $1 million. The Swiss-based dealer Walter Feilchenfeldt made a tentative approach to the Stadelschen Kunstinstitut in Frankfurt, the museum which had owned it prior to Göring's programme of purging 'degenerate' art from the Reich's art houses, on behalf of the Kramarsky family. When the deal collapsed, *Portrait of Dr Gachet* went back into the shadows, surfacing in far more dramatic circumstances in New York thirty years later. Meanwhile the Cézanne, *La Quarrière*, was sold in 1964 and *Daubigny's Garden* was snapped up exactly a decade later by the Hiroshima Museum of Art in Japan. In 1990, with prices for Impressionist works soaring, *Portrait of Dr Gachet*, the last of Franz Koenigs' three purchases of 'degenerate' art in 1938, made a final appearance on the market, for the time being at least. The portrait was sold at Christie's New York saleroom for an incredible $82.5 million to Japanese businessman Ryoei Saito, making it the most expensive work of art in history. In the same week, Saito had bought a Renoir, *Au Moulin de la Galette*, for $78 million at Sotheby's in New York.

Even though Anna Koenigs had filed a formal claim for her late husband's art only months before her death in 1946, the Netherlands took responsibility for the works formerly owned by Koenigs after the first large-scale repatriation of works by East Germany in 1987. Thirty-three drawings in all were returned in this consignment, with an assurance that no other Koenigs pieces were in the German Democratic Republic. The restored works – the first of the 526 prints taken to be returned to Dutch hands – were placed back in the Boymans Museum and became the property of Elen's employers at the Fine Arts Office, providing an impetus for a government claim for any further outstanding works. Another Koenigs drawing, *Holy Family* by Rubens, had been given back by Dr Jahn of the Leipzig Museum in 1946 but was later wrongly assigned to the separate Goudstikker collection. Along with the appointment in October 1987 of Albert Elen, a Dutch royal decree signed in April 1988 transferred efforts to find the other works from the ministry of finance to the country's cultural ministry.[48]

In the Woodner case, as in others, experts advising on art acquisition could easily have known about the status of certain works, even before they became the subject of newspaper stories, often in scandalous terms, in recent years. The very first decree issued by the Dutch government-in-exile on 4 May 1940 proclaimed that it had taken responsibility for all property belonging 'to natural or juridical persons in the Kingdom of the Netherlands . . . only in order to safeguard the rights of the previous owners'. Another bill issued only two months later gave further protection to those obliged to hand over their possessions to the occupiers or their agents by voiding any sale, forced or otherwise. Dutch people were forbidden from entering 'into an agreement with the enemy, with any enemy subject or with a person resident in enemy territory' without the permission of their exiled leaders.

To Christine Koenigs, the great collector's granddaughter, such declarations should have meant the simple resolution of the matter of ownership in her favour. In 1997, acting on behalf of her own father, Franz, and the two other surviving children of Franz Koenigs, Will and Heidi, she submitted a claim for all the drawings and paintings he had bought, especially those held in Dutch museums. Her request foundered on both the stubborn resistance of the Boymans Museum and the suggestion by officials from the Dutch cultural ministry that her grandfather had parted with his collection willingly, a conclusion with which she bitterly disagrees. 'What happened to the Koenigs' collection', she recalls, 'has always been a topic of sad irritation for my father. He would take me sometimes to the Boymans Museum when I was a little girl. He would whisper to me that this painting and that painting had been hanging in this room and that room in his father's house. The sense of loss has been with me almost since I can remember.'[49]

Today, she continues with her attempts to persuade those in authority to change their minds. In fact, her campaign is now a full-time occupation. An elegant, studious woman who orchestrates her efforts from a basement office at her central Amsterdam home, she talks about her family's heirlooms in a curiously dispassionate fashion, given the amount of time, effort and expense she has devoted to tracking them down. She makes no possessive allusions to the collection, never saying 'our paintings or drawings'; it is always simply 'the Koenigs collection', irrespective of any claims she may hold to rightful ownership.

The position of Dutch art officials thus far, she feels, gives the impression that the country which had pledged to respect the rights of art collectors and other citizens during the war has gone back on its word. 'My grandfather', she says, 'was a naturalized Dutchman who would never have sold his collection without being forced to do so. The bank who gave him the loan put pressure on him to settle because they feared the German invasion. The Dutch government had already gone abroad because of the same fears and yet they still believe that Franz Koenigs sold his art willingly despite lots of proof to the contrary.'

Others certainly had the proof. In 1946 a Dr Edgell of the Museum of Fine Arts in Boston wrote to Dutch officials handling the restitution of the country's art works. The museum had, he informed them, obtained a landscape painting by Herrie Met de Bles which had been among the nineteen works bought by Göring from those handling the collapse of the Lisser & Rosencrantz bank. Dr Edgell stated that he knew it had come from the Koenigs collection and offered to return the painting if the Dutch could confirm suspicions that the Reichsmarschall had gained it in irregular circumstances. The Dutch never even granted him the courtesy of a reply. In mid-July 1998 Christine Koenigs wrote to the Boston museum, asking it to return the work to the family. The board of trustees responded by again writing to the Dutch for clarification. One trustee claimed the museum 'simply doesn't want to have stolen property on our walls'. At the time of writing, the Netherlands has still not given its blessing or information to ensure a transfer.

The Netherlands art authorities did, however, produce evidence to back up their arguments for restitution in the case of the Baldung Grien drawing held by Ian Woodner. However, rather than pursue their claim in the courts as they had with Viktor Louis, they approached Woodner more discreetly, supplying documents which they hoped would induce him to yield. Far from doing so, he refused three times either to surrender the Baldung Grien or to provide information as to how he had acquired the drawing; so the Dutch went back to the courts, this time filing a suit in New York to demand its return. However, while the case was being prepared, Woodner died. His heirs and Dutch officials subsequently negotiated a settlement whereby The Hague paid an undisclosed amount in respect of the drawing, which arrived back in the Netherlands in March 1991.[50]

The Dutch realized that it would take more than a lawsuit to claim the largest chunk of the Koenigs collection still outstanding. From the end of the war onwards, suspicions abounded that Russian looting of German repositories was behind the disappearance of so many of the Koenigs' works. In 1989 Albert Elen produced a catalogue listing and illustrating the missing pieces. At the time, he was aware of where many were supposed to be. He said, prophetically as it turned out: 'The alleged presence of the drawings in the USSR and East Germany has been known since 1945. Since official steps taken through the Dutch embassies in those countries have been repeatedly denied by the respective governments there was no reason to drag on until either new indications emerged or the political situation changed.'[51] Both these conditions were to be met within two years of Elen's statement. In October 1989, the Iron Curtain was torn down. Popular revolutions throughout eastern Europe, some peaceful, some less so, inspired by the Soviet premier Mikhail

Gorbachev's principle of *glasnost* or openness, saw the Berlin Wall demolished. A new spirit of warm cooperation heralded the end of the Cold War.

As described in chapter 9, 1991 saw the first revelations by Russian art historian Alexei Rastorgouev of the existence of so-called 'trophy art' in Russia. Eighteen months later, Konstantin Akinsha and Grigorii Kozlov revealed the presence of secret repositories scattered across the Soviet Union. Items from the Koenigs collection, they had discovered, lay in the basement of Moscow's Pushkin Museum. Their dramatic revelations embarrassed the Russians into action. In June 1992, they established a state commission to look at restitution by Russia, and that October the Netherlands received the breakthrough it was seeking. Russian cultural minister Yevgeny Sidorov, apparently no relation to the Soviet professor who had owned several Koenigs works after the war, admitted in a newspaper interview that part of the collection was in Russia. The admission was to trigger the interest from Christine Koenigs which proved so embarrassing to the Dutch government.

Subsequent events initially moved swiftly and promised much. A fortnight after Sidorov's comments went to press, the Dutch ambassador in Moscow, Dr Vos van Steenwijk, was invited to view 150 Koenigs drawings which were, he learned, among some 300 or so which had been found in Russia. On 16 April 1993 a joint Russian–Dutch commission was established in order to assess the objects. One of the panellists was Dr Josefine Leistra, an official with the Netherlands Inspectorate of Cultural Heritage. (It is one of the ironies of the post-war business of restitution that the Inspectorate's headquarters was, until fairly recently, located in offices in The Hague which had formed the base for the Nazis' looting operations in the Netherlands.) Dr Leistra and her compatriots hoped that the accord with Russia would form part of a gradual process with only one conclusion. 'We decided first of all', she explained, 'to get the facts straight before we moved on to the possibility of restoration of the drawings to the Netherlands. That was our ultimate goal.'[52]

In late October 1993 art historians from the Netherlands and Russia, including Dr Leistra, spent four days in Moscow compiling an inventory of the 309 Koenigs drawings which remained at the Pushkin. A handwritten note prepared by the curator of the Pushkin hoard on 25 January 1957 lists '337 sheets [of drawings] from Linz'. Over the years the others had, it seemed, simply vanished, along with so much of the material taken back to the Soviet Union by the Red

Army in the days, weeks and months following the end of the war. Given the age and turbulent history of the Koenigs drawings, some were surprised that they were in such good condition. However, Koenigs' storage methods had been both advanced and environmentally friendly before their time. The specialists of the early 1990s found the drawings still in their acid-free cardboard boxes, custom-made in 1935, which prevented them from both being damaged and becoming warped.[53]

While the art experts exulted over the quality and preservation of the drawings, a legal framework was being constructed with the aim of seeing them returned to the Dutch. This sensitive discussion was causing some in Moscow to bristle and eventually brought the whole process grinding to a halt. A November 1993 report from Russian delegates on the joint Koenigs panel concluded that the Netherlands' claim to the drawings had a clear basis in fact; however, the Russian state's own restitution commission delayed any consideration of the findings. An indication of the prevailing mindset in Moscow was given by the response to plans to exhibit the Koenigs works in September 1995. Seated in her office, its walls lined with books, files and magazines documenting the enforced migration of art works from the Netherlands during the war and their gradual recovery, Josefine Leistra explained: 'As a condition of moving the Koenigs project forward, the Pushkin agreed to hold the exhibition. We offered to loan some of the drawings from the Netherlands to complete a more full exhibition. For instance, there were only two drawings of lions by Rembrandt: they had one and we had the other. We thought it appropriate to offer our drawing. But it became a political decision to refuse our approach. Perhaps they felt such relations might be taken as a possible indication of their willingness to hand the drawings they had back. Our offer had been made on artistic grounds, though.'[54]

As described in chapter 9, the Dutch decided to mount their own rival exhibition of Koenigs works in Moscow. It opened in November 1995, while the Pushkin's show was still attracting visitors. The effect, whatever the artistic sentiments which lay behind the decision to exhibit, was to suggest that the Dutch were thumbing their collective nose at the Russians. Their actions added insult to the injury already caused to the Koenigs family. While Dutch officials had sought information from the remaining heirs in compiling the Albert Elen book, neither Christine Koenigs nor the three surviving children of Franz Koenigs were invited to the Dutch show in

Moscow. The Pushkin director, Irina Antonova, was to make sure that an invitation to her own Moscow exhibition was forthcoming.

These differences were symptomatic of the impasse which had been reached in attempts to secure restitution, a hiatus which is acknowledged by Dr Leistra. 'There were several more meetings of the commission after the exhibition but most of the time was wasted,' she said. 'I personally feel that the work of the committee has been done. We did everything we had set out to do short of restoration: establish who the owners had been before the war, what works were in the Soviet Union and so on. The recent problems are due to politics not art.'[55]

The fact that the drawings and paintings both in the Netherlands and in Russia are referred to as the Koenigs collection is scant consolation for Christine Koenigs. She gleans little comfort either from the fact that one drawing, *The Judgement of Paris* by Albrecht Altdorfer, was effectively smuggled out of Moscow in 1995, after being recovered by Alexei Rastorgouev, by Dutch embassy officials seeking to avoid potentially abortive export procedures.[56] The sketch now sits in the Boymans Museum in Rotterdam. Another drawing by Hans Brosamer, *Red Bearded Man Wearing Broad-brimmed Hat*, also tracked down by Rastorgouev, has not succeeded in finding its way out of the country and lies locked in a vault at the former Stolichny Bank in Moscow.[57] Rastorgouev's discoveries leave the whereabouts of just 179 drawings from the original two and a half thousand unknown. The tally includes one Aldegrever which was offered to a museum in Vienna but disappeared without the sale being completed.

'It is silly to have to fight against one's own government,' says Christine Koenigs. 'The documents show the circumstances in which the collection was acquired, passed on and even recovered, yet the Dutch government does not want to accept that my family has a claim on the drawings and paintings. Meanwhile, it moves objects out of countries illegally. It has acted just like the Russians whom it criticizes. It does not want to answer questions in case it draws too much suspicion on what happened in Holland during and since the war.'[58] Christine Koenigs continues to dispute the official rejection of her claim. Like the heirs of her grandfather's agent, Jacques Goudstikker, she too is considering a legal challenge to the decision. Of the 1,100 paintings Goudstikker had owned before the Second World War, his grandchildren now have only one. In March 1998 the cultural ministry threw out their claim for the 300 or so works seized by Nazi looters and returned to the Netherlands after

Goudstikker died in tragic circumstances while fleeing the Germans. Four weeks later, their Amsterdam lawyer, Dick Schonis, lodged an appeal. The outcome may not be known for some time; and, given the attitude of the Dutch government in the Koenigs case, progress is not guaranteed. Robert de Haas, director of the country's Fine Arts Office, has been unequivocal in staking a claim for the works. Speaking at the launch of the Albert Elen catalogue in 1989, he said: 'The Koenigs' collector's mark is known by everyone working with Old Master drawings. It's a world famous collection after all. This catalogue will make it clear for once and forever that the missing drawings belong to the Netherlands.'[59]

Insensitivity is a charge which has been levelled against the Dutch government on other occasions. In December 1997 it emerged that civil servants in The Hague had in 1968 sold off jewellery and other valuables belonging to Dutch Jews killed in concentration camps. The functionaries were part of an agency supposed to oversee restitution of such objects to Holocaust survivors, yet auctioned off the items among themselves and at bargain prices. Critical newspaper headlines prompted the ruling government to launch an inquiry into the affair. On 29 January 1998 the Kordes Committee, established to conduct the investigation, concluded that although 'insensitive' and 'improper', the sale was perfectly legal.[60]

Such a tone had been struck at a similar but much earlier auction. In 1950 various artefacts looted by German forces and returned to the Netherlands from Allied collection points were sold off. According to the finance ministry's own figures, a total of 719 paintings went under the hammer at auction while eighteen were sold privately, along with '120 tapestries and an unspecified number of furniture and art objects', raising just over Fl 51,000.

It is not just the Dutch authorities who have come in for criticism over their handling of the restitution issue. France was the very country whose collaborationist Vichy officials helped seized the collections of families such as Adolphe Schloss. Even more criminally, officials at the Louvre obtained work looted from Jews in exchange for works from their own collection. The process of negotiation, not confiscation, lasted from the summer of 1943 until March 1944. Senior French personnel, including Jacques Jaujard, the man in charge of all France's museums, even met with Hermann Göring to discuss the exchanges. As described in chapter 3, in return for giving the Reichsmarschall the fifteenth-century wooden figure of Mary Magdalen by Gregor Erhart, known as *La Belle Allemande*, and the triptych *Presentation of Christ in the Temple*, the Louvre received five works. Most alarming was its acceptance as part of this deal of a painting by Charles Coypel, *Open Air Theatre*, which had been seized by the ERR from the Rothschild collection and entered on its inventory as 'ERR number R2251' before being acquired by Göring on 25 November 1942.[61]

It is somewhat bemusing, in view of its own past conduct, that France is still prepared to lay itself open to accusations of – apparently unwittingly – thwarting the efforts of heirs such as Jean de Martini from obtaining redress. In April 1997 President Jacques Chirac and the then Prime Minister Alain Juppé announced the opening of an embarrassing exhibition of 2,000 works from the so-called Musée Nationaux de la Récupération, or MNR.[62] As the exhibition opened at Paris's five principal museums – the Louvre, Georges Pompidou, Musée d'Orsay, Sèvres and Palais de Versailles – the country's heads of state and government were determining finally to find the owners of these and 1,000 other works handed back to France at the end of the war and return their property to them. Even allowing for the extra archival material now available and the undoubted abilities of certain very talented researchers to use it, the chances of reuniting all those works with their rightful owners seem slim.

Even those claiming strong ties to the MNR works have found it difficult to get their former possessions back. In April 1997 a letter sent by fax from curators at the Louvre accidentally found its way to the office of Dr Sabine Fehlemann, director of the von der Heydt Museum in Wuppertal. It concerned a pencil sketch of a nude by Renoir, missing since 1945: one of 352 drawings which had been taken from local museum walls. Dr Fehlemann made her way to Paris and, without alerting the attention of her French counterparts, confirmed that the Renoir on show was the same one she had been seeking. She also discovered eleven paintings which had disappeared from apparently safe storage in Koblenz at the end of the war. Two of them, *Arab Blacksmith* by Eugène Delacroix and a *Head of Zeus* by Ingres, had passed through the hands of the collaborationist dealer Martin Fabiani on their way to the Palais du Louvre. The others included works by Teniers, Theodore Rousseau and Narcisse Diaz. Dr Fehlemann thought she had a clear case for repossession. The Louvre clearly thought otherwise and refused to hand over the works, citing an edict from Charles de Gaulle of 1943 invalidating all business done during the German occupation as reason enough to retain Wuppertal's art. 'The works may have been bought in good faith,' she claimed, 'but clearly they have been retained in bad faith.'

Her bitter complaints prompted a joint Franco-German group to study whether Dr Fehlemann should ultimately have her way.[63]

One potential solution to the predicament of the MNR works which has already been discussed is an auction with funds raised going to Jewish communities or Holocaust charities. As described in chapter 8, such a sale was held in Austria in October 1996 to dispose of thousands of art works formally owned by Jews and returned to Austria where, instead of being handed back to their rightful owners, they had been kept in storage. Unfortunately for the Austrian government, the auction begged as many questions as it answered and focused an uncomfortable degree of attention on other areas of its post-war policy towards those who had lost out after the Anschluss of 1938. Even those families who had reclaimed their art at the end of the Second World War were obliged to give some back: claiming a right under the Export Prohibition Law for Art, passed at the end of the First World War to prevent a flood of national treasures leaving the country, Austrian civil servants taxed those keen to flee from the prospect of a second coming of the Third Reich. The widow of Alphonse de Rothschild had to leave 170 works in Vienna in order to take more to her new home in the United States. Another prominent collector, Eric Lederer, had to leave behind works by Giovanni Bellini, Egon Schiele, Rudolf von Alt and Gustav Klimt when he tried to take his collection to a new refuge in Switzerland. It was, in effect, looting by a more pernicious route, assuming a spurious tone of respectability conferred by the authority of peacetime common law.[64]

In early September 1998, under renewed pressure to act over the continued retention of art taken from those who suffered doubly during and immediately after the war, the Austrian government announced a fresh initiative. Those of the country's museums which still had works taken by the Nazis would return them to their rightful owners. A draft law was submitted to parliament and passed in late October. The impetus to act came from the embarrassment inflicted on the Austrian art establishment by the seizure of two works belonging to one of the country's most prominent collectors, Rudolph Leopold, in New York where they had been on loan, as described in chapter 10. Education and culture minister Elizabeth Gehrer explained: 'The clear and determined political will is there to give back those works of art that were held because of the export ban.'[65]

Gerbert Frodl, director of Vienna's famous Belvedere Gallery, went further. 'Owners were not permitted to export their possessions. Museums said owners could remove their collections if particular works were "donated",' he said. 'That wasn't exactly high moral standing.' The Belvedere housed seventeen of the art works which the Rothschild family were forced to hand over in order to take the rest of their collection abroad.

Other governments, too, have not escaped censure and legal action over their treatment and obstruction of, and confiscation from, Hitler's victims, including those who sought their help. One legal case, which commenced in mid-June 1998, is even more horrific for the fact that it does not involve a forced sale or strong-arm seizure by the Nazis or their agents. Like the case of Friedrich Gutmann discussed in chapter 11, it deals with the sale by auction of works sent away for safe keeping. In this case, however, Rudolf Bedo had not sent his collection to occupied France. The 200 paintings, sculptures and antiques that he had amassed at his home in the Hungarian capital of Budapest between the two world wars were despatched to London to keep them out of the rapacious grasp of the advancing Nazi forces.[66]

Rudolf Bedo had lost a leg fighting on the German side during the First World War. However, by the time Hitler had established plans for the extermination of Europe's Jews, Bedo and his family needed false papers to avoid the fate which befell two sisters of his wife, Maria, who were dragged off to concentration camps. One, Alice, died in Bergen-Belsen; the other, Edith, survived Ravensbruck. A third sister, Sara, died in 1945 from illness contracted in the Budapest ghetto.[67] In all, more than 85,000 Jews in the city died as a result of the Nazi occupation. Even before war commenced, Bedo had seen fit to move his collection of art out of harm's way. According to his surviving son, Gabor, there was only one destination worth considering. Rudolf Bedo, he said, considered London 'the country where there is absolute freedom for everyone. We regarded Churchill of course as the great man of our century. He always told us the collection he sent to London was a lifeboat if we had to flee either from the Nazis or because the war destroys everything, or both.'

The decision proved justified in October 1944 when the Hungarian Nazis, the so-called Arrow Cross Party, seized power. On one occasion Rudolf was arrested at home and taken off for questioning about his valuables. Gabor recalled: 'In came two Hungarian Nazis with guns. One was holding his gun to me. They called my father. They took him to the Party headquarters. He was questioned where he put his gold treasure because somebody said he had much gold. He could not do anything but surrender it to them. It was somewhere hidden. Otherwise he would have been shot to death. My father thought life is more appreciated than gold and gave it to them.'

However, once the war was over, Rudolf Bedo discovered that he was disadvantaged on three counts. First, he had lived in fear of the Nazi purge of Jews during the war. Second, the Soviet authorities who took control in Budapest in the years which followed the war branded Jews as 'class enemies'. Gabor Bedo believes that any action to regain the family possessions would have proved dangerous. Speaking from the same Budapest flat his family shared during the war, he said: 'He dared not to make steps because he knew that if here he was suspected to have connections with the West he would be suspected of being a spy. It was our tragedy to be always afraid, first of the Nazis then of the Communists. We were afraid that if we wrote it would fall into the hands of the censors.'

Third, and perhaps saddest of all, he was betrayed by Britain. In the wake of the ruthless Soviet suppression of the Budapest uprising in 1956, Rudolf Bedo discovered that the family 'lifeboat' had been sunk. Under the 1939 Trading with the Enemy Act, the assets of people living in enemy and occupied countries were frozen. Those living in the occupied territories had their property returned, but the British authorities held on to £30 million worth of bank accounts, valuables and other property belonging to citizens in Bulgaria, Romania, Hungary and Germany, whether they were victims of Nazi policy or not, as reparations. The amount formed part of the estimated £350 million of frozen enemy assets. Action against German properties was sanctioned by international law, established at the Paris Reparations Conference in 1946, but the treatment meted out to Hungarian assets had been decided on by Britain alone. By 1947 the man in charge of overseeing implementation of the seizure and the monies it provided to a near-bankrupt Britain was the future Labour Prime Minister, Harold Wilson.

Eventually, people from the four targeted countries were also allowed to claim exemption from the provision; but they had to satisfy certain strict conditions, including that they had been deprived of liberty, had not acted against the Allies and had left their own country. From behind the Iron Curtain, this proved well nigh impossible to do so, and the Bedo property in England was confiscated. It included a Barclays Bank current account containing £489 and 'fifty-four packages of household goods'.[68] These packages were auctioned off in 1955 and contained items far less prosaic than their description suggested. One sale, held at Philips' auction house on 22 November 1955,[69] contained seventy lots from the Bedo collection and raised £4,500. A catalogue from the sale shows they included a 'flower piece' by Renoir which, even allowing for inflation, was bought for a spectacularly low £10, a Teniers landscape sold for precisely the same sum and a van Dyck which fetched £14. A painting by Luca Giordano, *St John of Capistrano*, was bought by the London gallery Colnaghi and sold on to a private buyer for £120. Another great undervaluation involved a fourteenth-century work by Jacopo di Cione, sold for £230. In the following three decades, it surfaced during exhibitions at the Galleria Bellini in Florence and the Wadsworth Athenaeum in Hartford, Connecticut, before being sold again, this time for £36,036 at Sotheby's in New York in January 1985. The work was later bought again by Colnaghi for £100,000, and was at the time of writing still stored in London.[70]

Rudolf Bedo was spared the details of what had happened to his collection. He was merely informed that he no longer had any entitlement under English law to the works he thought had been saved for his family by being spirited off mainland Europe. His son remembers: 'It was a shock for him. He could not understand that a democratic country like England could confiscate a fortune of a person who was a Jew, was persecuted by the Nazis and by the Soviets, the Communists. How was this possible? The blow came from those he regarded as friends. It was a fantastic irony. Those from whom we expected our liberation, they took it away.'[71]

In 1976 Rudolf Bedo died in penury, a broken man. Gabor Bedo remained in the dark, a victim of communism, until the Berlin Wall fell in 1989. The following year he decided to contact the London storage house which had been the repository for his father's possessions. He was told that no records remained. Early in 1998 he approached the Holocaust Educational Trust, a London-based group led by the former Labour MP Greville Janner, now Lord Janner, which specializes in tracking down Jewish assets. The previous year the trust had produced two scathing reports detailing how successive British governments had appropriated the property of those it deemed war 'enemies'. By scouring sales catalogues, art databases and auction archives in much the same fashion as Jean de Martini, Christine Koenigs and other claimants, researchers discovered the truth. The result was a lawsuit which Gabor Bedo filed against the British government, claiming £5 million in compensation. He explained: 'I think that something should be done. If it is impossible to get anything back then a certain sum should be given as compensation. It was a great fortune which was confiscated and it should not have been because we were not enemies, we were friends.

I think a part of it should be compensated. If I were to get back just one of these works of art it would mean a lot to me. I loved these things. It would be a great joy to get just one or two back.'[72]

13

A CAN OF WORMS

'Once you start digging, you find stuff you don't want to know. The whole aspect of war loot is such a dirty issue. There is no place where there isn't dirt and that's one of the things which Jewish people find so uncomfortable about the whole situation.'[1]

What is troubling Tom Freudenheim over breakfast with the authors in a Manhattan café in July 1998 is a matter which potentially undermines the drive to resolve the so-called 'Holocaust art' issue: the suggestion that Jews themselves have taken advantage of the confiscation of property from other Jews by the Nazis. After all, most of the effort associated with attempts at restitution deals with materials seized from Jews; the topic of plundered art treasures was given impetus by research into and, ultimately, consideration at the highest levels of the gold stolen on a similarly large scale. The very notion that Jewish entrepreneurs and opportunists were trailing behind the German looting units like carrion, picking up profits as some of their own kind were shuffled off to Hitler's death camps, is one which many commentators who have considered the matter find extremely distasteful. However, it is one of the many hideous truths of a particularly horrific period of twentieth-century history.

The extensive reanalysis of the Holocaust in recent years has led to the old records being raked over in search of some comfort or explanation in the face of the near-extermination of a continent's entire Jewish population. Those who have spent many hours poring over the thousands of files on the subject have been forced to relearn history as unknown or long-forgotten details fill in a gory chapter in their past. The revision has prompted many changed perceptions, even revulsion at some figures whose legacies gleaned during the war remain intact. It has also created fresh energies, and fresh divisions. Instead of wartime profiteering, profile and credibility are now at the fore, along with the desire to be seen to 'do the right thing' for a persecuted creed. Governments have sought to take some of the credit.

It is a dim view of the restitution process, and some would prefer not to take it, remaining exclusively fixed on the basic need to achieve justice for the victims of the Holocaust. However, the background is essential to understanding whether justice will or indeed can ever be achieved for, or by, Jews. And, like the organized campaign of hatred which stripped it of its people and its property, the impact of this latest division is felt most deeply in the Jewish community.

Such sensitivities are very familiar to Tom Freudenheim. He now lives in New York, but was born a Jew in Stuttgart when the anti-Semitic policies of the Nazi party were beginning to take shape. His father had been an art dealer in Berlin in the 1920s; his mother's family possessed its own art collection which included works by artists whom the Nazis decried as 'degenerate', such as the Russian-born Cubist, Marc Chagall. Freudenheim's family left Europe along with many others in 1938, when young Thomas was still only nine months old, fearful for their safety. In November of that year their anxiety was terrifyingly justified. On the ninth and tenth of the month came Kristallnacht (the 'Night of Broken Glass'), when synagogues were attacked and Jewish businesses smashed or fire-bombed. Other firms were simply 'Aryanized' and taken over by Germans. The Nazis blamed the Jews for the damage and levied an 'atonement tax' (*Suhneleistung*) of RM1 billion on the community. Many paid in more than cash: thousands were rounded up and carted off to concentration camps, never to return. One of Thomas's aunts died in Auschwitz.

With art in his blood and the impact of Hitler's purges burned into the memory of his childhood, Freudenheim has during his career spent periods on all of the sides now involved in the debate about the return of works lost through confiscations and forced sales during the wartime years. Beginning as a historian and curator at the Jewish Museum in New York, he went on to become director of the museum at the illustrious Smithsonian Institution in Washington, before returning to New York to head a Jewish research organization. With such experience behind him, Freudenheim was one of those asked to help frame the debates for the conference on art loot in Washington, organized by the US State Department, in November 1998.

'No one cares', he says, 'about the stuff being looted in India, something which is perhaps a bigger problem in terms of scale. But the issue of Holocaust loot is different, because it has the interests of the Jewish community as its focus and the attention of the wider world community. It is an emotional issue and is driven by this need to do justice. But if there is going to be justice then there has to be injustice, and it is clear that some injustice was being perpetrated by Jews and that is where this whole thing becomes extremely awkward.

'It isn't just museums which have stolen art; there are lots of Jewish collectors who have in their collections items which should not be there. Then there are the dealers who sold and continue to sell articles of questionable provenance. It has proved to be a rallying point in recent years for Jews around the world and particularly in the United States, but it could backfire on those people who feel they're fighting for a good cause.'[2]

It is a fact that Freudenheim's good cause was known about in the earliest days of the war. As noted in chapter 4, intelligence began to reach Britain and the United States that the properties of Jews in Germany and Austria had been seized under strict racist laws even before war broke out. Some of the largest accumulations of art amassed on the continent belonged to grand Jewish families. The collections of Alphonse and Louis Rothschild, taken from Vienna shortly after the Anschluss of 1938, were the first great Jewish acquisitions for Hitler's Führermuseum. However, it was not until the war began that the process of acquisition began to accelerate. As a growing number of territories fell under Nazi occupation, so too did the art treasures of their most wealthy individuals, many of whom were Jewish.

The sheer quantity of looted art gathered by Nazi Germany will have by now become apparent to readers of this book. In the post-war years, however, as the remaining members of Jewish families picked their way back home across the bomb-cratered cities of Europe, there was only confusion. Berlin had made clever use of the category of 'ownerless' Jewish property for its own ends, deciding what items had been abandoned and which had not. By 1945, the religious and cultural genocide the Nazis had practised had rendered the wordplay gratuitous; many hundreds of thousands of property owners had perished.

A body was established with the responsibility of claiming heirless Jewish assets. The Jewish Restitution Successor Organization (JRSO) was founded in New York in 1947 to represent the interests of scores of Jewish groups throughout Europe. Researchers were faced with the gruesome task of combing though items and deciding where they should go. The task was anything but simple, not only because of the sheer volume of objects but also as a result of the insensitive attitudes of the Allies now occupying Germany. Word of the horrors that had been perpetrated at a network of twenty-two Nazi death camps spread across Germany, Poland, Czechoslovakia and Austria had already begun to filter down to Allied military commanders. Yet British and French authorities were against the idea of the Jewish organization being established. Even officials at OMGUS (the Office of Military Government, United States), who had given the scheme their blessing, gave the JRSO only three months to complete its duties.[3] Such perspectives stand in sharp contrast to the attitudes now being expressed by the same countries as the profile granted to the precise same process grows ever greater.

Saul Kagan's office in downtown Manhattan has become an important location for European émigré Jews like himself who settled in the New World. Mr Kagan runs the New York Office for Holocaust Claims, the clearing house in which thousands of demands for the return of outstanding property are still lodged. In 1944 he was a Polish airman flying over the D-Day beaches. Shortly afterwards, he and his contemporaries were among those who found themselves trying to piece together their former belongings from what was left after the war had ended.

'At first the emphasis for Jews and the organizations helping them was rebuilding their lives,' he says. 'Art was not an immediate priority. There were more simple concerns. Fewer than a thousand of the ten thousand Jews in Germany had managed to escape the slaughter. It was important for them to be able to put their lives back together: get homes, jobs, find out what had happened to their families. This was a very traumatic time. The only people who were worried about the fate of art in the post-war years were the rich families, the major collectors. They were able to use the money they had taken abroad, here to the United States, for example, and their connections with governments to get their claims settled quickly. Even those smaller collectors who expressed some interest had to wait and wait while the bigger, more important families were dealt with.'[4]

It is important to consider the role played by the wealthier elements of Europe's Jewish population. While they perhaps lost more valuable property during the Nazis' looting of Europe, in many cases they had sufficient funds to enable them to flee and thus avoid greater, more personal loss. After the war, they used the same resources to leapfrog others in the claims queue, according to historian Marc Mazurowsky who has become one of the key figures in the restitution of looted art. A quiet, well-spoken man, he has spent nearly twenty years poring over once-secret files now made available to the public at the US National Archives in Washington. That time has seen him accrue more knowledge than almost anyone else in the United States about the effects of the Holocaust on Jewish art collections. The papers support the personal testimony of individuals like Saul Kagan, he explains, about a two-tier claims process.

'Ordinary families filed claims for quite some time after the war but were met with resistance and obstruction from the authorities. If you weren't a Rothschild or a member of one of the other prestigious families, you were unlikely to get satisfaction. Even those top families didn't get everything back. They still haven't recovered all of their works. But it is a fact that the authorities were more willing to help them than the average families. It's the law of diminishing returns. The delay meant that many claimants simply gave up and the general lack of interest in the 1950s almost ground things to a complete halt. It's embarrassing really, because by failing to help the Holocaust survivors, the Allies lost the chance to help the one constituency who truly lost out as a result of the war.'

He continues: 'If they really had wanted to do something, the Allies would have had to be more forceful with the neutral countries such as the Swiss and the former allies of the Third Reich. That would have had serious implications for the free flow of goods and international markets until things were once more satisfactory and full restitution had occurred. We can see from their attitudes towards the restitution organization that the major post-war powers decided that was a ridiculous price to pay for the settlement of a few claims.'[5]

The sudden, seismic shift in the attitudes of the former Allies since the mid-1990s has much to do, Mazurowsky argues, with the politics of expediency – otherwise known as 'bandwagon jumping'. It will take much, he contends, to right the wrongs of half a century ago. His own efforts are now concentrated on one of the two organizations leading Jewish art restitution efforts. Both were launched in September 1997. Both are tackling the same subject from the same Jewish perspective. Both want to establish comprehensive sets of records to make it easier to find information about paintings, drawings, prints and sculptures which may have been stolen from their forefathers by the Nazis. However, the very existence of two groups highlights the chasm which exists between different sections of the Jewish community over the art issue.

On 4 September 1997 the National Jewish Museum in Washington DC announced the formation of the Holocaust Art Restitution Project (HARP). Spearheaded by the fruits of Marc Mazurowsky's endeavours in the hushed reading rooms of the National Archives, the project's aim is to conduct as thorough as possible a trawl of the papers in order to marshal an exhaustive wealth of detail in a state-of-the-art database available for instant, on-line consultation by academics and property-less heirs alike. In addition to Mazurowsky, the project is backed by another prominent tracker of war loot, Willi Korte. The Jewish Museum's director, Ori Zoltes, explained the decision to establish the project to a hearing of the US Senate's Banking Committee in February 1998, telling members: 'Simply put, the kind of research in which HARP is engaged means that questions of ownership history during the 1933–45 era, with respect to works in both the permanent collections of our museums and the loan exhibitions which we all seek, will not be as difficult to answer as they might have been in the past.'[6]

HARP may have the intellectual edge over its main rival, based in New York, but it has nowhere near the same financial resources. The Commission for the Recovery of Art (CRA) is based in bright, high-rise offices only a stone's throw from the exclusive shopping arcades of Fifth Avenue which cut a great commercial swathe through the centre of Manhattan. Its raison d'être is expressed to visitors by a series of images of the Holocaust which stare intimidatingly down from the walls of the reception area. The phones hum, but otherwise it's quiet, cool, organized and air-conditioned. The contrast with the cramped, busy rooms, some forty blocks south on the island, from which Saul Kagan operates is marked. Whereas the CRA is decked out with modern leather furniture and burnished wood, Kagan and his army of colleagues work among rows of old, grey metal filing cabinets jammed with envelope files and index cards which contain details of more than forty years of restitution work.

Instead of merely putting the tools of detection at the disposal of those who want to hunt down their heirlooms, the CRA will use its own database to do the hunting. The commission is the brainchild of the World Jewish Congress and is handsomely backed to the tune of $750,000 a year, some of which comes from the chairman of the CRA, Ronald Lauder. It was launched exactly a week after HARP, sparking a catty exchange which illustrated the tensions that the issue of restitution has created and did nothing to further the cause of either the groups or the issue. Ori Zoltes did his best to present a picture of close harmony between the two projects. They have, he has said, 'held substantive and very cordial discussions . . . and contrary to what has been suggested in some corners of the press, we anticipate a productive complementary working relationship'.[7]

However, attempts to paper over the cracks are rendered useless by the honesty of the CRA's director, Constance Lowenthal, a long-time specialist in chasing stolen art. Prior to taking up the CRA posting, she was in charge of the International Foundation for Art

Research. 'Most of us', she reveals, 'had no idea HARP was going to happen. It was announced right after a panel discussion in Washington organized by the National Jewish Museum. It appeared to us that we were being used. They alienated a lot of people in the field. I had no idea about Ron Lauder's scheme. When HARP heard, they wrote to him saying people are overdoing the efforts, why don't you give us your money. When that didn't happen they began saying Ron Lauder had stolen their idea. It was a mess.'[8]

The differences between the two bodies are not confined to mode of operation and available resources. They also have different attitudes when it comes to discussing the attitudes of the art world they are taking on. HARP's Mazurowsky is deeply critical of the stance of museums in particular. It is plain to see that he does not welcome the decision by the Association of Art Museum Directors to lay down new guidelines to police its members' responses to the war loot question. 'Getting them to look after or investigate their own dealings is like asking the Mafia to regulate its own operations,' he begins. 'These new guidelines are all voluntary. No one will really take them seriously. It's asking the art world to break ranks from a previous policy of indifference. All they have decided to do is ask their curators to inspect their collections for acquisitions from 1939 onwards with a view to establishing what could have been war loot. Once they have done that, it's game over. They will have done what they set out to do. Then they will probably say that there are no claimants anyway. They don't want to part with those collections.'[9]

Constance Lowenthal is less sceptical. In June 1998, she greeted the museums' decision as a 'great and welcome step forward. The guidelines are strong, clear and, where they are not specific, they are flexible.' She does have reservations, but is prepared to believe the directors are acting with the best of intentions. 'It's up to each museum to find the will and resources to do something about it. They say they don't yet have the cash, but they do have staff they can move from other tasks to conduct that research. I think the museums were taken by surprise to think that their things may be looted but they decided, I think, that if there is looted art then they want to deal with it fairly and resolve the problem.'[10]

The museums have responded in kind to Lowenthal's readiness to give them the benefit of the doubt. In his speech to the Banking Committee in February 1998, Philippe de Montebello of the Metropolitan Museum in New York paid tribute to her role in raising awareness about what has happened to Nazi Germany's booty.[11] However, while Lowenthal has undoubtedly helped move the debate on what should happen to those spoils of war which have still not found their way back to their rightful owners, her efforts constantly run the risk of being undermined by circumstances – or, more to the point, individuals – outside her control.

To say that the CRA's chairman, Ronald Lauder, is extremely well connected is something of an understatement. A middle-aged businessman with wealth independent of the family's multi-billion-dollar Estée Lauder cosmetics fortune to which he is an heir, Lauder is a renowned philanthropist and is perhaps ideally placed to advise on the commission's claims. According to some, Lauder 'rediscover-ed' his Jewishness in the mid-1980s, after his spell as US ambassador to Austria, a country whose president at the time, Kurt Waldheim, Secretary General of the United Nations from 1972 to 1981, was tainted with allegations that he had taken part in Nazi war crimes while an intelligence officer in the wartime Wehrmacht. Lauder's reinvigorated sense of the spiritual led him to become treasurer of the World Jewish Congress and to set up his own charitable foundation to support Jewish initiatives in eastern Europe. A serious art enthusiast, his extensive private collection includes large numbers of Old Master works, sculptures, medieval armour and, perhaps most notably, Paul Cézanne's *Still Life, Flowered Curtain and Fruit*, purchased for $50 million in 1997.[12] He is also chairman of New York's Museum of Modern Art and has influential friends in Washington.

However, some consider that Lauder has a massive conflict of interest, demonstrated most clearly and most painfully during the tortuous battle, described in chapter 10, over the decision by New York District Attorney Robert Morgenthau to prevent two works by Egon Schiele being returned to the Austrian collector who had allowed them to go on loan to the Museum of Modern Art. Ronald Lauder had helped secure the loan to the museum of which he is chairman and which reacted bitterly to Morgenthau's action. He brokered the deal with Dr Rudolph Leopold and paid half of the cost of exhibiting a total of 250 paintings. Lauder is said to number twenty pieces by Schiele in his own collection. Despite the claims to the two works at issue being made by Jewish families on behalf of their forebears, one of whom died in a concentration camp, 'it was', Lauder told reporters, 'my strong view that the paintings should go back'.[13]

Lauder had to balance his responsibility to his fellow collectors and museum with his obligations as chairman of a group seeking to advance the demands of Jewish families who wanted their art treasures back. Thomas Freudenheim is sympathetic. 'I feel sorry for Ron Lauder', he says, 'because he is an example of a true casualty of the pressures exerted on Jews in any way connected with any aspect of this whole Holocaust art issue. He has done a lot of good work for Jewish interests overseas and he should be congratulated for that. But he is very involved in the museum world and has loyalties there too.'[14]

Lauder's own brother, Leonard, who is chairman of the Whitney Museum of American Art, a New York collection of fine arts founded in 1914, was also sympathetic. He told the *New York Times*: 'Ronald is in an impossible situation. On the one hand, he was trying to bring sense and sensibility to the restitution of works of art taken during the war. On the other, he is chairman of the Modern, which has a contract [to return the works].' Leonard Lauder's final comment sounded much like a warning to his sibling. 'This is an emotionally charged situation where the person in the middle risks getting knocked off.'[15]

Constance Lowenthal claims that, notwithstanding the potential distractions, she and Ronald Lauder are committed to the task in hand, the size of which is growing roughly at the rate of one fresh claim each day. 'When we find something we will try and get it back or tell the claimants because we can't afford lawyers. We have been talking to international law schools about trying to establish a principle of return. But we will be encouraging mediation.'[16] Lauder agrees: 'If we treat each case as front page news, we'll never succeed in getting this moving in the right direction.'[17]

The CRA and HARP are not the only groups seeking progress. The Art Loss Register was founded in London in 1990 in response to suggestions of the need for a central point of reference where the public, law enforcement agencies and insurance companies could check for stolen art. It checks, on a fee-paying basis, about 400,000 auction catalogues from across the globe each year on behalf of individuals and organizations, either for clues to the location of their possessions or to ensure their materials have a clean bill of health. A Japanese bank recently approached them to vet $1.4 billion worth of art it held as collateral for bad debts. Since 1991 the system has led to the recovery of £50 million worth of stolen art and antiques. On average, say its directors, one in every 3,000 lots at auction is found to be stolen.

The Art Loss Register is principally financed by insurance companies and auction houses, the latter including the 'big three' in London of Christie's, Sotheby's and Bonham's. In addition to its

London base, it now has other offices in New York, Frankfurt and St Petersburg. The chief executive of its American operation is Ron Tauber, a lawyer and former partner for the major investment bank Goldman Sachs. Business in his office is conducted against a soundtrack of life in busy central Manhattan, with the distant throb of traffic snaking its way along Fifth Avenue, twenty-two floors below.

'Until about 1997', says Tauber, 'there really hadn't been much activity in terms of dealing with the World War Two looted art business. Our company was set up to help people find paintings and other objects which had been stolen in more contemporary times. In the last year or so, we began to think that maybe all hope was not lost in terms of getting things back. We started to see claims from victims of the Holocaust and their heirs. But the volume is only a small percentage of our total workload. We're talking about hundreds not thousands.'[18] The influx of cases has, however, been sufficient to require one senior researcher to be entrusted with the responsibility of chasing down wartime loot cases. In July 1997 the Art Loss Register's checks revealed that Christie's in London had failed to sell a work attributed to the sixteenth-century Italian artist Tiziano Vecellio, better known as Titian. The *Venus and Adonis* included for auction during a big Old Master sale was one of four by the artist on the same theme. One of the others was sold in 1991 to the Getty Museum in Los Angeles for $7.5 million.

The names of Carl Bümming and Hans Reemstma in the sale catalogue sounded the alarm bells for the Art Loss Register. Bümming was described in Allied reports of the 1940s as a 'book seller and dealer of Darmstadt' and the German representative of the notorious Theodore Fischer. He conducted negotiations on behalf of Fischer with Hitler's chief art adviser, Karl Haberstock, and Hermann Voss, head of the Linz project after the death of Hans Posse in 1941, to whom he sold a painting by Zumbusch, *Boy in a Sweater*. Reemtsma is identified as a source of financial support for the Kunstfund, the fund used by Göring to finance some of his own art acquisitions.[19] Possibly reflecting the increasing sensitivity in the art market towards work of questionable history, a process described as 'the smell test' by Christie's Stephen Lash,[20] the Titian, which had a reserve price of £750,000, remained unsold.[21]

According to Tauber, opportunists have sought to take advantage of the Art Loss Register's involvement to legitimize fraud. 'We had one person who had a sculpture and claimed to have bought it after the war from a soldier who got it in Germany. He said he was interested in selling it and wanted to know if anyone had made a claim to it. Everything seemed above board. He brought a picture of the sculpture itself and the box that it had come in, which had Nazi markings on it. We made enquiries of the appropriate experts, who told us the chances were high that the object and the box were fakes and this might be an elaborate scheme to pass them off as genuine by having the guy take our letter as almost a seal of its authenticity. We decided not to help him after all.'[22]

The Art Loss Register has so far not located any of the formerly Jewish-owned pieces referred to it for investigation, but Tauber is not disappointed. 'Zero is what we expect,' he says. 'The Holocaust pictures on our records have significantly more value than the works we would normally find ourselves dealing with. Our run-of-the-mill pictures are several thousand dollars. With the World War Two pieces, we're talking of some being in the region of several million dollars. They don't tend to surface that often.'[23] Lloyd Goldenberg, of the Washington art detection bureau Trans-Art International, agreed. 'There are massive amounts of stolen art traded each year by people who don't know its origins because they don't ask the right questions or enough questions. It's not necessarily a situation where there are thousands of Nazis operating underground, but the effect is the same; a lot of loot and not much recovery.'[24]

In spite of the seemingly slight chances of success, Tauber and the Art Loss Register are pressing ahead. Early last year, it struck an accord with both HARP and Constance Lowenthal's organization; the CRA is conveniently located just two stops away on the metro or a brisk five-minute walk up towards Central Park. Tauber explains: 'What we expect will happen is that claims processed by them will end up on our database and that claims that we initially receive will be given to them and the three organizations will be working together. Our intent is that when we search the international art market, which we do regularly, we will also be looking for losses dating from World War Two.'[25]

Although the Art Loss Register's two new partners may be latecomers by comparison, both are acclaimed as being at the head of the push for restitution to Jewish victims of the Holocaust. It is a fact which makes the bickering between the two all the more unfortunate, for it draws energies away from their professed aims and campaigns. Tom Freudenheim believes the differences run far deeper than the desire of each to be ahead of the other in their search for Nazi plunder. 'The tension between HARP and the CRA is due to issues which have nothing to do with art whatsoever,' he says. 'The recovery of paintings stolen or confiscated by the Nazis is just a whipping boy for totally different kinds of problems dealing with power struggles in the American Jewish community which they are part of.

'There used to be a whole network of organizations, such as the Council of Jewish Federations, whose work centred on supporting the synagogues and supporting Israel. You got an incredibly strong stranglehold which kept out other Jewish charities. That structure has begun to fall apart because of divisions in the Jewish community and a revision of the relationship with Israel. That created a vacuum which has been filled by others. People need to be coalesced around issues, they needed someone to love and someone to hate. Hence the huge public relations effort behind pushing the Holocaust art issue.

'Behind the World Jewish Museum is a group called B'Nai B'rith, which used to be a big player but is now at death's door. The World Jewish Congress has been around for a while, yet is only now being taken seriously along with an organization known as the Jewish National Fund, whose chairman is none other than Ronald Lauder. So, in effect, the two major players in reshaping Jewish life in the US are Edgar Bronfmann of the WJC and Lauder.'[26]

Stresses and divisions within the framework of Jewish life in the United States may have been slightly eased by the presence of a cause like restitution to rally around. However, deeper examination of the issue has only created fresh difficulties, with revelations of connections between certain Jewish dealers and Nazi art experts. Many Jewish art traders in Germany and Austria fled when it became clear that the anti-Semitic tirades emanating from Berlin were being turned into deeds. The purge of 'degenerate' art in 1937 was followed the year after by the seizure of private property and, of course, an increasing frequency in attacks on Jewish businesses and homes – which the authorities claimed were spontaneous outbursts and nothing to do with them. Of those who did not emigrate to the United States or Britain, many moved to countries such as the Netherlands where they believed they would be safe. That often proved to be so only if they entered into dangerous, delicate agreements under which they obtained the patronage of the Nazis' looters in return for helping to swell the collections of Hitler, Göring and other senior Nazis.

Myrtel Frank had been in the textile business in the Rhineland before he decamped to Hilversum, a city near Amsterdam prominent in the same line of business, with the help of a friend who secured him an exit visa to the Netherlands. He was later noted by the Allies as being 'the most important unofficial agent of the Dienststelle Mühlmann', the chief German looting organization in the Low Countries. During the later years of the war he became more confident of his ability to evade being denounced as a Jew and moved to The Hague. However, he still took precautions, changing his address constantly to avoid arrest.[27]

Among the scores of others who had sought sanctuary in the Netherlands and ended up working for the Nazis, several names stand out. The first is that of Dr Max Friedlander, the art historian and former Director of the Kaiser Friedrich Museum in Berlin. The records show that Friedlander had initially tried to escape from Germany to Switzerland but, having been refused entry, headed for the Netherlands where he made his way to The Hague. Friedlander, in his seventies, was subsequently arrested and shipped off to a detention camp at Osnabrück in north-west Germany. However, Allied reports detail how three principal figures in the Nazi art establishment, Walter Andreas Hofer, Bruno Lohse and Kajetan Mühlmann, fell 'over each other to claim the honour of getting him out of jail'. It was Hofer, Göring's main agent, who, acting on the Reichsmarschall's authority, had Friedlander set free, claiming the arrest was a simple case of mistaken identity. In return for his release and later being declared an 'honorary Aryan', Friedlander agreed to evaluate paintings for Hofer and his colleagues. 'He seems', suggested one post-war summary, 'to have been the connoisseur king of the German milieu in Holland.'[28]

Vitale Bloch, as described in chapter 12, was one of those involved in the disposal of the collection of Adolphe Schloss. A Russian-Jewish art dealer, he had been in business in both Berlin and London before the war, arriving in the Netherlands just before the fighting started. He too acquired protection, in this instance from Erhard Göpel, a member of the committee in charge of acquisitions for Sonderauftrag Linz. In exchange, Göpel was given first refusal on anything Bloch found on the market. Allied dossiers claimed the latter had been 'Friedlander's most intimate friend. Between them they formed the center of the collaborationist art world.'[29]

Kurt Walter Bachstitz was afforded some breathing space by his brother-in-law, Walter Hofer, for as long as it suited the latter. Chapter 11 described the events surrounding the dispersal of Friedrich Gutmann's collection, recounting how Bachstitz had bought two paintings from the German-born banker before the Second World War. Bachstitz's Munich dealing house was threatened with confiscation until Hofer paid for his sister to divorce him.

The luckless Bachstitz received an exit visa to Switzerland while Hofer's sister acquired the business and Göring received two sculptures and a Jan Steen painting for assisting the escape.[30]

In France, the names of those listed in declassified Allied files as collaborationist are even more illustrious. Paris-based Paul Graupe worked extensively with Hans Wendland before leaving the country ahead of the German invasion, heading first to Switzerland and then to New York, where he was involved in a plot to smuggle works from the Louvre into the United States.[31] Best known of all is Georges Wildenstein, whose renowned gallery in the French capital was 'Aryanized' under the custody of Roger Dequoy. There is no doubt that Wildenstein was, in part, a victim. His own collection was prey to Nazis keen to stock up the Reich's hoard of treasure. However, during his lengthy interrogation by the Allies, Karl Haberstock claimed that Wildenstein was eager to do business. Moreover, Dequoy was reported to have 'acted as intermediary between Haberstock and Wildenstein when they discussed the sale of the latter's pictures in the Hôtel du Roy Rene in Aix, in 1940', a year before Wildenstein departed for New York.[32]

The exact degree of contact and volition exercised by Georges Wildenstein has become the subject of much debate. The dealer's heirs were sufficiently moved by criticism to issue a lawsuit in 1998 against an author who had dared to print allegations that Wildenstein had falsely claimed manuscripts belonging to the family of another French collector, Alphonse Kann. Guy Wildenstein, quoted in the *New York Times* in April 1998, explained why a family known for the protection of its privacy had decided to speak out. 'For me,' he said, 'the honor of my family is at stake.'[33] The authors of this book subsequently made contact with the Wildenstein family in an attempt to obtain their version of events. The response came in a letter from their lawyer Richard K. Bernstein who is also a director of Wildenstein & Co. Mr Bernstein stressed that certain points had to be appreciated when considering the allegations made against Georges Wildenstein:

> Georges Wildenstein and his family were victims of the Nazis and the collaborationist Vichy regime no more nor less than any other French Jews. They were stripped of their rights as citizens of France, their property was seized under color of law, and they were forced to flee France or face the inevitable consequences. At no time from the fall of France in 1940 until his death in 1963 was Georges Wildenstein ever accused of collaborating or acting in league either with the Nazis in

occupied France or the Vichy government in unoccupied France. Consequently, he himself never addressed the issue. I believe that it is important to emphasize these points because they are unassailably true. Any of the accusations made against Georges Wildenstein that have surfaced in the past few years must be read against them . . .

In addition, Mr Bernstein explained why it is only now that the Wildenstein family had decided to respond to allegations first made about Georges Wildenstein in Allied intelligence reports more than half a century ago and which have become the subject of intense controversy in recent years:

[Karl] Haberstock was arrested by Allied authorities, but was never tried for his activities during the war. There are many good reasons to question the credibility of information attributed to Haberstock in which he purportedly made certain charges that he had proposed to Georges Wildenstein some sort of collusive and enriching arrangement with the German authorities to permit Mr Wildenstein to remain in France. Firstly, there was no reason for Haberstock to enter into any agreement with Mr Wildenstein; all of his property in France was already within the grasp of the Germans. Secondly, throughout this period of time, Mr Wildenstein was anxiously awaiting his visa to the United States to secure the safety of his two children and infant grandchild. Furthermore, the document containing this information appears to be an unsworn declaration by Haberstock, not an interrogatory. Haberstock, sitting in Allied custody and facing an uncertain future, hardly can be said to be unbiased in attempting to implicate others in his own work to minimize his own culpability. In any event, since he was never tried, Haberstock was never subjected to cross-examination on his claims. Consequently, it is likely that Georges Wildenstein never was aware of Haberstock's claims. Certainly, the Wildenstein family is not aware of any reliable evidence to the contrary. When these accusations against Georges Wildenstein began circulating a few years ago, the Wildenstein family treated them with contempt, and refused to dignify them with any comment. In retrospect, that may have been a mistake, since the family's silence appears to have been interpreted by some persons as giving some form of tacit assent to these accusations.

Spurred on by publicity surrounding the evidence ranged against figures such as Georges Wildenstein, the agencies involved in the restitution campaigns pressed ahead. The efforts of the researchers and community groups were taken up by the same governments who, fifty years earlier, had been notably reluctant about helping those who couldn't help themselves. On 25 June 1997, New York Governor George Pataki ordered the setting up of the Holocaust Claims Processing Office at the state's banking department. The aim of the scheme was to save those individuals trying to claim gold, art or cash from the difficulties they would encounter in pursuing such action alone.[34] In December 1997, London staged a three-day conference to review the progress of attempts to reclaim assets which had been looted by Germany and secreted in the vaults of Swiss banks, where they remained. One estimate suggested that £2.1 billion of gold, at today's prices, had been taken from Jews with a further £6.4 billion being taken from the central banks of territories occupied by the Third Reich. Forty-one countries were represented; but while the evidence of complicity against it was overwhelming, Switzerland still attempted to demur. 'I don't want the last chapter of the Holocaust to be about money,' Thomas Borer, the head of the Swiss delegation, was quoted as saying.[35] Eventually, in August 1998, Switzerland agreed to pay Jews £1.25 billion in compensation for the stolen assets which had found their way into its banks.[36]

Nine weeks later the US Senate held hearings of its Banking Committee on Nazi looting of art and other assets, including insurance policies. The American hearings were dismissed as a sham, as no more than a chance for the museums and politicians to express concern while escaping awkward questions. One journalist covering the hearing claimed that some political delegates to the committee 'turned up to check if the press from their locality was around and, if so, made a speech just so they could have a suitably compassionate opinion on the record'. According to Lloyd Goldenberg, the hearings 'were worse than a mutual backslapping session'.[37] 'It's amusing,' says Tom Freudenheim. 'On issues like this, everyone has to have a position. There is no right position where you can win all your constituents. It becomes a question of trying to assess if people who don't know about the issue but will vote anyway are more important than money in support of a political campaign from rich Jews who are private collectors. There is a lot of posturing going on.'[38]

HARP's Marc Mazurowsky is even more forthright. 'I didn't need the politicians to try and exploit people's misery to know what had happened. There was so much experience among the Jewish families and survivors of knocking their heads against a brick wall year after year that a great deal simply gave up. Now, of course, it's regained currency because of the interest in gold bars and bank accounts. But this is far more emotive a subject because people can relate to having things taken from their living rooms. They can visualize the paintings in a way that's impossible with either a bank account or a lump of gold.'[39]

Two weeks after the Senate hearings came a novel suggestion of how to deal both with the stolen Jewish art which had been left without owners to claim it after the genocide of the Nazi death camps and with similarly 'ownerless' materials found to have made their way into public or private collections. The World Jewish Congress, the representative body behind the CRA, proposed the founding of a permanent display in a purpose-built museum in New York. Not surprisingly perhaps, the idea, which came from the WJC's executive director Elan Steinberg, failed to win the support of the museum community. Jews also expressed disapproval of the idea. James Snyder, from the Israel Museum in Jerusalem, said: 'Creating a museum seems sad. The works should be seen as cultural heritage, not "appropriated heritage".'[40]

'It was a truly wacko idea,' suggests Tom Freudenheim. 'I was asked to write a comment piece in a Jewish newspaper about it. I said that it was great that the Jewish community was learning from the Nazis in having a museum of degenerate art. I added that I thought it was one of the dumber ideas to come down the pipe. What does art, if it's stolen, have to do with anything?'[41] Mr Steinberg and the WJC, however, seemed unbowed by the doubters. 'We have one very firm guiding principle,' he said. 'That which was stolen from the Jewish people must be returned to the Jewish people.'[42] If the plans for a museum of Holocaust art had any real impact, it was to refocus the minds of those trying to resolve the issue not on who was to blame, be they individuals or groups, but on the victims of the plunder which had accompanied the German armies into new and more lucrative territories.

There was another factor, not directly related to the wartime looting events themselves, which contributed to the resurgence of interest and activity in the business of restitution. Many researchers, including Willi Korte and Ron Tauber, believe the fifty-year rule applied to the national archives in both Britain and the United States, which kept key documents classified and out of reach of potential claimants searching for information, played a significant part in suppressing inquiry during the half-century after the war. The collapse of the Berlin Wall and the gradual seeping out of Second World War secrets from the countries of the former eastern bloc has also contributed to the knowledge not just of what items were taken but of where they went. As recounted in chapter 9, researchers digging into the massive archives of the former Soviet Union have confirmed that large numbers of objects were taken by Red Army trophy brigades back behind the Iron Curtain in 1945.

Marc Mazurowsky believes that the decision to bring to trial surviving Nazi war criminals like Klaus Barbie, the infamous 'Butcher of Lyons', has also played a part. 'The war crimes trials of the 1980s and 1990s have brought the issue back into the headlines and books and films have been made about the Holocaust. You feel you can discuss it again. If you are considering', he says, 'why this whole subject, of which looted art is an element, is being talked about and acted on once more, you also have to consider why it wasn't done forty or fifty years ago. The answer is that people decided to get on with their lives. They had been discouraged from pursuing claims by the hostility of the authorities. Importantly, they also did not want to keep revisiting the horrors of what had happened. The worst way to approach the matter during those years was to talk to the Jewish community.'[43]

Constance Lowenthal feels the momentum has everything to do with time and tide, and adds that the pressure to act may not necessarily have come from outside Jewish circles but rather from within. 'I feel', she says, 'that in a sense this pressure is generational. The people who were born at the end of the war and steeped in the immediate history of what had happened are now running countries and in a position to make policies. It's also millennial. The Holocaust is one of the most traumatic events of the twentieth century and as we're heading towards a new millennium the fall-out from it still hasn't been completely resolved.'[44]

'Perhaps', says Ron Tauber, 'the deciding factor which turned art restitution from a noble cause to a basis for government and state policy was the very fact that those who make policy took up the case. The subject followed on the heels of the progress made in pursuing the Swiss gold issue. Ministers and secretaries of state were reawakened to its importance and people realized that governments could do more than individuals, or communities even, acting on their own. The push was generated in the United States, championed first, it seems, by the American government and taken on board overseas. It's just so very sad that it took forty or fifty years for this to happen.'[45]

Harnessing the energy created by renewed interest in the subject is the next hurdle. While the Jewish community may have brought it so far, Lloyd Goldenberg claims that confining the potential benefits to Jews will be a grave mistake. 'Some people in the United States talk about the need for a so-called Jewish art law to address the issue of Holocaust loot. But is a Jewish claim more valid than theirs merely because of the Holocaust?'[46]

14

NO END IN SIGHT

The work of the Allies' wartime MFA&A staff and of the OSS ALIU proved to be prophetic as well as profitable. In addition to seeking out the principal figures in the Nazi looting programme, they were laying down the basic principles of restitution practice for their successors. When the war came to an end, Ardelia Hall was in charge of the US State Department's Office of International Information and Cultural Affairs, her task being to tie up the loose ends which the investigative efforts of the men and women from the MFA&A had created. The process was to last seventeen years until the operation was shut down by President John F. Kennedy's administration in 1962. Establishing what had happened to art looted during the Second World War appeared not to be considered one of Camelot's top priorities.

Yet in 1964, the matter was still occupying much of Ardelia Hall's time. At that point she warned, with great foresight as it turned out, 'the work will continue for many, many years. The Department as well as the National Gallery of Congress and Department of the Army calls me at least once a week on matters relating to art objects stolen during the war.'[1]

Prior to assuming the task, Hall had worked at the Metropolitan Museum in New York and the Museum of Fine Arts in Boston, two institutions which, ironically, have both featured in war loot cases that have made the news. At the time she was interviewed in 1964, large numbers of works of art, either confiscated or sold illegally in Europe during the Second World War, were still listed as missing or destroyed. Only 4,000 objects had been located by Hall and her colleagues at the State Department. A quarter of all Poland's art treasures remained untraced, while only fifty of the 650 works stored in Hitler's private shelter had been tracked down by the authorities. The Soviet Union alone claimed to have lost 98,000 works.[2]

More than thirty years later, Ardelia Hall has been proved correct in that the situation is still not rectified. At the time of writing, early in 1999, a large number of people are beset with the difficulties of obtaining restitution, while huge numbers of art works are still not back with their pre-war owners – reports have suggested that the figure may be as high as 300,000, including 'important' paintings by artists such as Titian, El Greco, Monet, Manet, Renoir, Rubens and van Dyck.[3] Other estimates claim that as many as 500 major works may have been in Britain since the end of the war. The restoration issue is furrowing brows of officials at the State Department once more; but the situation is no nearer resolution than it was in the early 1960s.

A rash of court cases, restitution appeals and the opening of previously classified documents have created fresh hope for the victims of pillage while causing fresh anxiety for those dealers, museums and enthusiasts whose collections contain the unreturned plunder. The rapid approach of a new millennium is also fixing minds on a date by which to draw the process of restitution to a close. So what chance is there of achieving a satisfactory conclusion to one of the twentieth century's most tragic and unfinished episodes of history?

Those at the centre of the process consider themselves to be as far away from solving the problem as Ardelia Hall was in the early 1960s. Attorney Thomas Kline, who has been instrumental in a string of successful returns of *objets d'art* which found their way into the United States, strikes a notably gloomy tone. 'There will be no final resolution to the problem of World War Two looted art,' he believes. 'There's simply too much art that was put in motion and too many of the owners were put to death. Also whilst there is a mountain of papers which have survived since 1945 and have been of some benefit to us, there are still insufficient records. If you're talking about a family or institution that fifty years later has the documentation to support a claim then that will go on. But if you're talking about the general problem, then the number of claims will relate to be a tiny fraction of the total amount of art stolen and still missing.'[4]

Kline's pessimism is shared by Josefine Leistra, who has been in charge of the Netherlands' restitution programme for the past decade. Since 1992, one of her main tasks has been coordinating the efforts of officials trying to bring about the return from Russia of more than 300 Old Master drawings taken out of the Netherlands in 1940 as a result of the forced sale of the collection belonging to Franz Koenigs. The attempts have so far been hostage to Moscow's internal political tensions; the moderates behind President Boris Yeltsin favour a return while the hawks, the rump of the old Communist Party, insist on retention as foreign reparations for war damage to Russia's own treasures. No end to the stalemate is in sight.

Inconclusive talks on the subject have stripped Leistra of her confidence. 'I don't think that the Russians will ever voluntarily surrender ownership of the drawings,' she says.[5]

The cause championed by Leistra and her colleagues has recently been taken up by some governments. Austria has been the target of much criticism for its failure to expedite the restoration of the thousands of objects looted by the Nazis yet given a home in its museums. In September 1998, following helpful comments by the country's culture minister, Elizabeth Gehrer, Austria's government established a commission to effect the smooth return of looted art to its rightful owners.[6] Gehrer was praised for her support of the campaign by members of the families striving to win back their possessions. Bettina Looram, daughter of Alphonse de Rothschild, one of the biggest losers in the Nazi plundering operation, was reported as saying the minister had shown 'extraordinary courage'.

Britain's Foreign Secretary, Robin Cook, gave the keynote address to the conference on the subject of looted gold held in London in December 1997, pledging similar attention to other areas of pillaging by the Germans and subsequently the Allies.[7] Two and a half months later, the US Senate's Banking Committee staged hearings to examine how much progress had been made on grappling with the thorny subject of stolen art and uncashed insurance policies. Even before taking evidence, Chairman James Leach was well aware of the core issue. He said: 'The committee today is reviewing what is considered one of the seven mortal sins: avarice'.[8]

Congress also set up a twenty-three-strong presidential advisory commission to report on the movement of Holocaust-era assets into the United States. Made up of senior lawmakers and representatives of federal agencies as well as private citizens, it was to take into account while making its deliberations the result of a major conference in Washington, trailed by the earlier London session. The four-day seminar was held in November 1998 and promised much. Organized by the State Department, the very organ of American government which terminated Ardelia Hall's work, the session was expected to be attended by delegates from thirty-nine countries and set itself the goal of 'deepen[ing] international research of that era, bringing together historians and other experts to share information on Nazi misappropriation of artwork, insurance policies and other assets'.[9]

Nevertheless, while the time set aside for talking and sharing knowledge was welcome, those involved seemed to be working against the clock, ushered on with indecent haste by politicians anxious to draw an abrupt line under another sorry, incomplete chapter of world history. Austrian minister Gehrer was obviously preoccupied with the turn of the century on 9 September 1998 when she announced plans for a law to back up her pledge on art returns. Parliament, she said, was expected to approve the bill by the end of October, enabling the restoration programme to begin before the end of the year. 'We want to document', she said, 'that at the end of the historically burdened twentieth century, we want to clear things up for once and for all.'[10]

J. D. Bindenagel, the State Department official who organized the Washington conference, reinforced the standard when describing the session as the government's attempt 'to come to grips with the unfinished business of the millennium'.[11] Stuart Eizenstat, US Under-Secretary of State, added to the sense of a deadline being established. He had, the previous year, compiled extensive reports on the international traffic in looted gold and was considered one of the more enlightened souls on the topic. Yet he too was reported to have described the Washington conference in similar fashion, as a 'catalyst to help reach consensus on further action and complete the unfinished business on this issue' by the end of the century.[12] Some did not believe it possible to condense what had not been achieved in the past fifty years into just over eleven months.

It takes only five minutes to walk from the State Department building to Thomas Kline's office on Pennsylvania Avenue, through the tight gridwork of streets which forms the effective base of power for the entire United States. With experience in painful and protracted restitution cases to guide him, Kline doubts whether it is practical to set dates by which the work must be done. 'The State Department has used 31 December 1999 as the deadline for the Holocaust Commission to give its report and for any subsequent legislation to be made. But there is not and should not be any demarcation with this subject,' he argues. 'It is unfair to the generations who suffered these losses and who are now dying off. There is still a lot of work to be done.'[13]

Once mention is made to Lloyd Goldenberg of the legislative attempts to accelerate restitution, the conversation instantly becomes animated. 'The laws are basically already there,' he says. 'If they were used properly, the questions of adequate research and ownership, for instance, would not need to be raised again. There is case law, precedent to back up a tough stance against those who have or deal in art objects taken during the Second World War. We should have full consideration of where we go from here with the process of restitution but there does not need to be any further law passed to tackle this.'[14] In fact, the United States has already sought to push the process along by adding to the contents of the statute book. A day after the Senate's hearing on Nazi plunder, the ink was drying on new legislation signed by President Bill Clinton granting $30 million of public money to fund organizations helping Holocaust survivors and detailed archival research into the movement of Nazi loot.[15]

America's financial contribution to the restitution drive contrasts sharply with the efforts of its former superpower rival, Russia. In a country bedevilled with economic problems which gave the Communist Party renewed plausibility with the public, 'trophy art' became another battleground on which the fight for political power raged in the spring of 1998. President Yeltsin vetoed a bill aimed at nationalizing the art works Stalin's forces had seized but which had not been handed back. As mentioned in chapter 9, these included works from both state and private collections as well as German repositories on the eastern edge of Hitler's occupied territories. However, just as his various nominees for the prime ministership were either rejected by the Duma or forestalled before they had even taken up the post, so Yeltsin was defeated by a ruling from Russia's Constitutional Court. Humbled, he was forced to allow the bill to become law.[16]

The blow fell hard on those assiduously working to retrieve their treasures from the former Soviet Union. Josefine Leistra from the Netherlands Inspectorate of Cultural Heritage, however, was not surprised. After six years of very slow progress towards a much hoped-for return of the Koenigs drawings from the Pushkin Museum, she realized that her negotiations with the Russians were as good as over. A loophole in the newly adopted Russian law was cold comfort. 'Works of art which were originally the property of charitable or religious institutions', she says, 'can escape being nationalized. Even those organizations, though, have to prove absolutely that they were the owners. Having done that, they will then be required to pay a fee to get those objects back. That's why I don't believe many will therefore be returned via that route either.'[17]

The process of incorporation of 'trophy art' into the Russian state collections had effectively begun even before Yeltsin's signature was committed to paper, making the bill law. As mentioned in chapter 9, Dr Anne Röver-Kann from the Bremen Kunsthalle reported having seen works belonging to her museum on show at an exhibition in the Hermitage in June 1997, already marked as elements of the state art inventory.[18] The collection of drawings delivered to the German embassy in Moscow with the assistance of Konstantin Akinsha and

Grigorii Kozlov is still there. According to Dr Röver-Kann, the German government appears unwilling to risk a diplomatic incident by bringing the drawings home as the Russians have apparently made it known that they would not be pleased if the works left the country.[19]

Russia, of course, would have had no room to manoeuvre if previous attempts to regulate the looting and restitution had possessed any real force or foresight. The London Declaration of 5 January 1943 merely issued 'a formal warning to all concerned, and in particular to persons in neutral countries, that they intend to do their utmost to defeat the methods of dispossession practised by the Governments with which they are at war against the countries and peoples who have been so wantonly assaulted and despoiled'.[20] At the time it was issued, the declaration was seen as a major positive step towards stemming the tide of plunder making its way out of the occupied territories and either back to Germany or on to nations such as Sweden, Switzerland, Spain and Portugal. Its supporters included Ardelia Hall, who believed that 'for the first time in history, restitution may be expected to continue for as long as works of art known to have been plundered during a war continue to be rediscovered'.[21]

However, half a century later, and bearing in mind the lack of impact it ultimately had in keeping art in its proper place, the declaration appears to have amounted to nothing more than the Allies screwing up their collective faces in disgust and wagging a disapproving finger at the pillaging Nazis. An estimated eighty per cent of art looted by Nazi Germany was recovered by the end of the 1950s. The remainder found its way quietly into the public and private collections of many countries who had been among the declaration's signatories, and to whom its terms, addressed to their wartime opponents, clearly did not apply. Hence Russia still holds several billion dollars' worth of art including Heinrich Schliemann's Trojan Gold and paintings by the Impressionist and post-Impressionist masters Degas, van Gogh, Gauguin, Renoir, Monet, Cézanne and Toulouse-Lautrec, while other unidentified missing works hang on museum walls in Paris, London and New York.

The Declaration of London had followed a previous stiff warning to looters everywhere signed in the Dutch capital on 18 October 1907. The Hague Convention, which came into force on 26 January 1910, was the first attempt prospectively to 'guarantee' the protection of cultural property during war. Thirty years later Germany, one of the countries which had signed up to the convention, began laying plans to rifle the private and state collections of a continent for its own national enrichment.

Attempts have been made more recently to lay down strict guidelines on the illicit movement of cultural artefacts. On 24 June 1995 in Rome, twenty-two countries signed up to the UNIDROIT Convention on the International Return of Stolen or Illegally Exported Cultural Objects. An initiative of the United Nations, it established a framework by which 'the possessor of a cultural object which has been stolen shall return it' in return for 'fair and reasonable compensation'.[22] Again, however, though noble in theory, its value in practice is limited at best. UNIDROIT was opposed by the international art market, a trade with an annual value of billions of dollars. It was welcomed by museums, but it is perhaps not difficult to see why. The current disputes about Holocaust art would be struck out under the convention which declares that 'any claim for restitution shall be brought . . . within a period of fifty years from the time of the theft'. Such a ruling would have spelt failure for many survivors of the Second World War and their heirs, whose cases for trying to win back their property are explained elsewhere in this book. Furthermore, while UNIDROIT was presented to seventy countries, fewer than a third of them became signatories. Britain and the United States, in particular, were not among them. Three years on, only five of the signatories had ratified the accord when it took effect on 12 May 1998. Ironically, they comprise some of the well-known centres of the black market in Second World War loot: Peru, Lithuania, Hungary, Paraguay and Romania.

Two months after UNIDROIT came the United Nations conference, also held in Rome, to establish an international criminal court. Under article 8 of the treaty founding the tribunal, provision is made for the prosecution of those considered to have been involved in the 'extensive destruction and appropriation of property, not justified by military necessity and carried out unlawfully and wantonly'. Also prohibited is the practice of 'intentionally directing attacks against buildings dedicated to religion, education, art . . . provided they are not military objectives'. The court was described as 'the missing link' in the international legal system.[23] Whether it will be judged as valuable by the 121 member states needed to bring it into being as it was by UN Secretary General Kofi Annan remains to be seen. In any event, its likely deterrent effect on those trading in looted art appears negligible.

As recent events in the United States have shown, more relevant legal activity is produced within national legal systems. It is not an overstatement to say that the seizure in January 1998 of the two paintings by Egon Schiele which had been on show in New York's Museum of Modern Art caused outrage. The ensuing case set the tone for a year of restitution claims, both won and lost by Holocaust heirs, and highlighted the pitfalls for museums in accepting loans and donations and purchasing art works. The Museum of Modern Art's director, Glenn Lowry, wasted no time in providing a glum forecast of what the lawsuit meant. It had, he told the US Senate's Banking Committee in February, the potential seriously to affect the future of loans of art in the United States. 'Unless', he said, 'we can assure lenders that works of art loans to American museums will be returned to them, they will simply not lend fearing the arbitrary seizure of their artworks.'[24] This position was described by Ori Zoltes of the National Jewish Museum, chairman of the Holocaust Art Restitution Project, as 'poppycock'.[25] Yet he too was critical of the New York District Attorney's action. The Museum of Modern Art, he argued, had been 'marvellously irresponsible' in preparing to send back the Schiele paintings without trying to settle the claims. Morgenthau, he concluded, by confiscating the works had 'effectively [taken] the Museum of Modern Art off the hook'.[26]

Zoltes' view, however, differed from that of HARP's director Marc Mazurowsky, who applauded Morgenthau's intervention. The museum had complained, he suggested, because 'they didn't want the courts or the federal government to become involved. They will do whatever to make sure that the market is not regulated or overseen or evaluated by another agency'.[27] Meanwhile, Mazurowsky's opposite number at the Commission for the Recovery of Art, Constance Lowenthal, was annoyed. She had been attempting to mediate a solution to the problem between the heirs and the museum – whose chairman, Ronald Lauder, also chairs the CRA.

Glenn Lowry's fears did appear justified to a degree. The loans process may not have come to a shuddering halt, but it continued with a great deal more scrutiny being applied. An exhibition by the French Impressionist Pierre Bonnard in June 1998 at Lowry's Museum of Modern Art saw two conspicuous withdrawals from the eighty-four pictures which had previously been on show in London: two pastel-coloured paintings, *Standing Nude* and *Grey Nude in Profile*. The Liechtenstein-based owner of the latter work wrote to the museum explaining: 'The news of the arrest of the two Schiele paintings in your museum made me very anxious and unsure and you certainly will understand why I'm not in a position to lend you my paintings under such circumstances.'[28] Lowry promptly attached the letter to a motion by the Museum of Modern Art to quash Robert Morgenthau's action and was successful when the subpoena was thrown out by a New York judge in May 1998. The Schiele paintings, however, remain in America pending an appeal.

Museums have since been taking no chances. The Washington-based United States Information Agency disclosed that there had been an increase in the number of institutions seeking the federal authorities' protection against confiscation for the works they had on show following the Schiele seizure. The agency's deputy general counsel, R. Wallace Stuart, announced a review of the guidelines on protection for exhibitions and was reported as saying: 'We are looking at what we require of museums. We're actively discussing how to fulfil the intent of Congress which was to encourage the exchange of art and the obvious problem of the appearance of protecting something taken in the Holocaust.'[29]

The Schiele case did not affect only works of art entering the United States. The Metropolitan Museum in New York contacted authorities in Berlin in late March 1998 before despatching more than thirty paintings by the Swiss artist Paul Klee for two exhibitions due to start in Mannheim and Essen three months later. Its staff also rigorously checked their own research materials and found that one picture had been seized by the Nazis. All the works made the trip to Europe, but only after an assurance that no claim was outstanding on any of the paintings in the shipment.[30]

As Morgenthau was making his challenge to the Museum of Modern Art, attention was also being focused on the international art market. The case of Japanese businessman Masatsu Koga and the $12 million worth of Bremen Kunsthalle drawings that he had tried to sell to US Customs agents in September 1997 prompted fresh concerns not just about the retention of 'trophy' material in Russia but also about the amount of loot seeping out from behind the borders of the former Soviet Union. Similar anxieties had been voiced after alleged KGB agent Viktor Louis turned up in London a decade earlier with a Holbein from the Koenigs collection, but these appeared to have little general impact. Together with the writs issued against Daniel Searle by the heirs of Friedrich Gutmann and against the Seattle Art Museum by Paul Rosenberg, the Koga incident added to the tumult building up in America. Further anxiety resulted from the assertion by Moscow-based art historian Alexei Rastorgouev that seventy per cent of west European art on the market in Russia stemmed from the massive amounts of precious objects brought back to the country at the end of the Second World War.

A similar warning note was sounded by Elizabeth des Portes, the outgoing French Secretary General of the International Council of Museums. She had written to members that the 'art market is the only sector of economic life in which one runs a ninety per cent risk of receiving stolen goods'.[31] Her successor in the post, Manus Brinkman, concurs. 'If you buy a car, you expect to receive documents detailing all its history,' he says. 'It has not been the case with paintings and that has to change.'[32]

Mr Brinkman, from the Netherlands, has a doctorate in international relations. It seems he will need it to pursue his agenda to the end. 'I know that there have been cases where looted art has turned up museums,' he adds. 'It's my opinion that where it is identified as such it should be given back immediately if at all possible. There is no clear ICOM policy at the moment with regard to World War Two looted art. I think we have to improve the moral tone in museums worldwide although I have no specific idea at the moment about how to do that. I would like to introduce a strong code of conduct for member museums which does more to accommodate victims of the Holocaust.' Even if Brinkman's plans are successful, there is a significant drawback: by his own admission, the international council is more or less a paper tiger. 'The only real power we have over our members', he concedes, 'is to tell them they are not members any more. However, we need to improve our standards of research to ensure that we do not continue to have in our possession any works which should not be there.'[33]

Lloyd Goldenberg believes the art establishment's concern with ensuring their collections have a clean bill of health can be attributed to one important factor. 'L.A.W.', he says. 'It is the law which is the driving factor here. Museums in particular are scared of receiving a lawsuit both because it could involve a claim for a painting which is worth millions of dollars and because it's extremely bad for business. The only way to defeat the law is by showing that you have made an appropriate inquiry as to whether the work was likely to have been stolen. That is, by showing due diligence. But in the art market that means asking questions about provenance which have nothing really at all to do with title.'[34]

Gary Vikan, Director of the Walters Art Gallery in Baltimore, agrees that the law does indeed play a more significant role than ever before in art acquisition. 'Nowadays, it's not just a question of showing good title,' he claims, 'it's all about having defensible title. The museums are being portrayed in some quarters as bad guys although they're not. The sheer volume of work involved in establishing even one full history to a painting is immense. The information on sales of one object alone dating from 1933 to 1949 can be many inches thick.'[35]

That operation, though, can now be short-circuited, according to Nick Goodman. He and his brother Simon and their aunt Lili cling to the belief that they may one day complete their task of tracking down the remaining pieces from Friedrich Gutmann's collection. They place great faith not only in the researchers who have helped them trace several paintings already but in the desire of the international art establishment to change itself. He says: 'Nobody wants to keep the status quo. The art business has been doing business in the same way for many, many years. Histories haven't been checked fully. But now there are the mechanisms available to do so now far more effectively than ever before. I think the art trade wants to change and avoid being stuck with the same slightly shabby label they have at the moment. They are seizing, quite rightly, upon the momentum which has been created. The whole Second World War thing has taken off. I just hope that it will help my family end our searching and find the works that we've been seeking for so long.'[36]

EPILOGUE

By the end of 1998, it had become 'the greatest treasure hunt in history'. The search for the remaining war loot had developed what seemed to be a critical momentum, one which could see all the old barriers to progress towards restitution finally overcome. No one could be sure whether it was the moral imperative, the genuine desire to do the right thing, or a more basic wish to avoid further embarrassment that had spurred the world's power-brokers into action; but it appeared that now they shared a common willingness to bring the issue of art stolen during the Second World War to a close. Austria, Switzerland and the Netherlands had all announced plans for research projects to vet their national collections, long suspected of harbouring unreturned Nazi booty. Vienna had gone one step further by passing a new law paving the way for objects discovered to have been acquired by the Third Reich to be returned to the families which had previously owned them. France, meanwhile, posted details of the 1,955 pieces of war loot it still held 'in trust' on the Internet.

What promised to be the most significant single event was to take place in the United States. The organizers of a four-day conference at the end of November hoped that the meeting would be the catalyst for dismantling most if not all of the outstanding obstacles to a full-scale return of stolen art. Hosted by the State Department and staged, appropriately, at the National Holocaust Museum, it followed twelve months after a similar conference in London which concentrated on the issue of gold seized and hidden away by the Nazis, much of which remained in bank vaults around the world. That gathering had certainly produced results: several months later, Swiss banks reached a $1.25 billion settlement with Holocaust survivors and Jewish interest groups. So it was with some confidence that more than fifty delegates from forty-four countries – including, crucially, representatives of the nations at the heart of the argument, whether as victims or confiscators – gathered in the American capital in November to address the question of looted art.

According to Madeline Albright, the US Secretary of State, the conference's intention was simple. 'We're here', she said, 'to chart a course for finishing the job of returning or providing compensation for Holocaust victims . . . our goal must be justice . . . we must dig to find the truth.' Her remarks were spoken not only in her role as a foreign spokeswoman for the world's most important nation, in effect making her the globe's chief policewoman, but out of a painful family heritage. Shortly before taking the stand to address the conference, Albright had learned that her grandparents were Jewish and, along with several aunts, had themselves perished in the Holocaust. She earned rapturous applause from her audience, as did others who followed her on to the podium to discuss some of the specific sticking points of restitution. Later, however, some of those present wondered just how much could really be achieved once the talking stopped.

The fundamental concern expressed by many was that for all the might of the United States and for all of its powers of persuasion, none of the countries with looted assets could simply be forced to give them back. This was not solely a matter of national boundaries. There was no threat of trading or other sanctions to ensure that the repentant tone struck by most of the delegations would be echoed in action. If they had withstood the shame of being publicly exposed by newspapers and authors for having absorbed criminally acquired collections into their own museums without question and managed not to flinch in the face of tearful appeals by individuals who had endured Hitler's death camps, would they really be cajoled into surrendering art of colossal value by some hours of relaxed debate in a lecture hall? The odds against such a dramatic change of tack seemed enormous.

France was one country singled out by US State Department officials at the conference for having taken 'courageous steps' towards resolving the problem. It could be argued, however, that it had not done so willingly. Investigations such as those undertaken by Hector Feliciano and publicized in his book *The Lost Museum* had provided unwelcome evidence of the French having failed to return some of the looted works of art they had received at the war's end. By the end of 1998, close to 2,000 looted and confiscated works of art remained in French national galleries, including the world-famous Louvre. Together the works form a collection known as the Musées Nationaux de la Récupération (or MNR, for short), which includes numerous paintings by some of the very greatest names in art – Renoir, Rembrandt, Goya, Picasso, Monet, Degas and others: artists whose works sell for tens of millions of dollars in today's art markets. In an attempt to locate owners for these 'homeless' treasures, which the French state considered it was only holding 'in trust', civil servants at the Cultural Ministry in Paris placed a list of them on the Internet in the apparent hope that they might at long last be claimed.

The pressure on France to do more intensified as the date of the Washington summit approached. Elan Steinberg, one of the most vocal advocates for restitution as head of the United States-based World Jewish Congress, was determined that Paris should be held to commitments dating from the London conference of the year before. 'France said they were temporarily holding these paintings,' he said. 'We expect that at this conference they will announce that they are releasing them.' In publicizing details of a study on how looted art held by France since the end of the Second World War had been loaned worldwide, Steinberg described the retained paintings, drawings and sculptures in unapologetically emotional terms. They were, he said, the 'last prisoners of war'. Exhibition catalogues stretching back more than forty years had been used to plot their movement around the globe. France, it could be concluded, was not overly concerned by the task of handing back what it did not rightfully own. Spectacular elements of the art denounced as 'degenerate' by Hitler, which fell into the hands of successive post-war French regimes, went abroad in apparent furtherance of the cause of art. *Head of a Woman*, one of Picasso's best-known Cubist works, turned up in Tokyo in 1996. The painting had been confiscated from the noted collector Paul Rosenberg and before being sent to Japan had hung on the walls of the Pompidou Centre. *Woman in Red and Green* by the Spaniard's fellow Cubist Fernand Léger was loaned to London's Tate Gallery in 1950. The Pompidou Centre was suitably embarrassed into promising to return the Léger work early in 1999 after freshly unearthed documents, found in German wartime archives, proved beyond any doubt that it had been plundered from the Rosenberg collection. Ironically, it meant the painting would almost certainly have to be removed from the walls of the newly opened Jewish Museum of Art and Culture in Paris, where it had been on loan from the Pompidou Centre. A bronze statue of Rodin's *The Kiss* was initially hidden in a storeroom before being placed, brazenly, in a back garden of the Hôtel de Matignon in central Paris. But this was still not to be a subject for public debate. The location, one of the most exclusive in the French capital, is the private residence of the country's Prime Minister. Perhaps most astonishing of all was the revelation that one painting by the Impressionist Maurice Utrillo had formed part of a show in Israel in 1954.

As with art works which had been retained by Austria until being auctioned at Mauerbach in 1996, Steinberg argued that the French holdings should be sold and the proceeds passed to Holocaust survivors. However, Steinberg had no evidence that this would actually happen other than some helpful pre-conference briefings by French officials and some good old-fashioned hope. And sure enough, his bubble was burst – by none other than the French President Jacques Chirac. Paintings looted by the Nazi forces occupying France during the war, he said, should remain in France. The country's government should become their owner, he went on, paying compensation to French Jews in lieu of the treasures. As if to prove a point, Chirac was speaking in Paris on the same day that the Washington conference began.

Chirac's stand antagonized Steinberg's World Jewish Congress which, along with other groups taking part in the seminars 4,000 miles away from Paris, rounded on France. Parisian government archivists, Steinberg explained, had consistently refused to hand over to him documents relating to the paintings so he could begin the work of chasing back down the paper trail to find their true owners or their descendants. This time, however, he levelled at France a more serious charge than stonewalling; he accused authorities there of 'fencing', of handling stolen goods. 'For fifty years', he raged, 'French museums have failed to return these works of art to their rightful owners. It is time to terminate their temporary custodianship over these works and transfer the research files on their ownership to people willing to return stolen goods.' Later, he asked: 'Can French museums be allowed to enrich themselves with the remains of Nazi plundering?'

Similarly strong accusations were made over French involvement in two individual cases which led to lawsuits, as yet unresolved. An exhibition of eighty-five works by the noted Impressionist Claude Monet arrived at the Museum of Fine Arts in the Massachusetts city of Boston in September 1998. They had been loaned by the Musée des Beaux-Arts at Caen in Normandy and were to remain on show until the end of December, when they were due to be shipped to London's Royal Academy, the next stop on their tour. But one of the artist's twenty-four celebrated waterlily paintings featured in the exhibition never made it to Britain. *Waterlilies (1904)* was withdrawn after British art investigators discovered it formed yet another multi-million-dollar element of the Nazis' war booty still in French hands. Soon after the Monets arrived in the United States, Sarah Jackson, research director at the London offices of the Art Loss

Register, came across the painting in the Boston exhibition catalogue and made a startling discovery. It was, she found, identical to one eagerly sought by the heirs of Paul Rosenberg, one of France's most celebrated and well-connected pre-war collectors – and, sadly, one of those who suffered most from looting by the rapacious Nazis. Miss Jackson's creditable alertness was allied to a keen investigative sense. A display plaque alongside the Monet in Boston told only of how the painting, which was estimated to be worth about $7 million, had been 'recovered after World War II and placed in trust with the Musées Nationaux de France'. Through her own research, she already knew that the waterlily work in question had been seized by German forces and later placed in the private collection of Hitler's Foreign Minister, Joachim von Ribbentrop.

The find caused fury in France and aggravation in Boston, but brought relief to the Rosenbergs – just as organizers of the Washington conference were throwing open their doors to delegates. Officials at the Boston museum staging the exhibition were horrified. One, quoted in an interview with a local newspaper, explained that there was no need to apprise the viewing public of the painting's full and terrible history. 'The public,' he reasoned, 'is not coming to this show to be informed about such issues.'

It was France, once again, which bore the brunt of criticism for the painting's inclusion in the exhibition. It emerged that Paris officials had objected to a fuller explanation of what had happened to the Monet after it was confiscated from M. Rosenberg. One of those who supported the provision of a more detailed history, Leonard Zakim, a director of the local Anti-Defamation League, was scathing. The display plaque, he said, 'whitewashes history from the French side . . . The real onus here is on the French to come clean.' Mounting indignation was fuelled by the discovery that a photograph of the painting had also been published in a book – *Art as Politics in the Third Reich* – written by a Baltimore college professor, Jonathan Petropoulos, several years earlier without any reaction from the French authorities.

A further twist to the tale came only days before the Monet exhibition was due to be packed into cases and transported across the Atlantic to London. The Rosenberg heirs lodged a formal legal claim in Paris asking for *Waterlilies (1904)* to be returned to them, thereby testing the French commitment to cede works should ownership be conclusively established. An embarrassing climbdown followed. Rather than have the painting shown in London to yet more catcalls, it was meekly withdrawn from the exhibition and returned to Normandy.

The heirs of another plundered collector, Alphonse Kann, also decided to pursue their objections to continued French custody of one of their works in the courts. It is perhaps ironic that Georges Braque painted *Man on the Guitar* shortly before enlisting in the French army to fight Germany in the First World War. By then, the artist had abandoned the Fauvist technique favoured by Henri Matisse for Cubism. The oil on canvas painting has hung in the Museum of Modern Art, better known as the Pompidou Centre, since being bought for £1.6 million from a Swiss art dealer, Heinz Berggruen, in 1981. But the painting, acquired by the museum less than twenty years after Braque's death, had like so many others a less than tasteful pedigree. Kann was a British Jew who had maintained a sizeable town house at St Germain en Laye, a few miles west of Paris, until he fled France in 1940 ahead of the German invasion, leaving his large art collection behind. Among those 'degenerate' works removed from his property to the Nazis' art collection centre at the Musée du Jeu de Paume in Paris, *Man on the Guitar* was exchanged by Reichsmarschall Hermann Göring in 1942 for a Dutch nativity scene more in keeping with his tastes.

Lawyers acting on behalf of Alphonse Kann's descendants lodged a claim for the painting but were shocked when the grounds on which it was based were summarily dismissed by Pompidou Centre officials. Jean-Jacques Aillagon, head of the museum, declared that the Kann suit was null and void under the French civil code. Ignorance of the facts, it seemed, was the ideal defence. Under the code, anyone buying a stolen object 'in good faith' was allowed to keep it unless the previous legal owners submitted a formal claim within three years of its latest acquisition. Aillagon said the museum 'had no idea that the painting had passed through the Kann collection'; so it could hang on to the Braque. Nor was there any suggestion that Herr Berggruen, who had sold the picture to the Pompidou Centre, had any clue as to its Nazi connections.

While the Kann heirs' decision to go to court represented a clear escalation in the dispute from their earlier firm but polite requests for their heirlooms to be returned, it could not guarantee success – only the strong likelihood that legal action would be costly and not necessarily a short process, as the Goodman family already knew. As mentioned in chapter 11, Nick Goodman, his brother Simon and their aunt Lili reached a settlement in 1998 at the end of an expensively protracted battle with Chicago-based pharmaceuticals empire heir Daniel Searle over ownership of a Degas, *Landscape with Smokestacks*. It appeared that this accord would be the end of the matter, and that a legal action which had cost Searle a rumoured $1 million was very nearly complete. But the Goodmans had not reckoned with a last-minute hitch. The painting had been bought by Searle for $800,000 and would fetch at least the same sum at auction. The valuation offer made to the family as part of the settlement was far below that figure. At the time of this book going to press, the Goodmans are still dug in, hoping that justice will finally be theirs.

The Searle/Goodman case had another, unexpected spin-off. As mentioned in chapter 13, Connie Lowenthal is director of the New York-based Commission for the Recovery of Art, established by Elan Steinberg's World Jewish Congress, and one of the dozens of individuals who kindly agreed to be interviewed for this book. Late in 1998, it was disclosed that Lowenthal had contributed to the Chicago case but in a way which appeared to conflict with her work on Holocaust-era art looting. According to rivals also investigating the same contentious period of history, she had actually helped Searle's defence against the Goodmans by providing him with an expert witness, Hermine Chivian-Cobb, who they hoped would prove whether or not the Degas landscape had ever belonged to Friedrich Gutmann.

The allegation looked, on the face of it, astonishing. Why would one of the leading activists in wartime looted art research apparently undermine her position by helping 'the other side'? Lowenthal was quick to quash any suggestion of impropriety. She explained that her role in the case stemmed from her time at the International Foundation for Art Research, an independent body at which she made her reputation as one of the world's finest art detectives before moving on to the CRA. 'Ralph Lerner, a New York lawyer with Sidley and Austin, the firm that represented Searle, asked me if I knew a Degas expert. I suggested Hermine, a woman I've known for over twenty years. At the Metropolitan Museum where we met, she was organizing a show of Degas collections. She subsequently had positions at Knoedler [a New York gallery], at Sotheby's for ten years and as a private dealer. Now she is an appraiser and is a woman of integrity and searching intelligence. I was happy to tell Ralph about her.'

Lowenthal went on: 'I hear a little tone in the rumour that it is somehow improper for someone who wants to recover art for claimants to do something for the "wrong" side. That is not my view. I think that the entire cause is best served when both sides have access to good information. Then, and this has nothing to do with any specific case, if the claim is valid, then great. If it isn't, then so be it.'

Nick, Simon and Lili Goodman's battle illustrates the difficulties facing families in making claims for confiscated art. It was with this in mind that Stuart Eizenstat, the US Under-Secretary of State charged with organizing the Washington conference, isolated art as one of the main topics for discussion. Delegates did make progress, agreeing to eleven principles which Eizenstat believed would impose a moral obligation on countries to track down, identify and then publicize Nazi-looted art. 'From now on,' he stated, 'the sale, purchase, exchange and display of art from this period will be addressed with greater sensitivity and a higher international standard of responsibility. This is a major achievement which will reverberate through our museums, galleries, auction houses and in the homes and hearts of those families who may now have the chance to have returned what is rightfully theirs.'

With the promise of a central register of information on the subject, probably on the Internet, it was generally accepted that the four days of talking in Washington had inched the issue forward. But just as question marks arose at the start, after Madeline Albright's opening remarks, so question marks lingered at the end. The principles agreed upon were not binding on the delegates who had attended, let alone on the multi-billion-dollar international art market which still profits from the fruits of Hitler's looting of Europe's treasurehouses. Observers recognized the obvious stake which Eizenstat had in the success of the conference. But even that could surely not account for his describing the newly announced guidelines as 'a breakthrough far exceeding our expectations', a verdict not borne out by the results.

Even a commitment from Russia to assist in the return of Holocaust-era art was not so progressive as it may have looked at the time. Valery Kulishkov, head of the Russian Cultural Ministry's restitution unit, pledged that his government would do what it could to assist in the founding of a central Internet database. Moscow, he stressed, would also welcome any approach from outsiders to trace the full true ownership of loot in its museums. However, there was a caveat. The wealth of material seized by Stalin's so-called 'trophy brigades' as German defences crumbled in 1945 was not up for discussion. Boris Yeltsin's previous attempts to free up materials in St Petersburg's Hermitage Museum and the Pushkin in Moscow had foundered on the resurgent nationalism among his parliamentary colleagues, which had shown no sign of ebbing in the run-up to the Washington conference. A frustrated Elan Steinberg explained: 'They are talking about the issue of what is essentially reparations for the destruction of [their] cultural property in the east.' The reassertion of the hard-line Russian position extinguished any immediate hope Christine Koenigs had of recovering the hundreds of Old Master drawings still missing from her grandfather's substantial collection. More than 300 are being kept at the Pushkin Museum, while another single work remains in a Moscow bank vault. Ms Koenigs holds out virtually no hope that the Dutch government will be able to retrieve them.

The Netherlands, too, was praised by Stuart Eizenstat; but it too has had to suffer complaints that it has dragged its heels over restitution. Worse still was the news that one painting had not only not been returned but adorned the official residence of the Dutch ambassador to Israel, of all places.

One of the most significant elements of the Koenigs collection resurfaced towards the end of 1998. *Portrait of Dr Gachet* by Vincent van Gogh had been purchased by Christine's grandfather at an auction of 'degenerate' art in 1938 and was one of several works which, according to her, Koenigs sent to the United States for safe keeping. Chapter 12 relates the story of the painting's later purchase and resale, culminating in its acquisition by Sotheby's in 1998. The art market, it appears, holds the key to the whole problem. Lucrative commissions are taken from the billions of dollars washing each year through auction houses and galleries around the world. Ronald Lauder, chairman of New York's Museum of Modern Art and a key player in the CRA, has estimated that war loot worth up to $30 billion is still to be traced. The value in doing business silently, then, is clear. But while much attention has focused so far on museums and galleries, auction houses and private collections have largely escaped scrutiny. In recent months they may even have considered that becoming more of a target for art loot investigators is a risk worth taking. Hiscox, an insurance syndicate working out of Lloyd's in London, offers up to $50 million of cover against claims of ownership through a new policy aimed at big collectors, but it is not cheap: premiums may be as much as two per cent of the value of a collection where there is adjudged to be a risk. However, with the chance of further documentation releases spurring further claims from families of Holocaust victims, it appears to be cover worth having.

Lord Janner, the former Labour MP Greville Janner who now leads the London-based Holocaust Educational Trust, believes that he and his colleagues endeavouring to root out the remaining missing spoils of war are not assured of success, despite all their efforts and overwhelming international goodwill. He has clear ideas of where the search may lead, even if it takes him to institutions previously thought to be beyond reproach. 'The Vatican, for example, has vast wonderful art galleries and so far we have not succeeded in persuading it sufficiently to look at the provenance of works of art in them. But we are always hopeful.' Ironically, says Janner, some of those who marshalled the Nazis' looting operations, including SS chief Heinrich Himmler, were allowed to profit from the theft. 'The art may have been returned to his heirs but the trail went dead for us,' he said. 'The hunt for Nazi loot has turned into the greatest treasure hunt in history. We don't know where it will end.'

NOTES

Chapter 1

1 Office of Strategic Services Art Looting Investigation Unit (hereafter OSS ALIU) Consolidated Interrogation Report (hereafter CIR) No. 4, Attachments A and B (PRO T 209 29).

2 William Shirer, *The Rise and Fall of the Third Reich* (London, Book Club Associates, 1983; first publ. 1959).

3 Charles de Jaeger, *The Linz File* (London, Webb & Bower, 1981).

4 OSS ALIU CIR No. 4, *Sonderauftrag Linz: Authority and Activity (1939–1945): Austria*, p. 5 (PRO T 209 29).

5 De Jaeger, *The Linz File*, p. 50.

6 Ibid., p. 28.

7 Ibid., p. 30.

8 Ibid., p. 44.

9 George Mihan, *Looted Treasure: Germany's Raid on Art* (London, Alliance Press, 1942), p. 86.

10 Ibid.

11 OSS ALIU CIR No. 4, *Sonderauftrag Linz: Authority and Activity (1939–1945): Austria*, p. 4.

12 OSS ALIU CIR No. 4, *Chief Dealers and Agents Abroad*, p. 47 (PRO T 209 29).

13 OSS ALIU CIR No. 4, *Personalities of the Linz Commission: The Directorate*, pp. 18–19 (PRO T 209 29).

14 William Stevenson, *The Bormann Brotherhood* (London, Arthur Barker, 1973), pp. 30–9.

15 OSS ALIU CIR No. 4, *Sonderauftrag Linz: Authority and Activity (1939–1945): Austria*, pp. 4–5.

16 OSS ALIU CIR No. 4, *Sources – Czechoslovakia: Confiscations*, p. 65 (PRO T 209 29).

17 OSS ALIU CIR No. 4, *Methods of Acquisition – Forced Sale: The Czernin Vermeer*, pp. 35–6 (PRO T 209 29).

18 OSS ALIU CIR No. 4, *Sources – Poland*, p. 65 (PRO T 209 29).

19 De Jaeger, *The Linz File*, pp. 57–8.

20 Andrzej Mezynski, *Archival Report: 'Kommando Paulsen', October– December 1939* (Sejm Library, Warsaw).

21 Ibid.

22 Ibid.

23 De Jaeger, *The Linz File*, p. 63.

24 OSS ALIU CIR No. 4, *Sources – Poland*, p. 66.

25 OSS ALIU CIR No. 4, *Methods of Acquisition – Forced Sale: The Mannheimer Affair*, p. 36 (PRO T 209 29).

26 Ibid.

27 De Jaeger, *The Linz File*, pp. 83–4.

28 OSS ALIU CIR No. 1, *Organisation and Authority*, p. 3 (PRO T 209 29).

29 OSS ALIU CIR No. 4, *Methods of Acquisition – Forced Sale: The Mannheimer Affair*, p. 37.

30 De Jaeger, *The Linz File*, p. 104.

31 Ibid., p. 106.

32 Ibid., pp. 106–7.

33 Ibid., p. 122.

34 Ulrike Hartung, *The Sonderkommando Künsberg: Looting of Cultural Treasures in the USSR* (Bremen, Research Institute Eastern Europe, University of Bremen, 1996).

35 *This Week* magazine (1943, n.d.), 'History's Greatest Theft'.

36 Ibid.

37 Ibid.

38 Lynn Nicholas, *The Rape of Europa: The Fate of Europe's Treasures in the Third Reich and the Second World War* (New York, Knopf, 1994), p. 191.

39 Hartung, *The Sonderkommando Künsberg*.

40 David Roxan and Ken Wanstall, *The Jackdaw of Linz* (London, Cassell, 1964), p. 145.

41 Ibid., p. 152.

42 Ibid., p. 148.

Chapter 2

1 OSS ALIU CIR No. 1, *Organisation and Authority*, p. 3.

2 Ibid.

3 Ibid., p. 4.

4 Ibid.

5 Ibid.

6 De Jaeger, *The Linz File*, p. 66.

7 MFA&A Branch, Control Commission for Germany (British Element), *The Bunjes Papers: German Administration of the Fine Arts in the Paris Area in the First Year of Occupation* (PRO T 209 26).

8 Ibid.

9 Ibid.

10 OSS ALIU CIR No. 1, *Methods Employed by the Einsatzstab*, p. 16 (PRO T 209 29).

11 OSS ALIU CIR No. 1, *The Goering Relationship*, p. 7 (PRO T 209 29).

12 OSS ALIU CIR No. 6, *Bruno Löhse*, p. 3 (PRO T 209 29).

13 OSS ALIU CIR No. 1, *The Goering Relationship*, p. 8.

14 OSS ALIU CIR No. 1, *Objects Acquired for Hitler*, pp. 23–4 (PRO T 209 29).

15 OSS ALIU CIR No. 1, *Official French Protests and German Justification*, pp. 18–19; see also Attachment 9 (PRO T 209 29).

16 OSS ALIU CIR No. 1, *Revision of the Mission: The M Action*, p. 9 (PRO T 209 29).

17 OSS ALIU CIR No. 1, *ERR Personnel Active in France: Executive*, p. 48 (PRO T 209 29).

18 Ibid.

19 De Jaeger, *The Linz File*, pp. 66–7.

20 Ibid., p. 67.

21 Ibid., p. 85.

22 Ibid., p. 86.

23 Ibid., p. 87.

24 Matila Simon, *The Battle of the Louvre* (New York, Hawthorn, 1971), p. 90.

25 De Jaeger, *The Linz File*, p. 88.

26 OSS ALIU CIR No. 1, *Exchanges*, p. 25 (PRO T 209 29).

27 Ibid., p. 26.

28 OSS ALIU CIR No. 4. *Gustav Rochlitz*, p. 2 (PRO T 209 29).

29 Ibid.

30 Ibid., p. 3.

31 Ibid., p. 5.

32 Ibid., p. 6.

33 Ibid., pp. 9–10.

34 OSS ALIU CIR No. 1, *Exchanges*, pp. 42–3.

35 Ibid., pp. 39, 44–5.

36 Ibid., p. 41.

37 Ibid., p. 44.

38 Ibid., p. 38.

39 Ibid., pp. 37–8.

40 Ibid., pp. 25–6.

41 OSS ALIU CIR No. 1, *Analysis of Confiscation*, p. 20 (PRO T 209 29).

42 Ibid.

43 OSS ALIU CIR No. 1, *Objects Brought to Germany: General*, p. 21.

44 OSS ALIU CIR No. 1, *Difficulty of Transportation and Storage*, pp. 21–2 (PRO T 209 29).

45 Ibid., p. 22.

Chapter 3

1 OSS ALIU CIR No. 2, *Belgium*, p. 92 (PRO T 209 29).

2 Ibid.

3 Ibid.

4 OSS ALIU CIR No. 2, *Personnel*, pp. 5–8 (PRO T 209 29).

5 OSS ALIU CIR No. 2, *Confiscations*, pp. 26–9 (PRO T 209 29).

6 Ibid.
7 Ibid.
8 Ibid.
9 OSS ALIU CIR No. 2, Attachment 1, Letter from Walter Andreas Hofer to Göring, 26 Sept. 1941 (PRO T 209 29).
10 OSS ALIU CIR No. 2, *Göring's Agents*, p. 57 (PRO T 209 29).
11 Ibid., p. 37.
12 Ibid., p. 49.
13 Ibid., p. 52.
14 Ibid., p. 35.
15 Ibid., p. 58.
16 OSS ALIU CIR No. 2, *Purchasing Agents*, p. 13 (PRO T 209 29).
17 Ibid., p. 14.
18 Ibid.
19 Ibid., pp. 14–16.
20 Ibid., p. 16.
21 Ibid., p. 31.
22 Roxan and Wanstall, *The Jackdaw of Linz*, p. 52.
23 OSS ALIU CIR No. 2. *Purchasing Agents*, p. 17.
24 Ibid., p. 20.
25 Ibid., p. 21.
26 OSS ALIU CIR No. 2, *Exchanges*, pp. 141–3 (PRO T 209 29).
27 Ibid.
28 Ibid.
29 Ibid.
30 Ibid.
31 Ibid.
32 OSS ALIU CIR No. 2, *Purchases – France: General Conditions*, pp. 33–4 (PRO T 209 29).
33 Ibid.
34 Ibid.
35 MFA&A Branch Report to the Foreign Office, 12 Sept. 1945, *Special Report on the Firm of Wildenstein et Cie, Paris Art Dealers* (PRO FO 837 1157).
36 Ibid.
37 Ibid.
38 Ibid.
39 Ibid.
40 Ibid.
41 Ibid.
42 Ibid.
43 Ibid., Attachment C, *Pictures from the Wildenstein Collection Acquired from the Einsatzstab Rosenberg by Marshal Goering.*
44 OSS ALIU CIR No. 2, *Holland*, p. 88 (PRO T 209 29).
45 Ibid., p. 72.

46 OSS ALIU CIR No. 2, *Italy*, p. 100 (PRO T 209 29).
47 Ibid., p. 102.
48 Ibid., p. 107.
49 Ibid., p. 108.
50 OSS ALIU CIR No. 2, *Confiscations: The Loot from Monte Cassino*, pp. 29–31 (PRO T 209 29).
51 OSS ALIU CIR No. 2, *Exchanges*, p. 139.
52 Ibid., p. 146.
53 Ibid., p. 148.
54 Ibid., pp. 143–6.
55 Ibid., p. 136.
56 Ibid., pp. 146–7.
57 Ibid., p. 147.
58 Ibid.
59 OSS ALIU CIR No. 2, *Sales*, pp. 149–50 (PRO T 209 29).
60 Ibid., pp. 153–6.
61 OSS ALIU CIR No. 2, *Transportation: The Flight from Berlin*, p. 171 (PRO T 209 29).
62 Ibid.
63 Ibid., p. 172.
64 Ibid., p. 173.

Chapter 4
1 'Looted Art Treasures Seized in Ship', *Daily Telegraph*, 10 Oct. 1940.
2 'Nazis' Looted Treasures – Trying to Sell Them in USA', *Daily Telegraph*, 20 Feb. 1941.
3 'Dutch Art Collection for Berlin', *The Times*, 21 July 1942.
4 'Ribbentrop has Corps of Art Thieves', *Daily Telegraph*, 6 Jan. 1943.
5 *A Record of the Work Done by the Military Authorities for the Protection of the Treasures of Art and History in War Areas* (London, HMSO, 1947).
6 Ibid.
7 Ibid.
8 Ibid.
9 Ibid.
10 John Richardson, 'Obituary: Douglas Cooper (1911–1984)', *Burlington Magazine*, April 1985.
11 Ibid.
12 Denys Sutton, *The Commission for the Protection and Restitution of Cultural Material* (PRO T 209 5).
13 Nicholas, *The Rape of Europa*, pp. 203–4.
14 Ibid., p. 211.
15 Ibid., p. 222.
16 *A Record of the Work Done by the Military Authorities for the Protection of the Treasures of Art and History in War Areas.*

17 Nicholas, *The Rape of Europa*, p. 221.

18 Ibid., p. 222.

19 *A Record of the Work Done by the Military Authorities for the Protection of the Treasures of Art and History in War Areas.*

20 Ibid.

21 Ibid.

22 Ibid.

23 Nicholas, *The Rape of Europa*, p. 211.

24 Ibid., p. 275.

25 Ibid., p. 278.

26 Simon, *The Battle of the Louvre*, pp. 123–4.

27 Written account of the events at the Château de Rastignac as provided by Philippe Sprang.

28 Ibid.

29 Ibid.

30 Ibid.

31 Ibid.

32 Nicholas, *The Rape of Europa*, p. 332.

33 Simon, *The Battle of the Louvre*, p. 183.

34 Thomas C. Howe, *Salt Mines and Castles: The Discovery and Restitution of Looted European Art* (New York, Bobbs Merrill, 1946), pp. 249–51.

35 *A Record of the Work Done by the Military Authorities for the Protection of the Treasures of Art and History in War Areas.*

36 Ibid.

37 HQ 1st US Army Report, 12 May 1945, *Chance Find of Mine Depository at Bernterode: Special Report* (PRO WO 220 607).

38 Ibid.

39 Ibid.

40 'Missing Nazi War Treasures: They Vanished Without a Trace', p. 19.

41 Craig Hugh Smyth, *Repatriation of Art from the Collecting Point in Munich after World War II* (The Hague, Gary Schwarz, 1988).

42 Ibid.

43 Ibid.

Chapter 5

1 148 (SD) Squadron RAF Record of Operations Book, Jan. 1944–May 45 (PRO AIR 27 996).

2 Ibid.

3 Letter of 2 Nov. 1944 from Lt Col. Sir Leonard Woolley, War Office Archaeological Adviser, to Lord Macmillan (PRO T 209 10).

4 Interview with Josef Grafl, 13 July 1998.

5 Nicholas, *The Rape of Europa*, p. 332.

6 SOE Report, History of CLOWDER Mission, sheets 20–1.

7 SOE Personal File on Albrecht Gaiswinkler (SOE HQ Ref. No. CL/X/ 45).
8 War Office GSI British Troops Austria Report, *Resistance in Bad Aussee.*
9 SOE Personal File on Albrecht Gaiswinkler.
10 Ibid.
11 Ibid.
12 Ibid.
13 Interview with Josef Grafl, 13 July 1998.
14 Ibid.
15 SOE Austrian Section Records (PRO HS 16 22).
16 Telephone interview with John Lennox, 6 Aug. 1998.
17 Ibid.
18 Interview with Josef Grafl, 13 July 1998.
19 Telephone interview with Bill Leckie, 10 Sept. 1998.
20 SOE Austrian Section Records (PRO HS 16 22).
21 Telephone interview with Bill Leckie, 10 Sept. 1998.
22 Interview with Josef Grafl, 13 July 1998.
23 De Jaeger, *The Linz File*, p. 127.
24 Interview with Walter Tarra, 14 July 1998.
25 OSS ALIU CIR No. 4, *Personalities of the Linz Commission: Lesser Functionaries*, p. 25 (PRO T 209 29).
26 Interview with Josef Grafl, 13 July 1998.
27 Johann Linortner, *Die Kunstgüter im Altausseer Salzberg 1943–1945* (Bad Aussee, Salinen, 1998), p. 7.
28 Ibid., p. 12.
29 De Jaeger, *The Linz File*, p. 128.
30 Linortner, *Die Kunstgüter im Altausseer Salzberg*, p. 12.
31 De Jaeger, *The Linz File*, pp. 133–4.
32 Interview with Josef Grafl, 13 July 1998.
33 Ibid.
34 Interview with Walter Tarra, 14 July 1998.
35 Kammerhof Museum, *Die Rettung der Kunstschütze im Altausseer Bergwerk* (Bad Aussee, 1995).
36 Ibid.
37 De Jaeger, *The Linz File*, p. 131.
38 Ibid.
39 Interview with Josef Grafl, 13 July 1998.
40 Kammerhof Museum, *1945: Ende und Anfang im Ausseerland* (Bad Aussee, Verlag Lutz Tietmann, 1995), p. 35.
41 Howe, *Salt Mines and Castles*, pp. 147–9.
42 Ibid., pp. 150–1.
43 Ibid., pp. 152–3.
44 OSS ALIU CIR No. 4, *Scope of the Collections*, pp. 78–9.
45 Howe, *Salt Mines and Castles*, p. 155.

46 War Office GSI British Troops Austria Report, *Resistance in Bad Aussee.*
47 SOE History of CLOWDER Mission, sheet 20.
48 Austrian Government Gendarmerie Central Command Report, 12 Dec. 1945.
49 *Rot-weiss-Rot-buch: Gerechtigkeit für Österreich* (Vienna, Druck und Verlag der Österreichischen Staatsdruckerei, 1946), p. 149.
50 Lt Col. Ralph E. Pearson, extract of diary published in *Kansas City Times*, n.d. [1958].
51 Simon, *The Battle of the Louvre*, p. 18.
52 Ibid., p. 23.
53 Letter from Robert Fohr, Direction des Musées de France, 18 Feb. 1999.
54 Nicholas, *The Rape of Europa*, p. 407.
55 Telephone interview with Craig Hugh Smyth, 1 July 1998.
56 Conversation with Robert Fohr, 22 Feb. 1999.
57 Documents from the French Foreign Affairs Ministry archive.
58 Telephone interview with Prof. Martin Kemp, 26 Feb. 1999.
59 MNR listing, French Culture and Communications Ministry.
60 Telephone interview with Robert Fohr, Direction des Musées de France, 26 Feb. 1999.
61 SOE Summary of Austrian Claims for Assessment, 12 Aug. 1945.
62 Ibid.
63 SOE Personal File on Albrecht Gaiswinkler.
64 Telephone interview with Cabinet Office, 23 June 1998.
65 Interview with Josef Grafl, 13 July 1998.

Chapter 6

1 Report of 10 March 1945 by Sqn Ldr Douglas Cooper, MFA&A Branch, Control Commission for Germany (British Element) to Lt Col. Sir Leonard Woolley, War Office, *Report of Visit of Investigation into Looted Works of Art and their Whereabouts in Switzerland* (PRO FO 837 1157).
2 Ibid.
3 Report of 2 March 1945 by Sqn Ldr Douglas Cooper to Commercial Counsellor, British Legation, Berne, *Looted Works of Art in Switzerland* (PRO FO 837 1157).
4 Ibid.
5 Ibid.
6 Ibid.
7 Ibid.
8 Letter of 12 Sept. 1945 from Wg Cdr Douglas Cooper, MFA&A Branch, to Mr Clark, Economic Warfare Department, Foreign Office (PRO FO 837 1157).
9 Report of 10 Dec. 1945 by Wg Cdr Douglas Cooper, MFA&A Branch,

Control Commission for Germany (British Element), *Report of Mission to Switzerland* (PRO 837 1157).

10 OSS ALIU Detailed Interrogation Report No. 9, 15 Sept. 1945, *Subject: Walter Andreas Hofer* (PRO T 209 29).

11 Ibid.

12 Ibid.

13 Ibid.

14 Ibid.

15 Report of 10 Dec. 1945 by Wg Cdr Douglas Cooper, MFA&A Branch, Control Commission for Germany (British Element), *Report of Mission to Switzerland*, Attachment A, *General Methods of Acquisition* (PRO 837 1157).

16 Ibid.

17 Ibid.

18 Ibid.

19 Report of 10 March 1945 by Sqn Ldr Douglas Cooper, MFA&A Branch, Control Commission for Germany (British Element) to Lt Col. Sir Leonard Woolley, War Office, *Report of Visit of Investigation into Looted Works of Art and their Whereabouts in Switzerland.*

20 Report of 10 Dec. 1945 by Wg Cdr Douglas Cooper, MFA&A Branch, Control Commission for Germany (British Element), *Report of Mission to Switzerland*, Attachment A, *General Methods of Acquisition.*

21 Supreme Headquarters Allied Expeditionary Force, March 1945, *Appreciation of Enemy Methods of Looting Works of Art in Occupied Territory* (PRO T 209 26).

22 Report of 2 March 1945 by Sqn Ldr Douglas Cooper to Commercial Counsellor, British Legation, Berne, *Looted Works of Art in Switzerland*, Appendix C, *Minute on the Subject of Looted and Smuggled Works of Art for the Consideration of the Commercial Counsellor* (PRO FO 837 1154).

23 Ibid., p. 44; report of 10 March 1945 by Sqn Ldr Douglas Cooper, MFA&A Branch, Control Commission for Germany (British Element) to Lt Col. Sir Leonard Woolley, War Office, *Report of Visit of Investigation into Looted Works of Art and their Whereabouts in Switzerland.*

24 Report of 10 Dec. 1945 by Wg Cdr Douglas Cooper, MFA&A Branch, Control Commission for Germany (British Element), *Report of Mission to Switzerland*, Attachment A, *General Methods of Acquisition: Exchanges* (PRO FO 837 1157).

25 Undated report [1945] by Wg Cdr Douglas Cooper, MFA&A Branch SHAEF (PRO FO 371 45769).

26 Report of 10 March 1945 by Sqn Ldr Douglas Cooper, MFA&A Branch, Control Commission for Germany (British Element), *Report of Visit of Investigation into Looted Works of Art and their Whereabouts in Switzerland.*

27 Ibid.

28 External Security Staff, Enemy Branch, Foreign Economic Administration, Aug. 1945, *Looted Art in Occupied Territories, Neutral Countries and Latin America – Revised* (PRO FO 837 1154).

29 Report of 2 March 1945 by Sqn Ldr Douglas Cooper to Commercial Counsellor, British Legation, Berne, *Looted Works of Art in Switzerland*, Appendix C, *Minute on the Subject of Looted and Smuggled Works of Art for the Consideration of the Commercial Counsellor.*

30 Letter of 18 April 1945 from Ministry of Economic Warfare to Commercial Secretariat, British Legation, Berne.

31 Ibid.

32 External Security Staff, Enemy Branch, Foreign Economic Administration, Aug. 1945, *Looted Art in Occupied Territories, Neutral Countries and Latin America – Revised.*

33 External Security Staff, Enemy Branch, Foreign Economic Administration, 5 May 1945, *Looted Art in Occupied Territories, Neutral Countries and Latin America – Preliminary Report* (PRO FO 837 1156).

34 Report of 10 Dec. 1945 by Wg Cdr Douglas Cooper, MFA&A Branch, Control Commission for Germany (British Element), *Report of Mission to Switzerland*, Attachment H, *Record of Conversation with Herr Emil Bührle* (PRO 837 1157).

35 Ibid.

36 Ibid.

37 Ibid.

38 Ibid., Attachment J, *Record of Three Interviews with Dr Hans Wendland* (PRO 837 1157).

39 Ibid.

40 Ibid.

41 Ibid.

42 Ibid., *Restitution in Switzerland.*

43 Ibid.

44 Ibid.

45 Ibid., Attachment C, *Report on a Meeting at the Federal Political Department.*

46 Ibid., Attachment F, *Report of Mission to Federal Political Department in Connection with the Questioning of Certain Persons Known to Have Dealt in Looted Works of Art.*

47 Ibid.

48 Ibid.

49 Ibid.

50 Ibid.

51 Ibid., Attachment C, *Report on a Meeting at the Federal Political Department.*

52 Report of 10 Dec. 1945 by Wg Cdr Douglas Cooper, MFA&A Branch, Control Commission for Germany (British Element), *Report of Mission to Switzerland*.

53 Ibid.

54 Ibid.

55 Ibid., Attachment H, *Record of Conversation with Herr Emil Bührle*.

56 Nicholas, *The Rape of Europa*, p. 419.

Chapter 7

1 External Security Staff, Enemy Branch, Foreign Economic Administration, Aug. 1945, *Looted Art in Occupied Territories, Neutral Countries and Latin America – Revised* (PRO FO 837 1154).

2 Ibid.

3 Adam LeBor, *Hitler's Secret Bankers: The Myth of Swiss Neutrality during the Holocaust* (New York, Birch Lane Press, 1997), pp. 58–61.

4 William Stevenson, *The Bormann Brotherhood* (London, Arthur Barker, 1973), p. 68.

5 Ian Sayer and Douglas Botting, *Nazi Gold: The Story of the World's Greatest Robbery and its Aftermath* (London, Granada, 1984).

6 US intelligence report, 13 Feb. 1945, *Report on Looted Works of Art in Spain: Miedl Case* (US National Archives).

7 Ibid.

8 Ibid.

9 Ibid.

10 US intelligence report (undated), *Miedl Case, Report No. 2* (US National Archives).

11 Memo of 24 Nov. 1944 from Mr R. Fenton, Ministry of Economic Warfare, to Miss Edith Clay, Macmillan Committee.

12 Ibid.

13 Memo of 4 Dec. 1944 from Mr R. Fenton, Ministry of Economic Warfare, to Miss Edith Clay, Macmillan Committee.

14 US intelligence report, 13 Feb. 1945, *Report on Looted Works of Art in Spain: Miedl Case*.

15 External Security Staff, Enemy Branch, Foreign Economic Administration, 5 May 1945, *Looted Art in Occupied Territories, Neutral Countries and Latin America – Preliminary Report* (PRO FO 837 1156).

16 US intelligence report, 13 Feb. 1945, *Report on Looted Works of Art in Spain: Miedl Case*.

17 Letter of 22 March 1945 from Ministry of Information to Macmillan Committee (PRO T 209 9).

18 US intelligence report (undated), *Miedl Case, Report No. 2*.

19 Memo of 17 Feb. 1945 from Mr J. Brooke Willis, Economic Warfare Division, US Embassy, London, to Miss Jane Mull, 'Alois Miedl and Looted Pictures'.

20 US intelligence report (undated), *Miedl Case, Report No. 2.*

21 Telephone interview with Aline, Countess of Romanones, 3 Sept. 1996.

22 Ibid.

23 Ibid.

24 Ibid.

25 Ibid.

26 Ibid.

27 Ibid.

28 Glenn B. Infield, *Skorzeny: Hitler's Commando* (New York, St Martin's Press, 1981), p. 183.

29 Ibid., p. 180.

30 David Robertson, 'He Smuggled Nazi Loot', *Daily Telegraph*, 14 June 1945.

31 Ibid.

32 Telephone interview with Michel Gardère, 15 July 1996.

33 Ibid.

34 Ibid., 14 Sept. 1998.

35 OSS ALIU report, 20 Aug. 1945, to Enemy Branch, Foreign Economic Administration (US National Archives).

36 Ibid.

37 External Security Staff, Enemy Branch, Foreign Economic Administration, Aug. 1945, *Looted Art in Occupied Territories, Neutral Countries and Latin America – Revised.*

38 Ibid.

39 OSS ALIU report, 20 Aug. 1945, to Enemy Branch, Foreign Economic Administration.

40 Ibid.

41 OSS intelligence report, 7 March 1945, *Transactions in Looted Art Objects in Portugal* (US National Archives).

42 Ibid.

Chapter 8

1 Kenneth Alford, *The Spoils of World War II: The American Military's Role in Stealing Europe's Treasures* (New York, Birch Lane Press, 1994), p. 18.

2 Report of 4 Sept. 1946 by Lt Walter Horn, MFA&A officer, to Chief, MFA&A Section, Restitution Branch, Office of Military Government, Bavaria (US National Archives).

3 Ibid.

4 Ibid.

5 Ibid.

6 Ibid.

7 Alford, *The Spoils of World War II*, p. 18.

8 Ibid., p. 19.
9 Ibid., pp. 19–20.
10 Ibid., p. 22.
11 Ibid., p. 23.
12 Ibid.
13 Ibid., pp. 24, 30.
14 Ibid., p. 25.
15 Ibid., pp. 25–6.
16 Ibid., p. 28.
17 Telephone interview with Dr Michael Maek-Gerard, Städel Museum, 26 Sept. 1996.
18 Letter and information supplied by Dr Michael Maek-Gerard, Städel Museum, 9 Oct. 1996.
19 Ibid.
20 Ibid.
21 Alford, *The Spoils of World War II*, p. 30.
22 Ibid., p. 229.
23 Ibid., p. 231.
24 Ibid., p. 232.
25 Ibid., p. 234.
26 Ibid., p. 236.
27 Ibid., pp. 241–2.
28 Ibid., p. 243.
29 Ibid., p. 259.
30 Ibid., pp. 259–60.
31 Ibid., p. 260.
32 Ibid., p. 261.
33 Ibid., p. 262.
34 Report of 15 April 1948 by Dr Erika Hanfstaengl, Munich Collection Point, to Chief, MFA&A Section, *Missing Painting by W. Liebl, Representing a Boy with Hat* (US National Archives).
35 Reports of 1, 10 and 22 Sept. 1948 by Edgar Breitenbach, MFA&A officer, to Chief, MFA&A Section, Restitution Branch, Office of Military Government, Bavaria (US National Archives).
36 Report of 29 April 1948 by MFA&A Section, Restitution Branch, Office of Military Government of Bavaria, to Kriminalpolizei, Munich (US National Archives).
37 Report of 13 Feb. 1948 by Edgar Breitenbach, MFA&A officer, to Chief, MFA&A Section, Restitution Branch, Office of Military Government, Bavaria (US National Archives).
38 Ibid.
39 Ibid.
40 Ibid.
41 Report of 16 Feb. 1948 by Edgar Breitenbach, MFA&A officer, to

Chief, MFA&A Section, Restitution Branch, Office of Military Government, Bavaria (US National Archives).

42 Report of 30 March 1948 by Edgar Breitenbach, MFA&A officer, to Ewan Phillips, MFA&A Section, Education Branch, HQ Control Commission for Germany (British Element) (US National Archives).

43 Ibid.

44 Report of 29 Sept. 1948 by Edgar Breitenbach to Chief, MFA&A Section, Central Collection Point, Munich (US National Archives).

45 Report of 4 Nov. 1948 by Edgar Breitenbach, MFA&A officer, to Intelligence Department, Central Collecting Point, Munich (US National Archives).

46 Report of 4 May 1949 by E. J. B. Doubinsky, French representative at the Central Collecting Point, Munich, to Stefan P. Munsing, Chief, MFA&A Section, Restitution Branch (US National Archives).

47 Ibid.

48 Nicholas, *The Rape of Europa*, pp. 437–8.

49 Letter of 1 Aug. 1945 from James Byrne, US Secretary of State, to Ernest Bevin, British Foreign Secretary (PRO FO 371 45770).

50 '$80,000,000 Paintings Arrive from Europe on Army Transport', *New York Times*, 7 Dec. 1945.

51 Nicholas, *The Rape of Europa*, p. 439.

52 Alford, *The Spoils of World War II*, pp. 257–8.

53 Ibid., p. 272.

54 Ibid., p. 275.

55 Jasper Gerard, 'Exhibition of Hate', *Sunday Telegraph*, 18 Aug. 1996.

56 Alford, *The Spoils of World War II*, p. 275.

57 Gerard, 'Exhibition of Hate'.

58 Habie Schwarz, 'Found: Family Paintings from a Nazi Hoard', *Sunday Times*, 3 Nov. 1996.

59 Press release, Christie's, 30 Oct. 1996, *Sale Held by Christie's to Benefit Victims of the Holocaust*.

60 Ibid.

61 Undated report [1945] by Wg Cdr Douglas Cooper, MFA&A Branch SHAEF.

62 Record of conversation, 9 Oct. 1945, between Wg Cdr Douglas Cooper and Mr Emil Bührle (PRO FO 837 1157).

63 Undated report [1945] by Wg Cdr Douglas Cooper, MFA&A Branch SHAEF.

64 Telephone interview with Michel d'Auberville, 16 Sept. 1998.

65 Letter of 24 July 1945 from British Legation, Berne, to Economic Warfare Department, Foreign Office (PRO FO 837 1157).

66 Telephone interview with Michel d'Auberville, 16 Sept. 1998.

67 Ibid.

68 Ibid.

Chapter 9

1 Konstantin Akinsha and Grigorii Kozlov, *Beautiful Loot* (New York, Random House, 1995) p. 22.
2 Ibid., p. 37.
3 Ibid., p. 38.
4 Ibid.
5 Ibid., p. 39.
6 Ibid.
7 Letter of 26 March 1945 from Sqn Ldr Douglas Cooper, MFA&A Branch SHAEF, to Lt Col. Sir Leonard Woolley, War Office (PRO FO 371 2556).
8 Letter of 28 March 1945 from Lt Col. Sir Leonard Woolley, War Office, to C. O'Neill, Foreign Office (PRO 371 2556).
9 Akinsha and Kozlov, *Beautiful Loot*, p. 102.
10 Ibid., p. 65.
11 Martin Bailey, 'Nazi Art Loot Discovered in Russia', *Observer*, 24 March 1991.
12 Akinsha and Kozlov, *Beautiful Loot*, pp. 84–7.
13 Ibid., pp. 120–3.
14 Ibid., p. 127.
15 Ibid., p. 131.
16 Ibid., p. 129.
17 Ibid., pp. 139–41.
18 Ibid., p. 142.
19 Thomas C. Howe, *Salt Mines and Castles* (New York, 1946) p. 24.
20 Ibid., pp. 90–125.
21 Akinsha and Kozlov, *Beautiful Loot*, pp. 142–3.
22 Letter of 30 March 1945 from Wg Cdr Jack Goodison, MFA&A Branch, Allied Commission for Austria, to Lt Col. Sir Leonard Woolley, War Office (PRO 371 2556).
23 Letter of 27 April 1945 from F. K. Roberts of Chancery, British Embassy Moscow, to A. J. Vyshinski, People's Commissariat for Foreign Affairs (PRO 371 46818).
24 Letter of 29 June 1945 from C. O'Neill, Foreign Office, to Lt Col. Sir Leonard Woolley, War Office (PRO 371 46818).
25 Akinsha and Kozlov, *Beautiful Loot*, p. 245.
26 Ibid., p. 246.
27 Nicholas, *The Rape of Europa*, p. 366.
28 Akinsha and Kozlov, *Beautiful Loot*, p. 167.
29 Ibid., pp. 162–3.
30 Ibid., pp. 183–4.
31 Ibid., pp. 177–8.
32 Ibid., p. 180.
33 Ibid., p. 182.
34 Ibid., p. 196.

35 Ibid., p. 206.
36 Ibid., p. 210.
37 Ibid., p. 216.
38 Ibid., pp. 233–4.
39 Ibid., p. 236.
40 Helen Womack, 'Stalin's Art Plunder Traced in Secret Video', *Independent on Sunday*, 28 April 1991, p. 1.
41 Helen Womack, 'The Hunt for Moscow's Secret Haul of Looted Art', *Independent on Sunday*, 28 April 1991, p. 13.
42 Helen Womack, 'Stalin's Stolen Art: The Veil Begins to Lift', *Independent on Sunday*, 28 July 1991.
43 Adrian Bridge, 'Rare Books Close Chapter of Plunder', *Independent on Sunday*, 28 July 1991.
44 Telephone interview with Alexei Rastorgouev, 29 Aug. 1998.
45 Akinsha and Kozlov, *Beautiful Loot*, pp. 239–40.
46 Ibid., p. 243.
47 Ibid., p. 247.
48 Letter and list of 31 July 1998 from Dr Anne Röver-Kann, Bremen Kunsthalle, to authors.
49 Akinsha and Kozlov, *Beautiful Loot*, p. 249.
50 Ibid., pp. 249–50.
51 'Stolen Artwork from World War II', National Public Radio, morning edn, 2 Aug. 1994.
52 Letter and list of 21 Aug. 1998 from Dr Anne Röver-Kann, Bremen Kunsthalle, to authors.
53 Akinsha and Kozlov, *Beautiful Loot*, pp. 219–26.
54 'In the Cellars of the Pushkin (Art Works Stolen from Germany are in Russia's Museum)', *The Economist*, 24 Dec. 1994.
55 Akinsha and Kozlov, *Beautiful Loot*, pp. 257–9.
56 Ibid., p. 257.
57 Netherlands Ministries of Foreign Affairs and Education, Culture and Science, *Counterparts: Old Master Drawings from the Koenigs Collection* (The Hague, 1995).
58 Hilary Hylton, 'Russia's Hermitage Displays World War II Art Booty', Reuters, 28 March 1996.
59 Telephone interview with Dr Anne Röver-Kann, Bremen Kunsthalle, 26 Aug. 1998.
60 'In the Cellars of the Pushkin', *The Economist*, 24 Dec. 1994.
61 Telephone interview with Dr Anne Röver-Kann, Bremen Kunsthalle, 8 Sept. 1998.
62 Louise Jury, 'Looted Old Master Must be Returned', *Independent*, 10 Sept. 1998.
63 Telephone interview with Herr Marcus Marshall of Axer Marshall, 9 Sept. 1998.

64 Telephone interview with Dr Anne Röver-Kann, Bremen Kunsthalle, 9 Sept. 1998.

Chapter 10
1 OSS ALIU Final Report, 1 May 1946, p. 5 (Getty Research Institute Box 910130, File No. 8).
2 Association of Art Museum Directors press release, 4 June 1998.
3 Judith H. Dobrzynski, 'The Zealous Collector – A Special Report: A Singular Passion for Amassing Art, One Way or Another', *New York Times*, 24 Dec. 1997.
4 Walter V. Robinson, 'New York DA Bars Return of Austrian Art', *Boston Globe*, 9 Jan. 1998.
5 Glenn D. Lowry, affidavit to Supreme Court of the State of New York, 16 Jan. 1998.
6 External Security Staff, Enemy Branch, Foreign Economic Administration, 5 May 1945, *Looted Art in Occupied Territories, Neutral Countries and Latin America – Preliminary Report.*
7 Foreign Office and Ministry of Economic Warfare, Economic Advisory Branch Report, 14 Feb. 1945 (PRO T 209 7).
8 Ibid.
9 MFA&A Branch Report to Foreign Office, 12 Sept. 1945, *Special Report on the Firm of Wildenstein et Cie, Paris Art Dealers.*
10 Special report on the firm of Wildenstein & Cie by Wg Cdr Douglas Cooper, Aug. 1945.
11 OSS ALIU CIR No. 1, *Interrogation of Karl Haberstock*, p. 34 (PRO T 209 29).
12 External Security Staff, Enemy Branch, Foreign Economic Administration, 5 May 1945, *Looted Art in Occupied Territories, Neutral Countries and Latin America – Preliminary Report.*
13 Ibid.
14 OSS ALIU CIR No. 1, *Interrogation of Karl Haberstock*, p. 58.
15 Nicholas, *The Rape of Europa*, p. 165.
16 Foreign Office and Ministry of Economic Warfare, Economic Advisory Branch Report, 14 Feb. 1945.
17 Musée d'Orsay, *Chefs-d'Oeuvres Impressionistes et Post-Impressionistes* (Paris, Editions de la Réunion des Musées Nationaux/Thames & Hudson, 1984; London, Thames & Hudson, 1995).
18 Foreign Office and Ministry of Economic Warfare, Economic Advisory Branch Report, 14 Feb. 1945.
19 Nicholas, *The Rape of Europa*, p. 3.
20 Foreign Office and Ministry of Economic Warfare, Economic Advisory Branch report, 14 Feb. 1945.
21 OSS ALIU CIR No. 4, *Sources (J – United States)*, p. 70 (PRO T 209 29).

22 *Federal Reporter, New York Supplement,* 2nd ser., pp. 804–20 (New York, 1966).
23 Ibid.
24 Ibid.
25 Ibid.
26 'Big Gifts are Growing and so are the Lists of Givers', *New York Times,* 9 Dec. 1997.
27 *38 Federal Reporter,* 3rd ser., pp. 1266–79, 1994.
28 Ibid.
29 External Security Staff, Enemy Branch, Foreign Economic Administration, 5 May 1945, *Looted Art in Occupied Territories, Neutral Countries and Latin America – Preliminary Report.*
30 Hugh Davies, 'Swiss "Helped Smuggle Nazi Loot to Argentina" ', *Daily Telegraph,* 6 Dec. 1996.
31 US State Department Report, *Supplement to Preliminary Study on US and Allied Efforts to Recover and Restore Gold and other Assets Stolen or Hidden during World War II,* June 1998.
32 Ibid.
33 Godfrey Barker, 'Eichmann is Linked to Looted Art', *Daily Telegraph,* 29 Oct. 1996.
34 External Security Staff, Enemy Branch, Foreign Economic Administration, 5 May 1945, *Looted Art in Occupied Territories, Neutral Countries and Latin America – Preliminary Report.*
35 Ibid.
36 *Globo Sao Paolo,* 9 Sept. 1998.
37 External Security Staff, Enemy Branch, Foreign Economic Administration, 5 May 1945, *Looted Art in Occupied Territories, Neutral Countries and Latin America – Preliminary Report.*
38 Nicholas, *The Rape of Europa,* p. 232.
39 External Security Staff, Enemy Branch, Foreign Economic Administration, 5 May 1945, *Looted Art in Occupied Territories, Neutral Countries and Latin America – Preliminary Report.*
40 Walter V. Robinson, 'Sweden Probes a Dark Secret', *Boston Globe,* 6 July 1997.
41 External Security Staff, Enemy Branch, Foreign Economic Administration, 5 May 1945, *Looted Art in Occupied Territories, Neutral Countries and Latin America – Preliminary Report.*
42 OSS ALIU, letter of 25 July 1945 to HQ US Group Control Commission Germany.
43 British Control Commission for Germany, *Schloss Celle – Losses* (PRO FO 1032 2024).
44 Alford, *The Spoils of War,* pp. 115–38.
45 Ibid., p. 65.
46 *678 Federal Reporter,* 2nd ser., pp. 1150–66, 1982.
47 Ibid.

48 Ibid.
49 Ibid.
50 Interview with Dr Willi Korte, 3 July 1998.
51 Interview with Mrs Lydia Braemer, 13 June 1998.
52 Walter V. Robinson, 'Theft Admission Ends Tug-of-War Over Artwork', *Boston Globe*, 13 May 1998.
53 Interviews with Dr Willi Korte and Mr Thomas Kline, 3 July 1998.
54 Ibid.
55 Robinson, 'Theft Admission Ends Tug-of-War Over Artwork'.
56 Foreign Office and Ministry of Economic Warfare, Economic Advisory Branch Report, 14 Feb. 1945.
57 Ibid.
58 Rajeev Syal and Jonathan Leake, 'Cary Grant was a Wartime Spy', *Sunday Times*, 28 July 1996.
59 Jane Turner, ed., *Dictionary of Art* (New York, Macmillan, 1996), vol. 26, p. 472.
60 Museum of Modern Art, *Forty Paintings from the Edward G. Robinson Collection* (New York, 1953).
61 Musée d'Orsay, *Chefs-d'Oeuvres Impressionistes et Post-Impressionistes*.
62 Sotheby's sale catalogue, 29 April 1964, *Impressionist and Modern Paintings, Drawings and Sculpture*.
63 Telephone interview with the Van Gogh Museum, Amsterdam, 1 Sept. 1998.
64 Foreign Office and Ministry of Economic Warfare, Economic Advisory Branch report, 14 Feb. 1945.
65 Telephone interview with Dr Jonathon Petropoulos, 27 Aug. 1998.
66 Will Bennett, 'Did the Nazis Loot This?', *Daily Telegraph*, 13 July 1998.
67 Telephone interview with Walter V. Robinson, 3 Sept. 1998.
68 Walter V. Robinson, 'Murky Histories Cloud Some Local Art', *Boston Globe*, 9 Nov. 1997.
69 External Security Staff, Enemy Branch, Foreign Economic Administration, 5 May 1945, *Looted Art in Occupied Territories, Neutral Countries and Latin America – Preliminary Report*.
70 Robinson, 'Murky Histories Cloud Some Local Art'.
71 Telephone interview with US Customs agent Bonnie Goldblatt, 5 Sept. 1998.
72 'Stolen Drawings Worth Millions are Recovered', *Star Tribune*, 10 Sept 1997.
73 Telephone interview with US Customs agent Bonnie Goldblatt, 5 Sept. 1998.
74 Walter V. Robinson, 'Sotheby's Takes Work Tied to Nazis off Block', *Boston Globe*, 25 Nov. 1997.
75 Ibid.

76 John Harlow, 'Revealed: Looted Nazi Pictures Went to British Museum', *Sunday Times*, 13 April 1997.
77 Martin Bailey, 'Nazi Loot in British Museum "Must Go Back" ', *Observer*, 21 April 1991.
78 Telephone interview with Richard Verdi of the Barber Institute, 2 Sept. 1998.
79 Bailey, 'Nazi Loot in British Museum "Must Go Back" '.
80 Transcript of Senate Banking Committee Hearing on Nazi Gold, 12 Feb. 1998.
81 Ibid.
82 Walter V. Robinson, 'Art Registry did not Inform Met of Claim', *Boston Globe*, 25 July 1997.
83 OSS ALIU CIR No. 1, *Interrogation of Karl Haberstock*, p. 5.
84 Telephone interview with Mr Nicolas Vanhove of Belgian Ministry of Economic Affairs, 18 June 1998.
85 Telephone interview with Sophie Sutherland of the National Museum Directors' Conference, 4 Sept. 1998.
86 Telephone interview with Press Office of Department of National Heritage, 8 Sept. 1998.
87 Telephone interview with Mr Thomas Hoving, 25 Aug. 1998.

Chapter 11
1 Interview with Mr Nick Goodman, 9 July 1998.
2 OSS ALIU CIR No. 2, *Interrogation of Karl Haberstock*, p. 1 (PRO T 209 29).
3 Interview with Mr Nick Goodman, 9 July 1998.
4 OSS ALIU CIR No. 2, *Interrogation of Karl Haberstock*, p. 25.
5 Interview with Mr Nick Goodman, 9 July 1998.
6 OSS ALIU CIR No. 2, *Interrogation of Karl Haberstock*, Attachment 16.
7 OSS ALIU CIR No. 2 *Interrogation of Karl Haberstock*, p. 65.
8 Interview with Mr Nick Goodman, 9 July 1998.
9 Ibid.
10 OSS ALIU CIR No. 4, *Linz: Hitler's Museum and Library*, Attachment 64.
11 Interview with Mr Nick Goodman, 9 July 1998.
12 Ibid.
13 Ibid.
14 Ibid.
15 OSS ALIU CIR No. 1, *Interrogation of Karl Haberstock*, Attachment 1.
16 Interview with Mr Nick Goodman, 9 July 1998.
17 Ibid.
18 Ibid.
19 Interview with Dr Willi Korte, 3 July 1998.
20 Ibid.

21 Hector Feliciano, *The Lost Museum: The Nazi Conspiracy to Steal the World's Greatest Works of Art* (New York, Basic Books, 1997).
22 Interview with Mr Nick Goodman, 9 July 1998.
23 Interview with Dr Willi Korte, 3 July 1998.
24 Telephone interview with Lloyd Goldenberg of Trans-Art International, 19 July 1998.
25 Telephone interview with Thomas Hoving, 25 August 1998.
26 Interview with Dr Willi Korte, 5 Sept. 1998.
27 Interview with Mr Nick Goodman, 9 July 1998.
28 Ibid.
29 Nicholas, *The Rape of Europa,* p. 160.
30 Interview with Ms Christine Koenigs, 22 June 1998.
31 Interview with Mr Nick Goodman, 9 July 1998.
32 Ibid.
33 Interview with Count Adam Zamoyski, 18 July 1998.
34 Ibid.
35 OSS ALIU CIR No. 2, *The Loot from Poland*, p. 31 (PRO T 209 29).
36 Ibid.
37 OSS ALIU CIR No. 4, *Linz: Hitler's Museum and Library*, Attachment 5.
38 Nicholas, *The Rape of Europa*, p. 69.
39 OSS ALIU CIR No. 2, *The Loot from Poland*, p. 31.
40 Nicholas, *The Rape of Europa*, p. 69.
41 OSS ALIU CIR No. 4. *Poland*, pp. 66–7.
42 Interview with Count Adam Zamoyski, 18 July 1998.
43 Ibid.
44 Nicholas, *The Rape of Europa*, p. 360.
45 Interview with Count Adam Zamoyski, 18 July 1998.
46 Ibid.
47 Nicholas, *The Rape of Europa*, p. 442.
48 Interview with Count Adam Zamoyski, 18 July 1998.
49 Ibid.
50 'Where is this Raphael?', *The Art Newspaper*, Feb. 1998.
51 Interview with Count Adam Zamoyski, 18 July 1998.
52 Netherlands Inspectorate of Cultural Heritage, *Origins Unknown* (The Hague, 1998).
53 Telephone interview with Dr Willi Korte, 5 Sept. 1998.
54 Interview with Mr Thomas Kline, 3 July 1998.
55 Elizabeth Simpson, ed., *The Spoils of War – World War II and its Aftermath: The Loss, Reappearance and Recovery of Cultural Property* (New York, Abrams/BGC, 1997), p. 136.
56 Ibid., p. 235.
57 Interview with Count Adam Zamoyski, 18 July 1998.
58 OSS ALIU CIR No. 2, *Confiscations: The Göring Collection*, p. 28.

59 OSS ALIU CIR No. 2, Attachment 1, Letter from Hofer to Göring of 26 Sept. 1941.

60 OSS ALIU CIR No. 1, *Methods of Acquisition: The ERR in France.*

61 'Heirs Sue Museum for Painting', Associated Press, 4 Aug. 1998.

62 Telephone interview with Lloyd Goldenberg of Trans-Art International, 19 July 1998.

63 Simpson, *The Spoils of War.*

Chapter 12

1 Interview with M. Jean de Martini, 15 July 1998.

2 Ibid.

3 Ibid.

4 Ibid.

5 OSS ALIU CIR No. 4, *The Schloss Affair*, p. 32 (PRO T 209 29).

6 Ibid.

7 Philippe Sprang, 'Le Trésor Nazi Refait Surface', *L'Evénement du Jeudi*, 7–13 March 1996.

8 OSS ALIU CIR No. 4, Attachments 29 and 29A (PRO T 209 29).

9 Ibid.

10 Sprang, 'Le Trésor Nazi Refait Surface'.

11 OSS ALIU CIR No. 4, Attachment 26 (PRO T 209 29).

12 Report of investigation by Directeur des Services de Police Judiciaire into Jean François Lefranc, 3 August 1945.

13 OSS ALIU CIR No. 4, *The Schloss Affair*, p. 31.

14 Roxan and Wanstall, *The Jackdaw of Linz*, p. 142.

15 Telephone interview with Prof. Craig Hugh Smyth, 1 July 1998.

16 OSS ALIU CIR No. 4, *The Schloss Affair*, Attachment 28.

17 Interview with M. Jean de Martini, 15 July 1998.

18 Dr Otto Kummel, *List of Most Important Old Paintings Destroyed in the Flakturm Friedrichshain 31st July 1945.*

19 Interview with M. Jean de Martini, 15 July 1998.

20 Letter of 21 May 1980 from French ambassador in Bonn to German government.

21 Interview with M. Jean de Martini, 15 July 1998.

22 OSS ALIU CIR No. 2, *Purchasing Agents in Italy*, p. 107 (PRO T 209 29).

23 Sprang, 'Le Trésor Nazi Refait Surface'.

24 Interview with M. Jean de Martini, 15 July 1998.

25 David D'Arcy, 'If not a Rembrandt at Least a Schloss', *Art Newspaper*, July/August 1997.

26 Walter V. Robinson, 'Portrait Nazis Stole is Hotly Disputed', *Boston Globe*, 5 May 1997.

27 A. Bredius, *Rembrandt: The Complete Edition of the Paintings* (Paris, Phaidon, 1984).

28 Conversation with Inspector Patrice Dallem, French Office Centrale pour la Repression des Vols d'Oeuvres et Objets d'Art, 24 Feb. 1999.

29 Conversation with Jean de Martini, 28 Feb. 1999.

30 David D'Arcy, 'The Very Comical Tragedy of the Schloss Collection "Rembrandt" ', Art Newspaper, Feb. 1998.

31 Fred G. Meijer, Still Life Paintings from the Golden Age (Rotterdam, Museum Boymans–Van Beuningen, 1989).

32 Letter of 16 March 1989 from Prof. J. H. Crouwel to Sol Chaneles.

33 OSS ALIU CIR No. 4, German Agents and Buyers, p. 46 (PRO T 209 29).

34 Interview with Christine Koenigs, 22 June 1998.

35 Foreign Office internal report of 3 November 1939 (PRO FO 371 23012).

36 Interview with Christine Koenigs, 22 June 1998.

37 Ibid.

38 Ibid.

39 Letter of 13 March 1940 from Dr Dirk Hannema to Mr van der Worm.

40 MFA&A, Additional Reports on Monuments in Province of Gelderland, p. 100 (PRO WO 220 614).

41 OSS ALIU CIR No. 2, The Goudstikker Affair, p. 71 (PRO T 209 29).

42 Interview with Christine Koenigs, 22 June 1998.

43 Simpson, The Spoils of War, p. 169.

44 Telephone interview with John Rowlands of the British Museum, 20 July 1998.

45 Interview with Christine Koenigs, 22 June 1998.

46 Ibid.

47 Cynthia Saltzman, Portrait of Dr Gachet: The Story of a Van Gogh Masterpiece (New York, Viking, 1998), p. 200.

48 Interview with Dr Josefine Leistra, 22 June 1998.

49 Interview with Christine Koenigs, 22 June 1998.

50 Interview with Dr Josefine Leistra, 22 June 1998.

51 Albert Elen, Missing Old Master Drawings from the Franz Koenigs Collection (The Hague, SDU/The Netherlands Office for Fine Arts, 1989), p. 20.

52 Interview with Dr Josefine Leistra, 22 June 1998.

53 Ibid.

54 Ibid.

55 Ibid.

56 Telephone interview with Alexei Rastorgouev, 29 Aug. 1998.

57 Ibid.

58 Interview with Christine Koenigs, 22 June 1998.

59 Elen, Missing Old Master Drawings.

60 Letter of 25 June 1998 from Dr Josefine Leistra to authors.

61 OSS ALIU CIR No. 2, Personnel, p. 20 (PRO T 209 29).

62 French Ministry of Culture and Communications, press release of 2 April 1997.

63 Telephone interview with Dr Sabine Fehlemann of Von der Heydt Museum, 28 Aug. 1998.

64 Hubertus Czernin, 'The Austrian Evasion', *ARTnews*, June 1998.

65 Walter V. Robinson, 'Austrian Move on Plundered Art', *Boston Globe*, 11 Sept. 1998.

66 Will Bennett, 'Budapest Jew Claims £5m for Art Seized by Britain', *Daily Telegraph*, 23 June 1998.

67 Holocaust Educational Trust press release, 17 June 1998, *Britain Confiscated £5m Jewish Victim's Art Collection*.

68 British government document, *Hungarian Owned Property Seized in the United Kingdom* (PRO BT 273 206).

69 Philips, Son & Neale sale catalogue, 22 Nov. 1955.

70 Holocaust Educational Trust press release, *Britain Confiscated £5m Jewish Victim's Art Collection*.

71 Ibid.

72 Ibid.

Chapter 13

1 Interview with Thomas Freudenheim, 2 July 1998.

2 Ibid.

3 Nicholas, *The Rape of Europa*.

4 Interview with Saul Kagan, 1 July 1998.

5 Interview with Marc Mazurowsky, 6 July 1998.

6 Transcript of US Senate Banking Committee hearing, 12 Feb. 1998.

7 Ibid.

8 Interview with Constance Lowenthal, 2 July 1998.

9 Interview with Marc Mazurowsky, 6 July 1998.

10 Interview with Constance Lowenthal, 2 July 1998.

11 Transcript of US Senate Banking Committee hearing, 12 Feb. 1998.

12 Judith Dobrzynski, 'Man in the Middle of Schiele Case', *New York Times*, 29 Jan. 1997.

13 Ibid.

14 Interview with Thomas Freudenheim, 2 July 1998.

15 Dobrzynski, 'Man in the Middle of Schiele Case'.

16 Interview with Constance Lowenthal, 2 July 1998.

17 Dobrzynski, 'Man in the Middle of Schiele Case'.

18 Interview with Ron Tauber, 2 July 1998.

19 Colin Gleadell, 'Did the Nazis Loot This?', *Daily Telegraph*, 13 July 1998.

20 Walter V. Robinson, 'An Ignominious Legacy: Evidence Grows of Plundered Art in US', *Boston Globe*, 25 April 1997.

21 Gleadell, 'Did the Nazis Loot This?'.

22 Interview with Ron Tauber, 2 July 1998.

23 Ibid.
24 Interview with Lloyd Goldenberg, 11 Aug. 1998.
25 Interview with Ron Tauber, 2 July 1998.
26 Interview with Tom Freudenheim, 2 July 1998.
27 OSS ALIU CIR No. 2, *Dealers*, p. 79 (PRO T 209 29).
28 Ibid., p. 88.
29 Ibid., pp. 87–8.
30 Ibid., p. 74.
31 OSS ALIU Final Report, 1 May 1945, p. 34.
32 MFA&A Branch SHAEF Report, 12 Sept. 1945, *Special Report on the Firm of Wildenstein et Cie, Paris Art Dealers.*
33 Alan Riding, 'Mighty and Secretive Art Dynasty Goes Public to Rebut Nazi Links', *New York Times*, 20 April 1998.
34 New York Banking Department press release, 25 June 1997.
35 Ivo Dawnay, Philip Sherwell and Adam LeBor, 'Search for Nazi Plunder Sends Shudder through Art World', *Sunday Telegraph* 30 Nov. 1997.
36 Louise Jury, 'Holocaust Campaigners Secure $1.25 Billion Settlement', *Independent*, 13 Aug. 1998.
37 Interview with Lloyd Goldenberg, 11 Aug. 1998.
38 Interview with Tom Freudenheim, 2 July 1998.
39 Interview with Marc Mazurowsky, 6 July 1998.
40 Robin Cembalest, 'Idea Emerges for Special Museum of Art Looted from Europe's Jews', *Forward*, 27 Feb. 1998.
41 Interview with Tom Freudenheim, 2 July 1998.
42 Cembalest, 'Idea Emerges for Special Museum'.
43 Interview with Marc Mazurowsky, 6 July 1998.
44 Interview with Constance Lowenthal, 2 July 1998.
45 Interview with Ron Tauber, 2 July 1998.
46 Interview with Lloyd Goldenberg, 11 August 1998.

Chapter 14
1 Milton Esterow, 'Europe is Still Hunting its Plundered Art', *New York Times*, 16 Nov. 1964.
2 Gleadell, 'Did the Nazis Loot This?'.
3 Ibid.
4 Interview with Thomas Kline, 3 July 1998.
5 Interview with Dr Josefine Leistra, 22 June 1998.
6 Karin Taylor, 'Austria Vows to Restitute Nazi Art Loot', Reuters, 9 Sept. 1998.
7 Dawnay et al., 'Search for Nazi Plunder Sends Shudders through Art World'.
8 Transcript of US Senate Banking Committee hearing, 12 Feb. 1998.
9 Joseph Schuman, 'Nazi-Plundered Art Hard to Trace', Associated Press, 17 July 1998.

10 Taylor, 'Austria Vows to Restitute Nazi Art Loot'.

11 Schuman, 'Nazi-Plundered Art Hard to Trace'.

12 Ibid.

13 Interview with Thomas Kline, 3 July 1998.

14 Interview with Lloyd Goldenberg, 11 Aug. 1998.

15 Marilyn Henry, 'Clinton Inks Bill to Aid Holocaust Relief Bodies', *Jerusalem Post*, 15 Feb. 1998.

16 'Yeltsin Calls Trophy Art Ruling "A Slap in the Face" ', Reuters, 7 April 1998.

17 Interview with Dr Josefine Leistra, 22 June 1998.

18 Interview with Dr Anne Röver-Kann, 2 Sept. 1998.

19 Ibid.

20 Inter-Allied Declaration Against Acts of Dispossession Committed in Territories Under Enemy Occupation or Control (also known as the Declaration of London), in Simpson, *The Spoils of War*, appendix 9, p. 287.

21 Ibid., p. 226.

22 UNESCO, UNIDROIT Convention on the International Return of Stolen or Illegally Exported Cultural Objects, 24 June 1995.

23 Press briefing in Rome, 18 May 1998, by UN Under-Secretary General for Legal Affairs, Hans Correll.

24 Transcript of US Senate Banking Committee hearing, 12 Feb. 1998.

25 Ibid.

26 Walter V. Robinson, 'New York DA Bars Return of Austrian Art', *Boston Globe*, 9 Jan. 1998.

27 Interview with Marc Mazurowsky, 6 July 1998.

28 Judith Dobrzynski, 'Lenders Pull Two Bonnards from a Show at the Modern', *New York Times*, 29 April 1998.

29 Ibid.

30 Ibid.

31 Walter V. Robinson, 'An Ignominious Legacy: Evidence Grows of Plundered Art in US', *Boston Globe*, 25 April 1997.

32 Interview with Manus Brinkman, 31 Aug. 1998.

33 Ibid.

34 Interview with Lloyd Goldenberg, 11 Aug. 1998.

35 Interview with Gary Vikan, 7 Sept. 1998.

36 Interview with Nick Goodman, 9 July 1998.

BIBLIOGRAPHY

Books, Journals and Catalogues

Aalders, Gerard and Wiebes, Cees, *The Art of Cloaking Ownership: The Secret Collaboration and Protection of the German War Industry by the Neutrals*, Amsterdam, Amsterdam University Press, 1996

Ader Picard Tajan, *Collection d'un Grand Amateur Deuxième Vente: Importants Tableaux Anciens*, 1989

Akinsha, Konstantin and Kozlov, Grigorii, *Beautiful Loot: The Soviet Plunder of Europe's Art Treasures*, New York, Random House, 1995

Alford, Kenneth, *The Spoils of World War II: The American Military's Role in Stealing Europe's Treasures*, New York, Birch Lane Press, 1994

Bazin, Germain, *L'Exode du Louvre 1940–1945*, Paris, Somogy, 1992

Bibliotheca Rosenthaliana, *The Return of Looted Collections 1946–1996: An Unfinished Chapter*, Amsterdam, 1997

Botting, Douglas, *In the Ruins of the Reich*, London, Allen & Unwin, 1985

Bower, Tom, *Blind Eye to Murder*, London, Andre Deutsch, 1981

Bredius, A., *Rembrandt: The Complete Edition of the Paintings*, Paris, Phaidon, 1984

Centre Georges Pompidou, *Guide des Collections Permanentes*, Paris, Éditions du Centre Georges Pompidou/Editions Scala, 1994

Centre Georges Pompidou, *Le Musée Nationale d'Arte Moderne*, Paris, Beaux Arts, 1996

Chamberlin, Russell, *Loot! The Heritage of Plunder*, London, Facts on File, 1983

Christie's Manson & Woods Ltd, *Mauerbach: Items Seized by the National Socialists to be Sold for the Benefit of the Victims of the Holocaust*, London, Christie's, 1996

De Jaeger, Charles, *The Linz File: Hitler's Plunder of Europe's Art*, London, Webb & Bower, 1981

Druck und Verlag der Österreichischen Staatsdruckerei, *Rot-Weiss-Rot-Buch: Gerechtigkeit für Österreich*, Vienna, 1946

Elen, Albert J., *Missing Old Master Drawings from the Franz Koenigs Collection*, The Hague, SDU Publishers/The Netherlands Office for Fine Arts, 1989

Fauchereau, Serge, *Braque*, Paris, Albin Michel, 1987

Feliciano, Hector, *The Lost Museum: The Nazi Conspiracy to Steal the World's Greatest Works of Art*, New York, Basic Books, 1997

Hartung, Ulrike, *The Sonderkommando Künsberg: Looting of Cultural*

Treasures in the USSR, Bremen, Research Institute Eastern Europe, University of Bremen, 1996

Higham, Charles, *Trading with the Enemy*, London, Robert Hale, 1983

Holocaust Educational Trust, *Ex-Enemy Jews: The Fate of the Assets in Britain of Holocaust Victims and Survivors*, London, 1997

Howe, Thomas C., *Salt Mines and Castles: The Discovery and Restitution of Looted European Art*, New York, Bobbs Merrill, 1946

Infield, Glenn B., *Skorzeny: Hitler's Commando*, New York, St Martin's Press, 1981

Italian Ministry of Foreign Affairs and Ministry of Culture. *L'Opera da Ritrovare*, Rome, Instituto Poligrafico e Zecca dello Stato, 1995

Kammerhof Museum, *1945: Ende und Anfang im Ausseerland*, Bad Aussee, Panther Verlag Lutz Tietmann, 1995

Kammerhof Museum, *Die Rettung der Kunstschütze im Altausseer Bergwerk*, Bad Aussee, Panther Verlag Lutz Tietmann, 1995

Kammerstätter, Peter, 'Materialsammlung über die Widerstands und Partisanenbewegung – Willy-Fred Freiheitsbewegung im Oberen Salzkammergut – Ausseerland 1943–1945', unpublished MS

Kunsthalle Bremen, *A Catalogue of the Works of Art from the Collection of the Kunsthalle Bremen Lost during Evacuation in the Second World War*, Kunstverein in Bremen, 1997

Lebor, Adam, *Hitler's Secret Bankers: The Myth of Swiss Neutrality during the Holocaust*, New York, Birch Lane Press, 1997

Linortner, Johann, *Die Kunstgüter im Altausser Salzberg 1943–1945*, Bad Aussee, Salinen, 1998

Louvre, Le, *La Peinture Européene*, Paris, Editions Scala, 1993

Meijer, Fred G., *Still Life Paintings from the Golden Age*, Rotterdam, Museum Boymans–Van Beuningen, 1989

Merrick, Kenneth, *Flights of the Forgotten: Special Duties Operations in World War Two*, London, Arms & Armour Press, 1989

Mihan, George, *Looted Treasure: Germany's Raid on Art*, London, Alliance Press, 1942

Ministère de Culture et Communications, *Pillages et Restitutions: Le Destins des Oeuvres d'Art de France pendant la Seconde Guerre Mondiale*, Paris, Adam Biro, 1997

Ministère de Culture et Communications, *Présentation des Oeuvres Récupérées après la Seconde Guerre Mondiale et Confiées à la Garde de Musées Nationaux*, Paris 1997

Ministère des Affaires Economiques, *Missing Art Works of Belgium*, Parts I and II, Brussels, 1994

Musée d'Orsay, *Chefs-d'Oeuvres Impressionistes et Post-Impressionistes*, Paris, Editions de la Réunion des Musées Nationaux/London, Thames & Hudson, 1995

Netherlands Inspectorate of Cultural Heritage, *Origins Unknown: Report on the Pilot Study into the Provenance of Works of Art Recovered from*

Germany and Currently under the Custodianship of the State of the Netherlands, The Hague, 1998

Netherlands Ministries of Foreign Affairs and Education, Culture and Science, *Counterparts: Old Master Drawings from the Koenigs Collection in the Museum Boymans–Van Beuningen in Rotterdam*, The Hague, 1995

Nicholas, Lynn H., *The Rape of Europa: The Fate of Europe's Art Treasures in the Third Reich and the Second World War*, New York, Knopf, 1994

Romanones, Aline Countess of, *The Spy Went Dancing*, New York, Century, 1991

Roxan, David and Wanstall, Ken, *The Jackdaw of Linz*, London, Cassell, 1964

Saltzmann, Cynthia, *Portrait of Dr Gachet: The Story of a Van Gogh Masterpiece*, New York, Viking, 1998

Sayer, Ian and Botting, Douglas, *Nazi Gold: The Story of the World's Greatest Robbery and its Aftermath*, London, Granada, 1984

Shirer, William, *The Rise and Fall of The Third Reich*, London, Book Club Associates, 1983

Simon, Matila, *The Battle of the Louvre: The Struggle to Save French Art in World War II*, New York, Hawthorn, 1971

Simpson, Elizabeth (ed.), *The Spoils of War World War II and its Aftermath: The Loss, Reappearance and Recovery of Cultural Property*, New York, Abrams/BGC, 1997

Smyth, Craig Hugh, *Repatriation of Art from the Collection Point in Munich after World War II*, The Hague, Gary Schwartz 1988

Stevenson, William, *The Bormann Brotherhood*, London, Arthur Barker, 1973

Watteville, Caroline de, *Collection Thyssen-Bornemisza: Guide des Oeuvres Exposées*, Fondazione Thyssen-Bornemisza, 1985

Wiesenthal, Simon, *Justice not Vengeance*, London, Weidenfeld & Nicholson, 1989

Woolley, Sir Leonard, *A Record of the Work Done by the Military Authorities for the Protection of the Treasures of Art and History in War Areas*, London, HMSO, 1947

Files in the Public Record Office, Kew, London

The files listed below are those discovered to be of relevance to the subject matter of this book. There are also a large number of files concerned with policy and establishments of MFA&A branches at various formation levels, and with MFA&A matters outside the scope of this book. Many files of the MFA&A Sub-Commission of the War Office were heavily 'weeded' after the war and thus contain little information of any use. Others are for some reason still classified and thus have not been released to the Public Record Office.

BIBLIOGRAPHY

AIR 27 – Air Ministry: Operations Record Books, Squadrons 1911–1977
AIR 27 996   Operations of 148 (Special Duties) Squadron RAF, January 1944–May 1945

HS 6 – Special Operations Executive: Operations in Austria
HS 6 20   January–February 1945
HS 6 21   March–April 1945
HS 6 22   May–June 1945

FO 1050 – Control Commission for Germany: Internal Affairs and Communications Division
FO 1050 1390 Monuments Fine Arts & Archives Branch Correspondence with G-5 Ops SHAEF (Forward)
FO 1050 1395 Planning and Coordination of MFA&A Branch
FO 1050 1396 Employment of US MFA&A Personnel in Germany
FO 1050 1397 USGCC MFA&A Branch: Control of German Administrative Areas in Two or More Zones
FO 1050 1399 US Council and Office of Strategic Services (OSS)
FO 1050 1401 Employment of Allied Officers by MFA&A
FO 1050 1402 MFA&A Branch: War Establishment, Vol. I
FO 1050 1403 MFA&A Branch: War Establishment, Vol. II
FO 1050 1434 Intelligence Reports
FO 1050 1439 Displaced Persons Branch: Liaison and Prevention of Smuggling of Works of Art by Displaced Persons (DPs)
FO 1050 1445 Belgian Advisory Committee for the Protection of Monuments and Works of Art
FO 1050 1447 Consolidated Progress Reports

FO 944 – Control Commission for Germany Control Office: Finance
FO 944 82   Restitution of Property Looted in Belgium
FO 944 85   Return of Identifiable Property Looted by Germans from Holland, Vol. I
FO 944 86   Return of Identifiable Property Looted by Germans from Holland, Vol. II
FO 944 972   Smuggling

FO 945 – Files Transferred to Control Office for Germany and Austria
FO 945 302   Paintings

FO 1030 – Supreme Headquarters Allied Powers Europe (SHAPE)
FO 1030 247 Restitution of Works of Art (United Kingdom High Commissioner's Office, Wahnerheide)

FO 1032 – Control Commission for Germany: Planning Staff, Military Sections and Headquarters Secretariat

FO 1032 1949 Removal of Works of Art by Allied Forces
FO 1032 2061 Confiscation of Nazi Property, Vol. II
FO 1032 2062 Confiscation of Nazi Property, Vol. IV
FO 1032 2538 Recovery and Replacement of Works of Art and Archives

FO 1057 – Control Commission for Germany: Reparations, Deliveries and Restitution Division

CZECHOSLOVAKIA
FO 1057 80   Looted Property
FO 1057 83   Paintings
THE NETHERLANDS
FO 1057 86   *Portrait of a Man* by P. H. de Koninck
FO 1057 87   Works of Art, Pictures and Furniture
FO 1057 88   Pictures
FO 1057 89   Pictures and Paintings
FO 1057 90   Works of Fine Art
FO 1057 91   Works of Fine Art
FO 1057 92   Pictures
FO 1057 93   Pictures
FO 1057 94   Pictures
FO 1057 95   Works of Fine Art
FO 1057 96   Pictures
FO 1057 97   Works of Fine Art and Paintings
FO 1057 98   Pictures
FO 1057 99   Works of Fine Art and Pictures
FO 1057 100   Works of Art
FO 1057 101   Pictures
FO 1057 102   Works of Fine Art and Pictures
FO 1057 103   Pictures
FO 1057 104   Pictures
FO 1057 105   Pictures
FO 1057 106   Pictures
FO 1057 107   Works of Fine Art
FO 1057 108   Works of Fine Art
FO 1057 109   Pictures
FO 1057 110   Pictures
FO 1057 113   Pictures
FO 1057 114   Works of Fine Art
FO 1057 115   Pictures
FO 1057 116   Works of Fine Art and Pictures

FO 1057 117   Pictures by J. B. Corot and Van Meegeren
FO 1057 118   Pictures
FO 1057 119   Works of Fine Art and Pictures
FO 1057 120   Pictures by Brandenburg and H. M. Hozee
FO 1057 121   Pictures
FO 1057 122   Pictures
FO 1057 123   Pictures
FO 1057 124   Pictures
FO 1057 125   Pictures
FO 1057 126   Pictures
FO 1057 127   Pictures
FO 1057 128   Works of Fine Art and Pictures by Piet van Wijngaard
FO 1057 129   Pictures
FO 1057 130   Works of Fine Art and Pictures
FO 1057 131   Works of Art and Pictures by Apol Louis, Rheymann
               and Vershner
FO 1057 132   Works of Fine Art and Pictures
FO 1057 133   Pictures
FO 1057 134   Pictures by van Huysum
FO 1057 135   Pictures by Pieter van Hulst
FO 1057 136   Pictures
FO 1057 137   Pictures by Leickert, Kool, van Borselen, Pieters,
               Scherrewitz and Willroider
FO 1057 138   Pictures by Mesdag, de Koninck and others
FO 1057 140   Pictures by Molenaer and Beerstraten
FO 1057 144   Pictures by Backhausen and others

DUTCH GOVERNMENT

FO 1057 179   Paintings
FO 1057 187   Paintings
FO 1057 199   Works of Fine Art and Paintings
FO 1057 200   Works of Art

FO 837 – Ministry of Economic Warfare: Enemy Property
Outside Enemy Territory

FO 837 1154   Looted Works of Art
FO 837 1156   Looted Works of Art
FO 837 1157   Looted Works of Art

SAFEHAVEN ACCORD

FO 837 1282   Spain
FO 837 1283   Spain
FO 837 1284   Interception of Loot: Iberian Peninsula
FO 837 1285   Interception of Loot: Iberian Peninsula
FO 837 1286   Interception of Loot: Iberian Peninsula

SWITZERLAND

FO 837 1288   Switzerland

FO 837 1289   Switzerland
FO 837 1290   Switzerland
FO 837 1291   Switzerland
FO 837 1292   Switzerland: Minutes of Meetings held in Washington
FO 837 1293   Switzerland
FO 837 1294   Switzerland
FO 837 1295   Switzerland
FO 837 1296   Switzerland
FO 837 1297   Switzerland: Negotiations 1 Oct.–31 Dec. 1950
FO 837 1298   Switzerland: Negotiations 1 Jan.–28 Feb. 1951
FO 837 1299   Switzerland: Negotiations 1–31 March 1951
FO 837 1300   Switzerland: Negotiations 1–30 April 1951
FO 837 1301   Switzerland: Negotiations May 1951
FO 837 1302   Switzerland: Negotiations June 1951
FO 837 1303   Switzerland: Negotiations July–Aug. 1951
FO 837 1304   Switzerland: Negotiations Sep.–Dec. 1951
FO 837 1305   Switzerland: Negotiations Dec. 1951
SPAIN
FO 837 1166   Property: Negotiations 1945
FO 837 1167   Property: Negotiations 1945–6
FO 837 1168   Property: Negotiations 1946
FO 837 1169   Property: Negotiations 1946–7
FO 837 1170   Property: Negotiations 1947–50
FO 837 1171   Property: Negotiations 1950–1

FO 1020 – Allied Commission for Austria: Headquarters and Regional Files
FO 1020 2766 Deposits (Works of Art, Archives, etc.) in Germany
FO 1020 2773 Restitutions and Reparations: Works of Art

WO 220 – War Office Civil Affairs: Monuments, Fine Arts and Archives
WO 220 584   The Macmillan Committee
WO 220 597   Allied Control Commission: Reports by Sub-Commission
WO 220 598   Parliamentary Questions on German Looting
WO 220 603   Field Reports on MFA&A: Nos 15, 16, 17 – France
WO 220 607   Field Reports on MFA&A: Nos 21, 22 – France
WO 220 609   Protection of Fine Arts in France
WO 220 612   Civil Affairs Reports and Field Report No. 7 – France
WO 220 613   Civil Affairs Reports – Germany
WO 220 614   Civil Affairs Reports – The Netherlands
WO 220 615   Civil Affairs Reports – Greece and the Balkans
WO 220 616   Civil Affairs Reports – Belgium and Luxembourg

WO 220 617	Civil Affairs Reports and Field Reports Nos 9–14 – France
WO 220 618	Civil Affairs Reports – Austria
WO 220 620	Civil Affairs Reports – Italy
WO 220 621	Enemy Propaganda: Alleged Disposal of MFA&A by Allies
WO 220 622	Extracts from Press Reports on Damage Done to Art Treasures
WO 220 623	Protection of MFA&A: Articles in Allied Newspapers
WO 220 624	Field Reports Nos 8, 9 – Italy
WO 220 625	Field Report No. 10 – Italy
WO 220 626	Field Report No. 11 – Italy
WO 226 627	Field Report No. 12 – Italy
WO 226 628	Field Reports Nos 13, 14 – Italy
WO 226 629	Field Reports Nos 15, 16, 17 – Italy
WO 226 630	Field Reports Nos 18, 19 – Italy
WO 226 631	Field Reports Nos 20, 21, 22 – Italy
WO 220 632	Field Reports Nos 1–7 – France
WO 220 633	Field Reports Nos 18–20 – France
WO 220 634	Field Reports Nos 22, 23 – France
WO 220 637	Sicily – Final Reports
WO 220 638	Italy – Final Reports
WO 220 639	Greece and the Balkans – Reports
WO 220 641	Situation Reports – Austria
WO 220 643	Report on MFA&A in Germany
WO 220 644	Report on MFA&A in Germany
WO 220 645	Consolidated Reports on MFA&A in Germany
WO 220 647	Lists of MFA&A in North-East Italy

T 209 – British Committee on the Preservation and Restitution of Works of Art, Archives and Other Material in Enemy Hands 1944–6 (the Macmillan Committee)

T 209 1	Proposals to set up a Committee on the Protection of Cultural Monuments and Works of Art
T 209 2	The Minutes of Meetings Book
T 209 3	Chairman's Notes
T 209 4	American Commission for the Protection and Salvage of Artistic and Historic Monuments in Europe (the Roberts Commission): Information
T 209 5	Commission for the Protection and Restitution of Cultural Material (the Vaucher Commission): Reports and Papers
T 209 6	Air Ministry
T 209 7	Ministry of Economic Warfare (later Economic Warfare Department, Foreign Office)
T 209 8	Foreign Office

FO 371 55826 MFA&A Branch Report – Feb. 1946

SWITZERLAND

FO 371 60519 Report by HM Consul-General in Zurich, on the Methods by which Persons Resident in Switzerland have made Clandestine Visits to Germany

POLITICAL: GERMAN ECONOMIC DEPARTMENT

FO 371 65055 Recovery of Works of Art Looted by the Germans in Occupied Countries

POLITICAL: GERMAN GENERAL ECONOMIC DEPARTMENT

FO 371 65336 'Safehaven' Negotiations with Spain

POLITICAL (ECONOMIC)

FO 371 45742 Control of Imports of Works of Art

FO 371 45769 Restitution and Replacement of Works of Art: Looted Works of Art

FO 371 45770 Restitution and Replacement of Works of Art: Looted Works of Art

FO 371 45771 Restitution and Replacement of Works of Art: Looted Works of Art

GERMAN GENERAL ECONOMIC DEPARTMENT

FO 371 70972 Liquidation of German Assets in Spain and Portugal under Safehaven Accord

FO 371 70981 Progress of Restitution of Property Looted by the Germans: Termination Date for Acceptance of Restitution Claims in British Zone in Austria

FO 371 70982 Progress of Restitution of Property Looted by the Germans: Termination Date for Acceptance of Restitution Claims in British Zone in Austria

FO 371 70983 Progress of Restitution of Property Looted by the Germans: Termination Date for Acceptance of Restitution Claims in British Zone in Austria

FO 371 70984 Progress of Restitution of Property Looted by the Germans: Termination Date for Acceptance of Restitution Claims in British Zone in Austria

FO 371 71029 Restitution Claims by Individuals in Respect of Works of Art

FO 371 71117 Proposal to Return German National Art Collections to German Keeping

GERMAN DEPARTMENT

FO 371 70442 Restitution from the British Zone of Austria of Property Looted by the Germans

FO 371 70463 German Fine Arts Material in Austria

FO 371 85520 Visit of German Museum Directors to the United Kingdom and Nazi War Loot on Display and Sale in New York

Files in the US National Archives, Washington

RG 59   Ardelia Hall
RG 239   MFA&A
RG 226   OSS
RG 331   SHAEF

Files in the Getty Research Institute

Box No. 860161 – Douglas Cooper Papers

File 42/1   War-Related Correspondence
File 42/2   Beltrand Appraisals of Paintings Confiscated by the ERR
File 42/3   OSS ALIU Consolidated Interrogation Report No. 2
File 42/4   OSS ALIU Consolidated Interrogation Report No. 4
File 42/5   War Office Report on Looted Art

Box No. 910011 – Dienststelle Mühlmann

Box No. 910130 – OSS ALIU Reports

File 1   OSS ALIU Consolidated Interrogation Report No. 1
File 2   Missing
File 3   Hitler's Museum at Linz and Interrogation Reports
File 4   Detailed Interrogation Reports
File 5   Treatment of Works of Art in Germany
File 6   Appreciation of Enemy Methods of Looting of Works of Art in Occupied Territory
File 7   French Report: Chronological Report Regarding Transfer of Art and Cultural Material in Contravention of the Hague Convention
File 8   OSS ALIU Final Report

Box No. 910172/8 – Alois Schardt Papers

Newspapers and Periodicals

Art and Antiques Dec. 1987, May 1989
Art & Auction June 1995, June 1997
ARTnews June 1998, Dec. 1984
Art Newspaper July/Aug. 1997, Feb. 1998, March 1998
Associated Press 17 July 1998, 4 Aug. 1998
Atlantic Monthly Sept. 1946

Beaux Arts Magazine Dec. 1995

Boston Globe 25 April 1997, 27 April 1997, 5 May 1997, 6 July
1997, 25 July 1997, 9 Nov. 1997, 25 Nov. 1997, 9 Jan. 1998, 13
May 1998, 11 Sept. 1998

Boston Herald 2 March 1998

Burlington Magazine April 1985

Cardozo Journal of International and Comparative Law

Daily Telegraph 10 Oct. 1940, 20 Feb. 1941, 6 Jan. 1943, 14 June
1945, 29 October 1996, 6 Dec. 1996, 23 June 1998, 13 July 1998

Der Spiegel

Die Zeit 16 Nov. 1984

The Economist 24 Dec. 1994

L'Evénement du Jeudi 7–13 March 1996

L'Express 28 Sept.–3 Oct. 1990, 21–7 Dec. 1990

Federal Reporter 38 3rd series; 678, 2nd series; *New York Supplement*,
2nd series

Forward 27 Feb. 1998

France-Soir 4 March 1988

Globo Sao Paulo 9 Sept. 1998

Histoarts

The Independent 13 Aug. 1998, 10 Sept. 1998

The Independent Magazine

The Independent on Sunday 28 April 1991, 28 July 1991

Jerusalem Post, 15 Feb. 1998

London Portrait Magazine

Minute 22–8 Dec. 1984

New York Times 7 Dec. 1945, 16 Nov. 1964, 29 Jan. 1997, 13 April
1997, 9 Dec. 1997, 24 Dec. 1997, 20 April 1998, 29 April 1998

Newsday

The Observer/Observer Magazine, 24 March 1991, 21 April 1991

Reuters 28 March 1996, 7 April 1998, 9 Sept. 1998

Star Tribune 10 Sept. 1997

Sunday Telegraph 18 Aug. 1996, 30 Nov. 1997

Sunday Times 28 July 1996, 3 Nov. 1996

Time magazine

The Times 21 July 1992

The Times Magazine 1 Aug. 1998

This Week magazine, 1943

Town and Country Monthly

Trace magazine

US News and World Report magazine

Vrij Nederland

Interviews (Personal and by Telephone)

Mr Gerard Aalders
Mr Henry Bondi
Ms Lydia Braemer
Dr Manus Brinkman
Ms Maria von Bummel
Mr Steve Coulton
M. Patrice Dallem
M. Michel D'Auberville
Ms Judith Dobrzynski
Det. Sgt Dick Ellis
Mr Roger Ellis
Dr Sabine Fehlemann
Mr Thomas Freudenheim
Mme Clothilde Galy
M. Michel Gardère
Agent Bonnie Goldblatt
Mr Lloyd Goldenberg
Mr Nick Goodman
Mr Cecil Gould (now deceased)
Herr Josef Hans Grafl
Mr Bernard Houthakker
Mr Thomas Hoving
Mr Saul Kagan
Mr Bill Kautz
Mr Lawrence Kaye
Prof. Martin Kemp
Ms Anna Kisluk
Mr Jeff Kleinmann
Mr Thomas Kline
Ms Christine Koenigs

Dr Willi Korte
Prof. Stuart Lane Faison
Mr Bill Leckie
Dr Josefine Leistra
Mr John Lennox
Herr Johann Linortner
Ms Janice Lopatkin
Ms Constance Lowenthal
Dr Michael Maeck-Gerard
Herr Marcus Marshall
M. Jean de Martini
Mr Marc Mazurowsky
Mr Jonathon Petropoulos
Dr Alexei Rastorgouev
Mr Walter V. Robinson
Aline, Countess of Romanones
Dr Anne Röver-Kann
Mr John Rowlands
Dr Dick Schonis
Dr Elizabeth Simpson
Prof. Craig Hugh Smyth
Mr Duncan Stuart
Ms Sophie Sutherland
Herr Walter Tarra
Mr Ron Tauber
Dr Gary Tinterow
M. Nicholas Vanhove
Mr Richard Verdi
Mr Gary Vikan
Count Adam Zamoyski

INDEX

Germany 182–3; destruction and looting as German forces forced to withdraw xi, 19–20, 68; purchase of works of art by Nazis 17–18; purchases for Göring collection in 18, 65–8, 70–1; return of works of art to 185; securing and protection of works of art by MFA&A in 85–6; target for Russian confiscations 194; tour of by Hitler (1938) 5, 6

Jackson, Sarah 345–6
Jaeger, Charles de 37
Jaffe collection 50, 133, 141
Jaffe, David 268
Jagielsky, Felix Roman 180
Jahn, Carlos 134
Janner, Lord 255, 311, 351
Janninck, Engbert 190
Japan 249
Jaray, Lea Bondi 229–30
Jaujard, Jacques 38, 59, 89, 306
Jerchel, Dr 34
Jewish National Fund 324
Jewish Restitution Successor Organization *see* JRSO
Jews 313–30; attitude of Allies on restitution of property of 317; collaboration with Nazis 313, 324–6, 330; and Kristallnacht 293, 314; legal justification by ERR of confiscations 30–1; plans for museum of Holocaust art by World Jewish Congress 328, restitution of assets 315–24, 327–30 *see also* Art Loss Register; CRA; HARP; resurgence of interest in restitution 328–30; role played by wealthy 316–17; seizure and confiscation of art treasures by Germans 7–8, 25, 31, 315; and Swiss gold issue 327, 329–30, 333, 342; two-tier claims process 316–17
Josipovicci, Leon 161
JRSO (Jewish Restitution Successor Organization) 315–16
Judgement of Paris, The (Altdofer?) 305
Juppé, Alain 307

Kagan, Saul 316
Kaiser Friedrich Museum (Berlin) 8, 15, 194
Kaiseroda mine repository 95–6, 202
Kaltenbrunner, Ernst 108, 111
Kamensky, Count 197–8
Kann, Alphonse 326, 347 *see also* Alphonse Kann collection
Karger, Nicholas 240
Karlsrühe Museum 6, 93
Karnzow repository 205–6, 219, 220
Kassel University 246–7
Katz, Nathan 69
Keitel, Generalfeldmarschall Wilhelm 15–16, 25
Kemp, Professor Martin 119
Kendall, Major General 176
Kennedy, Veron 176–7
Kesselring, Generalfeldmarschall Albert 18–19
Khrushchev, Nikita 214

Kieslinger, Dr Franz 57
Kirchner, Ernst 4, 5
Kirstein, Lincoln 113, 115
Kiss, The: bronze statue of 344
Klee, Paul 4, 5, 339
Kleininger, Lyonel 4
Kline, Thomas 247, 264, 268, 275, 330, 332, 334
Kneisel, Ernst 273–4
Köberl, Leopold 112
Koenigs, Anna 291, 292, 297, 300
Koenigs, Christine 268, 301–2, 303, 305–6, 350
Koenigs collection 65, 216, 291–306, 335; amassing of and contents 291, 292–3; claim of ownership by Christine Koenigs 301–2, 305–6; enforced sale of to Germans 253, 294–6, 301; exhibition held in Russia (1995) 222, 304–5; items sent to United States during war 293; items still missing 305; and *Portrait of Dr Gachet* 249, 292–3, 299–300, 350; reappearance and recovery of missing items 297–300; Russian refusal to send back 304, 332–3; in Russian secret depositories 302–4; taking of responsibility of returned items by Netherlands government 300
Koenigs, Franz 291–2, 292–3, 294–5, 296–7
Koga, Masatsu 251, 339
Köhler collection 221, 222
Königstein repository 201
Koninckx, Charles Georges 149, 150, 151
Konstantinov, Andrei 198, 209–10
Kordes Committee 306
Korte, Willi 247, 264–5, 266, 318, 329
Kowalski, Wojciech 276–7
Kozlov, Grigorii 215–16, 219, 220, 221, 303, 336
Kramarsky, Siegfried 293, 299
Kramer, Eckhardt 150, 152, 154
Krebs collection 59, 203–4, 221, 223, 224
Krebs, Otto 203–4
Krehl, Dr Wolfgang 162
Kreisauer Kreis 292
Kremsmünster monastery (Linz) 175
Kreutz, Dr Gottfried 173, 174, 175
Krinner, Albert 178
Kristallnacht ('Night of Broken Glass') 293, 314
Kronberg castle 243
Kulishkov, Valery 349
Künsberg, Eberhard Freiherr von 20, 21, 22, 36
Kunstammlungen zu Weimar (KZW) *see* Weimar museum
Kunstschutz 34–5; and ERR 36, 37; formation of 11, 26; in Italy 20; operations in France 26–7; role 26
Kuntze, Friedrich Franz 35
Kuzmin, Yevgeny 217

Labia, Count Paolo 67, 288
Lady with the Ermine (da Vinci) 11, 269–70, 270–1, 272
Lafarge, Lieutenant Colonel Bancel 86, 184
Lammers, Dr Hans 17, 36
Lanckoronski collection 3, 23